The
Light
in Their
Consciences

ROSEMARY MOORE

THE LIGHT
IN THEIR
CONSCIENCES

EARLY QUAKERS IN BRITAIN
1646—1666

THE PENNSYLVANIA STATE UNIVERSITY PRESS
UNIVERSITY PARK, PENNSYLVANIA

Library of Congress Cataloging-in-Publication Data

Moore, Rosemary Anne.
    The light in their consciences : the early Quakers in Britain, 1646–1666 / by
Rosemary Moore.
        p.   cm.
    Includes bibliographical references and index.
    ISBN 0–271–01988–3 (cloth : alk. paper).
    ISBN 0–271–01989–1 (pbk. : alk. paper)
    1. Society of Friends—England—History—17th century.   I. Title.
BX7676.2.M66 2000
289.6′41′09021—dc21   99–35185
                                                                            CIP

To the light in all your consciences I do speak;
which cometh from the Lord Jesus Christ,
who enlighteneth every man that cometh into the world.
—George Fox, 1652

CONTENTS

PART III: QUAKERS IN PRACTICE

PART IV: TURMOIL AND TRANSITION, 1659–1666

LIST OF ILLUSTRATIONS

PREFACE AND
ACKNOWLEDGMENTS

This book is an account of the first Quakers and their ideas and practices, starting from the obscure origins of the Quaker movement during the English civil wars and ending as it changed into the inward-looking sect of the later seventeenth century. The book's title comes from a distinctive Quaker phrase, one of the few that remained in use throughout the period. Quakers frequently admonished both friends and enemies to pay heed to "the light in your consciences," but the meaning shifted, and neither "light" nor "conscience" meant the same to the charismatics of the early 1650s as to the sober dissenters of the later seventeenth century.

Early Quakers have been variously described, at different times and by different scholars, as founders of a fundamentally new form of spiritual religion, as rediscoverers of original Christianity, as the radical end of the Protestant Reformation primarily related to spiritual movements on the continent of Europe during the previous century, as the radical end of the Protestant Reformation primarily related to English Puritanism, and as political revolutionaries. Any or all of these theories can be documented from the enormous quantity of source material, which, in the period covered by this book, includes some fifteen hundred mostly ephemeral publications together with large quantities of manuscripts, comprising letters, reports, epistles, and memoranda. My book is the result of an attempt to impose some order on this mass of material by the use of a computer database, listing practically all the printed pamphlets and several hundred manuscripts, and analyzing them with respect to date, to authors and other persons mentioned, and to subject matter. Contemporary sources were used almost exclusively in this study, because material from the later part of the century, notably George Fox's *Journal*, is liable to be misleading when dealing with the thoughts and feelings, and to some extent the history, of the early period. The resulting book is mainly an account of "establishment" Quakerism, but the existence of a "fringe" Quakerism, especially when it troubled the leadership, can also be discerned. Doubtful and disputed matters are considered in the notes, and a fuller account of the research is given in the appendixes. Readers who are not specialists in Quaker or seventeenth-century studies may ignore both notes and appendixes, if they so wish.

The starting date may be queried, on the grounds that the early history of the Quaker movement is uncertain. 1646 was chosen because the crucial meeting between George Fox and Elizabeth Hooton took place in that year, or early in 1647, and was followed shortly after by the first recorded instance of "quaking" and the conversion experience of George Fox. Most of what followed can be traced from these events. Studies of early Quakerism generally finish at the restoration of Charles II, but the distinctive characteristics of the early period did not come to a sudden end at this point, while some of the tendencies that led to the Second Period of Quakerism, to use the terminology associated with W. C. Braithwaite's classic histories, can first be discerned several years before 1660.

The first part of the book deals with the origins and early development of the Quaker movement, concentrating on the leading figures and their interrelationships. Parts II and III cover the beliefs and practices of the Quakers and the changes produced by internal and external pressures. The final part is concerned with the effects on the Quaker movement, first, of the political changes that followed the death of Cromwell and the restoration of the monarchy, and second, of the acute internal dissension that took place during the same period. The book finishes at a major punctuation mark in Quaker history, George Fox's initiation of major organizational reforms at the end of 1666.

Spelling and punctuation have been modernized, except in book titles. Biblical quotations are from the Authorized (King James) Version, as the translation most commonly in use in the mid-seventeenth century.

Parts of Chapters 1 and 2 have been published as "Leaders of the Primitive Quaker Movement," *Quaker History* 85, no. 1 (spring 1996). A form of Chapter 12 appeared as "Reactions to Persecution in Primitive Quakerism," *Journal of the Friends Historical Society* 57, no. 2 (1995). Much of Appendix 1 was included in "Evaluating the Evidence: The Reliability of Sources of Information for Quakerism before 1660," *Friends Quarterly* 27, no. 8 (October 1993).

I owe a great debt to Woodbrooke College, where I have been warmly welcomed on many occasions, and especially to Christina Lawson the Librarian (now retired). Edward H. Milligan, retired Librarian of Britain Yearly Meeting; Malcolm Thomas the present Librarian; and all the staff of Friends House Library have given me much advice and assistance, and special thanks are owed to Sylvia Carlyle for her expertise on suitable illustrations. I am very grateful to Rex Ambler and Hugh McLeod, my Ph.D. supervisors; to Larry Ingle and Michael Mullett, who kindly gave of their time and expertise to read and advise on drafts of the thesis; and to Kenneth Carroll, J. William Frost, and Douglas Gwyn, who performed a similar service in respect to the part of this book that deals with the period after the Restoration. Geoffrey F. Nuttall allowed me access to unpublished material, which is acknowledged in its place, and patiently assisted me by identifying obscure pamphlets and answering queries. John Punshon acted as my mentor in the early stages of the work when he was Quaker Studies tutor at Woodbrooke College. Hugh Barbour kindly presented me with a copy of the raw data used for the statistical appendix to *Early Quaker Writings*. Elsa Glines permitted me to use material that she is preparing for an edition of Margaret Fell's letters. Kate Peters, Joseph Pickvance, Stefano Villani and Ursula Windsor also helped with advice and information. The editor-in-chief, Peter J. Potter, and the anonymous readers of Penn State University Press made many suggestions that greatly improved the design of the book. My husband, Derek, who selected the computer hardware, installed the software, and acted as photographer and proof-reader, tolerated my state of distraction over many years with complete equanimity.

Assistance with the expenses of the study was provided by Worcestershire and Shropshire Monthly Meeting of the Religious Society of Friends, the Higher Education Awards Committee of Quaker Social Responsibility and Education, the Edith Haynes Scholarship Fund of Somerville College, Oxford, and the Edith M. Ellis Trust, which is a charitable trust established by British Friends.

To all these people and institutions, my grateful thanks. Errors and faults are my own.

PART I

QUAKER BEGINNINGS
1646—1659

Fig. 1 "The Land George Fox Knew." Drawn by Geoffrey Makins and first published in H. Larry Ingle, *First Among Friends: George Fox and the Creation of Quakerism*, Oxford University Press, 1994. (Reprinted by kind permission of the author)

1

GENESIS

Modern Quakers in search of their roots make pilgrimage to the "1652 Country," to the southeast of the English Lake District where George Fox climbed Pendle Hill to "sound the day of the Lord," and saw a vision of "a great people." To this day there are many sites of Quaker interest in the area, but it is not the true Quaker birthplace, for the movement that became Quakerism first appeared in the East Midlands of England some six or eight years earlier, during the Civil Wars.

One result of the Civil Wars was the abolition, for a period of some years, of controls on speech, printing, and ways of worship. Ideas could flourish unchecked, and the parliamentary armies provided a means for their discussion and dissemination. A favorite subject was speculation about the end of the present age of the world and the coming reign of Christ, and the practical political consequences of this, for theology and politics were not separate in most people's minds. Sects and informal religious groupings proliferated, causing great alarm among conventional people, especially the well-to-do. The sectarians, or "sectaries," introduced ideas of social equality into their teaching of the coming Kingdom of the Lord, that unlearned people could be called to preach the Gospel, and even that "all the earth is the Saints, and there ought to be a community of goods, and the Saints should share in the Lands and Estates of gentlemen, and rich men."[1]

Other ideas had percolated into England from the continent of Europe, generally by way of Holland. The "Family of Love," or "Familists," a body founded by the Dutchman Henry Niclaes and that had some similarities to the Quaker movement, had existed in England since the previous century, though so secretively it is difficult to judge its extent.[2] During the twenty years before the Civil Wars, a number of continental theological books, teaching spiritual religion and direct contact with God, and emphasizing the divine rather than the human Christ, were translated into English.[3] The influence of continental ideas on the English sectaries is uncertain, but the similarities, to Quakers in particular, were remarked on frequently in the anti-Quaker literature that was published from 1653 onward.[4]

At this time the regular parish ministry was organized on Reformed, or Presbyterian, principles. The Church of England hierarchy had been abolished, although the English Prayer Book continued in use, undisturbed, in many areas.[5] The chief rivals to the Presbyterians were the Independents, whose roots reached back to the last quarter of the previous century, when some Protestants became wearied of waiting in England for the true Reformation, and emigrated to Holland. During the reign of James I, conditions in England eased, and Independents began to return, so that by the time of the Civil War there were many self-governing "separated" or "gathered" churches, generally ruled by a "covenant," or local agreement. Many of the army officers, including Cromwell, supported the Independents, and after the Parliamentary victory a number of their ministers were appointed to parish churches.

Then there were Baptists (or, pejoratively, Anabaptists) of several kinds. Some were returned exiles from Holland who had met with Mennonites in that country and become converted to the practice of believers' baptism. They had also acquired in Holland the theology known as "Arminian," that salvation was possible for all people, and so these Baptists became known as "General Baptists" because they believed in the general possibility of salvation. They shared many ideas with Quakers and produced many converts to Quakerism. Other people who decided that there was no warrant for infant baptism in the Bible, and became Baptists, retained the Calvinist belief in salvation for a limited number of elect people, and were therefore called Particular Baptists. A few churches, while encouraging believers' baptism, did not insist on rebaptizing people who had been baptized as infants; John Bunyan's church was one of these. There were also Seventh-Day Baptists, who kept Saturday, the Jewish Sabbath, instead of Sunday. All Baptists emphasized a spiritual, Bible-based religion, but some had no objection to the parish ministry and even became parish ministers.[6]

At this time there were no hard and fast divisions between religious groups, and denominations in the modern sense did not form until later in the century. Parish ministers might be Presbyterian, Independent, or even Baptist or Anglican in their religious inclination. Churches "separated" from the parish ministry varied from congregations with trained ministers to small "do-it-yourself" bodies led by local men, or even women. Some might be called "Seekers," people who thought that the true church did not at that time exist, and looked back to recreate the New Testament church, or forward to the coming Kingdom of Christ.[7] Besides the Protestant churches, the Roman Catholic church had never been entirely suppressed, and was strong in some areas, especially the North.

There are no contemporary records of Quaker beginnings. The only sources of information are George Fox's *Short Journal* (which is not an ordered story), the early pages of Fox's *Journal* (which are not in the original manuscript), and a few other notes.[8] Fox's *Journal* gives 1646 to 1648 as the time when Friends' meetings were first appearing.[9] (To call them "Quakers" at this stage is anachronistic. They always called each other "Friends.") One record states, "Truth sprang up first in Leicestershire in 1644, in Warwickshire in 1645, in Nottinghamshire in 1646, in Derbyshire in 1647, and in the adjacent counties in 1648, 1649 and 1650," and continues, "We did meet concerning the poor and to see that all walked according to the Truth, before we were called Quakers, about the middle of the nation in Nottinghamshire and Derbyshire and Leicestershire."[10] This is an area some eighty miles square to the northeast of Birmingham, where Quaker tourists find little of interest, for this part of England changed beyond recognition during the Industrial Revolution. If the 1644–45 dates are correct, then proto-Quaker groups existed in the East Midlands before there is any clear record of them, and possibly before the first preaching of George Fox.

The first definite event in early Quaker history, for which there is evidence outside Fox's *Journal*, was a meeting between the young George Fox and a middle-aged woman named Elizabeth Hooton.[11] George Fox was born in 1624 at Fenny Drayton in Leicestershire, and at the age of nineteen, distressed by the failure of Christians to live up to their profession, he left home and wandered the country, an unhappy young man seeking faith. He may have deliberately arranged his route to avoid being drafted into one or other of the armies, and presently arrived in London where he visited his uncle Pickering, a Baptist, and must have heard, if not taken part in, the lively arguments that were going on.[12] Afterward he returned to the East Midlands, probably in 1645, which was the year of the decisive battle of Naseby.

While traveling in Nottinghamshire, probably during 1646 or early 1647, he met with a "shattered Baptist" church and a "tender people" ("tender," had, in the mid-seventeenth century, the sense of "susceptible to moral or spiritual influence, impressionable, sympathetic, sensitive to pious emotions").[13] Among these people was Elizabeth Hooton, whom Fox described as a "very tender woman," and who lived at Skegby, near Mansfield, some fifteen miles north of Nottingham. Religious meetings were held at her house, and her son Oliver described what happened:

> My mother joined with the Baptists but . . . finding they were not upright hearted to the Lord . . . she . . . left them, who in those parts soon all were scattered and gone. About the year 1647 George Fox came amongst them in Nottinghamshire and then after he went into Leicestershire where the mighty power of the Lord was manifest, that startled their former separate meeting and some came no more, but most, that were convinced of the truth, stood, of which my mother was one, and embraced it.[14]

The "mighty power of the Lord" was the "quaking" that later gave Quakers their name. "Startled" was a stronger word in the seventeenth century than it is today, and those who "came no more" had been utterly shocked and horrified. Those who "stood" were convinced that God had come among them in great power.

Fox in his *Journal* rarely mentioned his helpers and companions, and it is probable that Elizabeth Hooton was more important in the history of Quaker beginnings than the *Journal* indicates. The role of Margaret Fell as friend and supporter of Fox is well known, but before Fell there was

Hooton, another middle-aged, capable, strong-minded woman, who also opened her house to Fox. Elizabeth Hooton devoted the rest of her long life to the Quaker ministry, traveling twice to New England at a time when Quakers were not welcome, where she was whipped as a vagabond. She died in Jamaica in 1672 during a third visit to the New World.

About this time George Fox found faith, as he recorded later in his *Journal*:

> But as I had forsaken the priests, so I left the separate preachers also, and those called the most experienced people; for I saw there was none among them all that could speak to my condition. And when all my hopes in them and in all men were gone, so that I had nothing outwardly to help me, nor could tell what to do, then, Oh then, I heard a voice which said, "There is one, even Christ Jesus, that can speak to thy condition," and when I heard it my heart did leap for joy.[15]

Fox's *Journal* for the years 1647 to 1649 gives a picture of growing numbers of Friends in the East Midlands, presumably small, do-it-yourself religious groups, having no need for any ordained minister or prescribed ritual, and led by what they felt to be the power of God in their meetings. Most of these first Friends' meetings would later have been integrated into organized Quakerism, but one group, led by Rice (Rhys) Jones of Nottingham, a former Baptist, survived as an independent body for some years, during which time Fox and his associates had considerable controversy with them. They were known as the "Proud Quakers," or the "Castle Group" from their meeting place in Nottingham Castle. They allegedly did not believe in the human Christ, and they permitted greater laxity of conduct than the mainstream Quakers.[16]

These years were the high tide of the radical revolution. The Levellers, a London group advocating major political, economic, and religious reform, were strong in the army, and were suppressed with difficulty by Cromwell and his generals. War broke out again, and King Charles, who had escaped, was recaptured. Finally the king was executed in January 1649 as a tyrant, traitor, murderer, and public enemy. In order to obtain a majority for the execution, a number of members of Parliament were prevented from attending, leaving a "Rump" subservient to Oliver Cromwell and his associates.[17]

Besides the political disruption there was great economic distress, some of it caused by the wars, and some endemic. Beggary was common and

Fig. 2 Reproduction of a letter from Elizabeth Hooton to George Fox, dated York Castle June 11, 1653. Transcription appears on opposite page. (Source: ARB MSS, no. 14. Courtesy, Library Committee of the Religious Society of Friends, Britain Yearly Meeting)

seemed incurable. The church tax or "tithe," intended for the support of parish ministers, was a cause of much hardship, and there were tithe strikes in some parts of the country, including districts that later became Quaker strongholds.[18] The leader of the Digger or "True Leveller" movement, Gerrard Winstanley, whose writings show similarity to early Quaker teaching, inspired several communistic Digger communities for the "poor despised ones of the earth."[19] These communities, which had a brief existence in 1649, rapidly fell foul of alarmed landowners and were destroyed.

The disturbed political situation led to fresh ideas that the reign of

ffrom Yorke Castle ye 11: day 1653

deare Brother my tender love Remembered to thee, & to my sister Margaret ffell in whom dwelleth the power of truth, I writ to thee to let thee know the persecutions y^t are among us, ye rage of the enimie is great, & the preests sirreth [sic] up the people, to madnesse round about, now my desire is y^t thou wilt pray for us, and for me y^t I may stand fast to ye end, for ye enimie liyeth subtilly on every side, to betray ye precious seede within, and trample it underfoote, But ye lord doth keepe mee praised bee his name) divers freinds as the weare goeing to a meeting at Crake ye last first day, ye Preest having intellegence, raised ye toune with staves and Clubs and resisted them, and drave them out of there liberty, few y^t received any harme by them, but one Capt. Weddall had his horse stricken doune under him, and ye gave blowes to some others, then ye Cheeife Constable came and bad them depart, or else there would bee blood shead, and murder, then the went to another toune, likewise in the Citty great uproare, a frend haveing spoaken in ye streete, and after goeing into a freinds house, ye Rude people fell upon ye house and broake open ye dore, and fell violently uppon ym but there power is limited, and the are Chained, soe y^t the Cannot have there desires acomplished on us, now deare brother Remember us in ye lord y^t wee may bee tought with true wisdome, to stand in ye power of ye lord against all gainsayers, & falce accusations. many Comes in to find out our liberty, & many subtill spirits to betray us, pray y^t wee may stand in ye power of truth to ye end y^t love may abound among us y^t wee may all bee knit together, the lord hath Caused many in this Citty to one [own] ye truth of late, and mightily ye doe increase in ye Country Praised bee his name fforever &c. my ffellow prisoners all are in health & desires to have there love Remembered to thee, with Jane Vallance Elizabeth Tomlinson of selby hath her tender love to thee, remember my love to James Naylor.

thy deare sister Elizabeth Hooton

Transcription of letter from Elizabeth Hooton to George Fox.

Christ was about to come, or was even now present. About 1649 or 1650 some of those who taught the primacy of the indwelling spirit, the idea that God infused all things, received the name "Ranter." Their teaching, it was supposed, would lead to immorality, especially of a sexual nature, and there were indeed some people who held the view that if they were in the spirit, or elect, or justified, however they phrased it, then sin was impossible, for their behavior was of no consequence. The prevalence of such ideas was no doubt exaggerated by scaremongering.[20]

Eccentrics flourished in the aftermath of war, such as John Robins, who claimed to be God and had a group of followers who saw visions, and Thomas Tany, a pantheist who announced a divine command to change his name to Theaureau John as a Jew of the tribe of Reuben and who was drowned on a mission to convert the Jews. Such cases invite the question as to where exactly one draws the line between religious enthusiasm and mental disturbance.[21] Roger Crab, a pacifist vegetarian celibate whose death may have been caused by malnutrition, used language remarkably similar to the Quakers: "The Spirit of Christ . . . that redeemeth by Light and Life, and freely sets the soul at Liberty."[22] Many individuals tried different forms of church and sect and movement, and many people who finally became Quakers had been through such experiences.

In 1649, perhaps encouraged by the revolutionary climate to an even greater sense of the Lord's power, George Fox took action. He recorded in his *Journal*:

> Now as I passed to Nottingham . . . as I looked upon the town the great steeplehouse struck at my life when I spied it, a great and idolatrous temple. And the Lord said unto me, "Thou must go cry against yonder great idol, and against the worshippers therein." . . . And when I came there . . . the priest . . . told the people that the Scriptures were the touchstone and judge by which they were to try all doctrines, religions and opinions. . . . Now the Lord's power was so mighty upon me, and so strong in me, that I could not hold, but was made to cry out and say, "Oh no, it is not the Scriptures," and was commanded to tell them that God did not dwell in temples made with hands.[23]

Fox was arrested and imprisoned. This was the first of many occasions when Friends were in trouble with the law. They were not immediately crushed by sheer force, as happened to the Levellers, Diggers, and various Ranters, probably because they were operating further from the center of power in London, and were not as yet an organized movement, so that they were not yet recognized as a potentially serious threat to the social system.

In the autumn of 1650 George Fox was in Derby, together with some other Friends including Elizabeth Hooton, who left her home and her husband (with whom she was later reconciled) to travel with Fox. Fox again interrupted a church service, and with one of his companions, John Fretwell, was charged with blasphemy for claiming to be united with Christ, and was imprisoned.[24] Elizabeth Hooton was also imprisoned in Derby. Her letter to the mayor of Derby, threatening him with the Lord's vengeance, has survived, and is the first of many such attacks on towns and their authorities: "The day comes that shall burn thee, saith the Lord . . . friend, if the love of God was in you, you would love the truth and hear the truth spoke, and not imprison unjustly."[25] The nickname "Quaker" is said to date from this year, being first applied by the justice who tried Fox. The term came into general use, to the annoyance of Friends who disliked it, but to avoid confusion Quaker authors often felt constrained to include the phrase "by one of those in scorn called Quakers" on the title pages of their books.[26]

At this time came the first controversy with the Proud Quakers. Rhys Jones, their leader, quarreled with Fox, drew others with him, and went to fight at the battle of Worcester in 1651. This conflict may have been one cause of Fox deciding to move to another area when he was released from prison in Derby, for he was now becoming known beyond his immediate district.[27] After a short tour in the East Midlands he traveled north to Yorkshire. Elizabeth Hooton was also present in Yorkshire in 1652, when she was imprisoned with other Quakers in York Castle, so presumably she arrived with Fox.[28]

One or more groups, which may be described as "proto-Quaker" in their ideas, though there is no record of any "quaking," were already in existence in South Yorkshire, in the district of Balby. Balby is not to be found on a modern map but was an area near Doncaster, where the Friends' Monthly Meeting is still called "Balby." The local leader, as regards social position, was Thomas Aldam of Warmsworth, a substantial yeoman in his mid-forties.[29] In spite of imprisonments and several distraints for tithe, he retained enough wealth to pass on a considerable estate at his death. His surviving letters and publications show him to be a firm supporter of the Parliamentary cause, with a strict sense of right and wrong and no notion of compromise. He was strongly antagonistic to the established church, and it was probably this aspect of Fox's teaching that particularly attracted him.

The outstanding personality of this group was Richard Farnworth, who already knew Fox by correspondence, and was then aged twenty and in the throes of his own religious upheaval.[30] In his account of his religious journey he told how he could find no satisfaction in formal religion, and came to see, "by the breaking forth of the light of God in my spirit, that the steeplehouse was no church . . . that the Church of Christ was made all of living stones." He described his careful preparation for communion, but when he came to take it, it meant nothing to him, and, he wrote, "I saw then by the light of God in my conscience, that it was not the body and blood of the Lord but a carnal invention."[31] He was one of the most prolific of early Quaker authors.

Fox then got to know a similar group a few miles away near Wakefield, where he met another who was to become a leading Quaker, William Dewsbury (1621–88), shepherd, weaver, and, for a time, a soldier. He died in 1688, having survived a total of nearly twenty years in prison. He had long been seeking a true faith, and unlike most Quakers, he described his beginning in Calvinist terms, "conceived in sin and brought forth in iniquity." He joined the army, but, he wrote,

> The word of the Lord came unto me and said, put up thy sword into thy scabbard; if my kingdom were of this world, then would my children fight . . . which word enlightened my heart . . . that the Kingdom of Christ was within; and the enemies was within and was spiritual, and my weapons against them must be spiritual, the power of God. Then I could no longer fight with a carnal weapon against a carnal man . . . and the messenger of the Covenant . . . caused me to yield in obedience, to put up my carnal sword into the scabbard, and so leave the army.

This was an unusual experience among Quakers of the 1650s, for normally they were proud of their army service. Dewsbury returned home, still in great spiritual trouble, until at last, he said, "Jesus Christ purged away the filthy nature . . . so . . . I was made free from the body of sin and death. . . . I witness I am regenerate and born again of the immortal seed." This account was written in 1655, and although the imagery may be affected by Dewsbury's later Quaker experience, it appears likely that Dewsbury, like Farnworth, had found his way to a Quaker-type faith before he met Fox.[32]

James Nayler, one of the most important figures in the early Quaker movement, had been, according to his own account, a member of an Independent church at Wakefield. He had served eight years in the army, as a quartermaster with John Lambert, the most radical of the Parliamentary generals. He resigned because of ill-health, and in 1651, when he met Fox, he was about thirty-five years old, and working his farm.[33] The next year he joined in the Quaker traveling ministry. Little is known of his personal background, but he was highly intelligent, literate and articulate, and rapidly became a leader of the Quaker movement, many contemporaries considering him to be joint leader with Fox.

At the same time as the Quakers were becoming established in Yorkshire, another sect appeared in London, the only one of the Civil War sects, apart from the Quakers, to survive into the twentieth century. This was the Muggletonians, who, like Quakers, taught that the final age, the Age of the Spirit, had now arrived. Muggletonians had no regular worship, and when religious controls were reimposed after the restoration of Charles II, they were prepared to compromise with the laws requiring attendance at parish services. They remained a working-class sect, meeting mainly for social gatherings and not attempting to convert others. Their archives were preserved by amazing good fortune, being rescued by the last known British Muggletonian from the bombed headquarters of the sect during World War II, and stored for years in apple boxes at his farm.[34]

In later years Quakers and Muggletonians were rivals, Fox, Farnworth, and other Quakers being formally cursed by Muggleton, but in 1651 Quakers had no contact with London. During the winter of 1651–52, Fox made a tour in Yorkshire, returning to the Doncaster area in the spring. After this, members of the South Yorkshire group joined in active travel and preaching, including disrupting church services, and it was presumably the teaching and example of Fox and Hooton, coupled with the quaking or visible "power of the Lord," that inspired these previously law-abiding people to such activity.[35] Thomas Aldam, Elizabeth Hooton, and several others caused so much trouble that they were soon imprisoned in York Castle.[36] They were a turbulent and talented group, the most remarkable of them being Mary Fisher, a maidservant from Selby who was then aged about thirty. After her release she went to Cambridge where she was flogged for denouncing Sidney Sussex College as a synagogue of Satan, and declaring that she was the bride of Christ. In 1657 she traveled East to preach to the Turkish Sultan, who received her kindly, and she returned home safely. In 1662 she married another Friend named William Bayly, and had several children. After Bayly's death she remarried, and emigrated to South Carolina with her second husband, where she died in 1681.

In the spring of 1652 Dewsbury repeated Fox's autumn route, establishing several meetings, while Nayler and Farnworth joined Fox in a westward journey that led to the rapid growth of Quakerism in North-West England. Fox was not wandering at random. He planned his journey to meet up with potentially useful and sympathetic people and separated church groups, and to pass through one area where a long-running tithe strike was just beginning.[37] He was teaching that Christ had come, so there was no need for the intervention of parish ministers between God and believers. One valuable convert was Colonel Gervase Benson, Justice of the Peace, one time Mayor of Kendal, Commissary of the Archdiaconate of Richmond before the war, whose knowledge of the law made him a valuable Friend. His wife also became an active Quaker, giving birth to a child while in prison.[38] A few days later, after a meeting of Separatist church members at an old chapel on Firbank Fell near Sedbergh, two preachers, Francis Howgill (1618–69) and John Audland (1630–64), joined with Fox and, probably, brought their congregations with them.[39]

The speedy acceptance of Quaker ideas in the North is in marked contrast to the slow developments in the Midlands during previous years. Partly, no doubt, the success was due to Fox's increased experience as a leader, but also it was due to the nature of the area, which improved the chances of finding sympathetic colleagues. The North was remote and poor, the parishes were large and the few clergy underpaid.[40] Congregations might be led by local men with a gift for preaching, such as Francis Howgill and John Audland. Two Quaker meetings in this district wrote later that they had originated, one from "a meeting of a religious people separated from the common national worship," and the other from a "seeking and religiously inclined people."[41] Unorthodox opinions were difficult to check in this wild countryside, and not far away Roger Brereley, the curate of Grindleton, in the remote moorland to the east of Lancaster, had preached a doctrine with many similarities to Quakerism. It is possible that the Quaker minister John Camm may have previously been a Grindletonian.[42]

On their journey westward, Fox and his companions were invited to stay at Swarthmoor Hall near Ulverston, where traveling preachers were often welcomed, and the resulting "convincement," to use the Quaker term, of the mistress of the house, Margaret Fell, changed the course of the movement.[43]

Margaret Fell was the wife of Thomas Fell, wealthy and influential landowner and country gentleman, Judge of Assize and Member of Parliament, who, although he never was counted as one of the Friends, gave them considerable support, assistance and protection. Margaret Fell rapidly became the leader of an important Quaker meeting at Swarthmoor, as shown by the many letters addressed "to Margaret Fell and others." She was herself spiritually dependent on Fox, and with her household wrote a highly emotional letter to Fox after their convincement: "Our dear father in the Lord . . . in Christ Jesus thou hast begotten us through the gospel. . . . O thou bread of life without which our souls will starve. . . . O thou fountain of eternal life, our souls thirst after thee."[44] Ecstatic letters of this kind (see Chapter 6) became a feature of early Quakerism.

Despite such feelings of dependence, Margaret Fell was not merely Fox's mouthpiece. The many letters that she wrote to local and national digni-

Fig. 3 "Fox's Pulpit" on Firbank Fell near Sedbergh. The plaque on the rock was set up to mark the three-hundredth anniversary of Fox's sermon to the massed Separated congregation of the area in June 1652. The chapel where the Separatists held their meetings has long since disappeared but stood behind the wall to the left of the picture. (Photo by Derek Moore)

taries have a considerable theological content and show a thorough knowledge of the Bible. She was probably another of those who, like Farnworth, Dewsbury, and Nayler, had virtually arrived at a Quaker position before meeting Fox.[45] Her administrative ability, the shelter of her house and the use of her fortune proved indispensable to the success of the Quaker movement.

In the second half of 1652, using Swarthmoor as a base with the permission of Judge Fell, the Quakers spread across North-West England, despite fierce opposition from parish ministers and attacks by mobs. A warrant for blasphemy was issued against Fox, but at Lancaster assizes in September, with the help of Judge Fell and the Clerk of Assize, Colonel William West, the evidence was found untrustworthy and the charge was not proceeded with. Local gentry who supported Parliament were prepared to assist Quakers, for the North-West was strongly Catholic and Royalist, and Quakers were considered a useful counterweight.[46]

Fig. 4 Swarthmoor Hall, near Ulverston, home of Thomas and Margaret Fell, and the administrative center of the primitive Quaker movement. The window of the Great Hall is in the center of the picture, and the main entrance is behind the hedge to the left. The Hall is now owned by Britain Yearly Meeting of the Religious Society of Friends, and is used for Quaker retreats and workshops. (Photo by Derek Moore)

Fig. 5 Interior of Swarthmoor Hall, showing the Great Hall. (Photo by Geoff Harris)

Fig. 6 Reputed portrait of Thomas Fell (1598–1658), Judge of Assize and Member of Parliament, who was never counted as one of the Friends but gave them considerable support, including the use of Swarthmoor Hall as a base of operations. The picture is thought to have hung originally at Swarthmoor and is more likely to be authentic than any other portrait associated with the first Quakers. (Courtesy, Barrow-in-Furness Museum Service)

From this time many letters were preserved at Swarthmoor, and give a picture of the relationships between leading Friends. Thomas Aldam wrote to Margaret Fell and to Fox as one leader passing on news to others, but on practical matters he asked for Fox's advice. Aldam was worried because three of the women with him in York Castle had bought new clothes, having been given the money by another Friend. He felt that the money should be returned, and wanted to know whether the women should keep the clothes or if he should dispose of them. He asked George Fox to "judge of this thing which hath been of weight to me, how to order this thing," and "what the spirit of wisdom doth direct to do in this matter."[47]

Richard Farnworth wrote one of the earliest recorded Quaker letters, in July 1652 to "James Nayler and others," telling of his mission work in Derbyshire with a postscript to Friends: "Meet often together, for the presence of the Lord is oftentimes made manifest by meeting in his name." Later that year he wrote a long letter of spiritual counsel to Margaret Fell, and one wonders if she appreciated receiving such advice from the young and sometimes brash Farnworth.[48] Farnworth had a great respect for Fox, as shown by an interesting pair of letters that he sent to George Fox and James Nayler. The letter to Nayler begins: "Dear brother my dear love to thee," and continues as a letter from an affectionate colleague. But the letter to Fox starts: "My Heart, my life, my oneness, thou art ever with me," and continues in the same ecstatic vein.[49] This is particularly useful, as it is rare to be able to make a direct comparison as to how Fox and Nayler were regarded by another leading Quaker. Farnworth was also concerned with the embryonic Quaker organization. One undated early letter concerned arrangements for meetings:

> See that none do appoint meetings in their wills in any open place . . . for there will be many come to such meetings, some to carp some to cavil and some that may desire to be convicted [i.e., convinced of the truth] . . . take care that some be present there that is able to bear the burden and keep it for the life to thresh the heathen . . . and when there is a meeting desired by God in wild and unbroken places take not the body of Friends with you.[50]

Letters from James Nayler show his position of influence and leadership, as for instance in this letter of advice and warning to "Margaret Fell and others":

> O Friends, I see your minds drawn out from your conditions within, to look out at words; and there is presumption got up amongst you,

and boasting; but in the mean time the pure seed lies under. . . .
Richard Myers, thou gets above thy condition, mind the babe [i.e.,
the small beginning of spiritual influence] in you and it will tell you
so. And, Friend, thou that calls thyself a prophet art run up into the
air, lowly consider it.[51]

He wrote to Fox as an equal, his "dear brother," and is one of few Friends
on record as asking Fox to do something: "And if thou see Richard Hubberthorne, mind him to be faithful to the Lord, in what is committed to
him, that he may be serviceable amongst those my dear ones in the Lord,
that words get not up, and so presumption gets afoot, and so lead out from
the simplicity."[52]

Few of George Fox's personal letters survive, but he was already writing a
number of epistles for the nascent Quaker movement, advising local leaders
on the conduct of their meetings. One of these epistles is so like Farnworth's letter quoted above that the two leaders had surely been discussing
together the problems of disorganized meetings.[53]

So it appears that, in the second half of 1652, the leading influential
Friends were George Fox, James Nayler, Thomas Aldam, Richard Farnworth, and Margaret Fell, and probably also William Dewsbury, who is less
conspicuous in the contemporary records but who was occupied in stabiliz-
ing the Yorkshire meetings. Fox was treated with considerable respect by
the others with the exception of Nayler, who addressed Fox as an equal
colleague.

Many people who afterward became leading Quakers joined the movement in 1651 and 1652. George Whitehead (1636?–1723) was only
sixteen when he was "convinced." Less brilliant than some of the first
Quakers, but quietly competent and very long lived, he became a successful
London businessman and was the leading Quaker at the end of the century.
Christopher Atkinson was one who later "ran out," being described by Fox
as "that dirty man," but he was a capable minister in the first years, and
author of several popular pamphlets, six of which were included in a bound
collection of thirty Quaker pamphlets that was in use in Scotland in 1655.[54]
Edward Burrough (1633–63) from Underbarrow near Kendal, who died in
prison in 1663, became the chief political pamphleteer, and succeeded
Nayler as the most effective theologian.[55] William Caton (1636–65) was a
young member of the Fell household, most noted for spreading the Quaker
word in Holland and Germany. Richard Hubberthorne (1628–62), mentioned above in the letter from Nayler to Fox, was a former army captain
who had fought at the Civil War battle of Dunbar, near Edinburgh, in

1650, and his eloquence, both as a speaker and as a writer, made him one of the foremost Quakers until his early death in prison in 1662.[56] He left a contemporary account of his convincement in the shape of two letters seeking counsel from Fox and Fell, followed later by a more formal account of his conversion and call to the ministry, which together make up a remarkable spiritual autobiography. Many of the first Quakers had experiences of intense despair before reaching spiritual peace, but few could describe it so graphically:

> In my trouble I cried in the evening would God it were morning, and in the morning would God it were evening, and the terror of the Almighty being upon me, my acquaintance and familiers stood afar off me, for they knew not the power of the Lord . . . and the Lord raised in me a love to his word, by which all the powers of the earth did tremble, and the earth itself was shaken by it.[57]

There are no surviving Quaker pamphlets that can certainly be dated to 1652, although at least one was published toward the end of that year, for a letter from Farnworth to Fell dated December mentioned the printing of three hundred books that were now in use and being publicly read.[58] Some idea of the Quaker preaching of this time can be derived from the reports of the trials of Fox and Nayler for blasphemy in 1652–53, that were published in March 1653, but two anti-Quaker books give much more graphic detail. They were published in 1653, and refer to events of 1652.[59] The first of these, *Querers and Quakers,* was concerned with the area of Yorkshire first evangelized by Fox in the autumn of 1651.

Querers and Quakers described how people "all over Yorkshire" were being drawn into "absurd and unreasonable . . . principles and practices; by running up and down the country to act in quakings and trances, and drawing many people after them." "Wandering ministers" left their homes to preach and cry in the streets, "everyone that will, imagining he is called to it." "Men, women, boys and girls, may all turn into prophets by [according to] Quakers, and all other preachers and ministers are but deluded and without calling." They looked for "extraordinary raptures, inspirations, miracles," and they promised "the casting out of Devils." The author mentions and may have witnessed an occasion when the shopkeepers of Malton, who had converted to the Quakers, burnt their stock of ribbons as a testimony against worldly ways.[60]

The other adversarial book, Francis Higginson's *The Irreligion of the*

Northern Quakers, was a response to the Quakers' mission in Cumbria during the summer of 1652, and also described the trials for blasphemy of Fox and Nayler. Higginson knew of a number of Quakers by name, but especially George Fox, "the Father of the Quakers in these parts" and "the ringleader of the sect," and James Nayler, "principal spokesman in these parts." His description of Fox may be gossip but is worth quoting: "It has been his custom in these parts, to fix his eyes earnestly on such strangers as come into his company a good while together, as though he would look them through . . . his followers say he can out-look any man, and that he does it to know what is in them."

Higginson and the anonymous author of *Querers and Quakers* provided similar lists of the Quakers' "erroneous opinions." Quakers taught the possibility of union with God or with Christ, said that they had the "fulness of glory in this life," and claimed to attain a state of perfection so that "they neither do, nor can, sin."[61] They were antagonistic to the beliefs and practices of the church as then established, rude to people who were not their associates, and practiced social equality to a degree that was shocking to the stratified society in which they lived. Much the same could be said about other groups and individuals of the time. Quakers and Ranters were more alike than the Quakers cared to think: "The Ranter is . . . much of the make with the Quaker, of the same puddle . . . only the Ranter is more open, and lesse sour," wrote one fierce opponent of sectaries.[62] Quakers were also accused of teaching "a kind of popery," for Catholics were greatly feared in seventeenth-century England, and blamed for most untoward events.[63] Quakers were also described as related to Familists, continental Anabaptists, and heretics and fanatics of various kinds. Many such attacks followed during the next few years.

So the Quaker movement developed from a minor Midland sect and was poised to become a mass movement. There were four main factors in its early success. One was the personality of George Fox, and his ability to inspire other people. Another was the resonance of Quaker teaching with the wants and feelings of many people. Third was the quality of some of the individuals who joined the movement, above all Margaret Fell, for without Swarthmoor Hall as a base it is unlikely that there would ever have been a Society of Friends. Fourth, after Fox had moved from the Midlands to the North, there was an opportunity to consolidate the early gains by putting down deep roots, helped by the support of influential Northern gentlemen such as Judge Fell. By the time Quakers were recognized as a serious challenge to conventional society, there were too many of them to eradicate.

2

THE QUAKER EXPLOSION

In the course of 1653, the Quaker movement spread over much of North England, and in 1654 over much of the rest of the country, with an increasing number of Friends taking part in delivering the message. The mission depended on Friends being "moved" to undertake the work, but there was no shortage of volunteers.

George Fox was based at Swarthmoor, writing epistles of advice to ministering Friends, receiving their reports, preparing pamphlets for publication, and, presumably, laying plans for further Quaker expansion.[1] Most of Fox's epistles dated 1652 to 1654 were intended for local Quaker leaders and dealt with the general principles of consolidating and running meetings. In the late summer of 1653 Fox made a journey in the North, and soon was once more in trouble for alleged blasphemy, and imprisoned at Carlisle. Another conviction could have meant hanging, but urgent appeals were set in motion, the charge was not proceeded with, and Fox was released.

At the beginning of 1653 Nayler, together with Francis Howgill, was in prison in Appleby, also on a charge of blasphemy. The justice in charge of the case, Anthony Pearson, was converted to Quakerism by Nayler, and the justices agreed there was no blasphemy, although the prisoners were kept in prison until Easter to answer petitions that parish ministers had brought against them. After his release, Nayler's main function was to cover the areas in the North and Midlands where the Quaker movement was becoming established, and to deal with problems. Francis Higginson may have judged the situation correctly when he described Fox as "father" and "ringleader" of the Quakers and Nayler as their "principal spokesman." Nayler was the author of the most effective Quaker controversial books, or written disputes with opponents, and he also handled troublemakers. Rhys Jones's group in Nottingham was in dissension with the local Quakers who supported the national leaders, and Nayler went to visit Jones in the autumn of 1654, writing to Fox that "much confusion did appear in him," for Jones defended swearing and conformity to the world to "get a livelihood."[2] It is not certain if Nayler normally acted on his own initiative, or if he usually followed requests from Fox. Certainly, he valued his relationship with Fox, and often wrote that he was hoping to hear from him.[3]

Nayler was mentioned several times in the contemporary Quaker correspondence as an active and important minister of similar status to Fox, and in a letter from Dewsbury written in September, his name stood first.[4] Nayler was in no doubt about his own importance. His "Letter to Friends about Wakefield" begins: "James, a prisoner of Jesus Christ, unto all that love the appearance of our Lord Jesus Christ everywhere, grace and peace be multiplied from God our Father and from our Lord Jesus Christ."[5] None of his readers could have failed to pick up the similarity to the opening of Saint Paul's Epistle to Philemon, with echoes of other Pauline greetings.

Margaret Fell acted as the main troubleshooter for discipline and internal matters. Only Thomas Aldam ventured to give her advice, when some news from Swarthmoor must have caused him concern. He warned Margaret Fell "to beware of earthly mindedness" and told her, "Thy calling is to wait upon the Lord, and when he calls thee forth, to declare his name." She was "a handmaid of the Lord . . . and now must thou go forth as a valiant soldier to fight the Lord's battle, to thresh upon the mountains and to minister freely, as thou hast received freely." She must not neglect the work "lest the curse fall on thee."[6]

Margaret Fell did not take his advice to "go forth." Unlike Elizabeth Hooton she showed no wish to leave her home, and she was able to give much greater service to the Quaker movement as the mistress of Swarthmoor Hall and the wife of Judge Fell. She took full advantage of her social position, and wrote a number of letters to local dignitaries concerning the treatment of Friends. A Justice of the Peace named Sawrey ventured to complain to Fell's husband about her, after which he received from her several lengthy appeals to repent. She had great powers of vituperation, and a letter to a local parish minister, Gabriel Camelford, is a good example of her style. She began "Camelford—thou hast shewed forth thy poison and enmity that lodges in thee as no other can proceed from thee," continued for three sides of denunciation and ended: "O thou dissembling hypocrite, at that day thou shall give an account for these words, and before his presence thou shalt fly, for thy damnation slumbers not, nor thy judgement of a long time lingers not, 2 Peter 2:3."[7]

For all her force of character, Margaret Fell was perfectly capable of a tactful approach when necessary. In 1654 she made arrangements for a fund to be set up, known as the Kendal Fund, for the support of the Quaker mission, and there are a number of surviving letters concerning the fund and its accounts, including several well-crafted begging letters. The letter setting up the fund was addressed to "all my dear brothers and sisters," and used the "one body" theme of the First Epistle to the Corinthians, chapter 12, to remind them that many members of the body were in trouble, and that there was a need to bear one another's burdens. Friends at Kendal had been at heavy expense, and she had contributed herself, but now she was writing to other meetings in the North-West to ask them to take their share.[8]

She performed many administrative and financial functions. John Camm wrote to her: "Gervase Benson and thou must take care to write to some special Friends to make up about £20 and send it up to London for printing books." A letter to her from Thomas Willam, one of the Kendal Fund treasurers, covered a number of points, news of sufferings in Northumberland, and of Friends elsewhere, postal matters, news of expected parcels of books, and arrangements for the financing of Friends traveling in the ministry.[9]

Earlier writers on Quakerism underestimated Margaret Fell, being misled by Friends who often wrote to her as their "nursing mother." Her efficiency and importance, particularly with regard to the setting up of the Kendal Fund, were noted, but her formidable nature has only recently been adequately recognized.[10] She was not at this time writing books, but she engaged in theological dispute by correspondence, managed the Quaker finances, dealt with disciplinary issues, and, together with Fox, handled the arrangements for mission. (For Margaret Fell administering discipline, see Chapter 10.)

Of the other early leaders, Richard Farnworth continued with traveling and preaching, writing a number of pamphlets and many letters to Margaret Fell, George Fox, "and others," with reports on the development of the work and with general advice.[11] Thomas Aldam remained imprisoned in York castle until December 1654, and during the earlier part of that period he was very active, writing many letters to Fox and Fell and to other people concerning various aspects of the movement, including the arrangement for the publication of the first Quaker books in London.[12]

During 1654 Quakers spread south. No information survives about the preliminary planning of this mission, and Fox in the *Journal* said simply that the Lord raised the ministers up.[13] The traveling preachers went out in pairs, two men or two women together, generally an older person with a younger, and they were distributed to cover most of the country. The strongest teams went to the main cities, Francis Howgill and the young Edward Burrough to London, John Camm with John Audland to Bristol, the chief port, and later in the year Richard Hubberthorne with Christopher Atkinson and the teenager George Whitehead to Norwich, at that time the chief manufacturing town. In London and Bristol there was spectacular success, but in Norwich Christopher Atkinson became involved in an illicit love affair that became public knowledge, and Friends blamed this for the poor growth of the movement in the east of the country.

Sometimes the travelers would be welcomed by sympathetic people and local congregations, most often Baptist. Sometimes no one would receive them, and they preached in the open to anyone who would listen. In the early days the message would often be delivered in church after the minister had finished his sermon, which was allowable under current law, but this practice was made more difficult in 1655 by new laws aimed at Quaker preachers.[14] Sometimes their reception was actively hostile, women ministers being especially liable to abuse. Women preachers were not an entirely new phenomenon, but the large numbers of forceful, articulate Quaker women were another matter, and many ordinary people thought them disruptive of the social order.[15]

Nevertheless, the new movement had an instant success, and before the end of 1654 there were Quaker groups in many places. The government, having disposed of Levellers, Diggers, and Ranters, was alarmed by the appearance on the scene of Quakers, quite literally by the thousand. Ralph Farmer, a Bristol minister who suffered from the great Quaker success in that city, sent a report to the government, suggesting that Quakers were Levellers or something like it: "A while ago there came to this city of Bristol, certain Morris-dancers from the North. By two and two, two and two, with an intent here to exercise some spiritual cheats or (as may well be suspected) to carry on some levelling design. And our soldiers here, having nothing else to do . . . struck in with them in their quaking."[16]

The leading Quakers soon realized the possibilities of the press, and also that the published message would need to be authentic and self-consistent, for the first Quakers were a varied collection of people. Fox wrote to Friends: "Let not your wills and minds go before the light of God in you . . . write nothing but as you are moved by the Lord . . . let none print but what they can eternally witness."[17] Aldam, in a letter to Fox, wrote that he was glad to hear that Fox was to view all books before they were printed. This decision may not have been universally observed, but there are several later references to such checks being made.[18] Some thirty-six "books," mostly short pamphlets, were published in 1653. Farnworth contributed to thirteen, Fox to eleven, Nayler to nine, and Aldam to five. In 1654 some sixty Quaker pamphlets were printed, with Fox, Nayler, Hubberthorne, and Farnworth the most productive authors, together with important contributions from Edward Burrough and Francis Howgill, who all belonged to the inner group of leaders. In general, any statement of Quaker viewpoints that is based on the pamphlet literature represents the spread of opinions of the inner group, with which other Quakers, ultimately, agreed or departed.[19]

The Quaker pamphlets provided most of the subject matter for parts II and III of this book. In 1653 they consisted mostly of apocalyptic prophecies of doom, and diatribes against the parish ministry, which were closely related to the current political situation, contrasted with calls to obey the light of Christ within. The 1654 pamphlets, written for the mission to the south of England, tended to be a little more restrained in language, and included the first controversies with non-Quakers, and more ordered expositions of Quaker practices and beliefs.

Quaker preachers sent full reports to Swarthmoor, and letters describing the beginnings of the London mission provide a good example. Edward Burrough and Francis Howgill arrived in London in May 1654, and were diligent letter writers. They had meetings with Baptists, "Lockers"

["Lookers," i.e., Seekers?], Waiters, Ranters, a "Society of a great company of Philosophers," and a group called "the Bible People," who were making a new translation and judged it "by their reason," which, to Quakers, meant not according to the light of Christ. Their ministry was not easy, and they wrote that "none should come but that hath a sharp sword and well skilled to handle it," meaning the "sword in the mouth" that was the Quakers' weapon. Margaret Fell was asked to pass a message to George Fox about suitable ministers, that "none may come which are but weak, but as they are eternally moved." They had problems with Ranters, and also with Isobel Buttery, a woman who had been selling Quaker books in London the previous autumn but was now in prison, and not setting a good example. They were, they said, "constrained to stay in this city, but we are not alone, for the power of our Father is with us. . . . As yet we know little of our departing hence." They worked independently, sending Margaret Fell their news, but asking for no help or advice until they had a problem, as once when Howgill attempted to heal a lame boy, and failed. Howgill then wrote to Fox for advice: "I write to thee that if there be any deceit, thou may let me hear."[20] Later in the year, John Audland, visiting London, mentioned a meeting with Seekers, and also a meeting at "Lady Reynold's house." Evidently, Quakers were already attracting the attention of smart society.[21]

Not only Margaret Fell and George Fox got letters. Ministering Friends were writing to one another regularly. In the same letter as that quoted above, Burrough and Howgill said, "We receive letters every week from the prisoners at Chester [Richard Hubberthorne and companions], the work of the Lord goes on gloriously in that county. . . . Anthony Pearson writes to us of the like in the county of Bishoprick [County Durham]." In September Howgill wrote to another Friend, "We receive letters from every quarter. . . . Our dear brethren John Audland and John Camm we hear [from], and we write to one another twice in the week."[22] A national network, as much as a hierarchy, was developing.

Besides the network there was a central organization based on Swarthmoor, and a number of letters indicate the position of Fox and Fell as advisers and organizers. Both of them received letters of extreme personal devotion that emphasized their position as leaders (see Chapter 6). They were consulted concerning the direction of the mission, as in a letter to Margaret Fell from John Camm early in 1654, in which he said he had "drawings to go into the South again" and that George Fox believed he should go with speed. A letter from Ann Audland, John's wife, told that she had "some drawings to go to Bristol," but probably could not see Fox before she went, so asked that his blessing go with her, for she felt "his presence continually, which is her strength."[23]

Traveling ministers required immediate inspiration, or "drawings," but this did not prevent Fox directing their movements. His own letters are not available, but Nayler and Farnworth both referred to Fox's instructions in letters of their own.[24] Fox also tried to limit the amount of traveling by ministers: "If any amongst you have movings to do any service for the Lord, when they have done it, let them return with speed to their habitation, and there serve the Lord in their generation." He relied on reports from other ministers to let him know if anything was going wrong, as when Hubberthorne wrote, "Agnes Ayrey is not serviceable to go forth, for lust and filth and darkness rule in her."[25]

The only hint of criticism of George Fox's direction of the mission came from Burrough. In Summer 1654, when he was for a time in the North, he wrote, "There lies something upon me to write to thee. I have been speaking to my brother John Audland of it. I lie it upon thee, that none go forth but where the life is manifested and wisdom is grown to discern and order, for some have been here, and we heard of some in our passage in Lancashire, which give great occasion [i.e., cause trouble] and make the truth evil spoken of, and we have the worse passage. I lie it upon thee . . . to take care of it, especially into the country where none of our Friends have been. They two, Thomas Castley and Elizabeth Williamson, have given occasion. Call them in when they come out of prison."[26] Although both Audland and Burrough were evidently concerned about the matter, it was Burrough who took Fox to task. Friends did not usually "lie" things upon George Fox.

One influential non-Quaker who gave valuable support was Giles Calvert, a London printer and bookseller, who published most of the radical tracts of the 1640s and 1650s, and was a known supporter of radical ideas. He allowed his shop to be used as an address for London Quakers, and also acted as their banker, supplying them with money that was afterward reimbursed.[27] He was not a regular attender at the Quaker meetings, but it is recorded that on one occasion he attended the London meeting together with Judge Fell, and that afterward Nayler and another Friend, Alexander Parker, met with the Judge at Calvert's house.[28]

At the end of December 1654 Friends held a major general meeting at Swannington in Leicestershire. Presumably the place was chosen because it was conveniently central and some suitable local Friend could act as host.[29] This gathering of Quakers alarmed the authorities, who reckoned that about two hundred were present. Many leading Friends were there, although there is no mention of Nayler. Jacob Bauthumley the "Ranter" was in the area, and disputed with Fox, who wrote later that there were a number of "Ranters" in that part of the country.[30]

Nothing is directly known of the agenda for this meeting, but a number of contrasts in the organization of Quakerism between 1654 and 1655 makes it possible to suggest some items. One probably concerned the management of meetings, for in the following months there are signs of developing regional organization. Another item may have been arrangements for disciplinary procedure; in early years erring Friends were often referred to Margaret Fell for discipline, but this practice ceased about the end of 1654 (see Chapter 10).

A third matter under discussion would have been publications policy; since Giles Calvert attended the Swannington meeting and did excellent business there, it is likely that arrangements for vetting proposed publications, getting them to the printer, paying for them, and distributing them were all decided during the meeting. The development of the reporting system would also have been considered, for there was a great increase in the correspondence of Friends in 1655.[31]

It is more than likely that matters of faith were considered. Despite the increase in the number of authors, there is much less variation between individual Quaker writers in 1655–56 than in the earlier years. The disputes with the Ranter Bauthumley and others at the time of the meeting would have provided an excellent opportunity for the less experienced Quaker ministers and authors to study the arguments and methods generally used by leading Friends, and would have reinforced the vetting procedure.

It may be that the name of the movement was discussed. There was no regular name up to this time. Letter-writers most often referred to individuals as Friends, but Quakers as a whole were sometimes called the "children of light," especially by Nayler. The phrases "children of light" or "children of the light" occur frequently in the Quaker publications of 1655, and an effort seems to have been made to replace "Quakers" with "children of light" in the public consciousness, by using it frequently on the title pages of tracts. The phrase derives from several New Testament texts, especially Ephesians 5:6–14, referring to the chosen people of God. Quakers tried to lay claim to it, but it was also in use by others.[32]

After the Swannington meeting George Fox was arrested and taken to London. One of his associates, Alexander Parker (1628–89), originally from Lancashire, went with him to London, and thereafter was often mentioned in connection with the London meetings. Fox and Parker were able to satisfy Cromwell of Friends' good intentions, and Cromwell accepted a written promise from Fox that he would not take up arms against the government. This indicates that Cromwell thought of Fox as the leader, and able to control the other Quakers.[33]

The Quaker movement continued to spread, meeting fierce opposition in some places as well as success, and before the end of 1655 many Quakers were in prison for such crimes as interrupting church services, causing a public disturbance, alleged vagrancy, and rudeness to magistrates. George Fox himself spent much of 1656 in prison in Launceston, part of the time in revolting conditions.[34] The mission in London was particularly successful, and Howgill and Burrough hired a room that would hold a thousand people in an old tavern called the Bull and Mouth, in the City five minutes walk from St. Paul's Cathedral.[35]

In the country at large, both Fox and Nayler were becoming known outside Quaker circles. Dewsbury wrote to Fox in the winter of 1654, telling him that a Ranter "bound by the power of the Lord and cast into a lake" had called out "That is Fox's spirit." Nayler's name was often coupled with Fox's, so that in some parts of the country the names of Fox and Nayler were equally familiar. Both Fox and Nayler were known through *Saul's Errand to Damascus*, the account of their trials for blasphemy at Lancaster and Appleby, published in 1653 and reprinted in 1655. On one occasion, when John Camm and John Audland crossed from South Wales by boat to Bristol, they were directed to inquire for a certain house, and on arrival they were asked if they knew George Fox and James Nayler; a satisfactory answer was evidence of their credentials.[36] The introduction to Fox and Nayler's *Several Papers* described Fox and Nayler as both being "Ministers of the Eternal Word of God, raised up after the long night of apostacy to direct the world," but Fox's name on the title page is considerably larger than Nayler's, which indicates that either the editor or the printer considered Fox to be more important.[37] Anti-Quaker books either mentioned Fox and Nayler as equal leaders or gave slight prominence to Fox.[38] One newsbook, the *Weekly Intelligencer,* referred to Fox as the "great Quaker, who is said to be one of the ring-leaders of them," when he was arrested and brought to London after the Swannington conference.[39]

The Quaker correspondence of 1655 and 1656 provides ample evidence for the pre-eminence of Fox among the Quakers themselves, even when allowance is made for the fact that most of the letters were written to Margaret Fell, who clearly liked to hear Fox well spoken of.[40] During Fox's imprisonment at Launceston so many Friends were trying to visit him that the local authorities set up roadblocks to stop them.[41] This did not happen in the case of other eminent Friends suffering long and unpleasant imprisonments, such as Dewsbury in Northampton, and James Parnell who died in Colchester gaol before he was twenty.[42]

Even stronger evidence for Fox's position as organizer of the movement comes from letters suggesting that apologies and excuses were due to him as leader. The following two instances are both of interest in early Quaker history. The first occurred early in 1655. Thomas Stacey of Cinderhill near Sheffield wrote Fox a rather plaintive letter, excusing himself from helping Fox as requested.

> Before thy letter came to me I was gone forth, and have not been negligent since my coming from thee, and have not been three or four days at most at home. My passages and service [are] too large to relate [details], my father is not in health, but lies in bed and cannot stir without help. . . . I shall stay with him till I go to the meeting at Knaresborough, and he is very willing I should go and patient in his pain. I shall, as the Lord makes way, come to thee as shortly as I can.

News of this came to the Aldam family and their relations the Killams, and they also joined in the excuses: "And as for Thomas Stacy's not coming up to thee, he hath been much serviceable amongst Friends in several places since his departure from thee, and his father is very weak upon the gout, and having been much from him, he intends to come up to thee as shortly as he can without prejudice to his father."[43] A second example suggests that, although Fox was the acknowledged leader, there might be some resistance to his instructions. In April 1655 John Audland passed on a letter from Fox to John Wilkinson and John Story, to the effect that Fox wanted them in London.[44] They were to call at Giles Calvert's, or at an address in Reading, for further instructions. Audland continued: "Dear hearts, you know how the service is there and in this country [i.e., where the two had been working] and if G[eorge Fox] would send you to other places, lay it before him."[45] Audland evidently thought that Wilkinson and Story might be better employed by staying where they were.

In 1655 and 1656, by which time Quakers had covered Britain and were beginning to travel abroad, Margaret Fell continued to be the chief organizer. She received reports and handled money and dealt with all kinds of problem. One Friend taking ship to Barbados wrote, "I leave my little

mare here, either to be sold or to be sent into the North to Swarthmoor to
be disposed of as Margaret Fell sees fit."[46] Numerous newsletters describing
the progress of the mission were sent to her. There were also letters from
Friends concerning their personal needs, often assuring her that they "need
nothing." If Friends were in prison their wants would, however, be supplied, and one letter included the accounts for this. When funds ran low
she appealed for more donations "to be ministered . . . according to the
necessities of the Saints," for in so doing "you follow the practice of all the
Saints in the Light."[47]

Many letters from George Taylor, treasurer of the Kendal Fund, illustrate
Margaret Fell's authority. On one occasion, having told her about a complaint regarding his accounts, he wrote to her: "Now this thing is not
true. If thou own Lancelot Wordell for a Friend in the truth, reprove him
sharply." Other correspondence shows how closely she supervised Friends'
arrangements, and even their private lives. Several letters concerned the
arrival of a baby to Thomas and Elizabeth (Leavens) Holmes, who were
responsible for Friends' work in Wales. Margaret Fell evidently thought that
two Friends in the ministry, although married, had no business to have conceived a child because of the cost to local Friends. Thomas Holmes's letters
are most apologetic in tone, and refer to advice received from George Fox,
which Thomas Holmes evidently hoped would appease Margaret Fell.[48]

One letter illustrated Margaret Fell's status in relation to Fox and Nayler.
A Friend had written to Fox and Nayler with some criticism concerning
"lightness" in meetings at Swarthmoor. Fell wrote him a sharp letter to the
effect that he could have saved his trouble, "for they [i.e., Fox and Nayler]
do know us and see us and feel us in that which thou wanted to judge with
them."[49] Margaret Fell no doubt knew that Fox and Nayler would support
her.

Of the other leaders, Aldam, after his release from York Castle, was less
active as a Quaker, still a leading Friend, but not one of the most prominent half dozen. Farnworth continued in the traveling ministry during
1655, and in the autumn was in Banbury, supporting Ann Audland at her
trial for blasphemy, and was himself imprisoned for eight months. He, and
also Aldam, now wrote fewer letters to Fox and Fell, presumably indicating
that practical problems could now be managed without so much discussion.

Burrough and Howgill continued to act as an independent and efficient
pair, reporting regularly to Margaret Fell, but making their own decisions
about the course of their work, mainly in London but including a visit to
Ireland in the winter of 1655–56. An embryonic regional organization

developed. Camm and Audland exercised general oversight in the West from their base in Bristol. Hubberthorne was in East Anglia, where he was assisted by George Whitehead. Hubberthorne wrote many letters to Fox and Fell, and seems to have had a personal need to keep in touch with them.[50] Thomas Salthouse in the far west and Thomas Holmes in Wales also had regional responsibilities.[51]

An important new adherent was Captain George Bishop of Bristol, who joined the Quakers in 1654.[52] He came from a well-to-do Bristol family and had worked in intelligence-gathering in the early days of the Commonwealth, and took part in one of several Quaker delegations to Cromwell in 1655. He was not universally popular among Friends, and Thomas Willam, one of the Kendal Fund treasurers, wrote to Margaret Fell about "several in Bristol that are grown into such a high exalted spirit, especially such as George Bishop, that is great in the outward."[53]

Another valuable convert was Samuel Fisher, a Kentish parish minister turned Baptist minister turned Quaker, one of the few with good knowledge of Greek and Hebrew, and author of the immensely lengthy treatise on Quaker theology *Rusticus ad Academicos*.[54] Others were Thomas Curtis of Reading, a woollen-draper, and his wife Ann, who became leading Friends.[55] Another was Justice John Crook, whose house in Bedfordshire was first used for a large general meeting in the spring of 1655, to be followed by many others.[56] John Lilburne, a leader of the Levellers, was briefly a Quaker in 1656, but he died before he could have any real influence on the movement.

These were the most important of the newer Quakers, but except possibly for Bishop they were not yet equal in influence to the original northern leaders. In 1656, Fox, Fell, Nayler, and Farnworth were still the Friends who had responsibility for the movement as a whole.

In 1655 the total number of Quaker pamphlets, inclusive of reprints, exceeded one hundred, with Nayler the most prolific author followed by Fox, Farnworth, and Burrough. George Bishop's *The Cry of Blood*, published in 1656, was a detailed account of Quaker beginnings in Bristol, and with 163 pages by far the longest Quaker publication up to this date.[57] Many pamphlets gave descriptions of the sufferings of Quakers, but one letter to Margaret Fell advised that certain imprisoned Friends should not air their grievances, on the grounds that it would "but stir up more strife in the minds of those whom it concerns."[58] Anti-Quaker writings increased during these years and are an important source of information.

Financial support was still largely provided by the Northern Friends, but already there were signs that the balance of power was shifting to the South.

London was becoming the center, at first using as a base the house belonging to Robert Dring, a linen-draper.[59] It was London Friends who negotiated with Giles Calvert, handled the disbursement of money for activity abroad, and had access to the government and to the "good and great" of the time.

During the 1650s Quakers increased in numbers to between thirty and sixty thousand, out of a total population of some five million. Evidence for the socioeconomic status of the adherents of the movement is mostly late or circumstantial, but most Quakers appear to have been of the "middling sort," small businessmen and artisans.[60] People at odds with the parish ministry, especially over tithes, or finding no solace in other churches, would be attracted, and the small but influential number of well-to-do adherents would prefer Quakers to other radical groups, as Quakers did not attack property rights.

Reading between the lines of the ministers' correspondence, it seems probable that both the greatness of their success and also the fierceness of the opposition took Friends by surprise. The movement grew to such a size so rapidly that it was difficult for established Friends to handle, and was in danger of running out of control. Up to 1655 there were only minor crises, but it is not surprising that the following years were characterized by major upheavals and the construction of an elementary code of discipline.

During the following years there was a great expansion of Quaker work overseas.[61] The foreign mission developed naturally from the mission at home; when the Quaker preachers reached the limits of Great Britain they then went beyond. Irish Quakerism dates from 1654 with the work of William Edmondson, who found his converts mainly in Henry Cromwell's army. Edmondson had a poor opinion of the Irish: "We are here amongst a thick dull sottish people . . . the dragon stands ready to devour the man-child [i.e., the spirit of Christ] where he appears in any measure."[62] In 1655 Friends began to look further afield. They visited Holland and had considerable success there. The American mission began in 1655 with the arrival of Mary Fisher and a companion in Barbados, and the Quakers soon spread throughout the American colonies. From their Dutch base, Quaker missionaries attempted to evangelize much of Europe, and even the Middle East. A number of pamphlets were published in Dutch and German, but the mission to the European continent had no lasting success, although Dutch meetings persisted into the eighteenth century.[63] The present Yearly Meetings on the European continent are twentieth-century foundations.

3

THE CONSEQUENCES OF
JAMES NAYLER

The Quaker leadership, as described in the previous chapter, consisted in the first place of Fox as general organizer, then Fell as administrator in charge of finance, and thirdly Nayler as the chief publicist with Farnworth in support. Fox had vision, a powerful personality and a grasp of organization, but he could have done little without a base, finance, and a chief of staff, all of which Fell provided. He was not effective in theological argument, and therefore needed Nayler. Contemporary letters mentioned the value of Nayler's ministry and his power in dispute, and Francis Higginson's early assessment, that Fox was the "ringleader" and Nayler the "principal spokesman," evidently still held good in 1655.[1] Burrough and Howgill, Camm and Audland, and several others had regional responsibilities.

Meanwhile, the Quaker presence in London was growing, and the quantity of work was becoming as much as the resident Quaker leaders, the very capable Francis Howgill and Edward Burrough, could handle. The London ministry was of prime importance, and in June 1655 Nayler arrived in London to strengthen the team, presumably at the request of George Fox. Burrough and Howgill wrote to Margaret Fell, telling her that they were delighted to have Nayler to share the work. Sometime in the past there had evidently been a difference of opinion between Nayler and themselves, but they assured Margaret Fell that any difficulty between them and Nayler was now over.[2] Nayler enjoyed great success as a London preacher, and was soon moving in high society. He wrote to Margaret Fell, telling her of his meeting attended by "Lady Darcy" and other notables including Sir Henry Vane, a leading intellectual republican who was executed under the Restoration government.[3] One minister with whom he had a debate gave Nayler a warning that turned out to be prophetic: "Take good heed while thou forbears to have outward reverence of men, as capping and kneeing and the like, that thou steal not men's hearts away from God to thyself, and so lord it on their conscience that they have neither God nor Scripture . . . but take thee as a demigod and to make thee a mental idol."[4] Burrough and Howgill spent the winter of 1655–56 in Ireland, leaving Nayler to manage the London mission on his own. Possibly there had been a recurrence of personality problems, but if so, it left no trace in the surviving documents. Burrough and Howgill returned in the spring of 1656, having been deported from Ireland, at a time when Nayler was under much pressure, tired from bearing the main responsibility for the London meetings throughout the winter, and having conducted a difficult debate with the Baptist Jeremy Ives, during which he was challenged to prove his authority by performing a miracle or speaking in tongues.[5] He was then asked by Fox, who was at that time in prison at Launceston, to attend a meeting at York in June regarding a dispute among Friends.[6]

At this time a problem developed in connection with the ministry of one Martha Simmons. There are a number of published accounts of the events that followed, and this study is not concerned with the details, many of which are obscure, but rather with the repercussions on the Quaker movement.[7] Martha Simmons was a well-known London Friend, sister of Giles Calvert, and married to another printer, Thomas Simmons.[8] She was a more fluent writer than most of the early Quakers, men or women, as shown by this example from her spiritual autobiography:

For seven years together I wandered up and down the streets enquiring of those that had the image of honesty in their countenance, where I might find an honest Minister, for I saw my soul in death, and that I was in the first nature, and wandering from one idol's temple to another, and from one private meeting to another, I heard a sound of words among them but no substance could I find . . . about the end of seven years hunting, and finding no rest, the Lord opened a little glimmering of light to me . . . and then for about seven years more he kept me still from running after men . . . about the end of the last seven years the Lord opened my eyes to see a measure of himself in me, which when I saw I waited diligently in it, and being faithful to it I found this light more and more increase . . . and now hath given me a resting place with him.[9]

During 1655 she worked in East Anglia with James Parnell, and was for a time imprisoned in Colchester. Parnell wrote to William Dewsbury: "Our tender sister Martha Simmons is here in bonds in the town prison. . . . The Lord has shown his power much by her since she came here, she is a faithful heart in her measure. She was moved to walk in sackcloth barefoot with her hair spread and ashes upon her head, in the town, in the frosty weather, to the astonishment of many."[10] An anti-Quaker tract described her thus:

But their chief virago, is one who is called Martha Simmons . . . who cumbers herself with too much business of other folks matters, who runs and gads up and down with missives, and leaves letters, and sends them abroad to gain disciples; what a hubbub did she cause in Shoreditch church the last Lord's day, by boldly and impudently talking to, and against the Minister, till she was forced away by the church wardens and other officers.[11]

Martha Simmons has been described by most Quaker writers, both seventeenth-century and modern, as an emotional, unstable woman, but this is not consistent with her writing, nor with her position in the movement.[12] In 1655 she was a valued member of the Quaker community in the South-East. Some time in 1656 things went awry. Her ministry was found objectionable, and "she was judged by FH [Francis Howgill] to speak in her will."[13] Burrough, evidently exasperated, wrote to her: "This is the truth

from the Lord God concerning thee Martha Simmons, thou and who follow thy spirit, you are out of the truth, out of the way, out of the power,
out of the wisdom and out of the life of God, for you are turned from the
light of Christ Jesus in you and disobey it—You are become goats rough
and hairy, on the left hand you stand."[14] For the "goats on the left hand,"
see Matthew 25:31–33. This letter was not just addressed to Martha Simmons; the pronoun is "you" from the second line onward. Martha Simmons was the leader of a group of men and women in contention with the
Quaker leadership in London. The nature of the trouble is not known but,
in view of what happened afterward, it may be that Martha Simmons and
her friends were expressing the opinion that the return of Christ was imminent. The years 1655, 1656, and 1657 were often quoted by apocalyp-
tically inclined contemporaries as probable dates for the Second Coming,
and Burrough had written against this viewpoint in *Trumpet of the Lord,*
published early in 1656.[15] Leading Quaker ministers did not take kindly to
being contradicted. Martha Simmons may also have challenged the accepted Quaker views on spiritual and biblical authority, for she is recorded as
arguing with Hubberthorne about this early in 1657.[16] The following passage
by Martha Simmons illustrates the teaching of her "group." It was probably
published late in 1656, but it may express views that were current earlier.

> Why should it seem a strange thing to you to see Christ reign in his
> Saints . . . and make our bodies fit for himself to dwell in, seeing our
> hearts are ready to bow to his will? And is it not more for his glory,
> though it be a greater cross to your wills, to purify these bodies, and
> pour out the dregs thereof, than to bring down that body which was
> crucified at Jerusalem . . . by much tribulation, anguish of spirit, and
> sufferings of the flesh, has he now fitted a body for himself, who has
> conquered death and hell: so perfect is he that he can lay down his life
> for his enemies . . . this vessel is as precious to me as that which was
> tortured at Jerusalem, seeing the same Father has prepared them both.

The tract included a short paper by Hannah Stranger, another of Martha's
"group," in which she wrote, "As he suffered at his going away, so does he
at his coming again, for so says the scripture, *he shall come in like manner as
he went.*"[17]

The fact that Simmons was a woman may have exacerbated the dispute
but did not cause it. She was no more extravagant in her behavior than
other women ministers whose actions were recorded with approval.[18] Nor is

there any reason to suppose that Howgill and Burrough were personally opposed to women as ministers. They recognized that without the help of women it would be very difficult to keep the work in London under control and they wrote very warmly of women ministers whom they had encountered in Ireland.[19] It is probable that women ministers would be especially praised in letters to Fox and Fell, who both advocated the ministry of women, and it is possible that some Quaker men were less enthusiastic in private, but publicly women were accepted as equal in the ministry and compared to the prophetesses in the Bible. The few instances of men being specifically preferred to women as ministers date from the last months of 1656 or later, in some cases probably as a consequence of Martha Simmons's activities.[20] The exasperation expressed in Burrough's letter to Martha Simmons may well have been a male reaction to a troublesome woman, but his strong language equally suggests that a serious matter was at stake, and that it was a matter for "judging," whether men or women were involved.[21]

Simmons, on being rebuked by Howgill, asked Nayler for support. He at first refused to give it, but Hannah Stranger persuaded him to change his mind. Nayler stayed for a time at Martha Simmons' house, and appears to have had a mental breakdown. Several letters describing these events have survived.[22] George Fox was still in prison at Launceston, in the far southwest of England, and it is quite possible that if he had been free to deal with the situation, it would never have developed to a crisis. Leading London Friends decided that Nayler must be taken to see Fox. The party went by way of Bristol, where Martha Simmons followed them and caused a disturbance, being ejected from a meeting by local Friends. Nayler then continued his journey, but was intercepted by the authorities, and imprisoned in Exeter. Martha Simmons followed, and managed to visit Fox and harangued him, telling him to bow down to Nayler. Fox thought that Nayler had sent her, and consequently when Fox was released, and after some delay met with Nayler, there was utter misunderstanding, and they parted on very bad terms.[23] Fox wrote in strong terms to Nayler, "judging" what he had done, and "denying" Martha Simmons and her friends.[24]

Around this time, or possibly earlier, Martha Simmons and her friends decided that Nayler was Christ returned, or should enact Christ returned. In October Nayler, accompanied by Martha Simmons and other members of her group, and probably still in a poor mental state, rode into Bristol in recapitulation of Christ's entry into Jerusalem. Nobody can be sure what was going on in the minds of the participants in these events.[25]

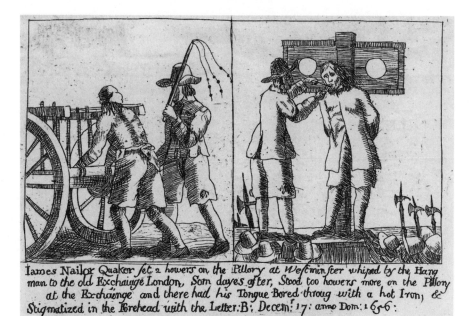

Iames Nailor Quaker set 2 howers on the Pillory at Westminster whiped by the Hang man to the old Exchainge London, Som dayes after, Stood too howers more on the Pillory at the Exchainge and there had his Tongue Bored throug with a hot Iron, & Stigmatized in the forehead with the Letter:B; Decem: 17: anno Dom: 1656:

Fig. 7 The punishment of James Nayler in 1656, following his trial before Parliament and conviction for blasphemy. This is one of many contemporary illustrations of the event. Nayler was the chief Quaker publicist in early years, but the events of 1656 split the movement. He was released from prison in 1659 and died in 1660. (Courtesy, Library Committee of the Religious Society of Friends, Britain Yearly Meeting)

Nayler received no support from local Friends and the whole party was promptly arrested. Nayler was taken to London, and after a famous trial before Parliament was sentenced to be whipped at the cart tail, pilloried, branded, and imprisoned, then to be taken to Bristol for further whippings, and afterward to be imprisoned again.[26] Because of Nayler's high reputation in London, members of Parliament thought that they had caught the leading Quaker, and were determined to destroy him. One Member of Parliament said, "Cut off this fellow and you will destroy the sect."[27] The first part of the sentence was carried out, but at Bristol a Friend was allowed to hold back the executioner's arm, thus reducing the severity of the punishment.

That is a brief outline of events. Up to the time when Nayler retired to Martha Simmons's house, the dispute was a straightforward matter concerning discipline within a meeting. The Quaker theological tenet in question was that the Light of Christ within, since it was the Light of Christ,

could not err nor be divided. It was usual in cases where there was disagreement about the interpretation of "the light" to follow the advice of leading
Friends, in this case Burrough, Howgill, and Nayler. Nayler had at first
agreed with Burrough and Howgill but, on being challenged by Simmons
and Stranger, he had, for whatever reason, wavered.

The latter part of the dispute was a power struggle between Fox and
Nayler, or possibly, since Nayler's health is in doubt, between Fox and the
supporters of Nayler. The relationship between Fox and Nayler up to the
autumn of 1656 was not well defined. Generally, they kept to their own
spheres, maybe by unspoken agreement.[28] If there were disagreements, they
were not publicized. During 1655 and 1656 Nayler's public reputation rose
compared with that of Fox; he was in London, much in the public eye, and
publishing a great deal. It is easy to see how some of those attending the
London meetings, in an atmosphere of apocalyptic excitement, developed
exalted ideas concerning Nayler. Fox, on the other hand, had not been
welcomed so readily in London, being considered odd in behavior and
appearance.[29] He spent most of his time in other parts of the country, and
for eight months of 1656 was in prison. Ralph Farmer in *Sathan Inthron'd*,
published early in 1657, said that Fox was not as well known in Bristol as
Nayler.[30]

Among Quakers in general, Fox was considered the leader. Margaret Fell
wrote to Nayler and advised him to submit to Fox; when it came to making a decision between Fox and Nayler, there was no doubt where her
loyalties lay.[31] The same applied to George Bishop. He had maintained
contacts with Fox while Fox was in prison, met him in Reading after his
release, and having seen Nayler when he passed through Bristol in August,
he knew which of the two he supported.[32] It was probably Bishop who had
Bristol Friends so well organized that no support was shown for Nayler in
October. It was Bishop who wrote to Margaret Fell with news of what had
happened. Not one of the leading Friends openly supported Nayler.

The Nayler affair was in fact an explosion waiting to happen, and Martha Simmons was merely the trigger. Disputes over doctrine and behavior
were characteristic of Quakerism at this time, and all such disputes were
concerned with the weight to be given a particular individual's understanding of "the light." Sooner or later such a conflict was going to involve some
of the leaders.[33] Differences between parts of the country may also have
been a factor; Quakerism had originated in the rural midlands and north,
and was now taking root in the very different environment of London.

Friends sent various documents to Parliament at the time of Nayler's trial. These included an obscure paper by Fox, supposedly written to defend Nayler, which was later interpreted by a friend of Nayler, a wealthy merchant named Robert Rich, to mean that Fox thought that he himself, George Fox, could call himself Christ, but that no one else should do so.[34] An alternative interpretation is that Fox had become aware of the need to defend the Quaker claim, and his own in particular, to have unity with Christ (see Chapter 6). He therefore found it necessary to argue in support of Nayler's right to claim that Christ was in him, without defending what Nayler had done in Bristol. Fox was attempting to make the best of a very difficult situation, and it is not surprising that his paper is unclear.

Friends were shocked by the severity of Nayler's punishment, and there is a marked contrast in the attitude of Bristol Friends when Nayler was sent back for the second part of his punishment in January 1657, compared with their attitude the previous year. George Bishop in his damage-limitation work, *The Throne of God Exalted,* remarked that if his opponents had their way they would have wanted Moses to have had Aaron whipped and burned for setting up the golden calf (Exodus 32).[35]

From July 1657 onward certain Friends were allowed to visit Nayler, who recovered from the punishment, and soon there was a movement in favor of reconciliation. In June 1658 Alexander Parker wrote to Fell that he had seen Nayler three times, and "he is made willing to lie under all [i.e., agree to any restitution], and would do any thing that might in the wisdom of God be seen convenient for taking of all occasion as much as in him lies, either by public recantation . . . or any other way."[36] However, Friends could not agree what to do. Ultimately, said Parker, it all depended on what George Fox thought, and Fox was firmly set against any move to reinstate Nayler. Nayler was finally released in 1659, but Fox would not meet him. Fox was not reconciled with Nayler until 1660, probably at the persuasion of Dewsbury, and even then he grudged it.[37]

Friends' ambivalence is shown by their attitude to Nayler's pamphlets of 1657 and 1658. These were printed by Thomas Simmons, one of the regular Quaker printers and also husband to Martha Simmons, and so presumably they were published under Quaker auspices, but they were all issued anonymously. From 1659 his pamphlets were published under his own name, indicating that Friends no longer regarded him as a pariah. Fox's influence did not prevent Nayler taking part in the Quaker ministry after his release, for Nayler was traveling with Burrough when young Thomas Ellwood was convinced in 1659. Ellwood, later a notable Friend and editor of the first published edition of Fox's *Journal,* recorded in his own autobiography that Nayler had impressed him more than Burrough.[38]

Many of Nayler's late works concerned his own sin and repentance, and were no doubt motivated by his desire for reconciliation with the main body of Friends, but his experience led him to a deeper understanding of sin and forgiveness than is found elsewhere in Quaker writings. Friends laid stress on the faithful following of the Light, and had little to say to backsliders. Nayler knew that it was not so easy: "I found by daily experience that my salvation was not complete so long as my soul was subject under any earthly lust or passion, nor the War over, but as by the mighty working of God in me by that Spirit this came to be subdued under the feet of Christ." It was possible and necessary to repent of sin, but God's punishment must be accepted, and God might take some time to show sins, and how to conquer them. The "ground and root of sin" was not removed at the first turning to Christ: "That ground was but removed as I grew in Christ and he in me . . . in which warfare I came to see the hardship of him that will be a soldier of Christ Jesus. . . . And in this journey I have seen the slothful servant overtaken with a fault which he had once cast behind him."[39]

Nayler died in 1660, following a mugging while he was traveling north. For George Fox it may even have been a relief that the problems of their relationship were now solved.

The conviction of Nayler had a serious effect on the reputation of Friends. Practically every anti-Quaker book of 1657–58 referred to it, with the consequence of increasing Nayler's importance in the eyes of the public. Several of these anti-Quaker works gave Nayler prominence over Fox, Nayler being described as the "Head Quaker in England," and "Your Archbishop Naylor that false Christ."[40] As for George Bishop's opponent in Bristol, Ralph Farmer, he could not restrain his glee; the Lord had indeed delivered his enemies into his hands: "Oh James, thou art already tried and weighed, and art found too light, George Fox and George Bishop, who have the eternal immediate and infallible spirit, have born testimony against you."

Farmer could not resist pressing home the point: "We all speak, and write . . . from that one unerring, infallible and undeceiving Spirit. Is not this your constant language. . . . How went the spirit from James Nayler? . . . how shall we know whether ever he had it? or whether George Fox has it, or ever had it? . . . And whom shall we believe? Tell us, wherein is Nayler behind Fox or wherein is he inferior?" He continued: "Will any people in the world, that are not infatuated, follow such for their guides and teachers (especially infallible ones) over whom the devil may have so much power?" He came to the conclusion that the division between Fox and Nayler was largely pretended, and implied that Fox was trying to save himself, for really, said Farmer, no one could find any distinction between the teaching of Fox and that of Nayler.[41]

This accusation that the "infallible, perfect spirit" was divided had to be answered. George Bishop replied to Farmer, and expressed what became the standard Quaker answer when divisions arose: "The people called Quakers have denied that spirit that led into temptation, and that woman, company, and their actions, as being gone forth, and out of the truth . . . and the people called Quakers, who abide in the truth, are one in the truth, where there is no division."[42]

This did not ease the practical problems. Friends, whatever George Bishop said, were deeply divided. Richard Farnworth was probably one of those affected; from 1656 until 1661 little was heard of him. It is more than likely that he was seriously upset by the Nayler affair, and not sure where his loyalties lay. During the autumn of 1656, when correspondence about Nayler was flying to and fro, the only surviving letter from Farnworth is one to Burrough and Howgill in which he explained at some length why it was quite impossible for him to come to London.[43] He did not mention Nayler, and it looks as if he wanted to keep clear of the controversy.

The Nayler affair caused repercussions among Quakers in various parts of the country and even abroad, and there were many references to difficulties with "weak Friends" during 1657.[44] Fox's first consideration after the trial of Nayler was to limit the inevitable damage to the Quaker movement. He not only had to contend with the loss of Nayler and with a divided movement, but also with the effective loss of Farnworth. In principle, all Quakers were sons or daughters of God and united with Christ, but everybody's "measure" was not equal, and Friends recognized that some people had special callings as "elders" or ministers to the flock. George Fox had an extraspecial calling, and only a minority of Quakers had quarreled with this assumption. Fox was determined that there should be no further challenge to his position.[45] Before the end of 1656, while the controversy over Nayler was at its height, he held several general meetings. A surviving report of what he said on one of these occasions shows that he covered the whole range of private and religious life, with particular emphasis on unity and order: "Therefore who are come now into the power of the Lord God, and to the seed that is royal, that was the elect before the world began, keep your meetings . . . in the power of the Lord God . . . that all uncleanliness whatsoever may by the power of the Lord be brought down and rooted out."[46]

There are no surviving letters discussing arrangements, but Fox's hand can be seen in the establishment of Richard Hubberthorne as leader of the London mission, releasing Burrough and Howgill, who may have been suffering from "burnout," to travel in the ministry. Hubberthorne was in charge of the London meetings by February 1657, perhaps earlier, and was presently joined by Alexander Parker. Both of them had always been close to Fox, and Hubberthorne could be relied on to write lengthy regular reports to Fox or to Fell about what was going on. They ran the London mission efficiently, without showing signs of strain or asking for help, coping with the aftermath of the Nayler affair and dealing with a number of difficult people, for Nayler's followers, led by Martha Simmons, continued to cause trouble in meetings. There was a great disturbance at the Bull and Mouth meeting that February, described by Hubberthorne, who wrote that Martha Simmons "and with her six or seven women, and there was also men of that company . . . they began to sing and to make a noise to stop the truth from the people, and they grew very bold, impudent and filthy and Mar[tha] took a bible and read a psalm and they sung it after her, as they do in steeplehouses."[47] Hubberthorne made an opportunity soon afterward to speak to Nayler's followers, and found that some "was simple and only captivated in their weakness and tenderness, the measure of God not being born up in them to judge of things that differ." These people realized that they did not seriously disagree with the main body of Friends, "so much of their proceedings are stopped . . . and several of them come to meetings and are quiet."[48] The disturbance of meetings grew less, though there were interruptions from time to time during the next year, especially by two women called "Mildred" and "Judy."[49] Nayler's supporters received no encouragement from Nayler himself, and disappeared from view, though many reappeared five years later as supporters of John Perrot (see Chapter 15).

Fox himself continued to travel the country, included London in his itinerary, and, presumably, overcame his earlier problems of acceptance there. Burrough, Howgill, and Dewsbury also traveled, having taken over much of the troubleshooting work of Nayler. The pattern of oversight and care of meetings by the leading ministers was retained, but there was a major administrative reorganization, which is described in Chapter 10.

The loss of Nayler and Farnworth made it difficult to keep up the stream of Quaker pamphlets, and the reduction in Quaker publications in 1657 may have been as much due to this cause as to the renewed official censorship. Fox's twenty-two publications in 1657, following eighteen in 1656, went some way to fill the gap, besides having the effect of publicizing the name of Fox. The general public would not again mistake someone else for the Quaker leader.

During 1657 and 1658 Fox wrote pamphlets on practically every matter of concern to Quakers, intending to demonstrate his ability to make a pronouncement on any topic. Besides expounding Quaker doctrine and writing attacks on the established church, Fox produced pamphlets on most of the specific Quaker ethical testimonies (see Chapter 9), he pronounced on the undesirability of Cromwell becoming king, and he advised the government on the right use of force, lawyers on the foundation of law, businessmen on their morals, and teachers and parents on the upbringing of children, providing them with a children's catechism for their use.[50] Fox, or his helpers, now began to take more care over presentation. Most of Fox's early pamphlets had been very rough, but his style became smoother from 1657 onward, and his pamphlets appear to have been written less hastily. Fox never wrote much with his own hand, and may now have found a new amanuensis.

The most important from this stream of publications was *The Great Mistery of the Great Whore*, compiled during 1657 and 1658, by far the longest book published by Quakers up to this time, and the longest work that George Fox published during his lifetime.[51] It is a neglected work, passed over in a few words in most studies of early Quakerism, but it represents Fox's considered thinking at the time when Quakerism was beginning its metamorphosis from early enthusiasm to later soberness.[52] The "Epistle to the Reader" by Burrough is important in its own right as an account of the history, principles, and practices of Quakerism, and was presumably included to make the whole work more accessible to non-Quakers. Burrough had by now become the most fluent and prolific of the Quaker pamphleteers, was the chosen author of official Quaker statements, and was better known in London than Fox. The choice of Burrough as author of the introduction underlined his position as the leading Quaker after Fox, and also that he was not a rival for the leadership.

The importance of *The Great Mistery* lies as much in its relevance to Fox's position as leader as in its theology (which is covered in Chapter 8). Up to this time Fox had not been an important writer of controversial books, but *The Great Mistery* brought him into this category, and would have been intended to establish his reputation in this field. Nearly all the books that Fox dealt with had already been answered by other writers, but he made no reference to previous answers by other Quakers, whatever their standing in the movement. It is not surprising that he would want to replace Nayler's pamphlets, but Hubberthorne and Burrough were treated in the same way; Fox wanted to provide his own answers to all important anti-Quaker works. *The Great Mistery* gave Fox's answers to seventy-nine known extant books, and to thirty-five other statements including lost books, books that cannot be identified with certainty, and various manuscript and oral sources.[53] Each section followed the usual plan of controversial books, picking up particular points in the opposing writer's book, often with quotations and page references, and answering them piecemeal. The disadvantage in this approach was that the agenda was set by the opposing side, and positive aspects of Quakerism might be neglected. As a systematic statement of Quaker theology *The Great Mistery* therefore had limitations, but its plan could have increased its practical use to individual Quakers, and to persons interested in Quakerism. When seeking a reply to an anti-Quaker work, all they had to do was to turn to the relevant pages in *The Great Mistery* to find an authoritative answer.

Quakers had become very concerned with their public image as an organized group, for after the fall of Nayler they were urgently in need of a "good press." The change in the ethos of the Quaker pamphlet literature between 1656 and 1657–58 is very marked, as it began to shift from prophecy to apologetics. Nayler's *Love to the Lost* of 1656 and Burrough's *Declaration to all the World of our Faith* of 1657 were both important statements of the Christian faith from a Quaker point of view, but Nayler's book was an unqualified exposition of the truth as he saw it, while Burrough, who could declaim equally dogmatically when he thought it appropriate, now put the Quaker point of view with frequent use of phrases such as "We believe so-and so." William Caton's *The Moderate Enquirer Resolved* carried the process further, being set out in question and answer format and designed as a "description of several Objections . . . concerning the contemned people commonly called Quakers, who are the Royal seed of God, and whose innocency is here cleared."[54] Fox's *Great Mistery*, likewise, was much milder in tone than the usual Quaker controversial pamphlets.

The Nayler affair marks the beginning of the end of early Quakerism. The new, more restrained, Quaker body attracted adherents from different backgrounds. William Smith, an Independent pastor from Nottinghamshire and one of the most important Quaker authors of the early Restoration period, joined with Friends in 1658. Isaac and Mary Penington came in the same year. Isaac (1616–79) was the son of Sir Isaac Penington, onetime Lord Mayor of London. He had moved from the parish church to the

Independents, but found no long-term satisfaction, and for a time he called himself a Seeker. He was a friend of John Crook, but was at first not impressed by Quakers. Finally, he agreed to attend a meeting, where, he wrote:

> I felt the presence and power of the Most High among them. . . . I felt the dead quickened, the seed raised, insomuch as my heart . . . said "This is he, there is no other, this is he whom I have waited for and often sought after from my childhood, who was always near me . . . but I knew him not distinctly, nor how to receive him or dwell with him." And then . . . was I given up to the Lord . . . to serve him in the life and power of his seed.[55]

Penington's life as a Quaker covered the transition from enthusiasm to sobriety, and his prolific works included political apocalyptic of the style described in Chapter 5, as well as fine devotional and pastoral writing. Thomas Ellwood, later the editor of Fox's *Journal*, attended some of his first Quaker meetings, as a young man in 1659, at the house of Isaac and Mary Penington.

PART II

SHAPING THE QUAKER FAITH

4

THE BIBLICAL
FRAMEWORK

Of the various influences that shaped the faith of the first Quakers, the
Bible was supremely important. In the mid-seventeenth century, the Bible
was built into the framework of everyday life, and apart from extreme
radicals few people questioned its literal truth and its importance as a
guide. In particular, the Bible, now accessible to any literate person, had a
considerable influence on political developments, especially when the many
passages concerning the "putting down of the mighty" were interpreted
according to the marginal references of the sixteenth-century Geneva translation, which was still commonly in circulation along with the new King
James, or Authorized, version.[1]

Quakers shared this worldview, and their attitude to the Bible was only marginally different from that of some Baptists and Independents, who said that the Bible could only properly be understood by the guidance of the Holy Spirit.[2] There could be no contradiction between Bible and Spirit, because the Spirit never changed, and so for all practical purposes the Bible was authoritative.

Thomas Rosewell, "a witness to the Truth, as it is in Jesus," answering a Quaker query about the religious state of people who were gathered to read the Scriptures but did not have the Spirit of God, thought that the Quakers were proposing an impossibility: "Is there not a sweet harmony and consent between them both, so that the gathering together with the one, cannot possibly exclude the other?"[3] Quakers differed from Rosewell in that they thought some people, those whom they disagreed with, did read the Letter, the actual words of the Bible, without the Spirit, and consequently did not understand the Bible. Christ was the Word, said Friends, and so the Letter, or Bible, was not itself the Word, but nevertheless the Bible was inspired by the Holy Spirit, and was to be obeyed. Opponents of Quakers said that Quakers "deny the Scriptures, though they cite them for their advantages," but in practice Friends accepted the Bible as true and as their guide for conduct.[4]

It was probably not so much the content of the Quaker teaching on the Bible that was provocative to orthodox believers, as its manner of expression. Fox in particular was vehement regarding the deadness of the Letter as opposed to the life of the Spirit.[5] Moreover, the frequency of references in the anti-Quaker literature to Quakers saying that the Bible was useless, or should be burnt, suggests that some of the more outspoken Quakers went beyond what their leaders approved. John Bunyan, for instance, wrote of "Anne Blackley, who did bid me in the audience of many, To throw away the Scripture."[6] As late as 1664, during a dispute with the mayor and aldermen of Hereford, a local Quaker reported to Fox that another Quaker, Katherine Crooke,

> stirred them up against us, not being guided by the wisdom of God in her words, they apprehended by her words that we did disown the Scriptures, and began to cry Blasphemy . . . and this was because Katherine said she had known the Lord if she had never seen nor read the Scriptures whereupon I wished her to forbear . . . and I called to the priest and mayor and people and said they misunderstood my friend and desired them to take notice that we did not deny the Scriptures . . . that which the Scriptures testified of . . . was that which

gave the knowledge of the glory of God in the face of Jesus Christ. . . .
And so I cleared many things which we hold to them by the Scriptures.[7]

All the protestations of the Quaker leadership would not counteract the
impression made by such incidents.

Quaker authors used the Bible in three ways: direct quotation, comment
in the text with references in the margin, and a continuous flowing paraphrase in which biblical phrases from different sources were run together
along with the authors' own comments.[8] To pick up all the biblical references from these paraphrases needs a knowledge of the Bible like that of
early Friends themselves, or else detailed line by line work with a concor-
dance.[9] Even direct quotations and marginal references are little easier to
trace because of the vast numbers of them. Frequently, especially in early
pamphlets, the margins were filled with biblical references, as many as
twenty to a page.[10]

This being said, a reader of early Quaker tracts is left with certain im-
pressions. Quakers interpreted the whole sweep of the Old and New Testament story, from Genesis by way of the prophets through to Christ and the
Book of Revelation, in such a way as to show that the story rightly ended
with the mid-seventeenth-century gift of the Spirit to the Quakers, the
same spirit that had inspired the prophets and apostles. Within the Old
Testament, particular favorites were the more lurid passages from the prophets concerning the coming "Day of the Lord" and also Jeremiah 23 and 31
for the promise of the New Covenant and for the mention of the "north
country." Passages on the North from Isaiah and Daniel were also often
quoted. Ezekiel 34 was in regular use against the "priests": "Woe be to the
shepherds of Israel that do feed themselves! should not the shepherds feed
the flocks? Ye eat the fat, and ye clothe ye with the wool . . . but ye feed
not the flock."

In the New Testament, Quakers made much use of the "Johannine corpus," that is, the Fourth Gospel, the three Epistles of Saint John, and the
Revelation, all books laying stress on Spirit, Light, and Word. Quakers
were especially fond of the prologue to the Fourth Gospel, passages from
the First Epistle concerned with sinlessness, and apocalyptic imagery from
the Revelation. They used the Epistle to the Hebrews for passages relating
to Christ, as the eternal High Priest appointed by God, passing into the
sanctuary of the temple and so making a way into the presence of God for
those who followed him.[11] The Pauline epistles were often quoted, but

references to the first three gospels were relatively rare. Quakers who wished to assert their belief in union with God without risking a blasphemy charge found 2 Peter 1:4 very useful. It reads, "Whereby are given unto us exceeding great and precious promises; that by these ye might be partakers of the divine nature, having escaped the corruption that is in the world through lust." It was turned into a jingle on the title page of Farnworth's *Discovery of Truth and Falsehood*: "Written by one whom the world calls a Quaker, but is of the divine nature made partaker."[12]

In the case of the more prolific Quaker writers, it is possible to compare the extent of their use of the Bible, and differences in their attitudes to it. Farnworth's early tracts are the most biblical of all, as regards direct quotation and even more as regards paraphrase. In his first tracts he did not discuss the distinction between Letter and Spirit; at this stage the issue seems not to have arisen for him, but by 1654 Quakers were being challenged on their attitude to the Bible, and Farnworth expressed the usual Quaker view: "God is not the letter, neither is the letter God: Christ is the new Covenant but Christ is not the letter . . . and the Gospel is the power of God unto salvation, but the Letter is neither the gospel nor the power, but declares it."[13] Francis Howgill, among others, likewise wrote that Matthew, Mark, Luke, and John were not the Gospel, for "Christ is the Gospel, yea the everlasting Gospel."[14] This use of "Gospel," derived from Pauline texts such as 1 Corinthians 4:15 and 2 Corinthians 4:4, was common among the radical sectarians and implied no disrespect to the Bible.[15]

Fox made nearly as much use of the Bible as Farnworth, but laid more emphasis on the Scriptures as the letter, as against the word of God. There was no real difference of opinion between Farnworth and Fox, but there was a difference of temperament. Farnworth's early tracts consisted mainly of spiritual advice and teaching for which frequent reference to the Bible was needed, whereas Fox was combative, announcing, "The Letter is a declaration of the Gospel, and many have the Letter but not Christ," and, "He that puts the letter for the light, when the letter says Christ is the light, is blind."[16] Such phraseology was not intended to be soothing. Years later, when he dictated his *Journal*, Fox wrote that he "had no slight esteem of the Holy Scriptures, but they were very precious to me, for I was in that spirit by which they were given forth, and what the Lord opened to me I afterwards found was agreeable to them."[17] Here spoke an older, more cautious Fox. Many of his early pamphlets do not suggest an "esteem" for Scripture, merely a considerable ability to use it for his own purposes. The young Fox had reacted sharply against biblical authority, as it was understood by the parish ministers whom he was confronting.

In using the Bible, Fox would accept straightforward quotation, but not the opposition's explanations: "We know the Scriptures, and own them as they speak, but all thy exposition of them we deny." God himself, not academic exegesis, provided the key to the Scriptures, and Fox decried, "such as you that would know meanings to the scripture, and cries for meanings, meanings . . . which must be scattered from the Lord God."[18] Biblical scholars for hundreds of years had been in the habit of interpreting difficult Old Testament passages allegorically, but Fox, probably because he was not a biblical theologian, would have none of this. Since the Scripture could only be understood in the Spirit, and since Friends had the Spirit, there was no need for complicated interpretations, nor, as Fox often said, for knowledge of the original languages. This also was a common stance among the radical sects of the time, who had a preponderance of members with no classical education. William Tomlinson, one of the Friends who did have a knowledge of Greek, indeed apologized when quoting from the Greek New Testament: "I desire tender spirits not to be offended, that I use words which they understand not; for I speak to those that do understand the literal sense of them; and must deal with them a little with their own weapons."[19]

Nayler made less use of the Bible than either Farnworth or Fox.[20] He tended to use his own words rather than running together biblical phrases, with fewer direct quotations and marginal references. Some of his most mature and careful thought was shown in *A Discovery of the Man of Sin,* the last part of a four-book controversy (see Chapter 8). The Spirit, he said, was not opposed to Scripture:

> You talk of the commands of God, but his commands you know not, who have them to seek in the letter; for his commands is in Spirit, and ever was, and yet this does not destroy the Scripture, but witness the same Spirit that gave them forth. . . . They that have had the Spirit of God in all ages, have made use of the letter . . . as we do at this day, and yet this letter is not the judge of the Spirit of God in them, for this were to set the letter above the Spirit.[21]

Burrough was very different in his general outlook from both Farnworth and Nayler, being primarily a polemicist who never lost touch with his

Calvinist origins, rather than a writer on Quaker spirituality. He was, however, like Farnworth in that he found it natural to take the Bible as sole
authority, and only said otherwise when, in debate, he was forced to defend
the Quaker position. He might say of his opponents, "They say the Letter
is the Word and the Scripture the Light," but he expressed this opinion
more mildly than Fox did. It was more natural to Burrough to say something positive about the value of the Bible, such as "The Scripture we own
to be a true declaration of life which they lived when they spoke them
forth," and "The Scripture I do own, and that Spirit which spake them
forth I witness."[22]

None of the remaining Quaker writers held a significantly different view.
As an example, Hubberthorne, like Nayler, tended to use his own rather
than biblical phraseology, but used the Bible to prove his points as necessary. Like both Fox and Nayler he was opposed to the kind of Bible study
that was likely to lead to ideas of one's "own brain": "The scribes and
Pharisees were learned men, they could not open the Scripture. Peter, an
unlearned man, he opened the Scripture." His attitude to biblical authority
was like that of Fox and Nayler: "The poor people is groping in the letter
to find life there, when the life was in them that gave it forth."[23]

Thus for Quakers, as for nearly everyone in the seventeenth century, the
Bible provided their spiritual and to a large extent their intellectual frame
of reference. It was customary to regard contemporary happenings as the
fulfilling of biblical prophecy, and Quakers did the same, though they
looked where possible for a straightforward literal meaning for Bible texts.
They would accept the explanation of an Old Testament text by a New
Testament writer, as when St. Paul wrote that the seed of Abraham meant
Christ and his church (Galatians 3:16 and 4:22–31), but they did not
admit the more elaborate allegorical interpretations current in some circles.
Where the Bible gave clear instruction, for instance regarding oaths, it was
to be followed exactly, for this was apostolic doctrine. Where it dealt with
the coming of the Spirit, it was to be understood by the Spirit, which
accounted for Friends' understanding of Baptism and the Lord's Supper
(see Chapter 11).

Quakers, especially Fox, were adept at using Bible texts to prove points.
A set of thirty-five biblical references for use in support of "quaking" was
compiled in advance for use as needed, probably by Fox.[24] Bible texts suitable for defending and explaining quaking are found in seventeen tracts of
1653 and 1654, by several authors, and there may be more. Such use of
"quaking" texts was condemned by several opponents, who said that most

of the examples were nothing to do with the quaking of Quakers, Pagitt claiming that Nayler had cited "all the places in the Scripture which mention either trembling or shaking, never so impertinent [i.e., irrelevant] and far from the purpose."[25] Habbakuk 3:16 was a favorite: "When I heard my belly trembled; my lips quivered at the voice: rottenness entered into my bones." Another favorite was Daniel 10:7: "And I Daniel alone saw the vision: for the men that were with me saw not the vision; but a great quaking fell upon them, so that they fled to hide themselves." A third was Acts 9:6: "And he [Paul] trembling and astonished said, Lord, what wilt thou to have me do?"

Fox could supply references for other subjects as needed, as for instance in an anti-Catholic pamphlet called *The Declaration against all Popery.* One of the points that Fox wished to make was that Friends disapproved of image making, so he included a two-page list of instances of the Children of Israel being commanded not to make images. A later example came from a pamphlet on the naming of children that was designed to show the wrongness and needlessness of water baptism and went through numerous examples from the Bible of how children were named, none of them of course being baptized.[26]

An ingenious new use for Bible texts was found in connection with the common seventeenth-century usage of describing weak and ineffective men as "women."[27] Two women ministers, Priscilla Cotton and Mary Cole, at this time in prison in Plymouth, wrote a pamphlet justifying women's preaching by arguing that when Saint Paul wrote that women should keep silence in the churches (1 Corinthians 14:34–35), he meant spiritually weak people, men or women, not actual female "women" as such.[28] This argument was, however, quietly dropped in due course, and Margaret Fell did not use it in her definitive *Womens Speaking Justified.*[29] No doubt it was just a little too shocking to the gendered society of the day.

Another inventive biblical explanation concerned the Quaker practice of refusing to remove the hat in the presence of social superiors. Quakers said that there is nothing in the Bible requiring one to remove one's hat in such circumstances. Asked to find a positive example of persons keeping their hats on before their superiors, they obliged: according to Daniel 3, Shadrach, Meshach, and Abednego were thrown into the burning fiery furnace, in the presence of Nebuchadnezzar, with their hats on.[30]

An example of Quaker practical use of the Bible occurred in 1655, in connection with the disownment of Christopher Atkinson for sexual misbehavior (see Chapter 10). Joshua 7, the story of Achan who had brought a "devoted" or "defiled" thing into the Israelite camp, was much used at that time by people of all religious persuasions in disciplinary cases.[31] Friends had been persecuted in East Anglia, and concluded that this was God's punishment for having brought the "defiled thing," that is, Atkinson, into the "camp," and that he must therefore be cast out.[32] What was defiled could not be allowed in the camp of the Lord, and if this happened, even unknowingly, it was only to be expected that God would show his displeasure. On numerous other occasions, however, Quakers decided that persecution was a sign of God's favor, since the Bible often told the people of God to expect persecution. Naturally, their opponents would then declare that Quakers were obviously suffering the punishment of God![33]

Besides the Achan text, Quakers had many favorite passages in common with their opponents, indeed, the same text could be used by Quakers and opponents against each other. For instance, 2 Timothy 3:6–8, concerning unsuitable ministers who "creep into houses and take silly women captive," was a regular Quaker text, and William Prynne used it in exactly the same way against Quakers in his *Quakers Unmasked*.[34] New Testament passages such as Mark 13:15–27, concerning the prevalence of false teaching and disturbances as a sign of the coming of God's kingdom, were used by all parties.

Two Quakers queried the accuracy of the accepted Biblical translations. John Audland, in the course of a dispute with Ralph Farmer of Bristol, wrote that the "Spirit was before many languages was, neither is those translations taught and guided by the Spirit."[35] The learned Samuel Fisher developed this thesis, writing that the Bible is in fact often mistranslated and may be fallible, and gave this as his reason for believing the only foundation of faith to be Christ.[36] This viewpoint did not find favor among Friends, who were generally most concerned to demonstrate their close adherence to every Bible text. The suggestion that there could be inaccuracies in the received version of Scripture was probably too revolutionary for most Quakers, who as time passed became more and more anxious to establish their claims to respectability. Indeed, George Whitehead, writing in 1661, contradicted Fisher, insisting that "The Scriptures . . . were given forth by the Spirit of God, and no whit altered by translation, they are a perfect Testimony of God . . . whatsoever is written ought to be believed and received for Truth."[37] Whitehead's view, rather than Fisher's, was probably more typical of Quakers, and definitely so as the century progressed.

Toward the end of the 1650s there was a change in Quakers' use of the Bible, in that they concentrated on fewer texts. There were not so many pamphlets whose margins were filled with biblical references. In controversies concerning tithe one passage was argued again and again. This was the story in Genesis 14:18–20, Abraham's meeting with the priest-king Melchizedek, and whether the offerings that Abraham made to him could be considered tithes in any proper sense of that word. The Quakers insisted that they were voluntary gifts made on a particular occasion, and that Abraham was not compelled to make them, nor was he making them regularly for the maintenance of Melchizedek.

The text that was most frequently discussed in general controversy was John 1:9: "That was the true light that lightens every man coming into the world." Controversial writing about the nature of the Quaker "light" became narrowed until it was nearly all focused on this one verse, which became known as the Quakers' text. Associated with arguments about the light were frequent references to the "holy men" of the Old Testament, who, the Quakers said, had fully possessed the light before the earthly coming of Christ. This narrower use of the Bible was to some extent forced on Quakers by their opponents, who insisted on debating these particular texts when arguing with Quakers. These debates are considered in Chapter 8.

5

THE KINGDOM OF THE LORD

The mid-seventeenth century, as noted in Chapter 1, was a time of much speculation about the end of the present world order and the reign of Christ that was to come, beliefs deriving from various biblical passages and especially from the Book of Revelation. Many people thought that the millennium, the thousand-year reign of Christ prophesied in Revelation 20:1–8, would arrive in the very near future, some believing, according to one contemporary author, "Independancy to be the beginning of Christ's Kingdom which is to be here on earth a thousand years."[1] During the Civil Wars the idea developed that the Saints who would bring in the Kingdom of Christ, and who were the true Body of Christ, were the army and their political and religious leaders. "God is now rising as a man of war in the

Saints, by whom he will destroy all the oppressors and oppressings of men," wrote a noted Seeker, William Erbury.[2] The execution of the king, the "man of blood," was seen by some people as part of the process of bringing in the Kingdom of God. Religion was politicized, and much political business was concerned with the conduct of religious affairs. The Quaker movement was therefore closely connected with contemporary politics, and its success was to a considerable extent the result of its political relevance.

The most extreme of the groups who understood the Kingdom of God in terms of practical politics were the Fifth Monarchists, so called from their emphasis on the Fifth Monarchy, which is the rule of Christ according to the Book of Revelation. It is not possible to draw a clear line between the early Quaker and Fifth Monarchist teaching, for both emphasized the part that the saints would play in the establishment of the Kingdom of Christ upon earth, and shared many common radical ideas. Most Fifth Monarchists were Calvinists with Baptist origins, and were more specifically millenarian than Quakers, producing some very precise political blueprints for the reign of Christ. Fifth Monarchists mostly came from the south of the country, and from towns, while the first Quakers came from the rural midlands and north.[3] Quakers were not, technically, millenarian, if that word is used in its exact sense, waiting for a thousand-year reign of Christ before the final judgment. Quakers generally described the coming end of the age in the language of Old Testament prophets combined with the less specific texts from the Book of Revelation, and they showed no great interest in the exact fulfillment of obscure prophecies.[4]

The events of 1653, a turbulent year in British politics, had a great influence on the development of Quakerism. In April 1653 Cromwell expelled the Rump Parliament, and after much discussion the so-called Nominated Parliament was appointed. This Parliament, also called the Parliament of Saints, or the Barebones Parliament after one of its members, Praise-God Barbones, consisted of 140 men chosen by the Council of State from a list of nominees supplied by the gathered churches, plus others of the Council's choice.

Cromwell addressed the opening session thus: "You are called with a high call; why should we be afraid to think that this may be the door to usher in the things that God hath promised?" There was a great surge of public expectation. Twenty-six of the thirty-six Quaker tracts published in 1653 dealt with the Kingdom of the Lord that they, and many other people, hoped would now appear on earth. Some Quakers were personally involved in the political aspects of the hoped-for victory of the Saints, such as Captain Amor Stoddart, one of the first army officers to join with Fox. Thomas Aldam kept in touch with the political situation, and evidently had early news of the army activity that preceded the expulsion of the Rump. Writing in February 1653 to Amor Stoddart, Aldam said that he rejoiced to hear the Lord's voice, "sounding through you, as in the demonstrance of the chief officers of the army, therein hearing a general convincement upon your spirits," that Christ "hath made himself manifest in flesh in you" and that the cries of the "poor oppressed Commonwealth" might soon be heard. He also wrote personally to General John Lambert, appealing for his influence in reforming "oppression in tithes and oppression in corrupt laws," and in dealing with rack-renting and oppression from gentry, priests, judges, and justices, who received rewards "contrary to the teaching of the Lord."[5]

George Fox was one with his contemporaries in that he saw politics and religion as two aspects of the same thing. The Nominated Parliament, in the event, did not immediately bring in God's Kingdom, and Fox, like other radicals, became dissatisfied with its progress. He published a collection of short pieces under the title *Newes coming up out of the North*, giving a warning to England and all nations: "The righteous seed of God is risen . . . which was dead and is alive. . . . Now is the great and mighty hand of the Lord stretched forth over the wicked. . . . Woe to the inhabitants of the earth." Fox's personal sympathies were made clear, for evil rulers, everywhere, would "be cut down with the same power that cut down the King who reigned over this nation, in whose family was a nurse for Papists and for bishops." This pamphlet contained Fox's political program for other matters besides reform of the church, notably law reform, which was a major concern of the Nominated Parliament. Those "set over the people" should be "men that hate covetousness, which are faithful to God, and that no drunkard or swearer bear office." No one should be put to death for theft, and there should be strict rules against popular sports.[6] The last point was common ground with many contemporaries.[7]

The most passionate of the early Quaker tracts with a strong political flavor was Benjamin Nicholson's *Blast from the Lord*, where knowledge of and concern about particular social evils were set squarely in an apocalyptic warning. Nicholson was one of the Quakers imprisoned in York Castle, and he died there during a second imprisonment in 1660. He began, "O England, take warning, the Lord is risen, he hath drawn out his sharp and glittering sword . . . to cut down all things that stand up in opposition against the pure being of his everlasting love and eternal happiness. Now is

the time of the breaking-forth of God's love upon the children of men."
This tract is worth quoting at some length, although its description of
specific ills was not representative of Quaker publications in general:

> O all ye powers of the earth, God is coming to overturn, overturn,
> overturn your power, and give it to him whose right it is: Jesus Christ
> shall have the rule and dominion over all nations. . . . Instead of
> covering the naked, and feeding the hungry, you set out laws to pun-
> ish them, my heart bleeds to think of the hard usage of my poor
> fellow creatures who have no abiding . . . if a poor creature steal a
> horse, ox, or sheep, he is either put to death or burned in the hand;
> but you never consider how many horses, oxen or sheep you steal
> from the Lord. . . . O you great men of the earth, it is along of you
> that there is so many thieves, for you hold the creation in your hands,
> and by all means go about to defraud the poor.[8]

Richard Farnworth was another who shared the belief that "the kingdoms of the world must be the kingdoms of the Lord and of his Christ,
and the earth shall be full of the knowledge of the Lord." In a tract "to be
read on the Market Cross at Rotheram, upon a market day" he wrote, "The
great day of the Lord is coming. . . . We look for new heaven and new
earth . . . and the nations that are saved shall wake in the glorious light and
liberty of the sons of God." He had great hopes of the new Parliament:
"Light is rising in Parliament and people, to see the deceits of the priests."
He also saw the turmoil from another point of view, as a spiritual battle
where the cosmic war, described in Revelation 12 and 20, took place
within the believers: "Now the kingdom of Jesus Christ is setting up in the
spirits of his people . . . Michael stands up . . . though Gog and Magog
join in battle against the Lamb yet he shall prevail and get the victory."[9]
Farnworth was severe on the rich, but less specific than Nicholson.
Shortly before the expulsion of the Rump Parliament he wrote that priests
and professors were "heady high-minded ones that fare sumptuously, grinding the poor to powder in taxation and oppression, you, that have got a
great deal of earth into your hands which is the Lords . . . [let] the poor
starve in the streets . . . did you but know Christ you would not suffer
him to want in his members, you would not imprison him to satisfy your
lusts."[10] James Parnell, the youngest of the Quaker preachers, expressed
similar feelings: "Woe unto you that are called Lords, Ladies, Knights. . . .
Your fellow creatures must labour like slaves under you. . . . [They] must

hunger and thirst and labour when you are eating, drinking, and sleeping, and here like Dives you sit at ease, and poor Lazarus lying starving without."[11]

Opponents, not surprisingly, came to the conclusion that Quakers were advocating community of property:

> They hold that all things ought to be common, and teach the doctrine of Levelling privately to their disciples. Those that know the leaders of the sect best, judge them to be downright Levellers, and that fear of suppression keeps them for the present from teaching that doctrine openly. Several of them have affirmed that there ought to be no distinction of estates, but an universal parity.[12]

Such accusations, and they were often repeated, were reminiscent of the extravagances of the Anabaptists of Münster in Germany during the previous century, when an attempt to set up a commune had ended in disaster. Nayler was charged: "There is much talk by some of your friends of dividing men's estates, and having all things common." Nayler replied this was not so, unless, "the power of the Gospel fall upon the rich or poor, and move them to distribute their own."[13]

Quakers, at least in their public authorized statements, did not share the extreme strand of radical belief represented by Gerrard Winstanley, that private property was evil, a consequence of the Fall of Man.[14] Despite the examples quoted and others like them, issues of social justice were not a major topic in the majority of Quaker pamphlets, in which the poor always seemed to be "them," and not "us." Richard Hubberthorne once described his audience as being "the under sort of people," which is indicative of the usual Quaker attitude.[15] Very often phrases such as "grinding the faces of the poor" were included in lists of ill-doing that the Lord would at some time punish, and the language would be general and derived from the Old Testament, without much immediate reference.[16]

Quakers were in fact successful in attracting and holding many people with a clear interest in maintaining the economic and social status quo. Comfortably-off yeomen like Aldam, and wealthy gentlefolk like Margaret Fell, did not feel threatened by Quakerism as regards their personal possessions, and this support from members of the well-to-do classes made a considerable difference to the ultimate success of Quakerism. Fox and other influential Quakers were not so much concerned with the ownership of wealth, as with the fact that extreme poverty existed alongside wealth misused to obtain luxuries or political influence, and Fox himself seems to have had adequate funds.[17] It is likely that any of the extreme political radicals who may have been attracted to Quakerism were prevented from proclaiming their views in print; this would have been one of the functions of the Quaker censorship of publications. Anti-Quaker literature and reports of court proceedings suggest the existence of a more radical oral Quakerism, but the main political interest of the Quaker leadership, and indeed for most Quakers and for many other radicals, was church reform, and specifically the abolition of tithe and other church dues. Such reforms were supported by many people in a good social position.

Objections to the tithe system were nevertheless often interpreted as attacks on property rights and the social system. Quakers, always sensitive to such charges, argued that this was not what they themselves meant, but in practice, the economic and religious aspects of the campaign against tithes could not be separated. One rebel against tithes was Isaac Grayes, who was pursued for unpaid tithes during the Civil War period, and escaped by joining the army "in the hope of gaining not only victory . . . but also to have seen an end of that power by which tyranny and oppression is still promoted." After the war he went home, but his adversary heard of it, and sent to arrest him, and "did by force of arms break into my house upon me, but being by me strongly resisted with sword and pistol, they durst not proceed the attempts to come up into my chambers." He escaped, and took refuge "at a Friends house" until he was betrayed and arrested.[18] Evidently there were Quakers who would assist tithe rebels, even if they performed acts of violence.

If the tithe system was to be abolished, another way had to be found of financing the parish ministry, and a main task of the Nominated Parliament was to find a system that would be agreeable to all parties. In the early months of 1653, radicals of all complexions shared the hope that the hated tithes would soon disappear for good, but it proved impossible to agree on an alternative. In November the Parliament was dissolved, with the tithe system still intact, so that Quakers and other radicals, greatly disappointed, had to rethink their strategy. The last word on 1653 belongs to Nayler's *Lamentacion over the Ruines of this Oppressed Nation*, written in November 1653: "Oh England! how is thy expectation failed now after all thy travails? . . . as power hath come into the hands of men it hath been turned into violence, and the will of man is brought forth instead of Equity." Although he still believed that the Lord would "arise . . . gather the outcasts . . . and . . . bring them to possess the gates of their enemies,"

Nayler and others were beginning to realize that this was not going to happen yet.[19] But political failure was not the end of all hope. For Nayler the Kingdom of God was more spiritual than political; he was, after all, some years older than most of his colleagues and had long experience of the gap between political aspirations and reality. Even before the collapse of the Parliament he was writing of the Kingdom: "You have been seeking without, but it is within you, and there you must find it . . . and the way to the Kingdom is within you, and the light that guides into the way . . . is within."[20]

In the course of the next few years, most Quakers came to share this point of view, for a political apocalypse was not now an immediate practicality. Cromwell was appointed Lord Protector, with the assistance of a Council of State, and a period of relatively stable government set in. During 1654, the Quaker proclamation shifted away from the coming of the Kingdom of God on earth, toward emphasizing their belief that the Kingdom was to an extent already realized among Quakers, the sons and daughters of God, as Fox termed them. Quakers did not invent the idea that the Kingdom of God was, in a sense, spiritually present in the church, for this belief can be found among the gathered churches from which many of them had come, but they transformed this idea into a belief that they, as the only true Saints, had a special destiny to lead the spiritual transformation of the world, as the necessary preliminary to the coming of the "new earth" that they still hoped for.[21] There is no direct evidence, but it is not unlikely that the Quaker national mission of 1654 had its roots in the failure of the Nominated Parliament the previous autumn. If the Kingdom of the Lord could not be established by Parliamentary action, then the Quakers had an alternative.

Farnworth adapted to the new situation immediately, and from 1654 he described salvation in purely spiritual terms, so that the Kingdom of the Lord, or the New Jerusalem, was for him entirely present and within, unrelated to the world of events.[22] There was less obvious difference between Fox's 1653 and 1654 writings, for 1654 was the great year of storming Quaker success, when Fox wrote, "Repent, for the day of the Lord is coming. Awake ye worldlings, hearken to that in your consciences. . . . Tremble and quake all ye nations, for the whirlwind is gone forth . . . the day of the Lord is appearing that shall burn as an oven." Nevertheless, the spiritual and inward aspect of the Kingdom was more noticeable in Fox's writings than in the previous year, with more passages of this type: "You turn from the light of Christ within you (which he hath enlightened you withal), and do not wait for the Kingdom of Jesus Christ to be made manifest within you."[23]

Nayler's works of 1654 used much apocalyptic biblical language, with imagery from the Book of Revelation, probably because he was now much engaged in public controversy, and found this imagery more suited to answering his opponents. But he made it clear that for him the Kingdom of God was really present and spiritual, and wrote of the "more glorious discovery and manifestation of Christ, to see him appearing in this second time in the spirit without sin unto salvation."[24]

In 1654 Francis Howgill and Edward Burrough were conducting an immensely successful mission that must indeed have seemed like the breaking-in of the Kingdom of God, and their pamphlets witness to the success of their war against the powers of darkness, as heralded by the coming of the Quakers from the North:

> And now has the Lord God of power drawn his sword, and a new open war is proclaimed in the North parts of England even betwixt Michael our Prince and the Dragon, the Trumpet of the Lord is sounding, and he is appearing in power for the deliverance of sin . . . woe, woe misery and lamentation and howling . . . is coming upon the Beast and the false prophet, and upon corrupt law and rule.[25]

The two tracts of William Dewsbury published in 1654 provided a good example of the ability of some of the first Quakers to believe simultaneously in a political-apocalyptic upheaval expected in the near future, together with a present-spiritual view of the Judgment. In the *True Prophecy of the Mighty Day of the Lord,* as might be expected from that title, there was thunder in the style of the Old Testament:

> Now is the Lord appearing in this day of his mighty power to gather his Elect together out of all Forms, and Observations, Kindreds, Tongues and Nations . . . and exalting Jesus Christ to be the King of Kings . . . to lead before his army which he hath raised up in the North of England . . . to cut down High and Low, Rich and Poor, Priests and People . . . that . . . walk in disobedience to the righteous law of God, the pure light of conscience.

In complete contrast is this passage from *The Discovery of Man's Return to his First Estate*: "Friends, Babylon is within you, the mother of harlots is within you . . . the beast which all the world wanders after, is your wills, that makes war against the Lamb of God in you, which is the light that makes manifest the evil of your hearts."[26]

Overall, Quaker beliefs in the mid-1650s ranged from expectation of the imminent coming of the Day of the Lord to the belief that the Kingdom of God had already come in the spirits of the believers.[27] Most typical was the belief that while the Kingdom of God was already beginning to be present in the Quaker movement, a final consummation in the (probably near) future was also to be expected; "the Kingdom is come and coming" was the typical Quaker phrase. These variations support the view that Quakers derived from several backgrounds and brought something of their original beliefs with them.[28] These views were all within the limits tolerated by the leadership, and suggestions such as those put forward by Martha Simmons (see Chapter 3) were not acceptable.

Non-Quakers took particular note of the Quaker belief that the Kingdom had actually come. "They judge themselves already glorified," wrote Ralph Farmer, a Bristol minister who was one of the bitterest opponents of Quakers.[29] In 1655 and 1656, which were years of high millenarian expectation, Quakers stood apart from the rest of England. The Quakers' reaction to their compatriots' expectations was to emphasize their distinctive view that the Kingdom of God was already, to an extent, present in themselves, and that the full consummation would be attained by spiritual transformation rather than by either secular politics or a final Judgment.[30] The outstanding example of this viewpoint comes in Nayler's detailed and thoughtful *Love to the Lost* of 1656, in which the final Judgment is almost entirely internalized: "True Judgement . . . is a gift from the Spirit of God, set in the heart of every one who dwells in the Light of Christ: which Judgement passes upon all that's in the Creature, contrary to the life of God, and so, as it is received, springs up with Light and Salvation, to the redeeming of the heart from all uncleanness."[31]

By 1656 Burrough had become a pamphleteer second only to Nayler, and one of his most important works was *Trumpet of the Lord Sounded out of Sion,* a denunciation of all that was bad in current political and religious life. Burrough commented on the contemporary belief that Christ would come again in person: "His Reign and his Kingdom is not of this world . . . the suffering of Christ must you know, before you can see him Reign, and through his war must you strive, before you can obtain his victory, and him must you own, in his convincing you of sin, before you can witness his Reign in glory upon earth over sin."[32] The emphasis on the spiritual nature of the kingdom was similar to Nayler's, but it was typical of Burrough to lay more emphasis on the conquest of sin, so that entry to the Kingdom was a conversion experience. For Burrough, there was more tension between the "now" and the "not yet" of the Kingdom. Burrough looked for a theocracy, but was not disheartened by the failure of the political road to the Kingdom of God. The Kingdom would come as the result of all individuals "owning" Christ.

During the mid-1650s, while the Quakers' understanding of the Kingdom of God was becoming spiritualized, they found less and less sign of the hoped-for Kingdom of God upon earth, for they were forced on the defensive, and had to struggle for their position in relation to the civil law. This had been a point at issue from their beginning, when Quakers were accused of denying the authority of civil magistrates, but it was less urgent while Friends were few in number and confined to the North.[33] As Quaker preachers spread throughout the country they were considered public nuisances, and were dealt with by local justices under any laws that might apply. The Quakers would not take off their hats in court, and the magistrate who tried Dewsbury and his companions at Northampton was one who believed that "if thou and Fox had us in your power, you would soon have your hands imbrewed in blood. . . . You are transgressors of the law, in that you are not subject to Government, and authority, in refusing to put off your hats."[34]

Quakers wrote a number of tracts dealing with legal matters, to the effect that, while civil government was to be respected, it had no rights over the church (themselves) and wicked laws need not be obeyed.[35] Burrough was particularly clear concerning this.

> Magistrates and Magistracy we deny not, but give respect for conscience sake; for who bears the sword of justice, who use their power to be a terror to the wicked . . . are Ministers of God. . . . But to such as act by their own wills in corrupt laws . . . we cannot be subject, but choose rather (than to transgress the law of God which is written into our hearts, by submitting to such mens wills and laws) to suffer by the corrupt wills of men, under corrupt laws.[36]

No government can accept the right of people to choose which laws they will obey. Despite Burrough's declaration of respect toward magistrates, the Quaker attitude to law appeared to the government as an invitation to anarchy. Cromwell was tolerant of eccentric sects, but the Quaker mass meetings, now appearing in many places, seemed likely to provoke public unrest. Thus, Hubberthorne was charged in Norwich: "That the people in a great number gathered about me, which might have proved of evil consequence, they being the under sort of people."[37]

Quakers had special problems because of the institution of the Oath of Abjuration in April 1654. This order required people to take an anti-Catholic oath, to be administered as and when local justices thought fit, and there are a number of records of Friends being gaoled for refusing it. London Quakers issued a pamphlet pointing out to Cromwell that they could take no oath because they "own the doctrine of Christ Jesus, who said Swear not at all," but they assured him "we do deny and condemn, with the light, all popish ways and their supremacy."[38] These matters are discussed more fully with other Quaker practices in Chapter 9.

Quakers sometimes deliberately stirred up trouble for themselves, as when Burrough took a distinctly inflammatory tone in a leaflet aimed at the large and discontented army.

> All you Governors, Captains, Officers and Soldiers, consider how you walk answerable in obedience to the Lord, from whom you have had power to overcome your enemies. . . . O consider and perform your covenant to the Lord . . . the rulers and lawyers have done violence, and oppressed the innocent, and trodden the poor underfoot. . . . Ye soldiers take warning, this is the word of the Lord to you all; uphold them not . . . how little is yet accomplished? For great is the suffering of the Lords people . . . even such men as have been in actual arms against you, are now exalted . . . and work tyranny over the Lords people.[39]

This would be unacceptable to any government, and the Protectorate was always afraid of disaffection. It is therefore not surprising that Burrough wrote to Fox that government spies come "to hear and carry the best report they can to the heads of the city and the nation." He told Fox that he had met with Gerrard Winstanley, leader of the ill-fated Digger colonies, who believed "we are sent to perfect that work which fell in their hands."[40] A coming-together of Diggers and Quakers, if observed by government spies, would reinforce their suspicions. Burrough may have been trying out Fox's reaction; Fox's opinion of Winstanley is not recorded, but he did not approve of Levellers, counting them with Anabaptists, Independents, Presbyterians, and Ranters, as people not living in the Light of Christ.[41]

As the government became increasingly troubled by the disruption caused by the Quaker mass movement, measures were taken against Quakers. A proclamation of February 1655 forbade the disturbance of public worship. The Lord's Day Act of 1656 extended these provisions to disturbance of ministers before or after worship, and people were required to attend an approved place of worship. The Vagrancy Act was applied in 1657 to persons traveling without due cause, and the existing law against traveling on the Lord's day to persons "vainly or profanely walking."[42] The effect was to make it harder for Quaker ministers to travel, for Quakers to enter or to meet near churches, and for them to go any distance to meetings.

Various Friends wrote to Cromwell and met with him, but got little satisfaction.[43] Fox's first contact with Cromwell followed his arrest after the Swannington meeting (see Chapter 2), when he wrote giving an assurance that Friends would not take up arms against the government.[44] Then came a pamphlet, beginning tactfully, "To thee, Oliver Cromwell, into whose hands God hath committed the Sword of Justice, that under thee all may be godly and quietly governed. A terror to the evildoers, and for the encouragement of them that do well."[45] Quakers declared that they posed no threat to civil order and would not be involved in armed insurrection.[46] One wrote, "The seed that the Lord has brought out of the North Country has grown to thousands and ten thousands in all parts of England . . . yet not one of these soldiers has so much as a stick in their hands; but they have a sword in their mouths and with it they slay the nations."[47]

It was the "sword in their mouths" that caused much of the trouble. Quaker language could be extremely militaristic and full of warlike metaphors. Military metaphors came naturally to mind among a group with so many members who had experience of soldiering, so soon after what many had believed to be a holy war. Burrough, who was too young to have fought, entitled one of his pamphlets *To the Camp of the Lord in England*, meaning an army camp, and wrote,

> Put on your armour and gird on your sword, and lay hold on the spear, and march into the field, and prepare yourselves for battle, for the nations do defy our God, and say in their heart, *Who is the God of the Quakers, that we should fear him and obey his voice?* . . . Stand upon your feet, and appear in your terror as an army with banners . . . cut down with the right hand and slay on the left, and let not your eye pity, nor your hand spare.[48]

This kind of talk could be taken literally. There were also rumors of Quaker relationships with Papists and other troublemakers. A warrant for the arrest of "Franciscans" was made out in connection with riots in Bristol, while Miles Halhead and Thomas Salthouse were arrested in Plymouth on suspicion of being Cavaliers, in spite, as they said, of their having certificates from the captain of the fort at Bristol, giving them permission to travel.[49] Consequently, Friends became very disillusioned with Cromwell's government, and one wrote,

> To thee Oliver Cromwell, thus says the Lord, I had chosen thee amongst the thousands in the nations, to execute my wrath upon my enemies, and gave them to thy sword with which I fought for the zeal of my own name . . . and therein for a time thou wast zealous. . . . But thou art fallen from thy first integrity, and in the spoil of my enemies art exalted, and art set up in the glory of the world, which is not pleasant in my sight. . . . But now . . . in thy name do my seed suffer . . . woe to them that are their oppressors.[50]

As time passed with still no sign of the Kingdom of God upon earth, radicals of all complexions came to feel that something had gone wrong. "Not many years since, Jesus Christ began to shine forth . . . and bondage of the law and the teachers thereof passed away, and liberty and peace in him broke forth," wrote one Separatist, but now this liberty was being "turned into wantonness and liberty in the flesh."[51] In 1656–57, there was a movement to promote the idea that Cromwell should become king, and the radicals, Quakers among them, thoroughly disapproved. "Keep kingship off thy head," Fox advised. "Oh Oliver! take heed of undoing thyself, by running into the things of this world that will change."[52]

In April 1657, a group of Fifth Monarchists led by Thomas Venner, as disillusioned with the Protectorate government as the Quakers but with different ways of showing it, attempted a revolt.[53] Their rebellion was a fiasco, but Quakers now had practical reasons for declaring their distance from this movement, for the state papers of April 23, 1657, noted that, "Its said the Anabaptists and Quakers were chiefly active in the conspiracy."[54] Burrough wrote that the Kingdom of the Lord was spiritual, and definitely not to be advanced by violent means, but rather by suffering. To some extent it was already present:

> The Kingdom of Christ is setting up, and it is not of this world, neither shall be exalted, nor advanced, by worldly policy, and worldly

wisdom, nor by carnal weapons. . . . You that are waiting for the Kingdom of Christ . . . seek for it where it may be found . . . through suffering must the Kingdom of Christ be set up, and not by rebellion through crafts, and plots, and secret policy, and turbulent arisings.[55]

One Friend met Fifth Monarchists in prison, and was shocked by their ideas:

The word of truth to you . . . who pass under the name of Fifth Monarchy; there is a precious seed stirring in many of you, but verily it is hid in the earth. . . . The murderer is got uppermost, and in this you are waiting . . . an opportunity . . . to take up the carnal sword to begin an offensive war. . . . Some of your fellowship declared to my face in this prison, and said that the kingdom of Christ was a bloody kingdom; woe be to you bloodthirsty ones. . . . You are of your father the devil . . . to make Christ the Lamb . . . a murderer like unto thyself.[56]

The Quaker establishment took a cautious line, protesting at government policies but distancing themselves from involvement in rebellion. A few Quakers, who had possibly slipped their pamphlets past the censorship (both Quaker and official), continued to use strong language, as, for instance, Thomas Zachary:

Unto you who at first were raised up by a mighty Spirit, to go forth with the sword in your hands, to recover some long lost liberties of the good people of England, from under the tyrannical powers of kings and bishops. . . . Your true interest lies in the broken, poor, despised people of God dissenting from the worlds worships and ways: while you were true to them and their liberty, you did abide in your first principles of faithfulness, but in as much as you have quit that interest, you have forgotten yourselves and your own original.[57]

For most Quaker pamphleteers, however, the idea of the Kingdom of the Lord became disconnected from political practicalities. In the final years of the Protectorate, the hope that the Kingdom would come by means of a change of heart in the government, probably preceded by divine intervention, was not dead, but government restrictions on publications and the unsympathetic political climate drove it underground, whence it rarely emerged until after the death of Cromwell. Quakers could see the Lord active in the success of their mission, and could wait for him to complete his work.

As a postscript to this chapter, one other aspect of the English under-standing of the Kingdom of God needs to be mentioned. This was a recon-sideration of the position of the Jews, who had been expelled from England some centuries before. Romans 11 suggests that, before the Kingdom of God can come in fullness, the Jews must be converted. In 1656, English people were discussing the possibility of allowing Jews to return to En-gland, as a preliminary to their conversion and the coming of the King-dom. Margaret Fell, George Fox, and other Friends shared this interest, and wrote tracts explaining to the Jews, from a Quaker point of view, where their beliefs had gone wrong, and what was necessary to return to the true fold.[58] Contacts with Jews were a feature of Quakerism during the rest of the century.

6

PUTTING EXPERIENCE
INTO WORDS

Not all the themes that made up the early Quaker faith can be described in terms of politics, for the Quaker movement had been born in an immensely exciting, usually corporate, experience (see pages 6, 144). It was the charismatic phenomena of their meetings, more than anything else, that distinguished Quakers from the other radical sects with which they shared many ideas. Moreover, many of those who became Quakers went through intense personal religious upheavals on their way to the new faith. The Friends had to find ways of accounting for these experiences in terms that made sense within the bounds of current thought and theology. Their emphasis on the present and spiritual Kingdom of the Lord, described in the previous chapter, represented one method of rationalizing what had happened to them.

Fox often expressed the Quaker experience in terms of sonship to God, a close relationship like that of Christ to the Father. ("Daughtership" would equally have applied, but the seventeenth-century custom was to assume that the masculine included the feminine). Fox is on record as calling himself "the son of God" on a number of occasions, and there are two such references in the original *Journal* manuscript, which were omitted from the first printed edition, and another in the *Short Journal,* which was written in 1663–64.[1] He retained this form of expression throughout his life despite the fact that it could be considered blasphemous.

Sometimes he varied the terminology. According to the earliest contemporary record of Fox's teaching, from the charge-sheet of his trial at Derby in 1650, Fox and his companion John Fretwell asserted that they were united with Christ, and in the course of questioning they said that they had no sin, for Christ was in them and had taken away their sin. When asked if they were Christ they replied, they were nothing, Christ was all, and when asked if stealing was sin, they said that all unrighteousness is sin. The Derby magistrates clearly thought that the men before them were of the Ranter kind, but Fox and Fretwell evidently meant that, if Christ was in them, it was not possible for them to act in ways that not only they, but most people, would consider wicked.[2]

A curious paper by Fox is important to the understanding of the original Quaker theology. It is not in the collected edition of his epistles, presumably having been suppressed as unacceptable when these were published at the end of the seventeenth century. It was addressed to "Margaret Fell and every other friend who is raised to discerning" and is dated 1653.

> According to the Spirit I am the son of God and according to the flesh I am seed of Abraham which is Christ, which seed is not many but one, which seed is Christ and Christ in you. The mystery which has been hid for ages but is now made manifest . . . which seed bruised the serpent's head. . . . According to the spirit I am the son of God before Abraham was, before Jesus was, the same which doth descend, the same doth ascend.[3]

There is much more in the same vein, and it is by no means entirely clear, but it shows that Fox in these early days transgressed the current blasphemy law in expressing his sense of unity with Christ, something that is not obvious in his published *Epistles*. Sometimes, like other Friends, Fox used the convenient text 2 Peter 1:4 when writing of Friends' unity with God:

"All dear Friends everywhere who have tasted of everlasting power and are made partakers of the divine nature, be faithful."[4]

The two early anti-Quaker books, the anonymous *Querers and Quakers* and Francis Higginson's *Brief Relation of the Irreligion of the Northern Quakers*, provide further evidence that the earliest Quaker teaching was mainly concerned with direct union with Christ or with God, expressed in terms of the Body of Christ, or of divine sonship, or of divine indwelling. Higginson emphasized Quaker teaching on the union of believers with Christ, or with God, and *Querers and Quakers* referred to the Quaker belief in "regeneration." In 1653 both Fox and Nayler were tried for blasphemy, and in the pamphlet *Saul's Errand to Damascus*, published early in 1653, they defended themselves against the charges. Both Fox and Nayler had said that God was in them, and both, probably, were blaspheming according to the law, despite their equivocations as to what they had meant. It was fortunate for them that, as noted in Chapter 2, certain judges in the North gave limited support to Quakers, and stretched the law a little in their favor.

There are a number of surviving letters, mostly to George Fox and to Margaret Fell, in which the recipient is addressed in the language of popular devotion as Christ would be. In later years they were an embarrassment, for the original scripts show attempts, probably made by Fox himself, to delete the offending passages. Quaker theologians and historians have also found them an embarrassment. These letters were written by a number of different people, mostly during the earlier years by people who first knew Fox in 1651 or 1652, but include some written by later converts. As an example, a letter from Farnworth to Fox (already quoted in Chapter 2) begins: "My Heart, my life my oneness, thou art ever with mee thou lies within my bowels thou knowest where I am, I cannot be hid from thee, thou knowest my secrets my beloved. . . . Thou art as a father unto me," and continues in the same vein, with the word "father" in some instances apparently meaning "God" without equivocation.[5] A rapturous letter to Fox from Camm, in addition to saying that Fox is "beautiful and comely and glorious" and "beyond what I can yet comprehend, express or utter," also describes dreams in which Fox had embraced and kissed him "with the kisses of thy mouth."[6] This is a reference to the Song of Songs 1:2, and today one notes a sexual connotation, and indeed, an unexpressed sexuality was probably at the root of other such letters by early Friends.

There were similar letters to Margaret Fell, some also with use of the Song of Songs. Another, from Ann Audland, includes the passage, "Oh that I could hear from thee, let my sufferings be refreshed by thee. . . . My joy is full, when I see thee present with me, near me even in my very heart . . . and with thee and in thee I am bound up and sealed for evermore."[7] Owing to the small number of surviving letters that passed between other Friends, one cannot be sure whether any other Friends were habitually addressed in these terms (apart from Nayler, by his followers, in the summer and autumn of 1656). The one piece of firm evidence, the dual letter from Farnworth to Fox and Nayler that was quoted in Chapter 2, suggests this was not generally so, and that these ecstatic letters indicate the special relationship between Fox and Fell and other Friends, and cemented their leadership. However, there are a few surviving letters in which other Friends were addressed in more than normally emotional language, for instance, this from Audland and Camm to Burrough and Howgill: "You are clothed with beauty and you grow in a pleasant place the hand of the Lord is with you and no weapon framed against you shall prosper," and that every day, "we feed with you upon the bread of life and we drink with you of the eternal fountain of life and we lie down with you in the arms of our father's love."[8]

The plain meaning of these letters is that the Quaker sense of their unity with God, or with Christ, extended to a strong sense of unity with each other, and especially with George Fox who was the visible focus of this unity.[9] This was not just a vague sense of undefined spiritual unity; body and spirit together were one with Christ. However, it is a fact that the special qualities of George Fox, including his supposed abilities as a miracle worker that are described in documents dating from later in the century, were never used by Quakers in the 1650s to support their arguments. Quakers preached the Light of Christ, not of Fox, and despite the many adoring letters that he received there is nothing in the published literature to indicate a personality cult centered on Fox. Quakers made great use of the concept of one's own "measure" of the Light or the Spirit, and while Fox's "measure" may have been greater than anyone else's, it was not different in kind. Son of God he may have called himself, but he directed others toward the Christ in themselves.

It was perhaps the experience of several trials for blasphemy, and possibly the advice of such people as Judge Fell, that persuaded Quakers to adapt their language. The more extreme language describing union with God or with Christ was confined to letters, while material for publication was more cautiously expressed. Apart from inviting prosecution under the Blasphemy Act, such language risked encouraging Ranterish behavior, and the many exhortations to Friends not to go beyond their measure, and to pay attention to the light in their consciences, indicate that the leaders of the movement were well aware of the risk. Christopher Atkinson was one who continued to write about unity with God: "As the Father and the Son are without distinction, so are they that are begotten by him . . . the children of light . . . whom he has begotten unto himself through the word of faith, in whom we live and abide for ever."[10] Atkinson, as will be described in Chapter 10, "ran out" in spectacular circumstances in 1655, justifying Friends' qualms about this kind of theology.

Friends therefore took care how they expressed their sense of unity with God. Fox continued to think of salvation in terms of divine sonship, and despite the blasphemy trials this surfaced from time to time in his writings. Publicly, he was now careful to use biblical language (1 Corinthians 1:24 and John 1:12): "You that are turned to this light which doth enlighten you, you are turned to Christ the power of God . . . and you that receive the light, shall receive power to become the sons of God."[11] The description of the relationship of believers to Christ as "Bone of his Bone and Flesh of his Flesh," a phrase Fox used more than once, comes from the older version of Ephesians 5:30, "For we are members of his body, of his flesh, and of his bones."[12] Fox's liking for New Testament passages that describe Christ as having come as a prophet like Moses, which has been noted by previous commentators, is also relevant; the idea of Christ the prophet, active in the Quaker community, becomes much clearer if he was seen as especially embodied in George Fox.[13]

Nayler's writing did not show the intensity of personal religious experience of Fox, but, like Fox, he wrote of a real union with God, although he understood this as a rather static, mystical union, while for Fox it was a dynamic take-over related to his own prophetic call. Also like Fox, he became more cautious in his use of explicit language in the course of the years 1653 to 1654. In *The Discovery of the First Wisdom from beneath and the Second Wisdom from above,* written in the spring of 1653 while he was in prison at Appleby, he wrote, "You will come to the unity with all saints in measure, and so come to Christ the first-born. . . . The second [i.e., redeemed] man is spiritually begotten by the immortal seed, is the express Image of the Father and is known of him, not by relation of the Creature, but by the indwelling of God in him . . . according to the measure of light revealed in him."[14] According to this passage, there is no distinction in nature between Christ and the believer, although there might be variation in the believer's "measure." In *The Power and Glory of the Lord,* written somewhat later during the summer of 1653, Nayler was more careful of his terminology, and emphasized the Kingdom within rather than the indwelling God (Chapter 5). Belief in a real union with Christ was fundamental to Nayler, as it was to Fox. The difference between them was one of temperament. Fox, after his early experiences, was alert to realities and avoided further serious conflict with the laws of blasphemy, whereas Nayler, in 1656, expressed his faith in a way that inevitably led to nemesis.

Burrough and Howgill, answering a set of queries in 1654, chose their words carefully: "The nature and glory of the elect differs not from the nature and glory of the creator, for the elect are one with the creator in his nature, enjoying his glory. . . . The elect . . . lives by the dwelling of the Son in him, and with the Son the Father lives also."[15] The first sentence is close to blasphemy, but the second modifies the argument. Such arguments hinged on very fine distinctions, as shown by the following passages from a work whose author declared his opposition to Quaker theology:

> Though they be really united, the natures of Christ and of the soul are kept distinct, and not confounded together, nor converted one into another. And a believer is not thereby Godded, or Christed (as some speak obscurely, unfoundedly, and I suspect blasphemously) or made at least a piece of a God, of a Christ, of a Mediator. As for your [the Quakers] being partakers of the divine nature, that is in respect of similitude or quality (wherein stands the image of God in us), not of the substance of the deity, which is incommunicable.

Having thus clearly stated that Christ and the believer were not the same, he then proceeded to explain how closely they were, in fact, united, a union of "substance, essence and person," like the root and branches of a tree, and that "The whole person of a believer is united to the whole person of Christ, both body and soul with his Deity and flesh." He also used the quotation favored by Fox, that the believer is "bone of his bone and flesh of his flesh." Much of this section could have been written by a Quaker. Yet, in his summing up at the end of the chapter, the author insisted once again that Christ and the believer were not united in the way that Quakers meant. It is very difficult to pinpoint the distinction.[16]

The word most strongly associated with Quaker teaching is "light." Francis Higginson knew the phrase "the light within" as regularly used by the first Quaker preachers, and the word "light" is common in Fox's early papers.[17] However, "the light" in Quaker thought may not have had the prime importance before 1653 that it came to possess later. In the first years of the Quaker movement, as has been shown, Fox was mainly concerned with the unity between Christ and the believer, for which he was several times charged with blasphemy. When he spoke of "the light," sometimes he used the phrase as equivalent to Christ and sometimes he meant the way Christ made himself known. It may be that "the light" developed into the characteristic Quaker phrase because it was a safe alternative to "Christ," to be used with less risk of blasphemy charges.

Fox's favorite "light" phrases around 1652–1654 were "the light (or "the light of Christ") in your conscience," "the light that Christ Jesus hath enlightened you withal," "the light of Christ (or "God") within you," and, frequently, "in the light," "receive the light," "turn to (or from) the light," and, very often, simply "the light" (never just "light"). "The light" was an overwhelming invasive force, not a vague mental illumination.[18] It must be emphasized that the phrase "inner light," often used by modern Quakers, never occurs in early Quaker writings, and that "inward light" is rare. "Conscience," also, was a stronger word than today, with something of the sense of "consciousness." "The light in the conscience," if it was attended to and not resisted, involved a take-over of one's personality.

It is possible that some of the light-imagery, and specifically the phrase "the light within," derives from the proto-Quaker groups that were already in existence in Yorkshire before Fox's arrival. Farnworth favored this phrase, and also "mind the light of God in you," in his early tracts, at a time when Fox preferred other terms.[19] For Farnworth, as for Fox, "the light" was identified with Christ the teacher, and led to true righteousness and thus to salvation. The following celebration of "the light within" is an example. As was usual among early Friends, Farnworth wrote as the spirit moved, which in his case meant few full stops or paragraph breaks and little logical plan, simply a flow of ideas and much repetition.[20]

Everyone, mind the light of God in you, that shows you sin and evil, that which does convince you of sin and uncleanness, and checks you when you do amiss, and it will turn your minds within, and show you how you have spent your time, and call you to repentance . . . loving the light within, you love Christ; hating the light within, you hate Christ; thy light within, obey it, is your teacher, and will show you the way that leads to salvation; disobey the light within, is your condemnation; let the light lead you and guide you and it will cross your earthly wills in all things that are carnal, and teach you to deny ungodliness; and this is the grace of God, this light within; take heed of rejecting the counsel of the Lord, in disobeying the light within, lest you turn the grace of God into wantonness.

Now you have time, Prize it, and take heed of despising the day of small things.[21]

Nayler made less use of the word "light" in his early pamphlets, for he had a wide religious vocabulary, and by 1654 he was engaged in serious theological controversy and having to adjust his terminology to the people he was dealing with. Other Quakers who were beginning to write pamphlets picked up Fox's phrases, particularly "the light in the conscience" and "the light that enlightens every man," and this "light" was often identified with Christ. If the light really was Christ then it could not err. The stage was set for a theological battle, in which Quakers were required to define their terms and explain, exactly, what they meant by "the light," for theologically minded opponents thought that Quakers were writing about the light of conscience, which God had given to everyone, and which had nothing to do with the work of Christ.

Most early Quaker pamphlets and letters, however, did not use conventional theological language, but described a remarkable experience and a continuing consciousness of the presence of God. Quakers had an idiosyncratic use of some words, probably derived from Fox's chosen turns of phrase and particular interests. "Truth" is one such word. It is an alternative word for "Gospel" derived from the New Testament, and was in general use. Francis Higginson, for instance, wrote of Quakers that "These men . . . have powerfully seduced multitudes . . . from the Truth."[22] For Quakers it developed a special resonance, describing their personal faith and its realization in their lives. It was not often used in Quaker publications in the 1650s, except as part of a title, but it frequently appears in letters and epistles, particularly from Fox, Farnworth and Burrough, concerning their mission, which was "to declare the truth." Fox wrote, "Dwell in the truth," or "Walk in the truth" and warned Friends to fear God "lest the truth suffer," while unsuitable preachers would cause the truth to be "evil spoken of."[23]

"Seed" was another favorite word, also used in letters rather than publications during the first years. Fox generally linked it to Genesis 3:15, where the "seed of the woman," meaning Christ, is contrasted with the "seed of the serpent," or to Genesis 24, where the seed of Isaac is contrasted with the "seed of the bondwoman," or Ishmael.[24] Other writers were more likely to introduce echoes of the Parable of the Sower, as when Burrough wrote to Fox, "Here is a precious seed, but deep in the earth, rocks and mountains, and the cursed earth which brings forth briars thorns and thistles are standing above—O how I have been pressed under for the seed's sake."[25] There is a similar use of "precious seed" in the letter from Elizabeth Hooton reproduced in Figure 2.

The process of salvation was often described as a return to the state of innocence of the Garden of Eden. The Fall of Adam and Eve was treated as taking place in the hearts and minds of people, who had to come through and out of the Fall: "You are not yet come to witness the first promise fulfilled, but are still in the fall.[26] After the expulsion of Adam and Eve, the Garden was a guarded by an angel with a flaming sword, and the difficulty of passing this was a common image, and also much used by continental writers of the previous century.[27] Dewsbury made striking use of this metaphor when describing his early religious experience:

> Notwithstanding all my strict walking in observation in which I was seeking the kingdom of God, I found him not, but the flaming sword cut me down; so my sorrow increased. . . . The Lord discovered to me that his love could not be attained in anything I could do . . . so in all these my turnings in my carnal wisdom, seeking the Kingdom of God in observations without, thither the flaming sword turned, which kept the way of the tree of life, and fenced me from it . . . waiting for the coming of Christ Jesus, who in the appointed time . . . purged away the filthy nature . . . so through the righteous law of life in Christ Jesus I was made free and clean from the body of sin and death; and through these great trials my garment is washed, and made white in the blood of the Lamb, who hath led me through the gates of the city into the new Jerusalem . . . where my soul now feeds upon the tree of life which I had so long hungered and thirsted after.[28]

The new quality of life that Quakers were experiencing was often described as life in the New Covenant. Covenant theology is discussed more fully in Chapter 8, but the following quotation from Farnworth gives a taste of what many Friends were thinking: "God did fulfil his promise given forth by Jeremiah the Prophet of the Lord in the new Covenant [reference to Jeremiah 31:34], when it is said he would teach them himself . . . all that came to enjoy the second Covenant they did witness the substance of the first Covenant. . . . Christ was the Covenant and they found him revealed and manifested in them."[29] Farnworth was saying that, as a result of the sacrifice of Christ, the Second Covenant, as foretold by Jeremiah, was in operation, and the Friends were actually living in it; in fact, the Covenant was the Spirit of Christ within them. A real change had taken place in the minds, or hearts, of himself and his friends, an idea that is also to be found among some of the sixteenth-century radical reformers on the continent of Europe.[30]

The theological strands of many early pamphlets are difficult to disentangle, for only Nayler could write an ordered treatise. The problems can best be illustrated by an example from Fox's writings. Fox was a particularly unsystematic thinker, tending to pile up images with similar resonance, and the following samples come from a collection of short pieces published under the title *Newes coming up out of the North:*

(a)   I speak the same seed which is Christ . . . Jesus Christ the way, the truth and the life, he is the door that all must pass through, and he is the porter that opens it.

(b)   Look at the Captain Jesus Christ who hath passed before, who was tempted, the captain of our salvation, he is the forerunner. . . . He endured the cross, he despised the shame . . . he is the head of the church.

(c)   The same Spirit that raised up Jesus Christ, the same Spirit raises up the same seed in you.

(d)   To all you who can witness the second birth, and are born again, which all the promises of God are to, the seed . . . except you be born again, you cannot enter into the kingdom of God . . . but as many as received Christ, to them gave he power to become the Sons of God.

(e)   Everyone of you in particular having a measure, mind the light of God within you, for God hath given all of you a light, which will draw up all your minds to God.

(f)   In the first Covenant . . . there were priests that God commanded, which were Figures, Types and Shadows of Jesus Christ the everlasting priest. . . . Jesus Christ [is] the end of the Prophets, the end of the Law, the end of all types and figures and shadows . . . the life of God which is unknown to the world.

(g)   To all you that can witness the seed of the serpent is bruised with the seed of the woman . . . your light is Christ . . . your baptism is with the Spirit into one body, your communion is the blood of Christ which cleanseth from all filthiness and redeems from your vain conversation.[31]

These passages are given in the order in which they appear in the pamphlet. Extracts (a) to (d) come from "A Word from the Lord to all you yet in your first birth," (e) from some advice to the faithful called "Moved of the Lord," and (f) and (g) from "The Voyce of the Lord," a more theological piece addressed to "professors," that is, to people who "professed" the Christian faith but did not, according to Fox, manifest its fruits.

In the last passage (g), the two seeds come from Fox's favorite Genesis 3:15, referring to the cosmic battle between good and evil. The seed metaphor also occurs in three other quotations. In (a) the seed is Christ (Galatians 3:16), in (c) the seed, Christ, is being raised in the believer, and in (d) the seed is the believers collectively, or the children of Abraham (Genesis 17:4–7, Romans 4:11–14, Galatians 4:22–28). Fox was expressing, in carefully precise biblical language, that belief in unity with Christ that caused him to be tried three times for blasphemy.

This unity with Christ was also a rebirth. The "second birth" of (d) is the reverse of the "second death" of Revelation 2:11, 20:6, 14 and 21:8, the final judgment on evil, implying that the age of the Spirit, or the Kingdom of God, was now beginning. There is reference to John 1:12 and 3:3, and probably to 1 Peter 1:23. The concept of rebirth as a son or daughter of God was fundamental to Fox.

Quotations (b) and (f) show Fox's understanding of the work of Christ. Much of the imagery is from the Epistle to the Hebrews. The emphasis is on Christ as the eternal priest, replacing the Old Testament law (or old Covenant) with a new dispensation. This leaves (e), the universal light within, but did Fox mean Christ, Holy Spirit or conscience, and did he make any distinction in his own mind? In (g) he evidently meant Christ, and that the ordinances of baptism and communion had been replaced by the Spirit and Christ, working in the believers and leading to real righteousness.

It may have been a consequence of the appearance of anti-Quaker publications, but the theological diversity of Quaker writing decreased after 1654. Quaker authors, who now included many new writers, had to concentrate on answering the anti-Quaker books in the agreed Quaker terminology, which had probably been clarified at the Swannington meeting. Farnworth, for instance, had written in 1653: "By the blood of his son dearly bought and purchased . . . we were by nature children of wrath . . . but the Lord who is rich in mercy . . . he has slain the old man that did bear rule in us, and raised up the new man, the Son of his love in us, being begotten by the Immortal Word . . . and redeemed us from our vain conversation [i.e., way of life, from 1 Peter 1:18]."[32] Such language of Reformation theology, regarding the depravity of humankind and salvation by the blood of Christ, was less used during the second half of the 1650s, and rarely picked up by the newer converts. Quakers now concentrated on the message of salvation by the light, which was thought to lead to a real freedom from sin, and was available to all, including the heathen, Jews and formerly wicked people. The phrase "Covenant of Light" came into use, probably coined by Nayler but used by several other authors, and especially by Fox. It made a creative link between the universal light of the Quakers and the idea of "covenant," which was common to all Reformed churches.[33]

Quakers were united in their faith, and utterly self-confident about it. This example of a Baptist confession makes a sharp contrast: "Also we confess that we know but in part and that we are ignorant of many things which we desire and seek to know: and if any shall do us that friendly part to show us from the Word of God that we see not, we shall have cause to be thankful to God and to them."[34] The Quaker sons and daughters of God, living in God's new order, could never have entertained such doubts.

Quakers could describe salvation as being in the Covenant of Light, or as a matter of attending to the light in the conscience, or as having returned to the state of innocence before the Fall, but always, they said, salvation had consequences for conduct. This had been a preoccupation of Fox since his youth, and the strong Quaker emphasis on ethics probably derived initially from Fox's insistence, although it certainly struck a chord with many who joined with Quakers.[35] Moral perfection in this life was, said Quakers, a possibility, a consequence of the spiritual presence of the Kingdom of God in believers. Quaker leaders explained how to achieve this: "Mind the light of God in you that does show you darkness . . . to yield obedience to it and it will let you feel your disorderly walking in all things. . . . It will cross your wills in all things that are earthly and carnal, and crucify your lusts."[36] The practical results of this belief are described in Chapter 9.

Some Friends said that perfection was not necessarily wholly complete at first; Nayler especially was careful about this, and wrote, "God is perfect . . . whoever receives his gifts receives that which is perfect. And no farther than the creature is in this perfection can any be united to God, nor appear in his sight, nor be blessed."[37] Nevertheless perfection was possible: "What perfection canst thou have, who deniest the perfection of Christ to be thine . . . the least Child of light shall thee judge, who art setting the old Covenant above the new."[38]

Other Friends described their freedom from sin with no qualifications.

Martin Mason, discussing 1 John 3:9, which reads, "Whosoever is born of God doth not commit sin," claimed that the plain meaning of the Greek word translated as "commit" is that those "born of God" do not commit any sin at all, not that they do not practice sin, or make a habit of sinning, which was the usual interpretation put forward by most biblical commentators.[39]

Blasphemous claims of union with God, a mysterious "light," and assertions of sinlessness. It was not surprising that Quakers found themselves attacked from all sides. The resulting controversies are described in the next two chapters, when Quaker theology had to develop rapidly to defend Quaker ideas and practices against criticism.

7

HEATED CONTROVERSY

The first anti-Quaker writings, the anonymous *Querers and Quakers* and Francis Higginson's *Irreligion of the Northern Quakers*, both written early in 1653, have already been described. These were but the beginning of a stream of such "adverse" writings, as Quakers came to call them, over three hundred during the period covered by this book.[1] The numbers peaked in 1655–56, when the impact of the Quaker expansion was first felt, and again in 1659–60, when feelings against extreme sectaries, Quakers especially, were running very high (see Chapter 13). The numbers of adverse books dwindled after the Restoration, when the Presbyterian and Independent ministers, who made up a large proportion of the authors, were preoccupied with their relations with the Church of England. Dealing with these attacks had a noticeable effect on the development of Quaker ideas.

Disputes were usually carried out by an exchange of pamphlets, a "pamphlet war." Authors and their printers worked fast, and books were often answered within a few weeks. Sometimes, owing to the habit of printers of starting the new year date any time between mid-November and the beginning of March, the reply would apparently be published before the book it answered, and Francis Howgill turned this practice to his advantage when a book against Quakers called *Hell Broke Loose* came out in November 1659 with a 1660 date. Howgill, in his reply dated 1659, wrote, "To the intent that thy book might not grow old nor stick upon thy hands, as other such mouldy stuff has done, thou saith *London Printed in the year 1660* and so hath printed a lie in the frontispiece of thy book, thy book by that time thou may hang up with old almanacks or sell for waste paper."[2]

Some of the books that Quakers took exception to were not primarily aimed at them, but contained a passing comment on Quakerism while dealing with another topic, or expressed opinions that Quakers disliked. The rest fall into four main classes, and these are comments and appeals from church leaders, gossip and scurrilous attacks, reports of public debates, and serious theological criticism.

From the first group, the first anti-Quaker church petition came from Lancashire and is known from the Quakers' reply to it, the book *Sauls Errand to Damascus*, dealing with the trials of Fox at Lancaster and Nayler at Appleby, and also answering a number of other documents issued around that time. The Lancashire worthies said that Quakers had no respect for the law, drew people from the churches, and had strange fits in their meetings. *Sauls Errand* was a clever damage-limitation work, attempting to show that Quakers were neither law-breakers nor blasphemers, and rushed out early in 1653 just before Francis Higginson's *Irreligion of the Northern Quakers*, which deals with much of the same material.[3]

In 1652, the "gentlemen, freeholders and other Inhabitants of the County of Worcester," organized by the influential minister Richard Baxter, petitioned Parliament regarding organization of the local ministry.[4] Quakers took exception to Baxter's recommendation that tithes should be retained for the maintenance of ministers, and Baxter wrote them an immediate reply. He was contemptuous of Quakers: "I know it will be judged a great weakness in me, to regard the words of such men, so far as to mention them. . . . If the Governors of the Common-wealth do think this to be meet language and doctrine to be permitted by the press to be divulged to all their subjects, it seems . . . they take it to be not so intolerable as we do." Baxter, who saw only the disruption and the challenge to the established church caused by uneducated upstarts, had no patience with Quakers, and believed the tales that were circulating about Quakers being Papists in disguise, or likely to behave as the Anabaptists of Münster.[5]

A few years later, in the West country, the Particular Baptist minister Thomas Collier had several passages of arms with Quakers, and especially with the local Quaker "overseer," Thomas Salthouse, who did his best to poach members from Collier's churches. The problem for Baptists was the close similarity between some of their beliefs and the Quakers'. Collier, in a letter to his local churches, wrote of "the manifold mercies of God to his people . . . such as the Saints before us in many generations have not known. The breaking-forth of the glorious light of the Gospel . . . a mystery in great measure hid from generations past, but God has now revealed it by his spirit through the Scriptures, to the glory of his own name and joy of Saints."[6] This is close to Quaker teaching, and Salthouse invited Baptists "to be delivered from the bondage of corruption into the liberty of the sons of God, and likewise enjoined as a member of the Church of Christ." Collier replied by warning of "damnable heresies, even denying the only Lord God, and our Lord Jesus Christ, and under pretense of holiness and the light within, to undermining the whole truth of the Gospel . . . and to speak evil of dignitaries and government." Salthouse riposted, denying these charges and suggesting that it was harder to be a Quaker than a Baptist, for water baptism "does not make the consumer thereunto perfect," whereas "it's not so easy to be a member of our church (which is the true church) . . . there can no wise enter anything that defiles or is polluted."[7]

Salthouse and Collier at least conducted their dispute with reasonable courtesy, not a common thing in the seventeenth century. Relations between Quakers and the Bristol Broadmead church were much more acrimonious, largely due to the unpleasant tongue and pen of one Denis Hollister, a Bristol grocer, elder of the Broadmead church, and member of the Nominated Parliament who returned from London "with his heart full of discontent and his head full of poisonous new notions." When the Quakers arrived, he not only welcomed them into his house but went over to them, taking some twenty members of his church, a quarter of the membership, with him.[8] Hollister then addressed his former colleagues in a pamphlet tactlessly entitled *The Skirts of the Whore Discovered*, telling them that they were "seed of the Bond-woman" (i.e., of Ishmael, not Isaac, a reference to Genesis 21:10) and that their ordinances came from "the Inventions, Traditions, and Imaginations of man's carnal wisdom . . . being but Cain's sacrifice" (Cain's sacrifice was not acceptable to God; Genesis 4:4). The church leaders, very hurt, replied at length affirming their beliefs, and continuing:

> You . . . take it for granted, that Christ is now come in life, power, and spirit, in you and your party, but truly you must give better demonstration of it, before we or any other judicious Christians will believe you, for we have read much, and know something by experience through grace, what the sweet gentle, and dove-like spirit of Christ is, and we have seen and known by sad experience how unlike your spirit is to that.

Hollister's reply was yet another "railing" pamphlet, this time called *The Harlots Vail Removed.*[9]

Turning to the second class of anti-Quaker writings, gossip and scurrility, it is a fact that early Quakers gave an easy handle to people who disliked them, in that unstable people were attracted to their meetings and then told extraordinary stories of what had happened there. The first of these to go public was one John Gilpin of Kendal, whose story (see Chapter 11), together with other similar tales, was often repeated in anti-Quaker books of the next few years.[10] On one occasion, Quakers were accused of bewitching a woman and turning her into a bay mare, a charge that actually came to trial. Although the defendants were acquitted, the tale circulated for some years in various forms, verse included.[11]

From 1655 onward, newsbooks frequently had items on Quakers, usually derogatory, and many pamphlets were published attacking Quakers as crypto-Catholics, immoral, and engaged in witchcraft. Anti-Quaker titles included *The Quaker Unmasked, Quakers are Inchanters and Dangerous Seducers* and *The Quakers Dream, or, the Devils Pilgrimage in England,* which began:

> An infallible relation of their several Meetings, Shriekings, Shakings, Quakings, Roarings, Yellings, Howlings, Tremblings in the Bodies, and Rising in the Belly . . . the Strange and Wonderful Satanical Apparitions, and the appearing of the Devil unto them in the likeness of a Black Boar, a Dog with Flaming Eyes, and a Black Man without a

Head, causing Dogs to bark, the Swine to cry, and the Cattle to run, to the great admiration [wonder] of all that shall read the same.[12]

One of these publications, *The Quacking Mountebanck, or the Jesuite turned Quaker,* made great play of the name "Fox." It seems to have been written shortly after Fox's release in London early in 1655, and says of Quakers that they "are not tame but wild by nature, for a Fox, who was of late kennelled, but now he and his whole litter are abroad, and therefore 'tis fit they should be stoutly hunted." The author said they were "whelped in the kennel of Ignatius Loyola the Jesuit," that "they had now hired a large strong kennel to practice in" (this was the Bull and Mouth meeting house), and made many more references to foxes including a description that may derive from an eye-witness, that Fox "wears a bush, a long bush of Hair by his Ears like a Fox tail, which he strokes often and plays with and sports with it."[13] Several pamphlets by "Quakers," with no authors' names, were written as answers to such accusations.[14]

A common accusation against Quakers was that they were crypto-Catholics. Catholics were popularly considered to be the chief public enemy, so that any odd and possibly dangerous people were likely to be accused of belonging to this faith. Quakers were vulnerable in that certain of their doctrines and habits, such as their attitude to the Bible and their emphasis on human conduct rather than God's grace, were, to the suspicious mind, reminiscent of Catholicism. In one pamphlet there is a list of such similarities, neatly set out and bracketed, Papists on top, Quakers underneath.[15] After serious rioting in Bristol in January 1655, a warrant was issued for the arrest of "Franciscans," whom it was supposed were disguised as Quakers. This tale surfaced several times, and was known to William Prynne, a well-known Parliamentarian whose ears had been cropped under the previous administration. He began a pamphlet: "The Quaker unmasked, and clearly detected to be but the Spawn of Romish Frogs, Jesuits, and Franciscan Popish Friars, sent from Rome, to seduce the intoxicated Giddy-headed English nation."[16]

The third form of anti-Quaker writing consisted of reports of public theological debates, which were a form of popular entertainment in the mid-seventeenth century, a spectacle like a gladiatorial contest. Quakers soon began to take part in these, though at first they did not always play the game according to the accepted rules. Some Baptists wrote to Farnworth, "When you begin your speech you are as it were in a trance, declare in your answer somewhat of the reason of it."[17] Quakers, however, soon

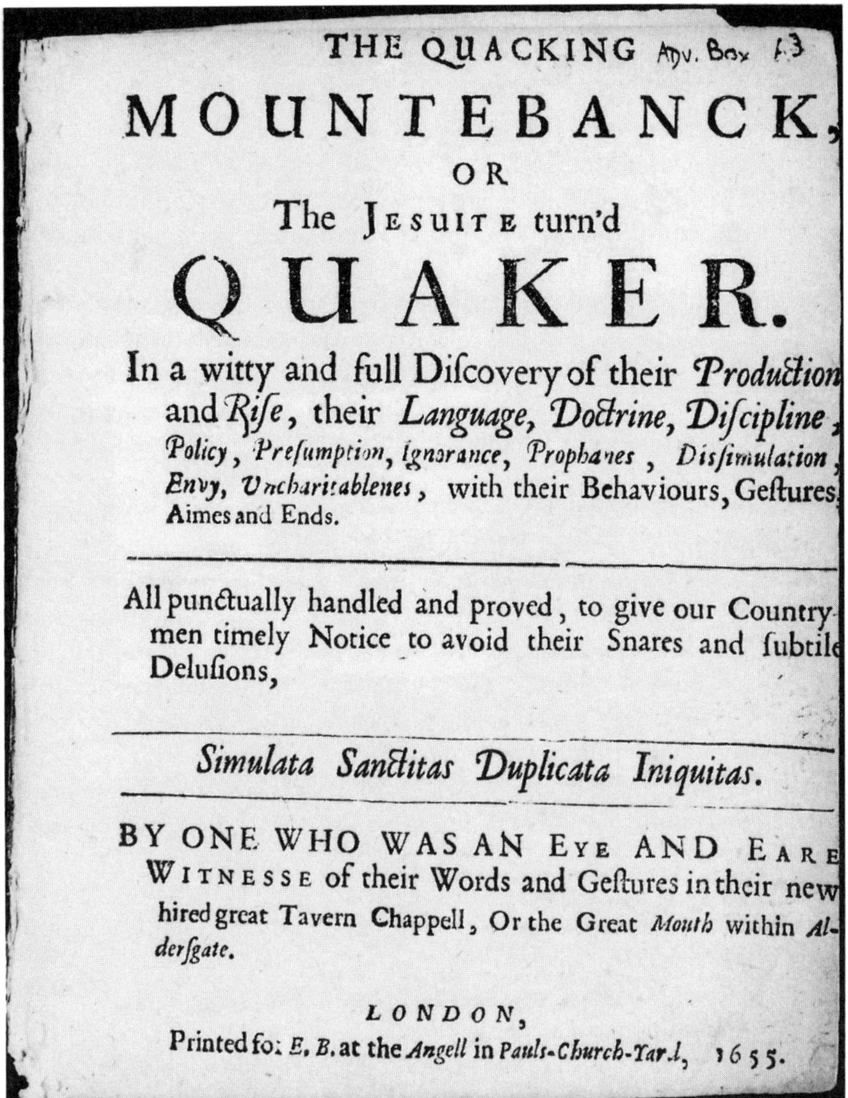

THE QUACKING ADV. Box 13

MOUNTEBANCK,

OR

The JESUITE turn'd

QUAKER.

In a witty and full Difcovery of their *Production*
and *Rife*, their *Language, Doctrine, Difcipline*,
Policy, Prefumption, ignorance, Prophanes, Dissimulation,
Envy, Vncharitablenes, with their Behaviours, Geftures,
Aimes and Ends.

All punctually handled and proved, to give our Countrymen timely Notice to avoid their Snares and fubtile
Delufions,

Simulata Sanctitas Duplicata Iniquitas.

BY ONE WHO WAS AN EYE AND EARE
WITNESSE of their Words and Geftures in their new
hired great Tavern Chappell, Or the Great *Mouth* within *Al-*
derfgate.

LONDON,
Printed for *E. B.* at the *Angell* in *Pauls-Church-Yard,* 1655.

Fig. 8 Title page of *The Quacking Mountebanck*, a typical early anti-Quaker pamphlet
written shortly after George Fox's release from prison in 1655. (Courtesy, Library Committee of the Religious Society of Friends, Britain Yearly Meeting)

learnt the art of making a quick reply, without waiting for special inspiration, and took the debates seriously. The importance of not missing such opportunities is shown by an urgent letter sent to the Quakers' London headquarters:

> I being at Arundel sessions friends informed me of a challenge made for a dispute with friends. . . . This was sent in writing by the greatest wicked baptist champion in the south, Matthew Caffin, and some friends returned answer to him in writing that he should be met for the purpose on the 19 day of this eleventh month at Chichester, where they give out they shall have the City Hall for the purpose, and that if friends do not meet them then they should for ever stop their mouths; so that in all likelihood the expectation of the people may be very great, and so of the greater concernement and the more to be taken notice of: this I thought fit to lay before you or one of you.[18]

One of the fullest descriptions of what happened during such debates was written by Philip Taverner, Vicar of West Drayton near London, "a grave and peaceable divine of unblameable life," who participated in a public debate with Burrough, Fisher, and others. In this debate, Taverner's friend Richard Goodenough, an army officer and Fifth Monarchist, was the "Objector," and Edward Burrough the "Defendant," with Samuel Fisher as his assistant. Taverner and another friend were present as "Hearers," and spoke "when they found Truth engaging them thereto." Taverner, who introduced himself in his "Epistle to the Reader" as one "who owns all Saints in the bond of love, under what distinction of Form soever," described the debate as follows:

> There were some things in the managing of the dispute (if it deserves such a name) just matter of reproof:
>
> 1. A disorderly and confused speaking of many, at sometimes together; both parties must confess guilty in this thing.
> 2. A great prejudice in each party against other; which appeared in this: neither party was willing to own what the other said, though (for substance) they held the same thing; so that what with passion, and prejudice meeting together, there seemed rather a contending for victory, than for truth: I fear, there is neither party can plead innocent in this matter.

Taverner noted that the contestants came very close in their understanding of Scripture, but their discussion of justification (see Chapter 8 for this term) was "a most wearisome and unprofitable discourse." It was getting late, Taverner was tired, and people began to go home. Somebody in the audience said, "You stand here, peck, peck, and to no purpose, you are all a company of novices; for if there had been any of the wisdom and power of God in either of you, one side would have silenced the other before this." "And here ended this confused dispute about justification," wrote Taverner, "in which point it is feared by some, that those called Quakers . . . have a Pope in their belly; if so, I heartily wish the Lord would show them their error . . . and deliver them from their delusion."[19]

Another controversy took Farnworth and Nayler to Cambridge, and involved a public dispute and an exchange of letters before both sides went into print. The opponents on this occasion were a group called the Manifestarians because they waited for the manifesting of the children of God, or in other words, they were of the Seeker kind.[20] They were also Mortalists, like many of the more intellectual theological radicals, believing that there was no distinct soul and that a human personality was effectively dead between physical death and the final resurrection of all bodies. This contest, involving the Quakers' best debaters, was higher in quality than many. Nayler said that, in contrast to the Mortalist belief, his body was already effectively dead to sin, but that God in his word was now manifested in the bodies of his saints, and that God was "a sufficient teacher and shield against sin."[21] Quakers were not Mortalists.

One of the most entertaining records comes from Shropshire. There had been a report circulating locally that "one Edward Laurence had overthrown the Quakers," so the Quakers published their own account of the matter.

> The aforesaid Edward wrote five positions, which he gave to one which is a Quaker, and promised to prove them at some of their meetings. . . . Noise of it spread abroad and people, a great multitude, were gathered together on the day appointed to hear both parties. The priest being come, who though he knew we were no upholder of steeple-houses, yet he pressed on us to go, telling us that it was a more fit and convenient place for that work, which was contrary to his promise, which was to do it at our meeting, to which promise we kept him. . . . He, seeing that we would not go from the place appointed, our meeting being without, he pleaded that he had but a weak body,

and was subject to be troubled with the toothache . . . upon which we proferred him to stand within the house, and to speak through the window, and we to stand without, but he, not being willing to engage, denied that, saying the wind would be sharper in the windows than elsewhere, and such like excuses, so went his way from us to the steeple-house and a great rude company with him. Many stayed with us waiting to see the event of the day, and after a while we sent unto him, that he would either come here or else he was a liar and did not fulfil his promise, and with much ado he came with two or three other priests with him and a rude multitude, and then he went to the window, though he had denied them before, and there began to prove his positions as he had wrote them down in his book. And ever when any of us Quakers did answer against what he had said, the rude multitude cried out hold thy tongue, hold thy tongue, we will not hear thee . . . and nothing would be heard but what the priest spake. . . . And when three of his positions were run over though not one of them proved, he . . . went to prayers . . . and when he had done he would not stay . . . and his wicked multitude thrusting one another fell a-fighting, but with patience we were through the love of God carried on, that day to bear the reproach of our enemies, and to rest satisfied in the truth.[22]

One wonders where the "rude multitude" came from, for this happened at Baschurch, a little village near Shrewsbury. Maybe the Shrewsbury lads had turned out to see the fun.[23]

Cambridge University is a far cry from rural Shropshire. One day Thomas Smith, the Keeper of the Cambridge Library, was going home to his rooms in Christs College when he saw George Whitehead preaching in the Quaker "common meeting-house," so he went in to listen, and afterward "confuted his doctrine" and proposed a formal debate. The Quakers accepted the challenge, and they planned to use the town hall, but the aldermen were unwilling to let it for this purpose as they feared a public disturbance. So it was agreed that the debate should take place in the Quaker meeting-house, but Thomas Smith by now was having second thoughts, as the aldermen thought that such a debate, anywhere, could lead to breach of the peace. However he was, naturally, accused of cowardice, and the debate went ahead. Smith did his best to tie the Quakers up in logical arguments, and in his own opinion succeeded, although he was unable to express himself in his usual manner as he was "necessitated to condescend to vulgar capacities, who cried out they would have no philosophy or scholars' terms." The audience enjoyed themselves, and both sides afterward published accounts of what had happened. Smith said that Quakers were bold, had little learning and could not argue, and "ran beyond all reason" in trying to argue for their strange opinions. George Whitehead said that a library keeper should not "utter such ignorance and scornfulness, and such gross untruths."[24]

Occasional debates took place after the Restoration, when opportunity offered. Among the prisoners in Lancaster Castle in 1663–64 was a well-known Particular Baptist minister and Fifth Monarchist called John Wigan. Finding himself imprisoned with Quakers, including George Fox and Margaret Fell, he hoped to live peaceably and avoid conflicts, for, whatever his opinion of their theology, he thought that they were entirely right in their stand for freedom of worship. When the Quakers requested a debate, he was doubtful about agreeing, because he knew the Quakers' habits of "railing," interrupting, and generally failing to conduct debates with conventional decorum. The terms of debate were agreed in an exchange of letters, the contestants agreeing to use scriptural proofs only and not to interrupt each other.

The debate took place on March 17, 1664, and Wigan undertook to demonstrate that the light that he believed to be in all people was not a light that gave salvation. John Stubbs spoke for the Quakers, but when Wigan replied, the meeting became disorderly, with several speaking at once, and, said Wigan, "they were so obstreperous," especially George Fox and Margaret Fell. Wigan described what happened:

> George Fox coming in about the time I was replying to John Stubbs, gets upon a seat with one foot, and to the table with the other, whereas I and others were standing on the ground about the table, he did not at all take off the strength of the Scripture alleged by me, but his endeavour was to prove That every man that cometh into the world hath the Spirit of Christ, in the management whereof he used many undervaluing and taunting expressions towards me. . . . He did miserably wrest and abuse several Scriptures.

The Quakers, of course, denied causing a disturbance and accused John Wigan of being the first to get on the table![25]

The topic of this debate, whether the light that Quakers believed in led to salvation, was one of the main subjects of dispute between Quakers and others, and continued as a matter of controversy for many years. Serious theological debate, which did not rely on point-scoring, needs a chapter to itself.

8

SERIOUS THEOLOGY

In order to understand the onslaught on early Quakerism by serious seventeenth-century theologians it is necessary to know something of contemporary theological controversies.[1]

Underlying much current theology was the concept of "covenant." The most important elements in relation to Quakers were the Old or First Covenant, or Covenant of Works, equivalent to the Old Testament dispensation under the Law of Moses, and the New or Second Covenant, the Covenant of Grace, brought in by Christ. The Old Testament tells of God's relationship with Israel, the covenant made with Abraham recorded in Genesis 17:1–14, the Law given to Moses, and the hope of something better in the future. The key text is Jeremiah 31:31–34:

Behold, the days come, saith the Lord, that I will make a new covenant with the house of Israel and with the house of Judah.

Not according to the covenant that I made with their fathers . . . which my covenant they brake. . . .

But this shall be the covenant that I will make with the house of Israel: After those days, saith the Lord, I will put my law in their inward parts, and write it in their hearts; and will be their God, and they shall be my people.

And they shall teach no more every man his neighbour and every man his brother, saying, Know the Lord: for they shall all know me, from the least of them unto the greatest of them, saith the Lord: for I will forgive their iniquity, and I will remember their sin no more.

Many seventeenth-century disputes concerned the extent to which this New Covenant was already in operation. Was it entirely for the future, in the millennium or thousand-year reign of Christ? Had it partly come into operation when the Holy Spirit was given to Jesus' disciples, and had its operation been wholly or partly spoiled when the church drifted into apostasy at the end of the apostolic age? What was the relation of this to the Law of Moses? Certainly, parts of the Law of Moses, the Jewish rituals of sacrifice and of circumcision, had been abrogated by Christ, and for most Christians the Jewish Sabbath had become the Christian Sunday. Did any of the Old Testament legal requirements apply in the seventeenth century? The New Testament is ambiguous on the question of the operation of the New Covenant and the passing of the Mosaic law, and it was a fruitful source of debate.[2]

Arguments over tithe hinged on this question; there is nothing about the upkeep of ministers by such contributions in the New Testament, but the Old Testament priesthood had been supported by tithing the congregations (Leviticus 10:30). Quakers maintained that the New Covenant was fully operational, and that tithe, being devised in connection with the Old Testament priesthood, was no longer applicable.

The idea of God's covenant was important to people of all shades of religious opinion, but opinion was divided as to who would benefit from it. The dominant faith in seventeenth-century England was a form of Calvinism, a belief that people were born in a depraved state, that only a predestined "elect" would be saved, and that everyone else would be damned. The elect were described as "justified," a translation of a difficult Greek term that is better expressed as "being in a right relationship with God."

Justification was said to have been made possible by the death of Christ on the cross, when, as a result of this sacrifice, the righteousness of Christ was "imputed" or accounted to sinful human beings, or at least to those of them who were among the "elect." They were "justified," not by their own efforts or virtues, but solely by the grace of God acting through Christ. Calvinists said that it was not possible to influence this election by one's own efforts. A godly way of life, a growth in holiness or a gradual "sanctification," indicated that, probably, one was among the elect, being predestined to appropriate behavior, but it was not impossible for sinners to be among the elect, and it was never possible to be certain of one's own election. Most of those who became Quakers were brought up to this faith, and described the unhappiness that came from doubts about their election. Remnants of Calvinist belief can be found in the writings of a number of Quakers, including Nayler, Burrough, Dewsbury, and Margaret Fell.

Arminianism, so called after its propounder, Jacob Arminius, was an alternative theory that God was willing to save anyone who turned to him, and that salvation was some extent a matter of human choice, to be influenced by one's own efforts. This doctrine was called "justification by works." In England this belief was associated with Archbishop Laud's party before the Civil Wars, but it also was taken up by General Baptists and other sectarians, including many Quakers. The Quakers' call to turn to "the light within," and their stress on the necessity of right conduct, was considered by their opponents to be advocacy of justification by works.

There was much argument about the exact operation of the grace of God, and what actually happened to sin, and the propensity to sin, in the course of justification and sanctification. Many English mid-seventeenth-century theologians emphasized the work of the Holy Spirit in the believer, but they generally considered that reception of the Holy Spirit followed justification, and was not an integral part of it.[3] The belief that the elect were incapable of sin, being entirely protected by the righteousness of Christ, was called Antinomian, meaning "opposed to law." Quakers taught this, though they emphasized the practical impossibility of sin for one united with Christ, and the real righteousness resulting, rather than a legalistic theory. Antinomian theory, or "Doctrinal Antinomianism," led to a great deal of theological in-fighting and hair-splitting, but there was another aspect, "Practical Antinomianism," the belief that, if elect and unable to sin, one might do as one liked, including performing all kinds of actions commonly considered "sins." People expressed a fear that popular belief in the rule of the Spirit and the end of divine Law would lead to immoral behavior, which certainly happened in the case of a few Ranters, such as the notorious Lawrence Clarkson, a renegade Baptist who said there was nothing wrong in having sexual relations with many women, provided he continued to support his wife. Quakers were regularly charged with being of a similar persuasion.[4]

The controversial literature in which Quakers were soon embroiled was but a small part of the contemporary theological pamphleteering. Their first major pamphlet war took place in 1653–54 between James Nayler and Thomas Weld of Newcastle-upon-Tyne. Weld was an experienced minister who had spent some time in New England. Each side wrote two books and the last book in the series, Nayler's *The Discovery of the Man of Sin,* as well as answering Weld's points, was the most systematic and careful statement of Quaker faith that had yet been published.[5] Weld opened by quoting various Quaker statements, that George Fox had said that he was equal to God and that Nayler had said that he was as good as God, and that Quakers had alleged that justification did not come through the righteousness of Christ being "imputed" to people, but by Christ, acting within people, enabling them to attain real righteousness, a perfection like that of Christ himself.

Nayler denied the charges of blasphemy, and replied that Quakers did not accept Weld's teaching that justification was something that happened outside the believer. Justification happened when Christ worked in the spirit within: "We own, Christ in us, according to the measure made manifest; our sanctification, justification, redemption from sin, and the hope of glory." Nayler did not deny that justification came from the sacrifice of Christ on the cross, for this was part of the frame of reference for anyone wishing to be considered a serious Christian theologian in the seventeenth century, and was not open to question. He was also still something of a Calvinist and was not going to admit that human choice played any part in the matter. He replied to Weld: "That we are "justified freely by his grace" we own; and that God has set him forth to be a "propitiation" . . . and his sufferings we own; and we witness what he did he does still in us, and bears and supports us . . . and by his mighty working in us, is the man of sin [the devil] cast out. . . . I deny justification by our own works, and own him who worketh in us to will and do."[6]

Weld, like many other theologians, taught that the only light that enlightened everyone was a light "natural" to humanity, that is, some knowledge of right conduct (Romans 1:18–20). Spiritual light was only for the elect. Nayler, referring to 1 Corinthians 2:14, "the natural man receiveth not the things of the Spirit of God," and to John 1:9, wrote, "The Apostle doth not speak there of a natural light and a spiritual light, for that which is natural is darkness, neither have you any Scripture to prove that to be a natural light, which enlightened every one that comes into the world." The light, wrote Nayler, "which we witness in us, is sufficient to lead out of darkness, bring into the fear of God, and to exercise a pure conscience before God and man in the power of Christ."[7] There was one light only, the light of Christ.

Was it possible for the elect to sin? Weld accused Quakers of saying that sinners cannot enter the Kingdom of Heaven, and that real Saints do not sin, which would exclude most of humanity from heaven.[8] The usual answer of Quakers to this charge was to counterattack, saying that the parish ministers "pleaded for sin," and told their congregations that perfect righteousness was not necessary in order to enter heaven. Weld said that parish ministers did not take sinfulness lightly: "There is a pressing and a continual wrestling and struggling in the power of Jesus Christ against [sin], which pressing is our constant practice to our people."[9] Nayler, who realized that there could be problems in demonstrating Quaker "perfection," stated that people's "measure" of light might vary, and that Quakers did not assert that every Saint was perfectly holy and without sin. Theoretically it was possible, but in practice unlikely. "For we witness the Saints' growth, and the time of pressing after perfection." All the same, Nayler insisted that Weld's understanding of justification was inadequate, and encouraged moral slackness. "You go about to make people believe, that though they die the servants of sin, yet they shall be complete in Christ, and made glorious, and perfect, and holy after death."[10]

This controversy between Weld and Nayler was just the beginning. In 1655 and 1656 at least eighteen books were published that made serious theological criticisms of Quakerism, and most were quickly answered by further pamphlets. The authors were of various theological persuasions, but their attacks on Quakers followed similar patterns. Their charges that Quakers used their own idiosyncratic understanding of the Spirit to interpret the Bible, did not respect civil authorities, and ignored biblical commands regarding church services and the upkeep of ministers are discussed in Chapters 4, 9, and 10. The remaining major cause of dispute was that Quaker teaching about "the light" was very confused, leading to a misunderstanding of the nature of Christ and his work, to belief in justification by works, and to impossible ideas about sinlessness.

The problems were exacerbated because Quakers were not consistent in the ways they used the word "light." They very rarely equated "the light" with the Holy Spirit, and were often unclear about its relation to Christ. Their commonest phrases were "the light of Christ" or simply "the light," and they often used the word in a way difficult to distinguish from "conscience." Opponents agreed that everybody had a conscience, but not that it was divine. Most writers who argued with Quakers, like Thomas Weld, wrote of two lights, a "natural" light of conscience, which was part of the human make-up, and a "divine" light that was the Holy Spirit.[11] Every writer who entered into serious argument with the Quakers picked up this point, which depended on the interpretation of apparently contradictory texts. Saint Paul, in Romans 1:18–2:16, suggests a natural, inbuilt conscience that is not the same as the spirit of Christ described later in the same epistle. John 1:9, "the light that enlightens every man," suggests one light, Christ.

The most careful discussion of Quaker theology at this time was *The Contradictions of the Quakers to the Scriptures of God* by John Stalham, an Essex minister who in 1655 was preaching in Edinburgh. He wrote that Quakers, "have a zeal of God but not according to knowledge. And some of them may haply be raised up by the Lord, to bear witness to the Ranters of the times, who have extinguished all common light of nature, and would level all with sin and hell." As well as hearing Quaker preachers he had studied a bound volume of approximately thirty pamphlets by leading Quaker writers, and concluded that Quaker teaching was not only opposed to the Bible but was also unclear and at times self-contradictory.[12] The nature of "the light" and its part in salvation was a main question at issue.

Farnworth, replying to Stalham, asserted rather than argued that the "the light" was not part of human make-up. "The light which doth disclose the natural corruption is not natural, as thou sayest, but it is spiritual, and such as love it bring their deeds to be tried by it."[13] Farnworth put more emphasis than most Quakers on the importance of the death of Christ, but failed to make a clear link to "the light," as when he wrote, "The death of Christ we witness to be of great effect. . . . Christ is light, and such as walk in him, receives the light of life," juxtaposing the ideas but not explaining the connection.[14] Farnworth retained the traditional Protestant beliefs in the unworthiness of man and the consequent necessity of the cross for salvation, but like many Quakers he found it difficult to explain how the necessity of the cross could be reconciled with the Quaker idea of a light available to all.

However strongly Quakers declared that "the death of the man Jesus which suffered at Jerusalem we own and witness, the same Christ that suffered at Jerusalem we own made manifest," they could not convince their opponents.[15] In the words of one anti-Quaker tract: "We gladly own Christ is in us by his spirit to crucify our flesh, and raise us up in our hearts . . . but we detect that doctrine that destroys the atonement in his blood, and the truth of his humanity."[16] "Thus, when Quakers say they own and witness the Christ that died at Jerusalem, they mean nothing more than the fact, it has no effect," wrote Ralph Farmer, one of the Quakers' fiercest critics.[17] Such criticisms were frequently voiced and never adequately answered.[18]

The most competent Quaker theologian was James Nayler, and by 1655 he was at the height of his powers, conducting written and public debates in addition to his regular preaching work. It is unfortunate that his pamphlet dispute with Richard Baxter did not measure up to the capabilities of either of the contestants. Baxter despised Quakers, while Nayler could not appreciate Baxter's teaching on the church as catholic, and the controversy degenerated, as often happened with these disputes, into "railing."[19] Nayler's mature thought was better expressed in *Love to the Lost,* a full statement of faith in twenty-five short chapters, the most comprehensive Quaker theological work up to that date and not easily summarized. Nayler began by describing the Fall of Man, and how the Devil was let into the world. Then Christ came to preach repentance.

> And as the mind is stayed in the light from hearkening to the earthly; so that seed which lies in death comes to hear the voice of the Son of God, and to receive life and strength from the Word . . . and as man beholds the seed growing, so he comes to see the new Creation, and what he lost in the Fall, and so is restored by the power of the Word, the Son of God . . . able to resist the devil, to choose the thing that is good, and delight in it.

The final line of this quotation, and especially the word "choose," suggest that Nayler had now departed from Calvinism, according to which people have no control over their own salvation. Like Fox, he described salvation as a new birth.

> That which is born of the heavenly, is heavenly, spiritual, eternal, and incorruptible; which is the state of the new man, which of God is begotten of the divine nature: and as is his nature, so is his works . . .

and so he that is born of this seed is born of God; and he that is born of God sins not in whom that seed remains. . . . And so the body of sin being put off through the body of Christ, the redemption is witnessed.

The use of "seed" in these passages is ambiguous. It is not clear if Nayler meant Christ or human potential. Nayler was approaching a fusing of the two concepts, putting forward a theory of human perfectibility, and like Fox, retaining as much as possible of the language of union with God. The phrase "body of Christ" is likewise ambiguous, perhaps deliberately, in that it could refer both to the human body of Christ and also to the Church. However, apart from a few such oblique references, Nayler did nothing to answer criticisms that Quakers devalued the human Christ. *Love to the Lost* has three pages on Christ, and they entirely concern the eternal pre-existent Christ, "He by whom all things were made, who is the life of all creatures, the beginning of all creatures who was before all creatures."[20]

The debate that dealt most fully with the Quaker understanding of Christ began with a public dispute between Edward Burrough and John Bunyan in Bunyan's home town, Bedford, on May 23, 1656, and was followed by four books written over a period of seven or eight months. Bunyan attacked the spiritualizing of Christ by Quakers and others, and emphasized that Christ had a fully human nature in unity with the divine, and made frequent use of the phrases "the man Jesus," and "the God-man." Burrough's reply, as so often with Quaker tracts, was highly abusive, and expounded the Quaker view of Christ as eternal, "before the world was," who "in time was manifest at Bethlehem." Bunyan restated his attack on Quakers as no different in essentials from Ranters, who "deny Christ to be a real man without them." Burrough riposted with an attack on Bunyan's understanding of Christ: "That body which was begotten of the Holy Ghost is not so carnal as thou supposest."[21] Here was the difficulty. The Quakers' intense experience of Christ, or the light of Christ, which led them to blur the distinction between Christ and themselves, was difficult to reconcile with a belief in Jesus as man.

After the disgrace of Nayler, Burrough became the leading Quaker theologian, and his main theological work, *A Declaration to all the World of our Faith,* was an exposition of the Quaker faith for non-Quakers, written in 1657. By this time Quakers, as was explained in Chapter 3, were beginning to care for their public image, and this book was a public relations exercise in which Burrough used conventional language. He said Quakers believed in one God, a Spirit, and that none could come to God but "his children who are born of his Spirit and are led and guided thereby." God had given his Son Jesus Christ as a free gift, and everyone could believe and be saved. Salvation, justification, and sanctification were only possible through Christ, and those who were saved were free from unrighteousness and had the witness of the Spirit in them. Christ was one with the Father, and "was, is, and is to come, without beginning or end." He was "made manifest in Judea and Jerusalem" where he did the work of his Father, was crucified, buried, rose again, and is ascended and glorified, and is to be waited for in Spirit. Salvation and the final judgment were telescoped, for all people on earth had a "time and day of visitation given, that they may return and be saved by Jesus Christ . . . they that do perish, it is because they do not believe in Christ, and destruction is of a man's self, but salvation is of God, through believing in his Son, who takes away sin." This book shows Burrough's difficulty reconciling the Quaker belief, in the possibility of salvation for all, with his original Calvinism. He still believed in election, at least in some sense. Performing good works, he said, was no advantage to the reprobate, while only "they that are chosen of God are delivered from wrath."

In this book, typical Quakerly references to "the light" are blended with traditional phraseology, as in a passage describing how those who came into the Kingdom of God were "washed and cleansed from all unrighteousness by the blood of Jesus, by whom their sins are remitted; for his blood cleanseth from all unrighteousness and sin, yea all such that walk and abide in the light which Christ Jesus hath lightened the world withal."[22] It is worth observing that, in an epistle intended for Friends, Burrough's language was very different. Instead of the blood of Jesus, he wrote of the indwelling of God and rebirth. "This is the whole salvation . . . that God dwells in us . . . according to his promise . . . salvation is come unto us . . . we . . . are begotten of the Word of God, and born of the immortal seed, and are new Creatures . . . [knowing] the Election which it is not possible to deceive."[23]

George Fox, as has been noted, was not given to theological subtleties, and at first he did not contribute to theological debates. His writings with a theological content were pastoral, calling people to share, as they could, in his experience.

> All people come to know the light in you, shining in your hearts
> to give you that knowledge of God in the face of Jesus Christ, and
> all people come to know the heavenly treasure in the earthly vessels,

which none do but them that come to the light which Christ hath enlightened the world, and all people come to know the second Adam, the Lord from heaven above the first Adam . . . and all people come to know the new Covenant that God hath prophesied by his prophet, the everlasting Covenant, and knowing the end of the first Covenant, know this Covenant which is everlasting.

This was typical of Fox, the call to all people, the ready use of the language of Saint Paul (2 Corinthians 4:6), his favorite text from the Fourth Gospel, and the reference to the New Covenant. Another well-known Foxian phrase comes a couple of pages further on in the same pamphlet: "God is come to take his people off from the teachings of men, and to teach his people himself."[24] Fox often insisted that he believed in the Christ that "died at Jerusalem," and indeed that the death of Christ brought salvation, but for him the atonement was spiritualized and not, as his opponents insisted, something that had happened at a particular moment in time. "Come hither . . . the power of God in you feel, and then you feel Christ Jesus who hath enlightened every one that comes into the world, then you will feel the covenant, which you have with God, which will blot out your sin and transgression, then you will feel the blood of Christ Jesus which cleanses you from all sin, which light discovers as you walk in the light."[25] The drama of salvation, based on a real historical happening for most contemporaries, was internalized by Fox to the point that the historical Jesus was almost an irrelevance.

Finally, in 1659, Fox entered the field of controversial literature with an enormous book, *The Great Mistery of the Great Whore*, a compendium of replies to over one hundred anti-Quaker books and statements. Its importance in the history of Quakerism was described in Chapter 3. *The Great Mistery* offers a possibility of comparing Fox's replies with earlier answers to the same books by other Quaker authors. Fox, although quite as capable of "railing" as any of his followers, now avoided much of the sheer abuse that had been a feature of both sides in the controversial literature. *The Great Mistery* contained a good deal of strong language, but it was balanced by a larger proportion of positive statements. Fox intended to present Quakers in a favorable light, and to minimize all those features of Quakerism that were particularly subject to attack, and that Fox did not consider essential to the truth that he was proclaiming. This change of tone will have been a policy decision, part of the regular campaign during 1657–58, for Quakers to present themselves as reasonable and responsible persons.

In this book, Fox avoided mention of the Nayler affair. Ralph Farmer's *Satan Inthron'd in his Chair* was one of the most vicious of all anti-Quaker books, oozing joy at the discomfiture of Quakers. In his answer Fox did not mention Nayler, or Quaker disputes, beyond a brief reference to "the rest of the stuff in thy book," and instead dealt solely with theological questions. Other books that had commented on Nayler were handled in similar fashion.

Fox minimized accusations of odd behavior, possible sorcery, Ranterish practices, and the like, which were common in anti-Quaker books, and where he could not avoid them, he tried to lift the discussion to a higher plane. An example is his treatment of an eccentric called John Gilpin (see Chapter 11), who had, for a short time, attended Quaker meetings.[26] Gilpin's alleged experiences had been reported in lurid language in a book called *The Quakers Shaken,* which had already been answered in strong terms by both Christopher Atkinson and Gervase Benson.[27] Fox, commenting on Gilpin, managed to bring in references to faith in the heart, reading and praying in the spirit, and salvation.

When accusations against Quakers were more general, Fox ignored them. For instance, accusations of Ranterism were made in Collier's *Looking Glass,* and Baxter's *Quakers Catechism,* and these accusations had been specifically answered in existing Quaker replies, but *The Great Mistery,* replying to Collier and Baxter, dealt only with positive aspects of Quaker ethics.[28] The practice of "walking naked" (Chapter 9) was lightly touched on, and made an occasion for attacking the legitimacy of the established ministry.[29] Fox's intention of presenting the more acceptable face of Quakerism became especially clear in the passages dealing with quaking. A number of the books answered in *The Great Mistery* described quaking, but in most cases, Fox in *The Great Mistery* entirely ignored what was said about this phenomenon. Twice he related quaking directly to salvation, leaving it slightly doubtful as to how far it was a physical and how far a spiritual happening.[30]

In the course of *The Great Mistery* Fox repeated, many times, his personal doctrine. Salvation came from the light, which was from Christ or was Christ. He used biblical language to describe the work of Christ, especially Saint Paul's first and second Adam metaphor: Christ was "the second Adam, the quickening spirit . . . the Covenant of God, of light, of life, of peace, who was glorified with his Father before the world began."[31] There was little distinction between physical and spiritual; the relationship between Christ and the believer was very close, described, in the same terms that Fox had used before, as being "flesh of his flesh and bone of his bone."[32] The following passage also slipped from physical to spiritual: "The blood of

Christ which satisfies the Father, which the Saints drink, and his flesh which they eat which in so doing have life is that which the world stumble at; which who drinks it, lives for ever."[33] Belief in a real union with Christ, however expressed, remained the keystone of Fox's theology.

Fox's theology was, however, obscure. The light was not Christ, but brought people to Christ. Was it the Holy Spirit? In one pamphlet proclaiming the Quaker faith Fox wrote, "The Father and the Son, and the Spirit of truth, and that of God in every one's Conscience shall bear witness unto us."[34] Such introduction of something like a Fourth Person to the Trinity caused problems when Quakers were attacked by conventional theologians who accepted the Trinitarian formula that God is three persons in one substance. What was this light, or "that of God," in everyone's conscience? Fox clearly did not equate it with the Holy Spirit, and while plenty of examples can be found of Fox equating the light with the spiritual presence of Christ, he by no means always did so, and he was often ambiguous. Most often he described the light as something that comes from Christ, or God, "the light that Christ hath enlightened you withal," without actually being Christ or God.[35]

Was the Quakers' "the light in the conscience" the same thing as the natural light of conscience? If so, it seemed impossible to their opponents that this natural light should be the same thing as the Holy Spirit, or Christ.[36] But Quakers said that the light was not just conscience, nor was it natural. They split hairs into imperceptible slivers when trying to explain that, when they talked about the universal light in the conscience, they did not mean conscience itself, and certainly did not mean that every one possessed the Holy Spirit and was therefore redeemed, a view that, they agreed with their opponents, led directly to the slippery slope of Practical Antinomianism.

Many Quaker writers in the latter part of the 1650s, responding to their opponents' demands that they should clarify their ideas on the meaning of "the light," came to pay less and less attention to the life and death of Jesus. Modern apologists for Quakerism often assert that the early Quakers accepted the true humanity of Christ, as well as his divinity.[37] It is true that Fox often expressed a belief in the Christ that "died at Jerusalem," and so, also, did Burrough, although as has been shown, their interpretation of this belief was unconventional. The majority of Quaker pamphleteers did not even pay lip service to traditional Christian formulations. During 1657 and 1658, about fifty Quaker authors (excluding Fox and Burrough), in some sixty pamphlets, gave their accounts of salvation. Of these perhaps eight ascribed any serious importance to the earthly life and death of Christ. All the others wrote of Christ and the light as though they were precisely equivalent terms, and several rarely mentioned Christ at all, concentrating almost entirely on the light.[38] Even some of Fox's writings showed, and doubtless encouraged, this tendency; his *Catechism for Children*, instead of being an account of the whole Christian faith with a Quaker leaning, is almost entirely about the operation of the light.[39] Pamphlets written in 1659 were if anything even more biased in this direction, and most Quaker writers of this time gave the impression of being far removed, in their understanding of Christ, from their Presbyterian, Independent, and Baptist contemporaries. They took to extremes the tendency derived from continental writers, which was noted in Chapter 1, to emphasize the divine eternal Christ at the expense of the human, and the contemporary accusation, that Quakers did not believe in a human Jesus, had much evidence to support it.[40] Part of the problem was the nature of the debates, when Quakers, forced on to the defensive, had to concentrate on trying to define "the light" and its operation.

Although, after the Nayler affair, Quakers moderated their language in some respects, they did not abate their claims to the possibility of moral perfection; this view is indeed to be found in Robert Barclay's *Apology*, probably the greatest Quaker theological work, which was published in 1676.[41] Fox wrote in *The Great Mistery* that the believer, being "in Christ," was like Christ, and was Christ, and so was perfect.[42] Burrough also showed no doubts. "Their sins are blotted out . . . for they cease to commit sin, being born of the seed of God."[43] Other writers, however, following the more placatory approach that became general from 1657, were more cautious. This is William Caton on the possibility of moral perfection:

> Perfection is that which they earnestly press after and have hope to attain unto the fulness of it, for they do not believe that God would command . . . which could not possibly be attained . . . these people . . . do see a possibility in the thing, and are not without faith but that they shall obtain it . . . if the Lord permit, who hath manifested in them that which is perfect, by which he will bring (and hath brought some of them) to the perfection of purity, and the beauty of holiness, where Hallelujah is sung to the most high.[44]

The last major Quaker controversial work from this period was Samuel Fisher's *Rusticus ad Academicos*, a huge tome, published in 1660, attacking John Owen, Richard Baxter, and two other eminent divines. It was never answered, for the world had moved on. However, before the end of the 1650s, at least one Quaker became aware of the damage that was being done to the reputation of Quakerism, by continually writing about the light to the exclusion of the rest of Christian doctrine. This was George Fox the Younger, who in 1659 published a pamphlet called *The Words of the Everlasting and True Light*. The author included a note on the last page that he really did believe in the human Jesus, crucified outside Jerusalem, whose blood gave remission of sins, but he could only write what God gave him to write, and this mainly concerned the light.[45] In due course other Quakers followed this lead, and attempts to restate Quaker theology, in a way that seriously addressed the concerns of other churches, are considered in the final chapter of this book.

PART III

QUAKERS IN PRACTICE

9

WALKING IN THE LIGHT

The people who flocked to the Quakers, seeking the Kingdom of God, were joining a movement that made strict demands on them. Some individuals left an account of how they came to be Quakers, for describing one's spiritual autobiography was a common seventeenth-century practice.[1] They had mostly been serious young people, concerned about their sins, searching for a true faith since childhood. Many had explored widely in current religious ideas and practices before finding a home, often after great trouble and distress, with the Quakers. Hubberthorne's religious search was described in Chapter 1, and it was typical of many.

Having found their way to faith, converts had to be prepared to change their way of life. "Walking in the light" involved absolutely right conduct, a necessary consequence of the experience of the teaching light of Christ. Right conduct acted as a substitute for formal church membership; people who did not behave according to "the light" were not part of the community. Opponents found the Quaker teaching on moral perfection impossible to accept, one writing, "Some of them affirms, that they are come up to so much perfection, that they have not had an ill thought nor spoken an ill word, for two years together."[2] Leading Quakers rarely disagreed about what constituted right conduct; indeed, if there had been serious disagreement, there could have been no Quakerism. When one or two people only were "walking disorderly" they were disowned; when a number of people with a definite leader were involved, as in the Rhys Jones controversy (Chapter 1), there could be no unity.[3] There were, however, frequent doubts within meetings as to the limits of right conduct, leading in due course to formal disciplinary arrangements. George Fox made this appeal:

> Judge not one another behind one anothers backs, neither lay upon one another weakness and nakedness behind one anothers backs . . . but everyone of you in particular with the light of Christ . . . see yourselves with it. . . . And that there be no backbiting behind one anothers backs . . . you that dwell in the light and see clear, speak to others whose minds is gone from the light.[4]

Quakers were often accused of being Ranters, and strongly objected to the charge. Many Quaker tracts included a list of sins to be avoided, among them usually drunkenness and swearing, two practices supposed particularly characteristic of Ranters.[5] Fox wrote, "Ranters, you had a pure convincement, I witness . . . but having fled the Cross, and now to it are enemies, which turns the grace of God into wantonness, and follows drunkenness, and cursed speaking, sporting yourselves in the day time, following oaths and swearing . . . and with the light to be condemned."[6] The important phrase is "fled the cross"; Ranterish types were not prepared to submit to the discipline required of Quakers, and indeed saw no need for it.

Quakers were extremely sensitive to any suggestion of sexual misconduct, which would in any case be a risk with groups of people, many quite young, some probably unstable, in a highly excited state. One letter, addressed generally "to Friends," concerned a couple who had

> covertly, closely deceitfully and filthily acted that which is abominable and detestable to all the Children of Light. . . . They have acted as

man and wife this long time, but did not to the world declare it . . .
and therefore they are cast out of the Assembly of the Saints . . . that
no disorder be among us . . . that the enemy of the truth may be
confounded. . . . True judgement may pass upon the head of the
wicked before ever they can be owned of the Children of Light or
received into the Assembly of the Saints.[7]

This is strong language by any standards, and not matched by letters concerning other misdemeanors. Accusations of sexual misbehavior were frequent in anti-Quaker pamphlets.

Quaker strictness clearly attracted some people who, repelled equally by Calvinism and Ranterism, were looking for a faith with high ethical standards. Thomas Symonds of Norwich left a record of his experience with a Ranter-type group:

The doctrine of free grace . . . was preached to me, that Christ had
suffered for sinners . . . so there was nothing for me to do but believe
these things. . . . It was pleasing to the fleshly mind. . . . I could be
merry, and . . . my staidness and soberness was turned into wantoness,
and laughter . . . it was the liberty of the Saints to be merry and
cheerly in the world.[8]

This life soon disgusted him, and he was convinced as a Quaker by Ann Blaykling, when he was visiting Cambridge. The situation of Thomas Symonds was probably not unusual, and goes some way to account for the rapid move of the Quakers toward staid respectability.

Many distinctive Quaker practices, as noted in Chapter 1, derived from pre-Quaker radicalism, but such practices rapidly became an essential part of Quaker self-understanding, linked to the belief that as Children of the Light they were separated from "the world," and must manifest in their lives the truth of the Gospel. Quakers were not expected to enjoy carrying out this witness; as many of them said, separation from "the world" involved a "cross to the will."[9] Children or servants who became Friends in a non-Friend household could have grave problems, as children and servants were expected to follow the head of the family in religious practice. Friends would try to find employment for those turned from home.[10]

Quakers were most frequently in conflict with civil and religious authorities regarding payment of tithe.[11] Fox's *Paper Sent Forth into the World* consists of eight pages of fierce and detailed attack on the church that ends: "All people that read these things, never come you more to the steeple-

house nor pay your priests more tithes till they have answered them, for if
you do, you uphold them in their sins, and must partake of their plagues."[12]
Refusal to pay tithes soon began to cause real hardship. "Treble damages"
could be exacted, and goods whose value far exceeded the amount due
might be confiscated, in one case, it was said, five oxen being taken for a
debt of fivepence halfpenny.[13]

Many tithes had been "impropriated," that is, the right to collect them
had been sold, often to a lay person. Quakers were not clear how they
viewed impropriated tithes.[14] Anthony Pearson, writing in 1653, recognized
impropriated tithes as a form of property, and suggested that their owners
should be bought out.[15] A parish minister who had a dispute with Quakers
in 1656 thought that Quakers generally objected only to payments to ministers, and not to impropriated tithes.[16] Fox, whose main objection to tithes
was that he disapproved of ministers being paid for their services, may have
been under some pressure to give a ruling on the subject, and in 1659 he
wrote a pamphlet in which he condemned impropriated tithes.[17] Payment
of such tithes remained a gray area, however, and came up again in one of
the Quakers' internal disputes in the 1670s.[18] The problem for Quakers was
that impropriated tithes were lay property, and they were careful to show
respect for property rights.

Quakers were noted for refusing to take oaths. This was and is the standpoint of Mennonites and other groups deriving from the Anabaptist movement that originated on the European continent during the sixteenth century. Some, but not all, English Baptists shared this witness. Oath-taking
was considered contrary to the Bible, and could also be a form of social
distinction, as oath-taking was rarely required of the gentry.[19] Oath-taking
also indicated a double standard of truth, a matter on which Quakers were
very sensitive.

By about 1655 Quakers had ceased to use the customary names of the
days and months because of their pagan origin, saying instead, "First day"
for Sunday, and "Tenth month" for December (by the old calendar). Some
Baptists did the same.[20] Other practices concerned forms of address.
Quakers did not care for personal titles, because they indicated social distinctions, but in earlier years they sometimes addressed men by their military rank, such as "Captain Stoddart" and "Colonel Benson." "Thou" was
the normal Quaker address to a single person, for "You," the normal address to social superiors, indicated social distinction and also, said Quakers,
was plural and should therefore, truthfully, only be applied to more than
one person.[21]

Quakers thus linked established radical practices, such as refusing oaths and using "thou," with actual truth-telling. Quakers also required strict honesty in business, including giving one fixed price instead of haggling. They came to use "truth" as the distinctive word for their faith. Fox's contemporary writings and also the *Journal* show the importance "truth" had for him, and it is probable that emphasis on "truth" in various senses was one of Fox's specific contributions to the development of Quaker faith and practice.[22]

Quakers would not give customary greetings, for they said that only God, not humans, should be so honored. Fox's 1657 pamphlets, when he was establishing his position as leader, included advice on this subject. On greetings, for instance, you might say "Good morning" to those in the light, but not to "evil workers, cursed speakers" and the like, for they were in the "evil day."[23] Often, especially when arguing with opponents, Quakers went beyond the omission of normal courtesies. "Railing" was the usual term. Ellis Bradshaw, one of Nayler's opponents, said that the Spirit should teach them courtesy, and that they "will with a most austere countenance call men damned, and carnal, and hirelings, and deceivers, and proud, when they can demonstrate no such thing, but in the judgement of charity might judge the contrary." Magnus Byne said that Quakers rudely refused to eat with people not of their company, calling them "Devils and Dogs." Richard Baxter wrote, "I have had more railing language from them in one letter, than I ever heard from all the scolds in the country to my remembrance this twenty years."[24] Quaker pamphlets were described as using language, "more fit for Billingsgate than the Press." (Billingsgate was the London fish market, and fishwives had the reputation of using worse language than anyone).[25] There is no obvious origin for this Quaker trait, unless it too derives from Fox, who could certainly be extremely abusive. But this was not a polite age, and the more vicious of the anti-Quaker pamphlets outstripped the language of the Quakers.

Quaker men refused to remove their hats in the presence of their social superiors, a practice perhaps not too unacceptable in the north of the country, but in the south, the rules of etiquette were strict.[26] If Quakers were taken before magistrates, it was usually in the first instance for alleged vagrancy or for disturbing worship, but when Quakers would not remove their hats in courts of law, there would be trouble. Richard Hubberthorne and George Whitehead were both imprisoned in Norwich for refusing to remove their hats in court, and in following years there were many other instances.[27] Eight tracts of 1655 dealt with this problem and explained why hats should be retained, since it was wrong to show respect to individuals. In 1657, Fox was his usual blunt self on the subject of hats: "Putting off the hat is but a custom got up amongst the Christians . . . in the apostacy. . . . If a Lord or an Earl come into your courts, you will hardly fine him for not putting off his hat . . . but it is the poor that suffer."[28]

Family life at this time was based on a patriarchal model with some flexibility in practice, and the Quakers generally followed this pattern. Farnworth, in one of his earliest pamphlets, described at considerable length the duty of a wife to be subservient to her husband.[29] Burrough, in *A Declaration to the World of our Faith*, one of the pamphlets written after the Nayler affair with the purpose of presenting a good view of the Quakers, wrote, "And we believe that obedience and subjection in the Lord belongs to superiors . . . and that children ought to obey their parents, and wives their husbands, and servants their masters in all things, which is according to God."[30] On the other hand, the Quaker marriage declaration, in which the man and woman used the same words to take each other, indicated greater equality between men and women within marriage than was usual at the time, and a second George Fox, called the Younger because he was "younger in the faith," may have given an accurate representation of the situation in a leaflet addressed to "Masters and Dames," equally in charge of a household.[31] It was accepted by Christians that duty to God might on occasion outweigh duty to a husband, and Quaker women such as Ann Audland followed this principle when they left their homes for the traveling ministry.[32]

Wealthy Quakers were expected not to be ostentatious. When Thomas and Ann Curtis, a prosperous couple from Reading, joined with Friends in 1657, Alexander Parker wrote to Fell that "they have formerly lived very high and very rich in apparel," but they were now "stripped of all," and "he has ripped his glass buttons off, and his wife has stripped off all her jewels and rich attire."[33] The distinctive Quaker dress did not, however, become mandatory until late in the century. Quakers had no objection to a comfortable way of living, and Thomas Ellwood, dining with the Peningtons before his convincement, noted that the food was very good.[34]

Except for "singing in the spirit," which is discussed in Chapter 11, Friends objected to music. Humphrey Smith, whose story is told in Chapter 12, was "one who had loved dancing and music as his life," but he came to the conclusion that music, poetry, and such-like were "the undoing of many poor souls." He pointed out that the father of music was Jubal, the son of Cain (Genesis 4:21), and that most references to music and dancing in the Bible are associated with false worship.[35] Solomon Eccles was a London music teacher and instrument builder who turned Quaker, and felt driven to make a bonfire of his instruments on Tower Hill. He later described his reasons, arguing, like Humphrey Smith, that music was associated with false worship, but that in any case the Lord had required him to take this action.[36] These pamphlets read as though abandoning music was a very painful duty for both Smith and Eccles.

Quakers became noted as serious people who only spoke when necessary and never joked. This practice seems to have derived from the personal predilection of Fox, shown in a paper from 1652, referring to Ecclesiastes 5:2: "[The] light will judge and condemn you for using many words, for he saith, let your words be few and seasoned . . . for you must give account for every idle word." A Quaker minister wrote later, "We must deny . . . all our vain words and light idle communication, jesting and foolish talking, lying and double-dealing . . . and this is a great cross to our own wills." Thomas Ellwood was surprised at the absence of conversation at the Peningtons' dinner table.[37] Other people made fun of the Quakers' solemn speech.

> Whether or no, that a book of the Quakers dialect or manner of speaking, ought not to be printed, for the better education of the brethren, to make others understand, that are not in the light? A taste of which I shall give you, it being a discourse between a Quaker and her husband in these words, *George, I say unto thee, Arise, and go to the wicket-chair, thereon hangeth my red-petticoat; in the pocket of which thou shalt find two brass-farthings; take them, and go unto our brother Simon, the tallow-chandler, and buy therewith two farthing candles, and light one of them, and bring hither, for I fear our son Peter hath fouled himself.*[38]

Quakers were expected to live a conventionally respectable hard-working life, and "idle persons without a calling" were among those evildoers they denounced.[39] Thomas Symonds of Norwich, whose journey to Quakerism has been described, described his business ethic thus:

> We doing unto all men what we would that all men should do unto us, not defrauding cozening, or cheating any, nor using deceitful words, to make any believe a lie, but in plainness of speech, with fewness of words, in singleness and uprightness of heart, we are ordered with the light of Christ in our house and conversations. . . .

> Where the truth of God is made manifest in the light of Jesus, and lived in the life and power, none can or dare take liberty to idleness, and slothfulness in business.[40]

Such people were attracted to the Quaker movement by the strict ethical standards that put much responsibility on the individual. Quakers were known to be honest, and so did good business, and some of them began to get rather rich. This was Fox's advice:

> Then is the danger and temptation to you drawing the minds into it . . . that you can hardly do anything to the service of God but there will be crying my business my business . . . and your minds will go unto the things. . . . So you do not come to the image of God . . . you go back into that what you were before and then the Lord God will . . . take your goods from you.[41]

Quakers are noted for their peace witness, but few Quakers were pacifists to begin with.[42] Howgill, who like Burrough tended to military language, put this very unpacifist message into the mouth of the Lord concerning the siege of Dublin: "I made thy walls as iron, and thy gates as brass, and thy batteries strong, and guarded thee . . . and brake the teeth of thy enemies . . . and I gave their carcasses to fall by the sword and for the fowls of the air to feed upon."[43] Soldiers were often warm supporters of Quakers, and the southwestern mission in particular owed much to their help.[44] Many Friends had been or were still in the army, and, like many of the Parliamentary soldiers, they thought they were helping to bring in the Kingdom of God. Nayler wrote of his army service, "I have served for the good of these nations, betwixt eight and nine years, counting nothing dear to bring the covenant into your hands [i.e., Cromwell's]."[45] Fox wrote, "To the Council of Officers of the Army, and the Heads of the Nation. . . . Now had you been faithful in the power of the Lord . . . then you should neither have feared Holland, nor France, nor Spain, nor Italy," and continued, regarding Quaker soldiers, "It has been said among you, That they had rather have had one of them, than seven men."[46] Most Quaker soldiers were finally expelled from the army, but because their discipline was suspect, not because they objected to fighting.[47]

There were occasional exceptions to Quaker militarism. One Quaker sailor, converted to Quakerism with some of his mates, and referring to the year 1654, wrote,

As yet we were not brought to testify against fighting; but we would take none of the plunder. . . . We called Quakers fought with as much courage as any, seeing then no farther . . . and I went into the fore-castle and levelled the guns. . . . But he that hath all mens hearts in his hand, can turn them at his pleasure; yea, he in a minutes time so changed my heart, that in a minute before, I setting my whole strength and rigour to kill and destroy mens' lives, and in a minute after I could not kill or destroy a man . . . for as I was coming out of the fore-castle door, to see where the shot fell, the word of the Lord came through me, how if I had killed a man: and it was with such power, that for some time I hardly knew whether I was in the body or out of it.[48]

Normal military duties might be permissible, but Quakers declared that they would not take part in civil strife. After the Swannington meeting, Fox assured Cromwell that Friends would not take up arms against him. "My weapons are not carnal but spiritual . . . with the carnal weapon I do not fight."[49] John Lilburne the Leveller, after his conversion to Quakerism, made a similar declaration. He caused great alarm in government circles when he became a Quaker, since it meant that one of the most notorious troublemakers in the country had joined up with the most intractable sect. His wife suggested that, like George Fox, he should write to Cromwell and promise not to draw sword against him, but at the time he did not wish to do so, for though he admired George Fox, he would not act in the same way unless moved by the Spirit. Presently he reached the stage when he felt he could make such a statement, and after many biblical references to the peaceable kingdom, he wrote,

I have now the faithful and true witness in my own soul, that the Lord himself is become within me. . . . By which divine teaching I am now daily taught to die to sin, and . . . do hereby witness, that I am already dead, or crucified, to the very occasions, and real grounds of all outward wars, and carnal sword-fightings and fleshly bustlings and contests; and that therefore I confidently now believe, I shall never hereafter be an user of a temporal sword more, nor a joiner with those that so do.[50]

This was a political document, and it is to be read in the context of the government's fear of armed insurrection; Lilburne was talking about civil, not international, strife. Nevertheless, while this passage should not be understood as pacifist in the modern sense, it was from experiences such as these, and from practice of passive resistance to what were considered unjust laws, that Quaker pacifism developed. Like other specifically Quaker testimonies, it probably owed a good deal to the personal attitude of Fox.[51] Further stages in the development of the Quaker peace testimony are described in Chapter 14.

For many Quakers, one consequence of their convincement was a call to engage in mission. This concentration on mission is one of the most distinctive features of early Quakerism. Other sects, especially Baptists, had itinerant preachers, but in this, as in other matters, the Quakers were more thoroughgoing. Quaker traveling ministers took with them lists of people who were likely to help them on their way, often Baptist contacts, but sometimes there was no one to help.[52] John Audland described his visit to Hereford with Thomas Ayrey: "We parted, having given up our lives into the hands of the Lord, not knowing when we should meet, and we had not the least knowledge of anyone in the city."[53]

The ministers were advised by Fox and financed as necessary by Margaret Fell, and kept under some sort of control if their message was not acceptable, but the actual call depended on the individuals being moved, as they understood it, by the Spirit. A number of letters refer to the need for work in a particular place, if anyone was moved to undertake it, and a letter from Farnworth throws light on how decisions were reached. He had received a request to visit a certain area, but wrote to Fox, "I found openings before it came that I might go into Lincolnshire, and I wait for it leading out. . . . I wait to receive orders from above, that I may have warrant from God, and I shall be freely willing to follow the leadings of the Lamb."[54]

The call, when it came, might be sudden and compulsive. One Friend described how he felt the call to action during a meeting:

> Upon the 10th day of the eighth Month, being on the first day of the week, about the second hour of the day, as I was peacable and quiet in my own spirit, and also sitting in a quiet and peaceable meeting among my brethren the people of God; the Lord moved his good spirit in me, and his word came unto me, (which was in me as a fire) saying, go to that congregation of people [location given] and declare unto them my word, and bear a testimony for me, and I had no rest nor peace in my own spirit, until I obeyed and went.[55]

There was complete equality as regards the ministry, at least in theory, between men and women, and there are no early records of men being preferred to women. There are, after all, many references to prophetesses in the Bible. There was no clear difference, as between men and women, in the experience of being called to minister, and in the delivery of their messages, although what the women did was more difficult, from the fact that they were moving into what was normally a male domain.[56] It is probable that the women were in general less educated than the men; in proportion to their numbers they published much less, and their pamphlets tended to be shorter and less theological, while only two women, Margaret Fell and Dorothy White, were in any sense major authors (see Appendix 3).[57] The account of the maltreatment at Oxford of two women Quakers, Elizabeth Fletcher and Elizabeth Leavens (Holmes), was written by Richard Hubberthorne, possibly indicating that the women concerned were not fully literate.[58] Women were more at risk of being badly treated by magistrates and hooligans, but other special problems and dangers in travel are not recorded, though Edward Burrough became rather concerned about "little Elizabeth Fletcher" who was traveling alone in Ireland, and wrote to Margaret Fell asking if some other woman might come and join her.[59]

Later in the decade the ministry of women was sometimes queried. Arthur Cotton from Plymouth, whose wife was an active minister, writing to Fox with a request for visiting ministers, asked for "rather men Friends, for they do not care to hear any women Friends."[60] Two years later, Margaret Fell was told that Friends in the ministry were wanted "by many who accepts rather of ministresses than none, although to some they are all one, both male and female . . . but thou knows as well as I, it is not so with every one."[61] Fox made his position clear: "The Spirit must not be quenched where it is poured upon the daughter."[62]

Traveling ministers carried books with them, to be distributed as appropriate. The author of an anonymous attack on Quakers in 1655 complained that Quakers "do disperse and communicate their erroneous books to such as they find inclining to them." The minister Giles Firmin had hoped it would be possible to ignore the Quakers in his parish, but "they would trouble me, sent divers of their books in to our town, invited my people to come and hear, and prevailed with some to hear." Twelve Quaker books were circulating, he said.[63] Among the surviving Quaker manuscripts is a request for copies of some fifty books "to be gathered up with speed to be sent into another country."[64] One result of the success of the Quaker mission was a flood of would-be new authors, and checking before publication was sometimes omitted, causing Fox to write, "All Friends everywhere, take heed of printing any more than you are moved of the Lord God."[65]

While the Quaker mission was highly successful, it also provoked extreme hostility. Traveling Quakers would appear from distant places, preaching an unfamiliar doctrine, maybe odd in appearance, many of them women. They were seen as threats to established society, and also easy prey as they did not resist. Local figures of authority, such as parish ministers and constables, were likely to turn a blind eye when hooligans set about Quakers.[66] In the spring of 1655 John Whitehead, one of Dewsbury's converts working in Wellingborough, wrote to Fox that he would probably be gaoled, and, "If thou find freedom to send any faithful friend among them, it will be a great service for the establishing of them, but persecution is likely to attend them that comes."[67] An important part of being a Quaker was learning to live with such situations, and the strategies developed to cope with persecution are described in Chapter 12.

In some cases the call to minister involved prophetic signs, the commonest being going naked or partly naked through the streets, or wearing sackcloth and ashes. This conduct was intended to signal the barrenness of contemporary society, and in some cases was not merely an illustration, but was intended to act like the signs of Old Testament prophets, and bring about the thing illustrated, the fall of the godless society and the coming of God's kingdom.[68] "As naked shall you be spiritually, as my body hath been temporally naked . . . as a sign of the nakedness and shame that is coming upon the Church of England," wrote William Simpson, who "walked naked as a sign" more often than anyone. Quakers who felt the call to this kind of witness often reported how difficult it had been to obey, and so did Simpson. "A necessity was laid upon me from the Lord God . . . to be a sign: But before I was given up to the thing, it was as death unto me and I had rather . . . have died than gone on this service."[69]

Most of the instances belong to the early period, 1652 to 1654. Thomas Holmes, for example, walked naked through the streets of Kendal, and the "grave and modest" Elizabeth Fletcher in Oxford.[70] There are few references to going naked as a sign in the anti-Quaker pamphlets and other records of 1655 and 1656, but there was an outburst in 1655 of such practices as going about in sackcloth and ashes.[71] George Bishop mentioned two women in Bristol, Sara Goldsmith and Temperance Hignal, who had done this, and Parnell reported Martha Simmons doing the same thing.[72] In all cases the practice was approved of, provided it was done "contrary to one's will." Presently, as Quakerism became less of an ecstatic movement, such practices became less common, though there were occasional instances later in the century.

Fasting was commonly practiced as a spiritual aid in the mid seventeenth century. Howgill fasted when in prison in Appleby, and the verdict at the inquest on James Parnell, who died in prison, was that he had brought on his own death by excessive fasting.[73] Nayler had been fasting prior to his "sign" in Bristol, and Farnworth issued a challenge to a fast in the course of a debate at Cambridge (see Chapter 7). The Swarthmoor family fasted, and Margaret Fell may have been the author of this passage: "I which am a Woman (the writer of this) fasted twenty-two days. . . . I will challenge all the Papists on earth, let them come out and go thirty days together without either bread or water . . . and try, and see if his belly be not his God; and the Quakers is known, they never had more strength than when they have fasted two and twenty, and thirty days together."[74] Unstable Friends sometimes caused trouble by their fasts; James Milner of Furness, having fasted fourteen days, prophesied, in full detail, the coming end of the world, an extravagance that was afterward held against Friends.[75]

Quakers felt they were living partly in the world of the spirit, and would often give their names as "known to the world as" so-and-so, having a real name in heaven. They might describe their daily work as their "outward being." Some Quakers took this to the point of basing their ethics on a matter/spirit dualism. Farnworth in particular often contrasted "within" and "without," or "carnal" and "spiritual." The same pairings were also used by other writers, and, later, by Fox. Most of the time Quakers, and especially Fox, seem to have meant the same as Saint Paul when he wrote of "flesh" and "spirit," that is, what is naturally human but turned away from God, contrasted with the naturally human turned toward God. In the seventeenth century the word "carnal" could either carry Saint Paul's sense or else it could mean "material," and some early Friends were not careful about the distinction.[76] Farnworth, for instance, wrote, "The world church is without thee, carnal lime and stone, and the call is outward, with a carnal bell, and a carnal man speaks the carnal letter, for money, to carnal minds. But the saints church is God the father . . . the saints teacher is within them . . . the saints law is within them"[77] There is no doubt about the "spiritual" side of the equation, but could anyone say with certainty whether "carnal" means "material" or "turned away from God," or indeed both at once? The distinction probably never crossed Farnworth's mind, and the same would have been true of many of his contemporaries who read Saint Paul's epistles and decided that they must give up all outward display. Nayler expressed similar views: "Keep your eye to the light, that it may lead you through all the visible things of the world . . . for the temptation lies in the carnal things, and there is the bondage of the creature to things that are corrupt."[78]

Fox, however, although equally strict about "taking pleasure in the flesh" regarding sports and games, had no doubts about the goodness of God's creation, and even wrote his own version of the Benedicite.

> Such as are turned to the light which comes from him who is the heir of all things . . . these come to see how all the works of the Lord praise him; . . . day and night praise him; summer and winter praise him; ice and cold and snow praise him; and that is the bad and evil that calls them evil . . . seed-time and harvest praise him; all things that are created praise him. This is the language of them who learn of him; hear him . . . who upholds all things by his word and power, by whom all things was made . . . that above all things he might have the preheminence.[79]

This passage is little known, and worth quoting as an indication that "walking in the light," and denying "the world," did not mean abhorrence of creation.[80]

10

FOUNDATIONS
OF THE
GOSPEL ORDER

The term "Gospel Order" was coined by Fox when he reorganized the Quaker network of meetings in 1666–68, and it is still in use among British Quakers. Fox was then building on foundations put in place during the 1650s, when, over a period of several years, Quakers developed a regular church order that governed much of their daily lives. Their first arrangements were designed to meet the needs of the moment, for, in the apocalyptic excitement of 1653, setting up a church organization designed for the long term would have seemed an irrelevance.

Quakers were quite clear about what was wrong with existing churches. The church building was not the house of God, formal worship of any kind was wrong, and ministers should give their services freely, like Jesus' disciples. Ministers need not attend the universities of Oxford and Cambridge, which were characterized as two evil mothers.[1] They should receive an "immediate" call to their work, as distinct from a "mediate" call authorized by human law and church authorities.[2] Quaker pamphleteers attacked parish ministers, whom they called "priests," for enjoying "Being Called of Men Masters" and "Having Best Seats in the Synagogue."[3] Ministry should rather be given freely in accordance with the New Testament.[4] Much of this was common ground with other radicals.

One of the earliest tracts, signed by Thomas Aldam and five others imprisoned in York Castle, included most of the Quaker complaints.

> All the holy men of God spoke forth freely and when any spoke for hire, it was a filthy and horrible thing. . . . Everyone looks for his gain from his quarter where he is. . . . Try your priests, and . . . see if they will not go to law with you? and if they do, you shall see that they were never taught of Christ, for he says, "If any man sue thee at the law and take away thy coat, let him have thy cloak also." . . . You do not read in all the holy scriptures that any of the holy men of God were Cambridge or Oxford scholars. . . . The professed ministers . . . are oppressors . . . they are the kings of pride in the towns where they are; and their wives . . . in their hoods, veils and rings, which are odious to the Lord. . . . Woe to the idle shepherds.[5]

Quakers insisted that they never denied church order and ministry. The Quaker ministry, and especially the upkeep of ministers, was a major issue in several disputes, for opponents argued that Quaker ministry was not really "free," since the ministers accepted maintenance from local Friends. Disputing with John Stalham, Hubberthorne wrote that people

> who are moved by the Spirit of God to watch over the flock, and ordained with gifts thereunto, may take the oversight of the flock wittingly. . . . The call to the true ministry and eldership is not by man, nor of man, but by the Lord. . . . The ministers of Christ do receive freely, and gives freely of what they have received from God, and having planted a vineyard, may eat the fruit of it . . . and when they go into a house, may eat such things as are set before them, and yet may not be chargeable to any man, and this is according to Christ's instruction, and not contradictory to the Scriptures.[6]

Many people at this time thought that the true church had been lost since the days of the Apostles, but Quakers declared that not only had the true church reappeared but that it was exclusive to their movement, in Nayler's words, "The spiritual kingdom of Christ in the consciences of his own poor despised little flock."[7] The Quaker claim to be the only true church met with strong opposition. Richard Baxter wrote that it was very unlikely that the only true Christians were "a few raging Quakers 1652 years after his [i.e., Jesus'] incarnation." He gave the example of the martyrs under Queen Mary as faithful witnesses from earlier days. Nayler replied that at that time "the light was not then come," though, indeed, the martyrs had denied the pope according to their measure.[8] Quakers were too conscious of the new beginning, and too sure that they alone constituted the true church, to be much concerned about what had gone before, although when pressed by opponents they conceded that God had always provided a few faithful witnesses to his truth.

After the Quaker movement had become established over most of England and Wales, in 1655, Quaker pamphleteers began to write about the superior virtues of the true church, in other words, themselves. One author made a detailed comparison between Quaker ministers and the ministers of the established and gathered churches. Quaker ministers had to leave their homes, deny themselves, wander, and expect persecution, declaring the word by the Spirit. Unlike ministers of other churches, who disagreed with each other, some baptizing by "sprinkling" and some by "dipping," these true ministers agreed in the Spirit, living "in the bond of love and peace . . . which leads up to one God . . . one faith, one baptism."[9]

The performance of miracles was considered to be a sign of the presence of the true church, as described in Matthew 11:5. Religious leaders could be challenged to show their powers, as Nayler was by Jeremy Ives (see Chapter 3). Accounts in Fox's *Journal* and "Book of Miracles" suggest that Fox performed healings that might be considered miraculous, but if sources of information from the 1650s are looked at, a different picture emerges.[10] Quakers knew that they needed miracles to support their claims, and were not good at performing them.

In the course of preparing the present study, just one report of a successful miracle was found in the contemporary Quaker correspondence, and none in their publications. The claim for a successful healing comes from Farnworth, aged twenty-two and very excitable, in July 1652.[11] Howgill tried and failed to heal a boy in London (see Chapter 2). Otherwise, there were some general claims for healings, but no specific instances.[12] An allegedly painless childbirth was put forward as a miracle, and on one occasion Farnworth was reduced to proposing a competition in length of fasting as a substitute for a more genuine miracle.[13] Quakers, lacking physical miracles, suggested that Quaker miracles were different from what people were expecting, being spiritual, and Fox wrote, "Among believers there are miracles in the spirit which are signs and wonders to the world."[14] Some of the healings that Fox claimed in later years may indeed be genuine, but he did not, in the 1650s, use such healings as evidence for the Quaker claims. He was probably too wise, for miracles might also be an indication of popery or of witchcraft, rather than of the true church. Accusations of witchcraft were frequently made against Quakers by anti-Quaker writers, from Francis Higginson onward.

Quakers used a number of terms besides "church" for themselves and their meetings. Most commonly, the first Quakers spoke of themselves as "children of light," "saints," "the people of God," "the righteous seed," or, when referring to the meeting of a congregation, the "assembly of saints" or "meeting of Friends." "Children of light" became less used after a few years, and for several years after the Restoration one of the commonest terms was "church of the first born," which derives from Hebrews 12:23.[15] Capitalization of such titles was random in the 1650s, and frequently absent, though a fashion for capital letters set in later in the century. "Friends" was their term of address, used for referring to one another, but it was not peculiar to them. Francis Higginson wrote to them, "Friends, for so I call you, since our blessed Saviour hath commanded us to love you."[16] A local meeting might be called the "church," as when Hubberthorne wrote to Margaret Fell, hoping that the "church in her house" might "know the true voice and power of God."[17] Toward the end of the 1650s, Fox stopped using terms such as "the children of light" or "the people of God" when writing for the general public, and used the word "Quaker" to prevent any misunderstanding: "The Quakers' mountain is the house of the Lord. . . . Quakers are not mountebanks but the Lords children. . . . The royal seed called Quakers . . . are in the power of God and in the authority of the Lamb."[18]

One after-effect of the Nayler affair was to advance the Quakers' understanding of themselves as a discrete organization. George Bishop wrote much on this theme. "James Nayler and those with him were really judged by George Fox and the people called Quakers, as gone forth from the truth."[19] The increasing self-consciousness of the Quaker body was now approaching the point where Quakers began to see themselves as a sect among others, while not diminishing their claims to be the one true church. Salthouse's dealings with Collier's Baptist churches have already been noted: "It's not so easy to be a member of our Church (which is the true Church)."[20] The following passage from Fox is admittedly special pleading, but it would not have been written a year or two earlier. It comes from a pamphlet protesting against Quakers being sued for nonpayment of tithe and charges for the repair of churches:

> Should all the Congregations, the Quakers, Baptists, Independants, Seekers, Brownists, compel the priests to maintain their meeting-places or give their speakers maintenance, and if the priest would not give it them, sue them at the law . . . or should the Quakers compel the Independants, or Baptists, or Seekers, or the priest, to maintain their meeting-house and their speaker . . . but they abhor such things, who have Christ and the Apostles for their examples.[21]

This beginning of a shift in the Quaker idea of the church eased the way to a thorough rethinking of their position in relation to other churches, which became necessary after the restoration of Charles II, and which is described in Chapter 17.

Quaker organization, as distinct from a loose linking of meetings, first developed from a need to handle problems, mainly care for their poor and matters of discipline. The Quaker movement attracted many argumentative people, and to begin with there was no agreed way of regulating "the light in the conscience," which was liable to indicate different things to different people.[22] As early as November 1652, Thomas Aldam had written that Jane Holmes "did kick against exhortation" from Farnworth, and "fell into a passion and lewdness, and said we was all in deceit."[23] While Friends were a purely northern body Margaret Fell would be asked to deal with difficult people, as when Richard Hubberthorne had problems in Westmoreland in 1653, and reported to Margaret Fell that Robert Collinson "did judge the word which I was moved of the Lord in his power to speak, not to be spoken from the power."[24] On other occasions, Thomas Lawson wrote to Margaret Fell to try to clear himself from allegations of sexual misconduct, and Nayler asked her to look after one Ellen Parr: "Let her stay a while with thee, and show her the way of love, which is much lost in the heights."[25] One letter to Fell concerned a difficult Friend, who had already been spoken to privately without effect: "I would have thee to send for him, for he is a burden to many tender consciences, for he is very much coloured [deceitful] and seems very tender but he is very deceitful, he speaks, sings often, in meeting."[26] There were other such instances.

As Quakers spread across the country, it became impossible to send all troublemakers to Margaret Fell. Some problems could be settled by a meeting of leading local Friends, when, as in a second case involving Collinson, the established leaders would exercise their authority. Occasionally, wrong conduct was dealt with by any suitable Friend who was to hand. Thomas Ayrey, once a traveling companion of John Audland, failed to live up to his profession and a woman called Ann Wilson rebuked him: "Thou art the prodigal who hast spent thy portion and now is feeding among the swine." "A mighty power did carry her through [i.e., "through her"]," wrote the correspondent, but Thomas Ayrey, "hardened himself against it," and said that this was not spoken in the power of the Lord. Audland himself wrote later to Fox about Ayrey, "He is hard and filthy, I spoke sharp terrible words to him and he was full of vermin and resisted the word of the Lord."[27] By 1655 and 1656 there are references in the Quaker correspondence to divisions in many places.[28] Much depended on the quality of local leadership. Howgill wrote to local church leaders, "Fathers, Elders and honourable Women":

> Watch over the flock of Jesus Christ in every place . . . where the Lord has set you, and govern them in all wisdom and righteousness. . . . And take care of them willingly, knowing this the Lord requires of you . . . to nourish the plants, and the young ones, and the babes: and that everyone may know their place, and watch and instruct in all wisdom, and correct and reprove in the name and power of our Lord Jesus, that no rebellious nor slothful may grow up nor be harboured among you.[29]

One major incident in Norwich, the disciplining of Christopher Atkinson in 1655, was fully recorded, and showed how Friends reacted when faced by a serious public scandal.[30] After Thomas Symonds had joined with the Quakers in 1654, Richard Hubberthorne, Christopher Atkinson, and other Friends came to Norwich, and by the end of the year there was a meeting of some twenty people. Margaret Fell already had doubts about Atkinson, but he was still accepted as a leading minister.[31] These Norwich Friends came into conflict with the civil authorities and several, including Hubberthorne and Atkinson, were imprisoned, but, as sometimes happened in seventeenth-century gaols, they were allowed a good deal of freedom. After they were released, one of Thomas Symond's servants confessed that sne and Atkinson had been having sexual relations while Atkinson was supposedly in gaol. Atkinson was immediately disowned at a meeting of Norwich Friends. He was induced to confess, and his signed confession was witnessed by two Swarthmoor Friends and by Thomas Symonds. Then, publicly in the meeting, Atkinson was denied by all the leading Friends. This was justified by reference to Joshua 7, which concerns the need to remove the "defiled thing" from the camp of the Lord in order to bring divine punishment to an end (see Chapter 4 for this use of the Bible).

There were some differences in the ways men and women reacted to discipline. Most of the people who are recorded as causing persistent disruption were women. They included, among others, Jane Holmes, Martha Simmons, probably Ann Blaykling, an unknown "little short maid" who gave problems to Burrough, and especially Mary Howgill (not a known relative of Francis Howgill).[32] Mary Howgill, who was active in East Anglia and the author of several pamphlets, caused problems to Friends in 1658 and again in 1660, when one elder wrote helplessly, "She much opposes us, yet for the world's sake she is borne, it were well she were stopped."[33] In all these cases, male elders had major problems in dealing with strong-minded women. It may be that these events are made much of in the records because men Friends were particularly sensitive to irregular behavior by women, for fear of bringing the movement into disrepute. However, the men never objected to women walking naked as a sign or going in sackcloth and ashes, and so forth, providing they were not exceeding their leading, and it looks rather as though there is a genuine gender difference here. These women, out of their usual sphere, would not fit into the male hierarchy, and so would not submit to the male discipline. The men, in their turn, would be unaccustomed to women behaving in such a way, and have difficulties in handling the situation.

Regular disciplinary matters could be dealt with by the area organizations that had been formed wherever Friends' meetings were well established. Several letters of 1653 and 1654 refer to the setting up of regular district meetings in the North "to declare what necessities or wants are seen in their several meetings, there to be considered on by friends there met, and as freedom and necessity is seen, so to minister," and with the appointment of people to care for the meeting who before long became known as "elders."[34] The structure was similar to the General Baptist organization of the time, but more formal.[35] Quakers of this time were much clearer about what was wrong with the old order than about what exactly should replace it. They knew that the church should be spirit-directed and therefore united, making much use of 1 Peter 2:5, "Ye also, as lively stones, are built up a spiritual house, an holy priesthood," but the many letters concerning doubts about the ordering of ministry, and how to handle difficulties, show that it took some years to work out the details. Such practical problems were dealt with more often in letters and general epistles rather than in pamphlets for the general public. Early Friends' meetings were liable to split apart; Friends in Bristol, for instance, were reluctant to divide into more convenient meetings for fear of causing divisions.[36]

A regular church order was needed to make arrangements for marriages. Friends' sensitivity to any hint of sexual irregularity has been described. The Nominated Parliament made provision for civil marriage, but some Friends were not happy about making a declaration before a magistrate. Fox gave the instructions. Those who wish to marry were to declare it "to the elders of the church where they are, that it may be examined." If this was agreed it could "be published in the meeting when the church of God is gathered." Friends could then go to the magistrate if they wished. However, if the rightness of the marriage was not clear to "the elders and overseers of the church," the couple were to wait.[37] Marriage was an affair of the church, not just of individuals, and when Thomas Holmes married Elizabeth Leavens "before divers Friends at Edward Morgans house" some Friends had doubts as to whether it had been done "in the light."[38] These regulations were repeated and refined in several disciplinary documents over the next twenty years.

The function of elder, a person appointed to look after the needs of a local church, was known among Friends at least since 1654, but the marriage regulations provide an early instance of the use of the actual word.[39] "Overseer" is a term that has been used in various ways among Quakers, generally meaning a person with responsibility for pastoral care. A different meaning of the word in the middle 1650s is made clear in a note to certain leading Friends who were asked to send copies of an epistle to all meetings "over which you are self overseers." This letter indicates a hierarchy, with one or more middle ranks of advisers, or "overseers," between the summit, that is the administration of Fox and Fell, and the local meeting at the base.[40] The system had grown up during 1653–54, as the Quaker message spread, but was now becoming formalized.

Thus a picture can be built up of a developing church order, of local meetings with leaders who included women, and whose members were otherwise equal and supported each other, gathering from time to time with other local meetings for a "general meeting," sometimes holding "monthly meetings" for business, and guided by experienced Friends, usually those who had first convinced them. This pattern was established in the North during 1653–54, and in the years following was extended to some other parts of the country where Friends' meetings were settled.[41] Women had only a limited part in these arrangements. Local women might have authority to "appoint meetings," but no women were regional overseers, and they were not normally signatories to official statements issued by Friends.[42] In some places they probably had their own local meetings for business, but there is no definite information except for London.[43]

The best evidence for the increasing institutionalizing of Quakerism in the second half of the 1650s comes from several highly prescriptive documents covering all aspects of church order and discipline, including people's private lives. The earliest, and probable model for the rest, dates from November 1656 and is known as the Epistle from the Elders of Balby. Farnworth wrote in October that Fox had ordered that a representative of each of the churches in Yorkshire, Lincolnshire, Nottinghamshire, and Derbyshire should attend a meeting at Balby (an old name for a district near Doncaster) "to consider of such things as might . . . be propounded unto them, and to enquire, into the cause and matter of disorder, if any be; (according to GF, his order or directions to me, etc.)."[44]

The Epistle, which was issued from this meeting was signed by Dewsbury, Farnworth, and several others.[45] It had eighteen clauses and a postscript, and began: "The elders and brethren send unto the brethren in the North these necessary things following; to which, if in the light you wait, to be kept in obedience, you shall do well."

The first two clauses dealt with arrangements for meetings, and the third with discipline. If miscreants did not reform after being spoken to by members of the local church, the case was to be sent in writing "to some whom the Lord has raised up in the power of the Spirit to be fathers." Clause four concerned ministry. If anything was spoken "out of the light" it should normally be dealt with in private. Clauses five and six were concerned with collections for the poor, and care for the families of traveling ministers and those in prison. Seven and eight concerned marriages, and the recording of births and deaths. Clauses nine to twelve dealt with relations within families, including servants and masters, and the care of widows and orphans. Thirteen and fourteen concerned relations with the state. Any Friends called before the civil authorities were to obey, and anyone called to serve in public office should undertake it willingly. Clause fifteen concerned the right conduct of Friends in business. Clauses sixteen to eighteen concerned personal relations between Friends, instructing them not to speak evil of each other nor be busybodies in other people's affairs. The Epistle ended with advice to elders, that they being made elders by the Holy Ghost should take up their duties willingly, as examples and not overlords, and then concluded with a quotation from 1 Peter 5:5. Finally, there was this postscript, frequently reprinted out of context, and today included in the introduction to *Quaker Faith and Practice,* the modern book of discipline of British Quakers: "Dearly beloved Friends, these things we do not lay upon you as a rule or form to walk by, but that all, with the measure of light which is pure and holy, may be guided: and so in the light walking and abiding, these may be fulfilled in the Spirit, not from the letter, for the letter kills but the Spirit gives life."[46] This was presumably added when the elders gathered at Balby paused to think. Were such detailed instructions as they had just approved really appropriate for a movement supposed to be guided by the light of Christ? The amount of prescription that was compatible with direct guidance was always a difficulty, and a subject of comment by anti-Quaker writers.[47] Just at the time the Balby Epistle was written, the problem was coming to a head in the dispute over James Nayler.

After the Nayler affair, attempts were made to extend the system of area gatherings, no doubt with the intention of making it harder for disaffection to take root.[48] Records were to be kept: "Them that are moved to record them that are borne or die, and them that are joined together by the Lord . . . so it all may be done by the power of the Lord God, and nothing out of it."[49] Some of these registers from the 1650s still survive. Friends were asked to organize by counties for purposes of managing finance and recording their sufferings.[50] Some big general meetings in the years 1658–60 were effectively national gatherings, and a statement from one such meeting was printed in 1658, a message to the pope "from the Elect and gathered Assembly of the chosen people in the Nation of England, called in derision and known amongst all false sects by the name of QUAKERS, and by a servant of the great God and of that people, this is written."[51] John Crook's house in Bedfordshire was used on several occasions for regional and national meetings.

Traveling ministers formed the link between the center and the periphery. George Fox in particular journeyed widely, and he was consulted on many assorted problems.[52] One curious occurrence was a Quaker baptism. A certain woman asked an ex-Baptist Friend called Humphrey Wollrich to baptize her, feeling that it was necessary for her salvation that this should be done, and that the ministration of the Baptist minister would not be adequate. He did as she asked, to the disapproval of some Friends, so he consulted George Fox. Fox was content to take no action since it was an isolated incident, but it was remembered, and remarked on during the internal disputes of the 1660s (see Chapter 15).[53] Fox was still expected to deal with any emergency, sometimes at very short notice. This was written to Fox in February 1659:

> This is to certify that there is a meeting here in Uxbridge on the morrow, it being the fourth day of the week, and this meeting was appointed by Edward Burrough for a monthly meeting, and now, he being absent and not in these parts, the meeting has been neglected because he is not hereabouts to supply it or to declare amongst the people: therefore it did lie upon me to write to thee: that thou mightest consider of it, and to send some friend in the ministry to the meeting if the Lord will.[54]

Until 1657 national finances remained largely the province of the Kendal Fund, under its treasurers George Taylor and Thomas Willan directed by Margaret Fell (see Chapter 2). Ministers were provided with things they needed, within reason. Robert Widder, for instance, wrote that William Adamson had had to borrow eight shillings so that "he would not be chargeable to weak Friends" and had spent four shillings on a Bible, "this he could desire might be paid [to him] again."[55] Like all treasurers, Taylor and Willan would query requests they felt to be excessive, as when Thomas Lawson wrote unhappily to Margaret Fell, asking that ten shillings, that he had borrowed from another Friend to buy a Hebrew lexicon, should be repaid, for, he said, "I saw George Taylor but could not mention it, for he is against me in his mind." Apparently a compromise was reached, for there is a note in the accounts of five shillings "to Thomas Lawson, which he said he wanted."[56] Adequate funds for the traveling ministry were available, and two ministers who were arrested for vagrancy wrote, "Is riding the straight road from Bristol to Plymouth, lying at the best inns, and paying for what they have for themselves and horses, a wandering?"[57]

Great care was taken to ensure probity in the financial administration. One example concerned a collection that Friends made for distressed Waldensians, who in 1655 were suffering severe persecution at the hands of the Duke of Savoy.[58] There were problems in handing over the money, and some of it went astray. Several letters from George Taylor dealt with the matter, and Fox warned in a general epistle that this kind of issue could easily cause divisions among Friends. George Taylor finally wrote to Margaret Fell, "Gervase Benson wrote to us that it was George Fox's and other Friends' minds, that what money soever was taken out of that money for Savoy, as we think, which was at London, should be made up again, and it go for what use it was intended."[59]

There were clearly difficulties in managing London finances from Swarthmoor. It is likely that there was some feeling of irritation between the original Quakers of the North and the new mass movement in the South. The Quaker center of gravity was, however, shifting. A regular business meeting for London men Friends was set up, probably in 1656, and was followed shortly afterward by a women's meeting, to handle practical matters of care for poor Friends.[60] The practice of submitting proposed marriages to the women's meetings, which caused much trouble when Fox attempted to introduce it to the whole country during the 1670s and 1680s, existed in London before 1663.[61]

During 1657 and 1658 the Quaker headquarters moved from Swarthmoor to London. The immediate cause of the move was disagreement between North and South over financial resources, particularly with respect to the support of traveling ministers. George Taylor's accounting was found to be less than satisfactory. Friends decided to cease central funding for ministers except for those traveling abroad, to raise money county by county, and to transfer responsibility for central funds to London.[62] Fox requested Friends to collect records of persecution and send them to Gerrard Roberts's house in London. This embryonic county organization became the basis for Quarterly Meetings, reorganized by Fox in 1667–68.[63] To help manage the business, a clerk was appointed in 1657. He was a young man named Ellis Hookes, who is counted as the first Recording Clerk, the equivalent of the chief executive of British Quakers, though the actual title came later.

The state papers of these years confirm the shifting center of Quakerism, recording several appeals to the Council of State for imprisoned Quakers, all signed by leading London Friends headed by Gerrard Roberts, whose name now appeared in connection with every kind of Quaker business.[64] He was a wine cooper, and his house, at the sign of the Fleur-de-Lys in Little St. Thomas Apostle, ten-minutes walk from the Bull and Mouth meeting house, replaced Swarthmoor as the nerve center of Quakerism.[65] One consequence of the move to London was a decrease in the number of surviving Quaker manuscripts, first noticeable about October or November

1657. This would have been a consequence of London becoming the administrative center, for many Quaker documents kept in London were destroyed in the Great Fire of 1666. What remains is probably heavily biased toward the interests of Swarthmoor.[66]

The shift of power to London affected Margaret Fell's position. She continued to receive full reports on the progress of the mission, both in this country and overseas, and to help find ministers.[67] She received regular reports about finance up to September 1658, when the financial reorganization was completed.[68] She was kept informed of the situation regarding James Nayler, and at least once was asked to intercede with Fox on his behalf.[69] But she was not actively dealing with problems, and few letters written by her with dates 1658 or 1659 have survived. She was still a force in the movement, but during these years less influential than she had been earlier, or than she became later, after the Restoration.

This administrative structure, which grew up during the 1650s, was primarily concerned with maintaining good relationships and spiritual health within the community of Friends, in accordance with the Quaker belief that divine grace was mediated through the worshipping groups. The meetings were from the start linked into a network and maintained by correspondence and by the intervisitation of Quaker leaders, for Friends were, collectively, thought of as the Body of Christ, which must be united. Presbyterians, Independents, and Baptists, by contrast, believed that divine grace was mediated through the word and ordinances, to some extent independently of a particular group. They concentrated on maintaining the quality of practice and belief within the individual church, but there was room for variation, as indicated by the Baptist confession quoted in Chapter 6. "Gathered" churches, Independent and Baptist, were therefore more loosely linked than the Quakers, usually associated with other similar churches in the neighborhood, but locally independent and governed by their own church covenants.

Later in the century the Quaker network was elaborated into a hierarchy of Particular, Monthly, Quarterly, and Yearly Meetings, and other Meetings with executive power. In the 1650s, it was still very dependent on those "raised up in the Spirit of the Lord to be fathers," but a recognizable forerunner of the modern Britain Yearly Meeting, with local and area meetings linked to a strong central organization, was in place by 1658. The difficulty of destroying this structure was an important factor in the survival of Quakerism during the Restoration period, for the Quaker meetings for business proved very strong, and were already beginning to take over from the charismatic leaders.

11

QUAKERS MEETING

Many of the people who became Quakers had had an early experience of emptiness in formal worship.[1] They wrote a good deal about what was wrong with other people's services, voicing opinions that were common among radical separatists.[2] Formal prayer was wrong, and so also was "singing David's psalms in metre," for there was no guarantee that David's thoughts would express the religious state of the singers. Preaching should come from immediate inspiration of the Spirit, not from study. Baptism was to be understood in a spiritual sense, and, except when specifically addressing Baptists, it was always "sprinkling of infants," not water baptism as such, that was mentioned, this being the practice of the Presbyterian parish ministers with whom the Quakers were most often in dispute. The

Lord's Supper, likewise, was to be understood in a spiritual sense. When challenged that this was clearly contrary to the Bible, Quakers said that the outward celebration of the Supper was not intended by the apostles to be a permanent arrangement, for it was not spiritual but a "carnal ordinance."[3]

When writing about worship Quakers rarely used the word "light," but preferred "spirit" and "spiritual," following John 4:23. Farnworth, for instance, wrote, "Those that are . . . baptised into one body which is spiritual, are made to eat all of one bread: which bread is Christ . . . their worship is spiritual, having fellowship with the Father and the Son . . . [and] the guiding and leadership of the Holy Ghost." Camm and Howgill wrote to Oliver Cromwell, "By the spirit of the living God are we gathered up together, up to God, to worship him in spirit and in truth, and are of one heart, and of one mind, and of one soul, and have all one teacher, and speak all one thing."[4]

Quaker worship had some roots in earlier practice. Free worship, or prophesying, had been common among the gathered churches for many years before Quakerism began, although only Quakers maintained the practice in the Restoration period.[5] The exiled Separatists in Holland had not permitted anyone preaching to use a copy of the Bible, in case this interfered with the free flow of the Spirit.[6] According to one contemporary author, some Separated churches used practices that later became characteristic of Quakers, calling churches "Steeplehouses," and having no use for learned ministers or set forms of prayer. Some of them would not sing psalms. Some allowed any "gifted men" to preach or prophesy, perhaps with several taking part, and then put questions to the preacher. Some even admitted women's ministry: "They commit the power of the keys in some places to women, and publicly to debate and determine ecclesiastical causes."[7]

A description of a meeting in Bristol of people "seeking the Lord" at the time of Camm's and Audland's visit suggests that it was similar to a Quaker meeting in form:

> There were many . . . which were seeking after the Lord; and there were a few of us who kept one day in the week in fasting and prayer; so that . . . we met early in the morning not tasting any thing; we sat down sometimes in silence; and as any found a concern in their spirits, and inclination in their hearts, they kneeled down and sought the Lord; so that sometimes, before the day ended, there might be twenty of us might pray, men and women, on some of these occasions chil-

dren spake a few words in prayer; and we were sometimes greatly
bowed and broken before the Lord, in humility and tenderness.[8]

There are a few other similar known precursors of Quaker meetings, and
it is likely that the people who met in Elizabeth Hooton's house church
would have had previous experience of free prophesy. Quakers, however,
according to Francis Higginson, might sit completely silent for as long as
two or three hours, and this report is consistent with later evidence.[9] There
are indications that this practice of lengthy silences was established during
the early days in the East Midlands, before George Fox and Elizabeth Hooton came to Yorkshire, but nothing to show how or why it arose. It was
clearly associated with Quaker dislike of unnecessary and uncalled-for
speech, which itself may have resulted from the coming together of some
like-minded people, Fox, Hooton, and perhaps others. It would also have
been related to the most striking phenomenon of early Quakerism, the
quaking, for the Lord did not show his presence in the Quaker meeting
through human speech.[10]

Quakers actually quaked, and this was the other main difference between
the early Quaker meetings and those of similar groups. It appears from the
fragment from Oliver Hooton's "History" that was quoted in Chapter 1
(page 6), that charismatic phenomena were an important part of the movement from the start. The coming of the "power of the Lord" and the
shaking of the worshippers was one of the most notable features of early
Quakerism, and there are a number of references to it in the early correspondence. Usually the quaking happened when Friends met together, as
when Farnworth wrote of a great meeting at Malton: "Twice the power of
the Lord was made manifest, almost all the room was shaken." Thomas
Holmes told Margaret Fell of another occasion: "Being met together waiting upon the Lord, the power of the Lord came upon divers, and made the
powers of the earth to shake. Many people came in when they was coming
from the steeplehouse and looked upon them that was trembling and crying, and they was astonished." The shaking could also happen when people
were alone; Margaret Fell recalled that the "power of the Lord" fell on her
when she was sitting with her husband, Thomas Aldam wrote to Fox that
he had been "taken with the power in a great trembling in my head and all
of one side," and another of the first Friends, Robert Widder, wrote to
Margaret Fell that "at night I was terribly shaken in my body."[11] The shaking, the "power of the Lord," was evidently something that had started to

happen unexpectedly. It was not common among the groups and sects of the time; there are few references to other shakers or quakers.[12]

The importance of such shaking in early Quaker worship has only recently been realized, perhaps as a result of Fox's habit, in the *Journal*, of hiding it under the apparently innocuous phrase "the power of the Lord."[13] The meaning of this can only be discovered from early letters where the "power of the Lord," unambiguously, meant quaking. The Quakers' use of the Bible to defend quaking was described in Chapter 5.

Quakers needed these Bible references because they were often challenged. "Where dost thou find that any of the prophets, apostles or saints did ever quake or tremble in their bodies and yell and howl and roar?" someone asked Hubberthorne.[14] Nayler had to deal with quaking in his controversy with Thomas Weld, who had evidently heard what Nayler considered to be exaggerated reports. Nayler wrote that "grovelling on the ground" and "foaming at the mouth" were not the habit of Quakers, but "quaking and trembling we own to be a condition the saints passed through."[15]

Quakers did not write accounts of their worship for the general public until the second half of the 1650s, for worship was something to be experienced rather than described. The earliest description of a Quaker meeting was given by Francis Higginson, and appears to be an eyewitness account. The spoken ministry might be like this:

> For the manner of their speakings, their speaker for the most part uses the position of standing, or sitting with his hat on; his countenance severe, his face downward, his eyes fixed mostly towards the earth, his hands and fingers expanded, continually striking in his breast; his beginning without a text, abrupt and sudden to his hearers, his voice is for the most part low, his sentenses incoherent . . . sometimes full of sudden pauses . . . his continuance in speaking is sometimes exceeding short, sometimes very tedious, according to the paucity or plenty of his revelations: his admiring auditors stand the while like men astonished . . . as though every word was oracular; and so they believe them to be the very words and dictation of Christ speaking in him.[16]

Spoken ministry, in the Quaker meetings, was expected to arise from the immediate impulse of the Spirit; Farnworth wrote to Margaret Fell that the waiting minister was a "white paper book without any line or sentence."

Until a sure inspiration came there must be silence, and if the call came it must be answered. John Stubbs wrote to Margaret Fell, "I never fell into more disobedience than the last meeting at thy house . . . for when the spring and well set open, then I did not speak, but in the dread [i.e., in his confusion and fear] I spoke, but the life was shut up, and I felt it to my condemnation."[17]

The problems came when these early Quaker meetings attracted unstable or excitable people. One such happening was recorded in print in 1653. John Gilpin of Kendal was "taken by a snare," as he put it, by which he meant that he had been drawn in by the Quakers, but escaped from their influence. He then wrote up his experiences as a warning to others. His particular mentor was Christopher Atkinson, who at this time was a prominent Quaker minister. Atkinson, Gilpin said, spoke from nine in the morning to three in the afternoon, and Gilpin noted that the word used for this was "speaking," not preaching or ministering.[18] Gilpin was told that he was to wait upon the inward light, so that he expected an actual light to appear. He wished to "fall a-quaking and a-trembling," and was worried when he did not. Suddenly he did start to quake, and cried out, "as is usual with them." He had dreams and visions and heard voices, and was thrown on the ground while John Audland was speaking, lying all night on the ground unable to move. Gilpin was then led to proclaim the Way, the Truth, and the Life in the street, saw devils, and thought he was carrying the cross and that Christ was in him. Finally he decided that the whole thing was a delusion.[19] Other odd things happened from over-enthusiasm, such as an incident that was recorded by Nayler in a letter to Margaret Fell in April 1654, when a young man had felt led to put his hand in a pot of boiling water.[20]

It may have been difficulties like these that caused Quakers to hold meetings for mission separately from meetings for people already convinced, or on the way to convincement (to use the Quaker terminology). Fox's advice of 1652 had recommended that when holding meetings in "unbroken places" only "three or four or six that are grown up and strong in the truth should go . . . and thresh the heathenish nature," while the remaining Friends should "wait in their own meeting place." This might prevent the spread of ideas and practices that were thought undesirable, but it was obviously hard to identify accurately those who were "grown up and strong in the truth," as could be seen from the trouble with Atkinson. Burrough had complained to Fox about other self-appointed ministers (see Chapter 2). A means had to be found of controlling the more bizarre manifestations of the light, and the disciplinary meetings described in Chapter 10 were the answer.

The only early printed Quaker work that deals with the conduct of worship is Fox's letter in *Several Letters to Saints,* which he dated October 1653:

> Your strength is to stand still, that you may receive refreshings, that you may know how to wait, and how to walk to God . . . by the Spirit of God within you . . . and Friends, everywhere meet together, treading and trampling all the deceit under your feet, and watch over one another in that which is eternal, and see everyone that your words be eternal life. . . . And you that are led out to exhort, or to reprove, do it with all diligence . . . and in your meeting wait upon the Lord, and take heed of a form of words, but mind the power . . . which will keep you in all unity walking in the Spirit.[21]

The best contemporary description by Quakers of early Quaker meetings comes in a letter dated September 13, 1654, from John Camm and John Audland, concerning their mission in Bristol. They had attended the Seekers' meeting described earlier in this chapter, and Camm wrote that these Seekers

> met together to seek the Lord, as they call it. There were many with the gloriousest words in prayer that I ever heard. . . . We bore them long till the power of the Lord took hold upon us both and I was forced to cry out amongst them. My life suffered and if I did not speak I should be an example among them, and in much tenderness I spoke unto them and silence was amongst them all . . . shame doth cover their faces for now they see themselves naked. There is a pure simplicity in them that would forgo all for the truth . . . we travail in pain unto Christ be formed in them and we are with them in fear and trembling lest their faith should stand in wisdom of words and not in the power of God.

On another day there were great open air meetings, and Audland wrote,

> The word of the Lord came to me, and when he had done, I stood up and all my bones smote together and I was like a drunken man . . . and I was made to cry like a woman in travail and to proclaim war

from the Lord with all inhabitants of the earth, and such a dreadful voice rang through me as I never felt before and the terror of the Lord took hold upon many hearts and the trumpet sounded through the city. The afternoon we met at the fort where soldiers are, the greatest meeting I ever saw . . . and all flesh was silent and not one dog moved his tongue[22]

From the first, Quakers had insisted that women's ministry was acceptable, and justified it from references in the Bible to women prophesying. "Let the truth declare itself, but let all flesh be silent till the Spirit be poured out on either son or daughter," wrote Farnworth, with a long list of women "ministers" from the Bible, but it has to be said that logical argument was not Farnworth's forte, and he did not properly address the difficult passage in 1 Corinthians 14:34–35. The ingenious Quaker argument, that Saint Paul, writing that women should keep silence, really meant that people weaker in faith should do so, was described in Chapter 4.[23]

In view of John Gilpin's account of a Quaker meeting, and taking into consideration all that the adversaries of Quakers had to say about the singing and crying out, it seems that the early Quaker meetings were often rather lively affairs. As the organization of Quakerism became more formal, so did Quaker worship calm down. A striking difference in the pamphlets of 1655–56 compared with those from earlier years is the decrease in references to quaking. With double the number of tracts there are only some twelve references, as against at least seventeen in the earlier period, and most of these references occurred in disputes, when adversaries continued to hark back to the early ecstatic meetings.[24] Quaking had not ceased, for Samuel Fisher as a new Quaker said he had himself witnessed trembling, and been made to feel the "weight of his hand in my own conscience," while Miles Halhead and Thomas Salthouse had "several peaceable meetings . . . and were made manifest with mighty power to that of God in the consciences of many to whom they were sent."[25] But these were exceptions. Fox wrote in 1656, "All Friends everywhere take heed of slothfulness and sleeping in your meetings, for in so doing you may be bad examples to others."[26] Sleep would hardly have been possible if "the quakings and tremblings, the roaring and crying, with other antic gestures" was still the regular practice.[27] Occasional descriptions of family and informal worship were published, and give a similar impression of quietness:

Reading we own, and speaking good words, exhorting one another, and prayer by the spirit of truth, and speaking the truth in love; that

we may grow up in him: in all things which is the head even Christ.
. . . Speaking about the things of God . . . that we do own, knowing
that by obeying the teaching of the spirit of truth, and also edifying
one another in love, building up into the most holy faith is well pleasing to the Lord, and comfortable one to another.[28]

Happenings in Bristol confirm the change. George Bishop had found the
beginnings of Quakerism in Bristol in 1654 as exciting as Camm had reported at the time: "Mighty were the outgoings of the Lord . . . in the
public meetings, and mightily was the Dragon enraged thereat, seeing his
Kingdom shortened." But already by the next year things were calmer: "We
meet together, and wait upon the Lord our Teacher, to receive his word and
testimony . . . and, in our measures, we know his voice from a stranger's,
and can try the spirits: and even those who oppose themselves have, and
may, come into our assemblies freely, and speak, whom we judge in the
Spirit of Christ Jesus."[29] The large numbers of new Friends affected the
arrangements for meetings, and Burrough and Howgill wrote to Margaret
Fell in March 1655 concerning their practice in London. Following Fox's
instructions of 1652, they held separate meetings for people at different
stages of spiritual development:

> Friends are so many that not one place can hold them on first days,
> where we can peaceably meet for the rude people. . . . We have thus
> ordered it . . . we get Friends on first days to meet together in several
> places out of the rude multitude, etc.; and we two go to the great
> meeting place which we have, which will hold a thousand people,
> which is always nearly filled, to thresh gainst the world; and we stay
> till twelve or one o'clock, and then pass away, the one to one place
> and the other to another place, where Friends are met in private, and
> stay till four or five o'clock.[30]

Camm and Audland hoped to arrange something similar in Bristol. Adversaries, however, were suspicious of Friends' motives in dividing their meetings: "They judging their novices, and all others besides themselves, unca-
pable to receive some of their principles as yet, and therefore they study
how to darken their sense by subtle glozing [deception with smooth words],
equivocating expressions and shuffles."[31]

Around this time, 1656, George Fox gave out much advice as to the
conduct of worship. This passage suggests a situation in which local elders
were being too discouraging of emotional ministry.

And therefore quench not the Spirit nor despise prophecy, where it moves neither hinder the babes nor sucklings from crying Hosanna . . . you that stop it yourselves do not quench it in others . . . the sighs and groans of the poor, judge not that . . . lest you judge prayer. . . . Every one exercise this gift and every one speak as the Spirit gives them utterance.

And Friends be careful how that you do set your feet among the tender plants that is springing up out of God's earth lest you do hurt them and tread upon them and bruise them or crush them in Gods vineyard.[32]

Dealing with inappropriate ministry has been a problem in Friends' meetings since their beginning. Fox wrote a paper on this subject, probably when he was in Launceston gaol in 1656, advising Friends to be tolerant if people were moved to "bubble forth a few words," and if they went beyond their measure, to bear it during the meeting. Only afterward, if necessary, should one or two people speak to them "in the love and wisdom that is pure and gentle from above."[33] The Balby Epistle (see Chapter 10) gave similar advice.

The conduct of meetings for worship was described in nineteen pamphlets published during 1657–59, for, since the Nayler affair, Quakers were writing more for the general public. Quaking was rarely mentioned. One anti-Quaker writer wrote that "nowadays it's rarely seen that they quake, yet it's well known to thousands, that the quakings and bodily trembling of single persons, and the greatest part of their assemblies, was very ordinary."[34] This was part and parcel of the tendency, already noticed, that the Quaker movement after the Nayler affair was calming down, developing into an organized body with its own distinctive practices, and concerned about its public image. The amount of disturbance at public meetings in London made it necessary to continue with big evangelistic "threshing" meetings, separately from the meetings of convinced Friends, but "threshing" meetings elsewhere seem to have ceased. People now knew what the Quakers stood for, those who were inclined to it were attending meetings, and other people who were interested knew where to go. Traveling ministers attended the silent meetings, and seem normally to have provided most of the spoken ministry. Friends at this time generally held their meetings in private houses, barns or out of doors, but before long, certainly from 1656 or 1657, they began to build meeting houses.[35]

Fox now began to write devotional pamphlets for the public, in similar terms to the manuscript epistles that he had been writing for some years to Friends.

Fig. 9 Broad Campden Friends Meeting House, Gloucestershire, is the oldest Quaker meeting-house in regular use at the present day. This building, originally a barn, was bought by local Quakers from two of their number in 1663 and may have been used for meetings before that time. (Photo by J. Rendel Ridges)

> Come out of the bustlings you that are bustling and in strife one against another, whose spirits are not quieted, but on fighting with words . . . wherein stands the several ways and distances of people one from another, and opinions and sects, wherein all come to throw dirt at one another, wherein is weariness, groans, burdens and travels . . . none . . . come to have their spirits quieted, but who come to the light that Christ Jesus hath enlightened them withall . . . such a one shall find mercy of God, when their minds are guided up to God, and their spirits and minds are quieted in silent waiting upon God, in one half hour, more peace and satisfaction than they have had from all other Teachers of the world all their life time.[36]

Friends tried to explain to the general public how people should be moved to speak in the meetings. One Friend wrote, "They only are to be said to speak as the oracles of God, who speak by inspiration or revelation of the Holy Ghost; or else in the Light speak these things which themselves have handled or tasted, both seasonably and aptly for the edification, or benefit of the hearers."[37] Burrough wrote that the length of the silence depended on the Lord. Sometimes it happened that everyone was "sitting silent before the Lord having received nothing of the Lord to speak one to another."[38] The long periods of silence often seemed strange to outsiders, and William Caton, in his introduction to Quakerism, *The Moderate Enquirer Resolved*, tried to put it simply:

> When they come together, they wait upon the Lord in his light, it may be sometimes two or three hours in silence, and sometimes it happens that in less space than one hour some of them may be moved to speak more, or less, to the edifying of the rest in the most holy faith, but their worship consists not in words, but in Spirit, and in truth. . . . And as for singing and praying, they do them both with the Spirit, and with understanding.

Caton continued that most people find it difficult to understand "what they are made partakers of in silent meetings, in which they witness the workings of the power of God . . . by waiting in the light of life, there are motions of the Spirit of the Lord known.[39]

It was thus in the silence rather than in the spoken ministry that Friends sought the presence of God. At least, this was the theory, but the long silences did sometimes cause problems, which were not mentioned in the printed publicity material. A letter from Ireland said that many had been convinced, but "Friends not staying with them, they coming to silent meetings, many is famished for want of words, and so they, not willing to wait in the silence, are turned back, and so cause the truth to be evil spoken of."[40]

The meetings were however not quite silent. Singing had always been acceptable, provided it was "in the spirit," and not pre-arranged. Hubberthorne wrote, "Singing with the Spirit, and with understanding, we own of such as are redeemed out of the World." John Whitehead said that praying with the spirit, and singing with the spirit, was practiced by Friends. Farnworth was particularly enthusiastic, but whether his method of learning to sing was practical is quite another matter: "If any want matter of praise and know not how to sing . . . let them wait upon the Lord to teach them."[41] This kind of vocal ministry continued for some time, for in 1661 George Whitehead agreed that "humming and hollow sighing" might be heard in meetings, and came from the Spirit of God, while John Whitehead wrote that the power of God sometimes came "with sighs and groans that are unutterable, sometimes with sensible words" (Romans 8:22 and 26), while "serious sighings, sensible groaning and reverent singing" was described as late as 1675, and approved of, providing it was not "immoderate."[42]

New Quakers needed training in how to behave in meetings, and this advice, given in the difficult circumstances of the early 1660s by Alexander Parker, is still in regular use by modern Friends:

> So Friends, when you come together to wait upon God, come orderly in the fear of the Lord; the first that enters into the place of your meetings, be not careless, nor wander up and down, either in body or mind; but innocently sit down in some place, and turn in thy mind to the light, and wait upon God singly, as if none were present but the Lord; and here art thou strong. Then the next that comes in, let them innocently and in sincerity of heart, sit down and turn in to the same light, and wait in the Spirit; and so all the rest coming in, in the fear of the Lord, sit down in pure stillness and silence of all flesh and wait in the light . . . a few that are thus gathered by the arm of the Lord into the unity of the Spirit, this is a sweet and precious meeting; where all meet with the Lord. . . . In such a meeting, where the power and presence of God is seen and felt, there will be an unwillingness to part asunder, being ready to say in yourselves, it is good to be here; and this is the end of all words and writings, to bring people to the eternal living Word. . . .
>
> And if any be moved to speak words, wait low in the pure fear, to know the mind of the Spirit, where, and to whom, they are to be spoken. . . . Thus, my Friends, as you keep close to the Lord, and to the guidance of his good spirit, you shall not do amiss; but in all your services and performances in the worship of God, you shall be a good savour unto the Lord; and the Lord will accept of your services, and honour your assemblies, with his presence and power.[43]

The Quaker meetings for church business were run on the same principles as the worship, with freedom for all to contribute, and a seeking for unity until all were agreed.[44] There are no surviving minutes of Quaker business meetings from the 1650s or early 1660s, for meetings started new books after Fox's reorganization of 1667–68, and any old ones that may have existed are lost. Records of church meetings of some General Baptist churches have survived from the mid-1650s, contemporary with early

Quakers, and procedure was probably similar. Comparing the Baptist records of the 1650s with the Quaker records of the late 1660s and the 1670s, it appears that much of the business of church meetings, for both Baptists and Quakers, was concerned with the misdemeanors of members of the church.[45]

A few months before his death in 1663, at a time of considerable dissension among Friends, which is described in Chapter 15, Edward Burrough wrote a lengthy paper about the development of the Quaker work in London, describing the origin and composition of the men's business meeting, and how it should conduct its business

> not in the way of the world . . . by hot contests, by seeking to out-speak and over-reach one another in discourse, as if it were controversy between party and party of men . . . not deciding affairs by the greater vote, or the number of men, as the world, who have not the wisdom and power of God; that none of this kind of order be permitted in your meeting. But in the wisdom, love and fellowship of God, in gravity, patience, meekness, in unity and concord, submitting one to another in lowliness of heart, and in the holy Spirit of truth and righteousness, all things to be carried on . . . as only one party, all for the truth of Christ, and for the carrying on the work of the Lord, and assisting one another in whatever ability God has given; and to determine of things by a general mutual concord.[46]

This was the theory, though in practice there were, and are, difficulties for inexperienced Friends. In the seventeenth century, the function of the clerk was simply to record decisions, not, as today, to assist the meeting in coming to agreement. As late as 1706 one exasperated Friend asked why should Friends not have a chairman at meetings, and put an end to the abuse of "twenty or thirty speaking at once, the loudest voice prevailing."[47] It was well into the eighteenth century before the developing function of the clerk in guiding the meeting, and greater experience in the method, eased this problem.[48]

12

"SUFFERINGS" BEFORE THE RESTORATION

It was characteristic of Quakers that they managed not only to exist under official and unofficial disapproval but that they also flourished. During the latter part of the 1650s, attacks on Quakers became more serious. The Quaker reaction to persecution was complex, involving their personal ethic, their church organization, their understanding of salvation and of the Kingdom of God, and their relations with the government. They learned their survival techniques well before the Restoration and the coming of serious anti-Dissent legislation.

Friends lived with persecution from the start. Whether they were the objects of what, according to the law of the land, was legitimate prosecution or whether they were the victims of spite or of hooligans, to Quakers it all appeared as persecution, the activity of the Antichrist, or the great Beast described in Revelation 13. The earliest Quaker message was a call to repent for the Day of the Lord was actually arriving, and their first reaction when they met with opposition was to deliver fierce warnings of coming doom. Francis Howgill, imprisoned in Kendal in 1654, wrote a pamphlet entitled *A Woe against the Magistrates, Priests, and People of Kendal . . . which may warn all the persecuting Cities and Towns in the North, and everywhere, to Repent and fear the Lord*. It begins: "The Word of the Lord came unto me, saying, write and declare against that bloody town of Kendal."[1] The same attitude was still evident to the end of the decade and later, in a number of similar denunciations of specified people and places.[2]

Anthony Pearson made an early appeal for imprisoned and persecuted Quakers to the Barebones Parliament in 1653.

> And as the wicked are thereby provoked, so are their cruel minds encouraged by the Lamb-like disposition of these people: for having the same spirit that was in Christ Jesus, . . . they do not resist the evil . . . bearing stripes, wounds, prisons, reproach and shame with joy, knowing that through many tribulations they must enter the Kingdom. . . . And being raised up in Christ, and made partakers of the life which is eternal . . . in the Spirit and power of the Lord they are carried into the public meetings of the world, to declare his word.[3]

Quaker meetings could arouse intense hostility, and were liable to be broken up by the authorities or attacked by hooligans. Evesham was the scene of particularly unpleasant persecution, and a local Friend wrote about the difficulties of holding a meeting for worship under such circumstances.

> Upon the next day we had a meeting with some friends, and likewise in the evening; and being many of us together in the fear of the Lord, until a constable came, and took away some of our friends, Humphrey Smith and Thomas Cartwright, he being the man of the house . . . on the sixth day we had a meeting in the street, where our Friend spake forth of the prison hole, at which time many threw dirt and stones.[4]

Presently the persecution eased off, and Humphrey Smith wrote that "Friends met peaceably twice or thrice a week, so that the ignorant began to be convinced . . . and much people received the truth in love." Then a new mayor was appointed, and persecution and arrests began again.[5]

Friends developed several strategies for minimizing the effects of such attacks. They gave maximum publicity to "sufferings," while trying to present a positive image of Quakerism, in order to enlist public sympathy. The organization that they were building provided discipline and mutual support. They lobbied for changes to the law, and used the law to have particular acts of persecution declared unlawful. They encouraged one another with thoughts of the dire fate awaiting persecutors. Finally, they developed a theology of suffering, the "daily cross" and the "cross to the will," a unity with the experience of Christ through which suffering came to be seen as a necessary part of salvation and entry into God's Kingdom.[6]

First, Quakers attempted to reduce the effects of persecution by seeking public sympathy. Those in trouble with the law frequently published their own accounts of what had happened, usually containing a description of the circumstances of their alleged crimes and of their arrest with copies of legal documents and correspondence with the authorities, together with accounts of what was said at their trials, and finally a record of what happened afterward. Descriptions of acts of persecution, to gain sympathy for people unjustly punished, to explain the legal position as Quakers saw it, and to increase publicity, were written from 1654 onward, serving the dual purpose of keeping the ill-treatment of Friends before the public eye and also providing evidence for the correctness of the Quaker faith. Many of the authors had fought for Parliament, and pointed this out in no uncertain terms.[7] Writers attempted to enlist the sympathy of their readers by their descriptions of violent acts and unjust processes of law. This was the beginning of Quaker "sufferings" literature, which by 1657 was a considerable proportion of all Quaker publications.[8]

The Saints Testimony Finishing through Sufferings was an early example of the genre.[9] It is a collection of several pieces concerned with events at Banbury, when Ann Audland was charged with blasphemy and acquitted and a number of other Quakers, including Farnworth, were prosecuted. In such cases it was evidently thought, as one would say today, that the sufferings had good publicity value. After William Caton and John Stubbs were arrested in Kent and flogged as vagrants, Stubbs wrote, "In the power of the Lord I was kept, in which power I was made willing to suffer for the testimony of the EVERLASTING TRUTH."[10]

Some pamphlets of this type, especially the earlier ones, were straightforward factual accounts, but as mistreatment of Quakers became more common the emphasis changed. The style became less confrontational. In 1655 there is the first record, in a letter to Margaret Fell, of an attempt to collect

A DECLARATION

Of the present

SUFFERINGS

Of above 140. Persons of the people of God *148*

(*Who are now in Prison,*) called *1900*

QUAKERS: *a part of many more*

With a briefe accompt of above 1900. more, being but
a part of many more that have suffered within these
six years last past, whose names and particular sufferings are not here set down.

21

Together with the number of 21. Persons who were imprisoned and persecuted until *Death.* All which was delivered
to *Tho. Bampfield*, then Speaker of the Parliament, on the
sixth day of the second Month, 1659.

By which all people may be made sensible of the great oppressions
of the Innocent, and lay them to heart, that the Judgments
of the Lord may be prevented, which otherwise will fall
heavy upon the oppressors, and all that are at ease in the
flesh, and unsensible of the day of *Jacobs* troubles.

As also an Accompt of some grounds and reasons, why for Conscience sake we bear our Testimony against divers customes
and practices at this day in use amongst men.

Also a cry of great Judgement at hand upon the oppressors
of the Lords heritage, as received from him on the 18.
day of the first Month called *March.*

With an Offer to the Parliament of our Bodies, person for
person to be imprisoned, for the Redemption of our Brethren, who are now in Bonds for the Testimony
of Jesus.

London, Printed for *Tho. Simmons*, at the *Bull* and *Mouth*, near *Aldersgate*, 1659.

information on all cases of sufferings of Friends. A detailed account of Quaker "sufferings," collected from all over the country, was published in 1656.[11] In 1657, Friends were again instructed by Fox to keep careful lists of "sufferings" and from now on to send them to Gerrard Roberts. Other collected accounts followed. These records, as well as forming the basis for pamphlets, enabled Friends to target relief where it was needed. This was their second method for minimizing the effects of persecution, for the system of local and regional meetings had as one function the provision of a network for the care and support of Friends in trouble. A check was kept on Friends whose goods were confiscated for nonpayment of tithe or who were imprisoned, their families were looked after, and the prisoners were visited.[12] Before long there were more deaths, from bad prison conditions, mistreatment by gaolers, or attacks by members of the public. A broadside of 1659 lists all fatal cases with the details picked out in red; there were twenty-six.[13]

The third strategy was use of the law. In the early years there were a number of appeals directly to the Protector, and to Parliament when one was sitting, but the later Protectorate Parliaments did not favor radical sectarians, and Cromwell, although he supported liberty of conscience, would not countenance public disorder. There was a further spate of such appeals in 1659, when the government was more favorable to radical sectaries, and many prisoners were released.

Appeals alone were not always effective. Friends looked for other ways of using the legal system, and frequently challenged the legality of the action taken against them. One interesting example was the case of Robert Widder. He had not paid his tithes and was proceeded against by being declared an outlaw, which made it possible for the aggrieved minister to apply for seizure of his goods. Advice was sought from Friends and sympathizers with legal knowledge, and with their help a means of setting aside the outlawry was found.[14] This case was a precursor of the practice of Quakers later in the century, when they regularly made use of specialized legal advice.[15] Some Friends had acquired considerable legal experience by the time the Meeting for Sufferings was set up in 1676. This survives to the present day as the national representative body of English, Welsh, and Scottish Friends, but its original remit was to deal with the legal problems of suffering Quakers.[16] There was doubt among some Friends of the time as to whether it was right to use the law in this way; such Friends believed that, if the Lord wished them to be saved from suffering, he would save them himself.[17]

The fourth tactic was to threaten disaster to persecutors. As was normal at that time, Quakers believed in the active intervention of God to punish evildoers, according to much of the biblical tradition, but in their early years they had to content themselves with general warnings, as their enemies were flourishing. It was not until the Protectorate came to an end in April 1659 that Quakers found a clear case of the intervention of the Lord on behalf of his people.[18] The Protectorate government had persecuted the Children of Light, and it had fallen, so the governments that succeeded were warned not to go down the same path.[19] It was common practice in the seventeenth century to collect "Examples" of the fate of wicked people, and about this time Friends began to do the same. The first collection was published in 1659 in a pamphlet by Edward Billing. He had found forty-two Examples, and he appended a further list provided by his friend Humphrey Smith "that he was an eye-witness of."[20] Also in 1659, Alexander Parker wrote to Margaret Fell about someone who had disturbed meetings. "Wicked Cumberland the common disturber is forced to fly for debt, and shut up his shop . . . and thus God blasts his enemies and confounds the devices of the wicked and brings them to naught."[21] The practice of collecting such examples gathered pace, and continued until 1701.

The final weapon used against persecution was the development of a theology of suffering. In the seventeenth century the first thought of people who suffered was to suppose that they were being punished by God for some sin. This had been Friends' reaction in Norwich at the time of the Atkinson scandal; they had welcomed the accursed thing into their company, therefore God was permitting their enemies to persecute them. James Parnell's death in April 1656 at the age of nineteen, from maltreatment in Colchester gaol, was a shock to Friends and concentrated their minds on the subject; their serious attempts to write theologically about suffering date from this event. They developed the idea that their suffering was a part of God's plan, so that Quaker faith and the Quaker experience of persecution were found to reinforce each other, instead of being opposed. Quakers knew themselves to be united with Christ. Since the wicked were flourishing, Quakers looked for biblical texts that described the persecution of the righteous as a sign of the coming of the Kingdom of God. These are plentiful, for Christ himself had suffered, and had said that the Kingdom of God would not come without a period of great tribulation for the church.[22] What more natural than that they, the Children of Light, God's elect, should also suffer; it was indeed a privilege, and evidence of their election. A letter from Burrough to Fox and Howgill, written during an imprisonment at Kingston-upon-Thames, provided an example: "I have no cause of trouble in it, but rather of joy and peace, knowing that it shall be for the furtherance of the gospel . . . my name is assuredly written in the Lamb's book of life."[23]

It has already been noted (Chapter 9) that Friends were commanded to become aware of the "cross to their will," and to "take up the daily cross." One typical Quaker wrote that he felt "the Lord . . . raise a swift witness in me, that the ways of man were evil continually, and that self must be denied, and a cross to it must be born; and so the life of Christ Jesus was manifest unto me."[24] This thinking was found in many non-Quaker as well as Quaker writers, for spiritualization of the cross dates from the Middle Ages. Understanding life as a "daily cross" no doubt assisted Quakers in dealing with the all too real sufferings that many of them were to undergo.

There was a contemporary accusation that Friends deliberately exposed themselves to abuse and suffering in order to appear more like ministers of Christ, actually going out of their way to seek a form of martyrdom, and this they denied.[25] Certainly, they were uncompromising. Records from the late seventeenth and early eighteenth century show that Friends who refused to pay tithe would not allow neighbors to pay their tithe for them, and would follow up members of their meeting who were thought to be weak in this witness.[26] Quakers were not expected to seek out suffering, and those who suffered did not receive special honor within the group, but it was known that inclusion in this group was likely to lead to a clash with the law, and that the consequences of this must be accepted and not avoided.

Knowledge of martyrdom was part of the inheritance of most English people in an age when children were brought up on John Foxe's *Acts and Monuments,* otherwise the *Book of Martyrs.*[27] The style of some Sufferings tracts may have been influenced by it, but Quakers in the earlier 1650s did not say that they accepted suffering because they were in the martyrs' tradition. The examples they referred to were invariably biblical. It was not until 1657 that Anthony Pearson wrote a pamphlet linking Quakers and earlier martyrs, and then he compared the Quakers only to John Wyclif, leader of the Lollards, a fifteenth-century English radical group, and to John Hus, the founder of Bohemian Protestantism, who were not supporters of the tithe system. Quakers at this date were ambivalent about the martyrs under Queen Mary, many of whom had been parish ministers and recipients of tithe.[28]

Quakers did sometimes put themselves into situations that would inevitably lead to trouble, most seriously in New England, where the authorities tried to stamp out Quakerism completely. When floggings, brandings, and imprisonments failed, a law was passed banishing Quakers under pain of death if they returned. Quakers repeatedly entered the colony in defiance of this law, and four people were hanged before the newly restored Charles II intervened. This appears to have been a deliberate seeking of martyrdom, although the Friends concerned were sure that they were called by God to this witness. Such was the claim by one of those executed, Mary Dyer, who said, "I came to keep blood-guiltiness from you, desiring you to repeal your unrighteous and unjust laws of banishment upon pain of death. . . . I came to do the will of my Father, and in obedience to his will, I stand even to the death."[29] The principle on which the New England martyrs acted was that Friends were not to seek confrontation with the authorities "in their own wills," but if they felt that the Lord was calling them to a certain course of action, then danger must not turn them aside.

An outstanding example from England was that of Humphrey Smith and his friends, who were accused of public preaching, unlawful traveling, and refusal to remove their hats. Humphrey Smith had been a parish minister before he joined the Quakers. Even before he encountered Quakers he had felt it wrong to take a minister's maintenance, but instead accepted a free gift from a local justice. He felt a call to travel in the ministry, and, worried about his wife and family, he "used all means possible to drive the power of God from me, and the thoughts of him, and his works out of my mind." "I have seen," he wrote, "Children, Wife, Farms and Oxen, to hinder from the Kingdom of God, but that which hindered most, was the love of outward goods." He went through a period of much doubt and trouble, as so often described by Quakers, for at this time he did not know about the cross "which crucifies to the world and all its vain customs" and so his preaching did not bring people to God. Then at last "I was brought to be silent from my public preaching and waited on the Lord, with a few contemptible ones in the eyes of the world." In due course he joined the traveling Quaker ministry, where he was "exposed to want, hardships, revilings, imprisonments, whippings, stonings and all manner of cruel torture."[30] He was the most productive Quaker writer of the year 1658, pouring out his heart from a horrible dungeon in Winchester, where he and several friends were imprisoned in revolting conditions for over a year. He continued to write prolifically until his death in 1663, during a second period of imprisonment.

In words reminiscent of Saint Paul in 2 Corinthians 11:24–27, Humphrey Smith wrote,

I have been brought before rulers, haled and beat out of the syna-
gogues, numbered among the transgressors, tried at an assizes as an
offender, yet there denied the liberty of a murderer, being six times
imprisoned, twice stripped naked and whipped with rods, and since
put into Bridewell [named from a London prison]; once put into, and
kept long in a dungeon for praying, often abused in prison; sometimes
near death; in trials often, in perils often, in loss of goods, in daily
reproaches . . . and yet I have been preserved unto this day by the
power of him who is the Light, and the only Son of God.[31]

In another pamphlet he wrote,

And this I say plainly unto you, that your long tyranny will never
weary out the patience we have received, neither can you inflict more
punishment than the Lord has enabled us to bear . . . for self we have
denied, and we have given up our bodies and souls a living sacrifice
unto God, to do or suffer his will. And him that kills the body we fear
not, much less those that can but whip or imprison for a few months,
for our life you cannot reach, neither can you disturb their rest whom
the Lord has crowned with honour. . . . Yea, and there is none can
make them afraid with all their threats, unrighteous laws, bonds . . .
long unjust imprisonments, or death itself.[32]

Note the phrase "neither can you disturb their rest whom the Lord has
crowned." In their dungeon, Smith and his friends had already found the
Kingdom of God.

Strong individuals, and there were many of them, accepted their suffering as God's will, and as evidence of their salvation, while at the same time
the organized Quaker movement fought persecution vigorously and to
some extent successfully. During the more serious troubles of the Restoration years, four hundred Quakers died in prison and several thousand were
crippled in health or ruined in fortune, but the movement survived. The
1650s had provided the Quakers with a valuable training exercise in living
with persecution.

PART IV

TURMOIL AND TRANSITION
1659 — 1666

13

THE DEFEAT
OF THE RADICALS

During 1657 and 1658 there had been a subtle transformation in Quaker-ism, as the shock of the Nayler affair led to a dislike of too much enthusi-asm. Quakers were settling down, and becoming as respectable as their consciences would permit them to be under the current laws. Practically everything the Quakers were thinking or doing was affected, and they were already showing signs of moving toward the eighteenth-century Society of Friends, a self-contained organization with a distinctive view of its place in the scheme of things.

The next few years were a period of upheaval. There were major political changes that had a drastic effect on Quakers, and the movement also suf-fered from acute internal dissension. The first developments came after the

death of Cromwell, when it rapidly became clear that the old Quaker enthusiasm was still alive beneath the surface.[1]

Oliver Cromwell died in August 1658. His successor was his eldest son,
Richard, who could not command the loyalty of the army, and a power
vacuum developed. In April 1659 the Protectorate fell. Many Quakers reacted to the events of the following months as they had in 1653, their hopes
for the Kingdom of God becoming so closely involved with their political
views as to be indistinguishable. They looked for the Kingdom of God on
earth, in which God would rule through human beings by his Spirit within
them.

Quakers in 1659 were more closely involved with national events than
they had been in 1653. In 1653 Quakers had still been a relatively small
group, mostly in the North, but in 1659 their headquarters were in London, near to the action. In 1653, the leading London Quaker was probably
Amor Stoddart, but by 1659 he had been reinforced by such men as Burrough and Hubberthorne, not to mention the underpinning provided by
Gerrard Roberts, Ellis Hookes, and other London Friends. In 1653, the
most capable pamphleteer was James Nayler, a man with long experience of
politics and politicians and the gap between expectation and realization,
and although for a few months in 1653 he had high hopes of the Nominated Parliament, politics did not rule his life. By contrast, in 1659 the
leading publicist was Edward Burrough, still only twenty-five, idealistic and
able, who flung himself enthusiastically into the tumultuous events of that
year.

The Rump Parliament, which had been expelled by Cromwell in April
1653 but never formally dissolved, was recalled in early May 1659 (see
Chapter 1). From then on, Quaker pamphlets appeared at a rate of several
a week, many by Burrough.[2] The earlier ones were full of high hopes and
wide-reaching requests, and indeed demands.[3] Several were issued on behalf
of Quakers as a whole, on the authority of the London men's meeting.[4]
Fox's *To the Parliament of the Commonwealth of England, Fifty-nine Particulars laid down for Regulating Things* was probably written in the early summer and concerned civil government, and was the clearest statement of
Fox's social and religious policy, but showed little interest in the practical
details of government except where the interests of Friends were affected. It
was yet another in the series of pamphlets that demonstrated Fox's ability to
advise on everything.[5]

Fierce apocalyptic warnings, and a feeling of excitement because God
was at last about to act, were characteristic of the majority of Quaker

pamphlets of 1659. Dorothy White, who published more tracts than any seventeenth-century Quaker woman except Margaret Fell, began her career as an author this year with four tracts. *Friends, you that are of the Parliament, hear the Word of the Lord,* is an example:

> Friends, you that are of the Parliament, hear the word of the Lord as it came unto me concerning you. . . . The Lord will overturn you by his powerful arm, for the decree of God and his purpose is . . . to throw down and break up Parliaments. . . . God himself will rule and bear rule in the hearts of men, and such as know God to rule . . . shall rule for God . . . for God will throw down and overturn, root up and consume both root and branch of all your Parliaments, until he hath brought in the Royal heir, the Prince of Peace, the Everlasting King of Righteousness and he will reign in the destruction of his enemies.[6]

During that summer of 1659 the radical sectaries felt that the Lord was at last vindicating them, and few people advised caution. Gerrard Roberts collected lists of potential Quaker Justices of the Peace, and of existing justices considered unsuitable because they were persecutors of Quakers, and sent them to the government.[7] The government was unstable, depending on army support, and the army itself was not united. Parker and Howgill asked Fox's advice on service in the militias that were raised that summer, or on accepting other office, and Fox replied that Friends should not become involved.[8] Despite this advice a number of Friends did serve, for Fox could not command all Quakers all over the country, who managed their own local affairs.[9] As fears of civil disruption increased during the summer, Fox wrote a general letter to Friends, advising them to keep clear of such disputes: "It is the word of the Lord God to you all . . . this power, life, light, seed and wisdom by which you may take away the occasion of the wars, and so know a kingdom which has no end, and fight for that with the spiritual weapons which takes away the occasion of the carnal."[10] Fox's attitude to armed conflict was not fully worked out at this time. He had warned Cromwell that his failures in war were due to his disobedience to God, and he had praised Quaker soldiers. He had not made any pronouncement against the use of force by the lawful government about its lawful occasions, nor against Quakers being soldiers, although he had consistently warned Friends not to take part in plots against the government, but to fight with spiritual weapons only. As the government began to collapse, it became increasingly difficult for Quakers to know their right course of action.[11]

Margaret Fell junior was in London that summer, and wrote to her mother on August 27 that George Fox was ill and "much out of temper." It seems that he had some kind of nervous breakdown. He stayed with Thomas and Ann Curtis in Reading for several months, and young Margaret Fell noted his return in a letter of December 3.[12] Fox's illness no doubt exacerbated the lack of communication among Friends, for he provided the main link between the center and the regions. His breakdown was probably due to the difficulties of the situation and to a feeling that the Quaker movement, like the country as a whole, was running out of control. He would have been dismayed by the behavior of Burrough and Hubberthorne, who were both too involved with active politics for Fox's taste.[13]

During Fox's illness Quaker business proceeded as normal. When he had been in prison in Launceston in 1656 the other Quaker leaders had been greatly disturbed by their inability to consult him, especially about Nayler, and Quakers who had tried to visit him had been intercepted by the civil authorities (see Chapter 3). In 1659 there were signs of greater maturity, and Edward Burrough and the London men's meeting could handle anything that had to be done.

Burrough was not only a pamphleteer, he was also a highly effective popular speaker. Many years later a London Quaker wrote down his memories of Burrough in action.

> I have beheld him filled with power by the Spirit of the Lord . . . at the Bull and Mouth, where the room, which was very large, hath been filled with people, many of whom have been in uproar, contending with one another, some exclaiming against the Quakers . . . others endeavouring to vindicate them. . . . In the midst of all which noise and contention, this servant of the Lord hath stood upon a bench, with his Bible in his hand, for he generally carried one about him, speaking to the people with great authority. . . . And so suitable to the present debate amongst them, that the whole multitude was overcome thereby, and became exceedingly calm and attentive, and departed peacably, and with seeming satisfaction.[14]

During the summer and early autumn there was growing hostility in the country toward radical sectaries, Quakers especially, as they were perceived to be taking over positions of power in the militia and in the country.

Quaker pamphlets of 1659 described the increasing severity of attacks on meetings, which were liable to be disturbed by people who thought it amusing to enter the room and try to make the worshippers react, sometimes by physical attack, and even on one occasion by fire-bombing with devices constructed by a local apothecary.[15]

A Royalist rising in August, under Sir George Booth, was put down by John Lambert, the most radical of Cromwell's surviving generals. The political situation became very confused. An unpublished broadside of Burrough's was probably written about this time, and may have been turned down by the London men's meeting as too strong. George Fox, if he had been present to discuss it, would not have approved it, for it included an indication that Quakers would not exclude the use of armed force in some circumstances. In this paper Burrough wrote that, if the government had reinstated Friends in their offices,

> we should have cause to own that you intend to establish righteousness . . . oh then we should rejoice, and our lives would not be dear to lay down; but till then how can we come between you and your enemies to defend you and establish you in power to oppress us . . . we must suffer till the wickedness of the wicked be finished, and the Lord have avenged our cause. . . . And now the Lord hath suffered the wicked to arise against you . . . now blood is like to run down, and the innocent like to be devoured, and this is because of your transgression.[16]

On October 6 came Burrough's most outspoken pamphlet, *To the Parliament of the Commonwealth of England who are in place of Authority to do Justice*. It was carefully thought out and expressed, and highly radical in viewpoint. No short quotation can do it justice. It began:

> Forasmuch as this nation . . . has long been held in bondage and captivity, and the free-born people have born the heavy yokes of tyranny and oppression, both in respect the foundation of government, and also in respect the practice thereof . . . the choosing of governors has been out of course. . . . And while thus it hath been in our nation that our Kings have attained to the throne of government hereditarily . . . and our parliaments and rulers have attained to the place of judgement over us, by such a way of traditional choice, as has been the custom in our forefathers days (that knew no better being in the

days of apostacy and great ignorance themselves) and thus has it continued for many ages, whereby the inhabitants have always been suffering under . . . great oppressions and vexations, being subjected under such a government, falling as aforesaid, from parents to children, after the manner of the heathen nations, and being subjected to such laws, made and executed by men, not truly called and ordained of God thereunto . . . the great and rich men have been set to rule over the poor, and while men for earthly honour, and for riches sake in birth and breeding, have claimed to be princes over us successively, and to be chosen our rulers according to custom, without respect to their virtue and goodness, and without true calling from the Lord . . . thus the government of our nation has been out of course, and not as the Lord required it, even to this day, while great darkness has remained upon the hearts of the people . . . that they have not known their own bondage, nor yet how to be redeemed into perfect liberty, while they have submitted themselves (through ignorance) to be ruled by such men as had no right from God to that place of rule and government.

Burrough continued with an apocalyptic warning. The Lord was beginning to appear, and soon would deliver his people:

For we look for a new earth, as well as a new heaven . . . all our bonds of oppression shall be broken. . . . And the Lord will appear to be the king and judge and law-giver over all, and will commit the giving forth and execution of good laws unto the power of faithful and just men ordained by God . . . who will judge for him . . . and the hand of the Lord will accomplish it, if not by you, then contrary to you.[17]

This may have been written with knowledge of the petition delivered to Parliament on behalf of Lambert's army on October 5. After the defeat of Booth's rebellion, this most radical section of the army felt that it was in a position to state its terms. The Rump was disinclined to compromise, and on October 13 Lambert's troops surrounded the Parliament building and prevented members entering. The country was now once again under army government, and there was an uncertain pause when no one knew what would happen next.

General Monck, the commander of the army in Scotland, refused to endorse the expulsion of the Rump, perhaps from a combination of personal dislike for Lambert, objections to the officers sent to serve under him, fear for the existing church settlement, and alarm at the prospect of a takeover by Quakers and other extreme radicals, for some of Lambert's soldiers were said to have been attending Quaker meetings.[18] Monck was a professional soldier who had served Charles I, before transferring his allegiance to the Commonwealth when it became the de facto government. He now purged his army of dissentient elements, moved it to the Scottish border, and waited. Lambert moved north to block Monck's route south. The pause continued.

By November Burrough was beginning to despair of secular government, and his next pamphlet was entitled *A Message to the Present Ruler of England whether Committee of Safety, (so called) Councell of Officers, or others whatsoever.* He wrote that it was "delivered unto them by an ambassador from the only right heir of the government." God was the ruler over all governments. As for the present government, it was just another horn of the fourth beast of Revelation 13. It would go the way of other governments if it neglected God. He ended:

> My master has a people, even a suffering people, that have born the burden of the cruelty . . . both of rulers and teachers. . . . He hath formed them for himself, and they cannot join any of the horns of the great beast, neither can a place of honour pervert them from the perfect way, but my Lord has kept them . . . till his pleasure is to make further use of them . . . therefore touch them not . . . This nation can never be happy. . . . while this people are held in bondage, and their sufferings are deeply considered of the Lord, and the season thereof is expiring . . . then woe unto the Kingdom of AntiChrist.[19]

This was a considerable retreat from his hope of a new earth as well as a new heaven that he had expressed only the previous month.[20]

Unable to govern effectively, the Council of Officers restored the Rump in December, but the political situation was still very uncertain. The London men's meeting issued an extremely cautious statement, written by Burrough, on December 20. Fox was not a signatory, although he had returned to London by this time:

> We are not thy enemies. . . . We have not the spirit of mischief and rebellion in our hearts toward thee, neither are we of one party or another . . . nor do we war against any by carnal weapons. . . . We do

declare that we are not for men or names . . . we rather yet choose to suffer by all . . . than to lose our integrity and innocence by joining to any in their unjust ways. . . . We have chosen the Son of God to be our King and . . . his Kingdom is not of this world neither is his warfare with carnal weapons, neither is his victory by the murdering and killing of men's persons, neither has he chosen us for that end, neither can we yet believe that he will make use of us in that way, though it be his only right to rule in nations. . . . For the present we are given up to bear and suffer all things . . . and our present glory and renown therein stands till the appointed time of our deliverance, without the arm of flesh or any multitude of a host of men.[21]

This did not entirely exclude armed action by Friends. Friends were clear that they should not take part in armed insurrection against a legitimate government, but at a time of near anarchy it was difficult to determine the right course of action.[22] There are indications that some Quakers were under arms in Wales, and that others were helping Lambert's army.[23]

By the end of the year there was utter confusion. Lambert was losing men from desertion, and his army fell apart. Monck crossed the border on January 2 and began to march his army south. Isaac Penington was one who kept his faith in a radical political solution. He still believed that it was not impossible for the present government to continue God's work that had begun with the civil war, writing on January 19: "The foundation of reformation which God has laid is glorious: and in these troublesome times is he raising up the building of his new Jerusalem."[24]

Political realities were different. Parliament invited Monck to bring his army to secure London, and he arrived on February 3. The day of the radical sectaries, though they did not as yet realize it, was over. Six months later Alexander Parker wrote to Fox, "Better had it been if all had been kept still and quiet in those times, for because of the forwardness and want of wisdom in some, is one great cause of our present sufferings."[25] It is always easy to be wise after the event.

Radical hopes did not collapse immediately upon the arrival of Monck's army. Monck still professed support for a republic, and on February 12 Penington wrote, "This is the thing which the Lord has determined to do . . . namely, to pull down the mighty from their seats. . . . This work has the Lord begun already; for his great and notable day hath appeared."[26] The political situation remained confused. Monck agreed to the return of the full Long Parliament, which dissolved itself in March, and a new Parliament was called. Many people thought that insurrection by Quakers and other extremists was still a serious danger, and it began to appear that a restored monarchy might provide the best means of achieving a calm and united country. Presbyterians and Independents were concerned to secure the religious gains of the past years, and there was much consultation between advisers in Britain and Charles II's court in Holland. Charles issued the "Declaration of Breda" on April 4, promising various concessions including freedom of worship and toleration provided that Parliament consented. The new Parliament, the "Convention" Parliament, assembled on April 25 and accepted the Declaration of Breda. This cleared the way for the Restoration, and Charles was proclaimed King on May 8 and arrived in London on May 29, to public rejoicing but to the gloom of the radicals.

The disappearance of their republic took the radicals, including Quakers, completely by surprise. There are no Quaker pamphlets dealing with British politics bearing dates between February and May 1660, although the following from Penington may have been written about this time. He wondered

> whether the kingdoms of the earth shall not one day become the kingdom of the Lord and his Christ. . . . Consider therefore whether these be the beginnings of the great and terrible day of the Lord God Almighty, or only some such ordinary shakings as use to happen according to the course of kings and states? . . . There may be some hopes and probabilities of a settlement again, but they will but provoke God to shake more effectively.[27]

Quakers were having a hard time. Meetings all over the country were attacked and broken up, as many letters testify. This is an example:

> Since G[eneral] M[onck] coming to London with his army, we have been very much abused in our meetings, as in the palace yard [Westminster], we were pulled out by the hair of the head, kicked, and knocked down both men and women in such a manner not here to be expressed, women with child crying out they were undone; many were the knocks and blows and kicks my self and wife received, and this was done by G. M.'s foot[soldiers], who came into the meeting with sword and pistol; being as they said, bound in an oath to leave never a sectarian in England.[28]

KING CHARLES II
triumphal Entry into the
City of London at his
Restoration.

Fig. 11 The triumphal entry of King Charles II into London in May 1660. The restoration of the monarchy took the radicals, including Quakers, completely by surprise, but for a time Quaker life continued much as before. (Courtesy, Guildhall Library, Corporation of London)

Monck declared that these soldiers had acted without authority, and on March 9 he issued an order that Quaker meetings should be left alone, but this did not help the situation outside London.[29] Trouble was exacerbated by the continued publication of abusive anti-Quaker books, notably Richard Blome's *Fanatick History*, which dragged up every accusation that had ever been raised against Quakers, as well as attacking their theology.[30]

Despite such problems, Quaker life continued much as before. Quakers published nearly as many pamphlets during 1660 as in 1659.[31] Some theological arguments continued, and Samuel Fisher published his enormous *Rusticus ad Academicos*. George Fox and two colleagues wrote *A Battledore for Teachers and Professors to learn Singular and Plural*, a huge large-format book demonstrating in thirty-one languages the correct use of the second-person singular and plural, in support of the Quaker usage of "thou" to a single person.[32]

Quakers attributed the political turbulence of the previous year to God losing patience with a succession of unsatisfactory governments, and the return of the King looked like another incident in the same succession. Consequently they felt quite confident and sure of themselves, despite increased persecution, and once the Restoration had been agreed, a number of Friends addressed pamphlets to the King and Parliament, advising them on carrying out their responsibilities, and warning them of the Lord's disfavor if they continued to oppress the Lord's people. A statement from Burrough in May was probably the first official one. He wrote that Quakers had nothing against the proclamation of the King, because the fall of the previous government had resulted from the purposes of God. The Quakers would be his obedient servants, being "sober, innocent and harmless." They hoped that the new government would offer liberty of conscience, but Quakers would bear persecution if necessary, and would in any case not use "carnal weapons" against any government.[33]

Besides the official statement, several Quakers proffered personal advice to the King. George Fox the Younger was one of them, writing from the perspective of an old Parliamentary soldier, and seeing no need to moderate his language when addressing the King: "Concerning thy father and those that took his part, there was an eminent hand of God in breaking them down." Unfortunately, the next government had done no better: "Alas, covetousness and self-seeking lusts sprang up in most of them. . . . And thus the just hand of the Lord came upon an hypocritical, deceitful, professing people." Charles should therefore consider the hand of God in his coming to power again: "Let no man deceive thee by persuading thee that these things are brought to pass because the kingdom was thy own proper right. . . . For I plainly declare to thee, that this kingdom and all the kingdoms of the earth are properly the Lord's, and that he may and does give them unto whomsoever he pleases." The King must not persecute the Lord's people: "For the Lord God has brought forth a people in these nations . . . and if thou oppressest this people, the Lord will surely take away thy power and avenge their cause."[34]

Other Quakers wrote publicity pamphlets, explaining the nature of Quakerism in simple language, presumably intended for the benefit of Royalists who had returned from exile knowing nothing of Quakers: "The Lord hath sent forth many of his servants (called Quakers) and by believing obeying and following the light within, they have received power from God, and by the power of God are they led out of their ungodly ways . . . and are brought into the life and power of truth, and can witness their sins forgiven by the Lord."[35]

The change in government had come so quickly after the excitements of 1659 that the Quaker leaders were anxious, with reason, about their followers' reactions. Burrough distributed a general epistle to Friends in May, "To be read in all the assemblies of those that meet together to worship the Father in the Spirit and Truth, in the silence of all flesh." He warned Friends that they were in God's hands and should wait upon the Lord.

> Neither are we of one party, or against another, to oppose any by rebellions or plottings against them, in enmity, and striving with them by carnal weapons; nor to destroy any men's lives, though our enemies, and so we war not for any, nor against any, for the matters of the world's kingdoms. But our kingdom is inward, and our weapons are spiritual.[36]

Meanwhile, George Fox was traveling in the north, moving from east to west as he held general meetings at Balby, Warmsworth, Skipton, and Arnside. Given the probable involvement of Quakers in the Northern Plot two years later, it is likely that he was aware of disaffection, and was trying to ensure calm. The authorities caught up with him at Swarthmoor, where he was arrested as a potential troublemaker and imprisoned in Lancaster Castle. Margaret Fell came to London to try and obtain his release. She saw the King and published a declaration, signed by a number of leading Quakers including Fox and Hubberthorne but not Burrough, that although Quakers would take no oaths, they declared their allegiance to the government, that their weapons were "not carnal but spiritual," and they asked for liberty of conscience.[37] George Bishop was annoyed that official statements were being published without general consultation among Friends, and wrote from Bristol to London, "It will be well if no papers come forth, but such as stand in the authority of God . . . and if anything be done, wrote, or printed in the name of Friends, let them first see it, as is right, and be satisfied, for there is a great body of Friends."[38]

Richard Hubberthorne had an audience with the King, who was very approachable, and he received the King's promise that Quakers should not suffer for their opinions. Fox was released in September and arrived in London the following month, and Ellis Hookes wrote to Fell that the King would need to be assured that the Quakers would not take up arms against him. Hookes also consulted with Fox concerning an updated collection of material relating to Quaker sufferings, to be laid before the government, and this was considered by a committee of the Council in November.[39]

That autumn the new religious settlement was being negotiated. The King was thought to favor toleration, but other powerful interests did not. Nevertheless, the situation did not look hopeless for Friends. Early in December a leading London Friend, Thomas Moore, had a formal audience with the King and the Council to deliver a statement about Quaker sufferings, and the King permitted him to keep his hat on. But there were ominous incidents, such as an occasion in October at the Oxford Quarter Sessions, when a judge revived the ancient writ of praemunire in order to deal with Quakers who refused to take the oath of allegiance. "Praemunire" was a fourteenth-century penalty, by which guilty people were outlawed, their estates forfeited to the Crown, and they themselves imprisoned during the King's pleasure. It proved a much more effective way of dealing with recalcitrant Quakers than any of the new penal laws that were eventually enacted against them.

Then, in January 1661, a band of Fifth Monarchists led by Thomas Venner rose in revolt in London, leaving forty dead before he was captured and hanged. All hope of a settlement favorable to Quakers and Baptists disappeared. For several years their very survival was in question, and radical activity was forced underground.[40]

14

SURVIVAL

After Venner's revolt, orders were immediately issued banning all Quaker, Baptist, and Fifth Monarchist meetings, and a sweep was made all over the country picking up anyone suspected of such opinions, so that four thousand Quakers were crowded into prisons. Quaker businesses were investigated, and a Bristol ironmonger named Roe came under deep suspicion because of the large quantity of powder and shot that he was holding, for his business, as he said. Quaker meetings and their voluminous correspondence were considered suspicious.[1] Most of the imprisoned Quakers were released within a few weeks, but official suspicion of Quaker disaffection was not abated, and the order banning meetings continued in force.

Fox acted quickly, and in a few days prepared and had printed the *Decla-*

ration from the Harmless and Innocent People of God called Quakers, a strong
statement of Quaker abhorrence of violence, and assuring the King that

> that Spirit of Christ by which we were guided, is not changeable, so as
> once to command us from a thing as evil, and again to move unto it.
> And we do certainly know, and so testify to the world, that the Spirit
> of Christ which leads us into all truth, will never move us to fight and
> war against any man with outward weapons, neither for the kingdom
> of Christ, nor for the kingdoms of this world.[2]

This statement was signed by twelve leading Friends, and thus for the first
time Quakers committed themselves, unequivocally, not to fight. Like Margaret Fell's declaration of the previous summer, the signatories included
Hubberthorne but not Burrough, which may or may not be indicative of
Burrough's opinions. It was an advance on the statement of the autumn of
1659 in which Quakers had said that they thought it unlikely that the Lord
would call them to fight, and on a number of earlier statements pledging
Friends not to engage in civil insurrection but making no mention of war
in general. The problems with this statement were, first, that it was distinctly economical with the truth, for it was common knowledge that a
number of Quakers had been involved with militias raised in 1659, and,
second, that whatever Fox declared, he could not bind all his followers. The
issue was by no means closed.

  Isaac Penington, acutely intelligent and in less of a hurry than the Quaker
leadership, could see the problems with this new statement. Fox, and the
other signatories to what modern Quakers call "The Peace Testimony,"
wanted to clear themselves from involvement with Fifth Monarchists, and
they did not consider the consequences for the country if everybody accepted the "Spirit of Christ" and refused to fight, any more than Thomas
Lurting and his friends had done (see Chapter 9). Penington did consider
this, and came up with an answer. Quakers should be defended, in case of
need, by others who had not been called to the witness for peace. He wrote
that it is one of the functions of magistrates to defend those who cannot
care for themselves. Women, children, the sick and the aged, and priests,
did not have to fight to defend themselves, and so he suggested that "fighting, which came in by the fall [of Adam], should come to an end in such,
whom God draws out of the fall, and that magistrates . . . should not
require fighting of them, whom the Lord has redeemed out of the fighting
nations, and chosen to be an example of meekness and peaceableness in the

places where they live." When this spirit had spread all over the earth, fighting would stop. In the meantime,

> I speak not this against magistrates or peoples defending themselves out of foreign invasions, or making use of the sword to suppress the violent and evil-doers within their borders (for this the present estate of things may and does require . . . and while there is need of a sword, the Lord will not suffer that government . . . to want fitting instruments under them for the managing thereof) . . . but yet there is a better state, which the Lord has already brought some into, and which the nations are expected to travel towards.[3]

The Convention Parliament had been dissolved in December 1660, and in May 1661 the new Parliament, known as the Cavalier Parliament, assembled. This Parliament was determined to establish the worship of the Church of England and admit no other. The full details of the repressive legislation that followed, known as the Clarendon Code after Charles II's first minister, need not be described here. Parliament's first action was to move against the Quakers, by bringing in an act, the Quaker Act, "for preventing the mischiefs and dangers that may arise by certain persons called Quakers and others, refusing to take lawful oaths." The preamble to the act states:

> The said persons, under a pretence of religious worship, do often assemble themselves in great numbers in several parts of this realm, to the great endangering of the public peace and safety, and to the terror of the people, by maintaining a secret and strict correspondence among themselves, and in the meantime separating and dividing themselves from the rest of his Majesty's good and loyal subjects, and from the public congregations and usual places of divine worship.

The act made it unlawful to refuse to take a legally tendered oath, or "by printing, writing or otherwise go about to maintain and defend that the taking of an oath in any case whatsoever, is altogether unlawful," and forbade Quakers above the age of sixteen years to assemble together "under pretence of joining in religious worship, not authorized by the laws of this realm." The penalties were fines and imprisonment, with the sting in the tail being:

> If any person . . . hath been twice convicted of any of the said of-
> fences, shall offend a third time, and be thereof . . . convicted, that
> then every person so offending and convicted for his or her third
> offence abjure the realm; or otherwise it shall . . . be lawful . . . for his
> Majesty . . . to cause him, her or them to be transported in any ship
> or ships, to any of his Majesty's plantations beyond the seas.

The bill was discussed in committee during July 1661, and Fox, Burrough, and George Whitehead all lobbied members of Parliament against
it.[4] After the act came into force, in May 1662, matters rapidly became
much worse for the Quakers. Meetings were regularly raided, people attending them were beaten, and many Friends were imprisoned. When the
oath of allegiance was tendered, writs of praemunire were used against a
number of Friends. The King ordered the release of most Quakers in August, but a further raid on the Bull and Mouth soon filled the London
prisons again. One man died from his injuries. Solomon Eccles, a musical-
instrument maker who had already felt called of the Lord to burn his
instruments on Tower Hill, walked naked as a sign. Then there was talk of
a Quaker and Baptist plot in October, and hundreds more were arrested.

Edward Billing, one of the more politically active Friends, who was described by an informer as a "very suspicious dangerous man," made things
worse.[5] He and some other Friends had been asked to sign a paper saying
that they would not take up arms against the King. Apparently, as Hookes
wrote to Fell, "They said they were not free to engage nor promise anything being a free people," and, when reminded of Fell's paper to the King,
they "denied it to be our principal to promise any such thing . . . and this
spirit has got up to a great height at present and they threaten, I hear, to
call in that paper which R.H. and thee wrote, and declare against it as not
to be our principle, and thus many are liable to suffer, and do suffer, which
is likely might have been released."[6] Clearly, the peace testimony was by no
means established among Friends. Other Quakers tried to undo the harm
caused by Billing, publishing the *Briefe Declaration of the People of God
called Quakers,* renewing the peace declaration, and specifically denying the
possibility that the Lord might send them fresh instructions, telling them
to fight. There is an oblique reference to Billing and his friends, "to prevent
the joining of the minds of any that are weak to the temptations of the
enemy."[7]

In the crowded, unhealthy prisons there were soon deaths, and the cost
to the Quaker leadership was heavy. Richard Hubberthorne was one of

those arrested in London during the summer of 1662, and he died in August. Hubberthorne had been devoted to Fox and Fell, a close and reliable colleague, whether as manager of the London meetings during the difficult period after the death of Nayler, as a competent controversialist, as a valuable supporter in times of internal dissension, and as possessed of a good prose style that had been particularly useful during the past two years when official statements had to be drafted in a hurry.[8]

The second loss was even more severe. Edward Burrough returned to London in June 1662 to share the suffering of his fellows, and was promptly arrested. He was not among those released in August. In January there were further releases, but again Burrough was considered too dangerous to be set free. He died in February 1663, leaving Friends in a state of shock, so that after his death, Fox distributed a letter "for the staying and settling of Friends minds," in which he wrote, "Be still and wait in your own conditions, and settled in the seed of God that does not change, that in that you may feel dear Edward Burrough among you in the seed, in which . . . he begat you to God."[9] Burrough had on several occasions shown independence of thought, and in view of the omission of his name from both peace statements, it is possible that the authorities were right in considering him not reconciled to the new order. On other matters, his opinions coincided with those of other Quaker leaders. He had been active in the formation of the London men's meeting, and close to it ever since, and, if he had been released and accommodated himself to the political situation, he would have been a powerful ally for Fox in the controversies over reorganization during the years to come. Or would he have sought the freer atmosphere on the other side of the Atlantic, perhaps as an associate of William Penn?

With both Hubberthorne and Burrough gone, George Whitehead, still under thirty years of age, became the most prominent of the long-serving leaders based in London. Fortunately the early months of 1663 were relatively peaceful for Quakers, and George Fox and Margaret Fell were able to make long journeys across the country. The government was by no means secure, and presumably one object of Fox and Fell was to try to keep Quakers quiet, and prevent them becoming involved in plots. Francis Howgill, also traveling in the ministry and probably with the same aim, was arrested in July, about the time the authorities became aware of the coming Northern Plot. Owing to the incompetence of the plotters it was a fiasco, but twenty-six men were executed in connection with it for treason.[10] There was considerable, and probably justified, suspicion that Quakers were involved: "They will be up in a few days, the Quakers to a man are engaged in it, who with other sects are fully agreed in this business."[11] But nothing could be proved against those Quakers who were currently active in the movement. Howgill knew exactly how far Friends were involved, and the following year wrote to Fox: "I have borne a great weight many months upon my back, about this plotting and the like, and some that were too much inclined, I knew, to it, whom I could not wholly reject as believing in the truth, neither yet justify; so that I have been as on a rack betwixt my friends and enemies."[12]

Fox and Fell were arrested in January 1664, and Fell was praemunired in August (her estates were later returned) and imprisoned in Lancaster Castle. She was released in 1668. Francis Howgill was praemunired in Appleby and imprisoned for life. He died in the prison there in January 1669. Fox was recommitted, and in May 1665 was transferred to Scarborough Castle, where the authorities held him isolated from his friends in very harsh conditions.[13]

Meanwhile, Parliament had passed the Conventicle Act, which came into force in July 1664 and extended the provisions of the Quaker Act to all nonconforming worship. It became the practice to try to secure two convictions quickly, and then a third, which would carry the sentence of banishment. Within a few months some two hundred sentences of banishment were passed on Quakers.[14] Very few were actually carried out because of difficulties in finding willing shipmasters, and in one case the Quakers were put ashore as the captain and crew decided that Quakers were unlucky, but at the time the threat seemed appalling.[15] Ministers wrote to the meetings to stand firm, and William Bayly's *Epistle General*, written in August 1664, is an example, addressed "unto all as are or may be under the judgement and sentence of banishment for the testimony of Jesus Christ": "Take no thought for your life, what you shall eat, what you shall drink, or wherewithal you shall be clothed, and, for your relations and friends, what they shall do in your absence, for the Lord (for whose sake you suffer) will provide both for you and them . . . but consider how great and weighty a work and service the Lord at this time has called you unto." Those who were still free should "keep your meetings together, in the name and fear of the Lord, and be not daunted, or terrified, in any thing from your adversary." God would come to save them, and they should wait quietly for his coming.[16]

The various tactics, that had been developed by Quakers to mitigate the lesser persecution of the 1650s, now proved their worth.

First, there was publicity. This included writing accounts of trials and suffering in prison, full details of the trials of Fox and Fell, and many papers entitled *For the King and both Houses of Parliament*, containing lists of those suffering and further statements of why it was that Quakers could not pay tithes nor go to steeplehouses, with assurances that they were not rebels.[17] At the same time, Friends issued papers to the public, broadsides intended to bring the state of the Quaker prisoners to public notice, and listing their sufferings, 3179 imprisoned and 32 dead up to 1660, and 5000 imprisoned and 22 dead since the King returned.[18] Juries in some cases came under pressure to convict, and the Quakers published the details.[19]

It was important also to write pamphlets giving a good and positive image of Quakerism. Two on Quaker faith were John Crook's *Truth's Principles*, a straightforward account of Quaker beliefs, and Farnworth's *The Spirit of God Speaking in the Temple of God*, addressed to "the Christian reader" and giving an explanation of Quaker worship. William Smith, in *Some Clear Truths particularly demonstrated unto the King and Council*, wrote that Quakers are "serviceable people in their place," good examples of righteous people, and just dealers. Such descriptions of Quakers as useful citizens became more frequent as the years passed.

A Testimony from us the People of God whom the World calls Quakers, signed by Fox and other leaders, was probably written about the time of the Northern plot to allay suspicions of the good faith of Quakers regarding the use of "carnal weapons"; people who advocated this, declared the authors, were "not in our fellowship in the spirit." While Fox was in prison, other Friends issued, anonymously, a "Remonstrance" in answer to a letter from the government to local authorities, ordering them to enforce the laws against dissenters more strictly. In this pamphlet they declared that they loved the King and denied, as "not to be of us" any one involved in plots or sedition. They were not so foolish as to wish the land to be run by foreigners.[20] Their meetings were for worship and their collections for their own poor. They "cannot strive with carnal weapons of war, being redeemed out of these things."[21]

The second technique, in use since the previous decade, was to use a disciplined church order to succor the afflicted. There is some difficulty in knowing how well the structure set up in the 1650s, which was new and incomplete, stood up to the rigors of the 1660s, but there are indications.

One is the persistence of the central organization managed by Ellis Hookes, which maintained effective links with the regions. Hookes realized that the printing press was better than hand copying for disseminating information. He wrote to Fell, concerning a paper of Fox,

> I see a good service in the paper to go amongst Friends for the taking answer of scripture and stumbling blocks, which have been laid in the way of the simple . . . for the better spreading of it (having not time to write so many copies as there was occasion for) therefore I have committed it to the press, to the end that it may do its service for which the Spirit of the Lord gave it forth.[22]

Committing papers to the press became his regular practice, and consequently many papers have survived that were intended for private circulation, marked "This is only to go among Friends." The manuscripts came to London from all over the country, often having been written in prison, and once printed, presumably made their way back again by similar routes. These pamphlets acted to some extent as a substitute for the actual presence of ministering Friends. Such papers were usually intended to be read in meetings, and were printed with addresses such as "*The Word of the Lord to his Church and Holy Assembly to whom this is sent to be carefully and distinctly read, in the fear of the Lord, when they are met together.*"[23] These epistles formed an important part of the Quaker pastoral writing that is described in the next chapter. In the autumn of 1662, when Hookes was temporarily at odds with London Friends and had been given notice (see Chapter 17, pages 223–24), he wrote to Margaret Fell, "In the meantime I go on with my work and I think to print some Friends books and have printed 4 or 5 lately towards my maintenance." It is worth noting that printing Friends' books, in the year 1662, would bring in a living.

The authorities made great efforts to suppress underground publications, which were produced by dissidents of all kinds. Friends' regular printer at this time was Robert Wilson, and his premises were raided in October 1661, he himself being arrested and his stock of books burned by the common hangman.[24] For reasons of security, Friends rarely published the printer's name after 1663, and the government's efforts to suppress Quaker publishing were remarkably unsuccessful. Around 1663–64, Friends' printing was being done by William Warwick, who had apparently taken over Thomas Simmons's press at the Bull and Mouth. When these premises were raided in the summer of 1664, Hookes was able to find three alternative printers immediately, possibly spreading the books around to minimize the risk of loss.[25] There were problems, and he may have been doing some of the work himself, for he apologized for books "wrong stitched up." Warwick was back at work in the spring of 1665, though Hookes said that there were still difficulties as Warwick was "under restraint."[26] Up to 1664 Hookes and Warwick had continued to publish Quaker pamphlets at approximately the same rate as in the 1650s. In 1665 there was a slight fall in numbers, but the reduction of titles to around thirty in 1666 may have been due to the effects of the Great Plague and the Great Fire as much as to the activities of the authorities.[27]

The London business meetings, both men's and women's, were certainly operative, being mentioned on several occasions in the letters and pamphlets of these years.[28] In the country at large, it would have been impossible to hold large regional meetings, and probably there were difficulties with monthly meetings, which were groupings of several individual meetings, but the rapidity with which they reappeared in 1667–68 suggests that, where they existed, they had remained basically intact. The county organization survived; this is indicated both by the address of the "Testimony of the Brethren" (see Chapter 17, page 224) and by a remark of Fox that Quarterly Meetings already existed when he commenced his reforms of 1667–68.[29]

Local meetings functioned, sometimes despite severe persecution, with many arrests, damage to meeting houses, and interruption of meetings. There is a good deal of evidence that Quakers met persecution in a highly disciplined way, meeting out of doors if the meeting house was inaccessible, and caring for those imprisoned. The women and children, and at Reading the children alone, maintained the meetings if the other adults were arrested.[30]

A third stratagem of Quakers concerned the use of the law, lobbying for changes, declaring certain procedures unlawful. Quakers reminded the King of the Declaration of Breda, which had never been implemented. Friends continued to make their traditional appeal to their persecutors: "Why do you prevaricate with the light of God in your consciences, which lets you see the abomination of this thing?"[31] Several pamphleteers suggested that the Quaker and Conventicle Acts did not apply to Quaker meetings, because their meetings were not, in fact, held for the purposes described in these acts.[32] These meetings, they said, were not seditious gatherings. They argued in court that a silent meeting was not a conventicle. Quaker arguments, admittedly, cut no ice with judges who were out to secure convictions, but at least the attempts were made, and experience gained. Albertus Faber, a German doctor living in London who had joined with Friends, wrote that the Conventicle Act was badly drafted and could apply to other kinds of meeting. William Smith warned juries to be very careful on convicting in cases leading to transportation, and to be sure there was really a proof of actions leading to conviction under the Act, such as causing "discord and strife." He pointed out that persons in a position to inform on conventicles should note that there was no penalty for not informing.[33]

Richard Farnworth had returned to active Quaker work in 1661, and in 1664 he arrived in London. He must have been studying the law, for he produced some clever pamphlets, arguing in legal terms that Quakers should be exempt from the new laws, and was one of the most effective Quaker authors in calling for general religious toleration.[34] Friends were now joining regularly in such appeals, an important new development in their understanding of themselves in relation to other Christians, which is discussed more fully in the final chapter of this book.

Another technique was to issue warnings of the dire fate awaiting persecutors. Quakers did not accept the new laws meekly, and the commonest reaction was defiance. It was difficult to feel the actual presence of God's Kingdom in these circumstances, and there is much strong apocalyptic language, warning of a coming catastrophe, more of it in the pamphlets of the early 1660s than in pamphlets written in the middle 1650s.[35] To the government, such language was seriously threatening. Even in 1664, when the persecution was intensifying and some Friends were beginning to weary of waiting for the Lord to act, there were still many defiant apocalyptic warnings, as Quakers continued to give out threats of the Lord's coming vengeance and their own triumph. Margaret Fell, imprisoned in Lancaster Castle, had no doubts: "This Lamb is now arising and raising up that which was fallen down . . . worthy is the Lamb that was slain . . . he has redeemed us out of every kindred, tongue, and nation, and has made us unto our God, kings and priests, and we shall reign on the earth." [36] She was not alone in making such proclamations. William Bayly wrote a pamphlet called *The Great and Dreadful Day of the Lord God Almighty (which is hastening like a flood . . .):* "This is your warning once more to repent with speed . . . so while you have an inch of time, prize it." George Whitehead struck the same note: "Where will you hold yourselves . . . in the great day of the Lamb's wrath which assuredly will come upon them who make war upon him and his followers?" George Bishop's warning was strangely prophetic: "Meddle not with my people because of their conscience; and banish them not out of the nation, because of their conscience: For, if you do, I will send my plagues upon you; and you shall know that I am the Lord."[37]

In 1665, at last, it seemed that the Lord was taking action, for a serious plague epidemic broke out in London, just after the first Friends had been transported to Jamaica. Pamphlet after pamphlet ascribed the plague to the Lord's doing, and pointed out that it was no use calling for official fasts and days of repentance, if the cause of the visitation, the banishment order against Friends, was not lifted.[38] However, Quakers as well as their enemies were victims of the plague, and they wondered why the Lord should treat them so. The most famous Quaker to die that year in the plague was Samuel Fisher, but the worst case was when a number of Quakers, destined for transportation, were confined on a ship where plague broke out, and half of them died. It was difficult to believe that God was really supporting Quakers when such terrible things were happening. Ellis Hookes wrote to Margaret Fell, in November when the epidemic was easing,

> So as a brand is plucked out of the fire so has the Lord delivered me, for I have often laid down my head in sorrow, and rose as I went to bed and not slept a wink for the groans of them that lay a-dying, and every morning I counted it a great mercy that the Lord gave me another day. . . . [of Friends, now there is] not above one a day buried, whereas there used to be 16, 18 and sometimes 20 in a day buried for several weeks.[39]

George Whitehead wrote an epistle "to be read distinctly in the life and authority of God (from whence it came) among Friends." God was with them: "And so none of you be discouraged . . . because of that common calamity and late mortality which has befallen many of the righteous as well as the unrighteous . . . for God's testimony and glory shines and will shine . . . God . . . chastens and tries not in anger and fury, but in love, fatherly care, and pity."[40]

The Great Fire of London in September 1666, when much of London was burnt in a four-day blaze, was thought by dissenters to be another instance of the Lord's intervention. Francis Howgill, hearing of the fire, wrote to Margaret Fell, "I am satisfied in the righteous judgement of the Lord upon that great and rebellious city, and indeed I looked for great judgement to come some years since, and one woe came, that great pestilence, but I felt they had forgotten it."[41]

The last of the Quakers' techniques for easing the impact of persecution

Fig. 12 The Great Fire of London in September 1666, from a German print showing London ablaze, viewed from the South beyond the river. Most of the city and a considerable area west of the city wall was burnt in a four-day blaze. To Quakers and other dissenters, the fire was a sign of God's anger against their persecutors. (Courtesy, Guildhall Library, Corporation of London)

was the use of theological argument. Quakers, now joined by other persecuted dissidents, developed their belief that suffering is the way to the Kingdom of God. Most pamphlets on this theme come under the heading of pastoral writing, and are considered in Chapter 16. A few were written for the general public, although none with the fervor of Humphrey Smith (see Chapter 12). One was Rebecca Travers's *This is for any of those that resist the Spirit*. She wondered what would happen if the persecutors were under the same stress as the Quakers, and how they would stand up to it: "Well, Friends, if ever you should be tried as God is trying us by you, you will have need of our strength . . . and this upholds us, we cannot fear what man can do unto us, for the Lord is with us."[42] Quakers were now willing to see themselves as standing in the tradition of earlier British martyrs, and

Ellis Hookes wrote two books to encourage this sense of unity with those who had gone before.[43]

How long the Quakers could have held out under such pressure is a question to which one will never know the answer. There is a strained note in some of the pamphlets published toward the end of the period, and one unhappy epistle, written from the gaol at Bury St. Edmunds during 1665, continues for pages in the same vein:

> Oh when will the Lord cause the days of my mourning to be over, and the night of my soul to pass away. . . . The thing which the Lord has purposed must be accomplished in his season, and the thing that he has determined must be fulfilled in spite of all the powers of darkness; Oh that all thy babes and lambs may willingly wait thy appointed time Oh Lord God almighty, Oh dear God keep all thy people retired in thy name, that so whatever thou suffer to befall their bodies, their souls may be bundled up in the bundle of life.[44]

Fortunately, persecution was never applied consistently over the whole country, much depending on the attitude of local authorities, and it eased generally toward the end of 1664. The Great Plague and the Great Fire gave encouragement to all dissenters that the Lord had not forgotten them. In the autumn of 1667 there was a change in the government, and ministers more inclined to toleration came to power. Despite sporadic persecution for another twenty years, the dissenting churches were never in serious danger again. As for the Quakers, George Fox was released by order of the King in September 1666, giving the movement a new lease of life.

15

THE CONSEQUENCES OF JOHN PERROT

At the same time as the serious persecution described in the last chapter, the Quakers had to cope with a major internal upheaval. Many modern Quakers consider it a petty affair badly handled, that throws no credit on Fox and the other leaders, and some seventeenth-century Quakers shared this opinion, although their views did not prevail.

Incompatibility between the "the light" as it appears to an individual Friend and the corporate "light" of a meeting, which was at the root of the Nayler affair, was and is a potential source of difficulty among Friends. After 1656, and for most of the rest of the seventeenth century, this recurring problem generally took the form of a challenge to the authority of George Fox, although in fact the authority of Fox was always backed by powerful Friends. The next episode in this history was sparked off by the return to Britain of a traveling minister named John Perrot.[1]

Perrot was an Irish Baptist who had been convinced during Burrough's and Howgill's mission to Ireland in 1655. In 1657, feeling the call to go further afield, he joined a party traveling to the south of Europe and beyond. One member of this group was Mary Fisher, now returned from America, who reached Constantinople and had audience with the sultan before returning safely to Britain. Perrot and his companion John Luffe were less fortunate, for after traveling in Italy they were picked up by the Inquisition. Luffe disappeared, probably dying in prison.[2] Perrot was imprisoned in the Prison for Madmen in Rome, where he was chained, beaten, and tortured over a period of three years. The effect on him was devastating.

He managed to do some writing while in prison, and his papers were brought back to England and published, mostly in 1660 and 1661.[3] Several of them are rambling and incoherent with weird associations of ideas, and in one case, a most peculiar title. Even in the seventeenth century, when odd titles were common, the reader might have trouble in comprehending *A Wren in the Burning Bush, Waving the Wings of Contraction, to the Congregated clean Fowls of Heavens, in the Ark of God, holy Host of the Eternal Power, Salutation.* One pamphlet, which Friends apparently refused to publish, included passages such as "and now the countenances of an illustrious off-spring, and comeliness of a numberless train of the most enamoured beautiful virgins, doth compass my waist, as with the cincture of ravishment." Such ambivalence about sex and gender did not endear Perrot to the Quaker establishment.[4]

Inevitably, during three years alone in horrible conditions, Perrot became turned in on himself, and his personal spiritual life, which held firm, came to mean much more to him than the Quaker habits of communal worship, which were already becoming set traditions. Besides the pamphlets that were eventually printed, several letters and general epistles made their way back to Britain, and one contained the following passage:

> If any Friend be moved of the Lord God to pray in the congregation of God fallen down with his face to the ground, without taking off the hat, or the shoes, let him do so in the fear and name of the Lord, and if the world be contentious, ask them why take off your hat without precept, and not your shoes, being it was a precept which God commanded Moses, saying, take off thy shoe from off thy feet.[5]

Logic would seem to have been on Perrot's side. Given the Quaker under-standing of worship, that it was directly inspired by God, there was no reason why men should not be moved to pray without, as was customary, removing their hats, or indeed, why they should not alternatively remove their shoes in the presence of God, as Moses had (Exodus 3:5), and there was no reason for any difference of treatment between men and women. Saint Paul, in 1 Corinthians 11, had said that men should pray uncovered and women covered, but Quakers had no problem in finding an alternative explanation of other biblical precepts that did not fit in with their ideas of God's wishes.

At this time, in nearly all churches, it was customary for men to keep their hats on except during prayer and the singing of psalms. Friends had discarded most conventions in worship, and there are some indications that in the early days this practice also may have been in doubt. For most Friends, however, whatever the logic of the matter, keeping on one's hat during prayer was quite unacceptable; it showed a lack of humility toward God. Keeping on one's hat also meant disunity with the prayer, and had been one of the signs of disapproval used by Nayler and his friends in 1656.[6]

Perrot's letter caused great offense to George Fox, who wrote a strong reply.[7] At first sight this is odd, for Fox was tolerant of mild eccentricity among Quakers. He had warned elders not to discourage Friends who were moved to "bubble forth" a few words in meetings, and advised that if correction was necessary, it should be delivered carefully and in private.[8] He had dealt very gently with Humphrey Wollrich, who had felt moved to baptize a woman (see Chapter 10). His views on the payment of impropri-ated tithes appear to have been easy-going (see Chapter 9). There were three differences in Perrot's case, first, that Perrot had not submitted his opinion to the judgment of Fox or of other leading Friends, second, that Perrot's practice would affect the normal conduct of public meetings, and third, there was a probable link to early and now discredited practice that may have been associated with Nayler.[9] Friends had discovered some years earlier that to avoid Ranterish and possibly lunatic behavior it was advis-able to keep meetings to a regular order.

Perrot was released from prison in Rome in June 1661, possibly through the intervention of Charles II, and returned to England, famous as a near martyr. He then traveled in England, his ministry having great success, and he became well known outside the Quaker circle. Some anti-Quaker writers addressed a set of queries equally to Fox, Fisher, Perrot, and Burrough.[10]

Perrot then wrote another letter on the subject of hats in meetings, probably as a preparation for discussions with Fox and other leading Quakers:

> The purpose of God is to bring to nought all the customary and
> traditional ways of worship of the sons of men which have entered
> into the world and stand unto this day in the curse and state of
> apostacy from the power of the living worship.
>
> For which cause I preach the cross of our Lord Jesus Christ unto
> that reasoning part in all seeming to stand in opposition to that which I
> have received by express commandment from the Lord God of heaven
> in the day of my captivity in Rome, (viz), to bear a sure testimony
> against the custom and tradition of taking off the hat by men when
> they go to pray to God, which they never had by commandment from
> God, and therefore unto them may be rightly said, Who hath re-
> quired this thing at your hands? . . . God is one and the same, both in
> the male and in the female and looks not to the uncovery of the
> external heads in the female.[11]

This was a direct challenge to the Quaker leadership. Perrot spent some
weeks in London, and a number of meetings were held in an attempt to
clarify the issues. He began to hold his own evening meetings instead of
joining other ministers at Gerrard Roberts's house, which was a further
cause of annoyance. According to Perrot's account, Fox, supported by Hubberthorne and others, twice verbally abused him for several hours at a time,
not only regarding the conduct of meetings but also concerning the possible misuse of Friends' funds for traveling ministers. In addition, Fox
disliked some of the verses and other writings that Perrot had sent from
Rome, considering them "hard."[12] Perrot left London in January 1662 and
traveled west, spending some time with Isaac Penington before going on to
Bristol and Ireland. He may have thought the London discussions had
settled the issues, but further letters from Fox followed him, and others
were sent ahead to Bristol to warn Friends there of his coming. A main
reason for the alarm of the Quaker leaders was that they seemed to be
heading for a re-run of the Nayler case. Perrot was a popular and attractive
preacher, and Friends who had been Nayler's supporters re-appeared as supporters of Perrot. Perrot even grew a beard, as Nayler had done. Beards
were uncommon ornaments at that time.

Perrot was soon back in England, and like Burrough he was arrested in
London and sent to Newgate prison in June. John Crook and Edward

Burrough were also imprisoned there, and both of them received the impression that Perrot had made his peace with the main body of Friends, although later they discovered that they had been mistaken.[13] During meetings in the prison Perrot "forebore the wearing his hat" in prayer, and the three Friends together, as "prisoners of the Lord," published an epistle to Friends, calling on them to keep their meetings "for the day of your deliverance hasteneth."[14] Perrot then decided to obtain his freedom by accepting the government's offer of voluntary exile, and departed for Barbados in October. He never returned to Britain, but traveled in America, where his presence led to more dissension, which is outside the scope of this book.

Meanwhile, Fox distributed an epistle to Friends in which he wrote that this argument was like the disputes under the old covenant about eating particular foods and observing days. It was a "jangling": "They that are come to Christ, are in a state beyond Adam before he fell; far before outward coverings, for Christ was with the Father before the world began, before Adam was made." Did that mean that hats do not matter? Not at all, for they "that have a fellowship in keeping on the hats, and observing of meats, those outward things guards them from [i.e. keeps them away from] the power." Moreover, and this was the important point, "You, with your earthly spirits, and earthly form, have given occasion to the world to say, that the people of God called Quakers are divided, some with their hats on, and some with them off."[15]

Perrot's departure did not bring the dispute to an end, for his followers fanned the flames. George Whitehead wrote to Margaret Fell in November 1663 about troubles he was having with various adherents of Perrot in East Anglia.

> That spirit of discord which has made the hat its chief cloak against us, not so much at work as it has been. . . . B. Furly has written very perversely and revilingly against me (especially) and partly against thee, and sent his letter by London open, and I fully answered him and returned his absurdities and falsehoods upon him, and sent my answer to London in like manner, for such to see as had seen his . . . scarce any of the ancient labourers will be left in these parts Norfolk and Suffolk. Will Salt has published in print a book against first day meetings, and that none should meet but as they are immediately moved etc. I suppose thou mayest have heard of or seen Jo. Harwoods scandalous, reviling pamphlet in print against thee.[16]

Benjamin Furly was a wealthy businessman resident in Holland, a leader of Dutch Quakerism, and the paper mentioned by Whitehead was probably a general epistle to Friends to the effect that Fox and Whitehead were making a fuss about matters of no importance: "Is this a time for us (who are gathered into the unity of the one spirit and life and truth of God) to be found smiting one another about things in which neither our unity with God nor with each other is established?"[17]

The "book against first day meetings" was William Salt's *Some Breathings of Life*.[18] The movement against incipient formality in Quaker worship now extended, beyond the question of hats, to objections to the arranging of meetings for a specified time. There is also evidence that some of Perrot's followers disliked the Quaker practice of shaking hands in greeting and at the close of meetings.[19]

Some Breathings of Life included a posthumous poem by George Fox the Younger, attacking people who thought too well of themselves. It is probable that George Fox the Younger had been a friend of Perrot, for Perrot, while in London, had said that Francis Howgill had accused him of "writing the secrets of my mind to George Fox the Younger," and it was "J.P.," probably Perrot, who wrote the "Epistle to the Reader" in Fox the Younger's collected works, published in 1662. But George Fox the Younger died in July 1661, the month that Perrot returned to England from Rome, and his opinion of Perrot cannot be known for certain.

The most outspoken assault on the Quaker leadership was what George Whitehead called John Harwood's "scandalous reviling pamphlet," *To all People that profess the Eternal Truth of the Living God, tis is a true and real demonstration of the cause why I have denied, and do deny the Authority of George Fox*.[20] Harwood was one of the original Yorkshire Quakers imprisoned in York Castle in 1652, who had recently been disowned as being "begotten by, and unto an unruly, heady high spirit, and was never to our feeling thoroughly subjected under the power of the truth."[21]

As with a number of printed papers of this time, Harwood's epistle was not intended for the general public, but was "only to go among Friends . . . where George Fox's papers of enmity against the innocent hath passed." It is a mighty attack on Fox.

> And whereas George Fox hath called himself the Son of God . . . I do desire Friends to judge impartially of his fruits, whether or no the Son . . . of God ever brought forth such things as these that follows; And whether or no such have not been . . . deceived, who have esteemed . . . him infallible;

And though he hath been in his day and time serviceable in the work of the Lord, yet that will not save him from judgement in the day of his transgression. So long as he stood innocent and faithful, God honoured him with the glory of his presence, and prospered his work in his hand . . . but since he hath sought to exalt himself, and throw down others to set himself in the highest place in the seat of God . . . his glory hath faded, and he suffered to be ensnared, and to fall into divers temptations, as hereafter will . . . appear.

Harwood followed this with a long list of instances of Fox's high-handed behavior and misjudgments, and also accused him of possible sexual misbehavior with Margaret Fell. Regarding hats, which was the important issue, Harwood referred to a previous book of Fox's, *The Honour amongst the Jews.* In this book, Fox had said that hats were earthly, and not of importance, but now he was saying that he could only have unity with men who put off their hats at prayer.[22]

Fox promptly answered Harwood, point by point. He would certainly never deny that he called himself the Son of God, for it was scriptural usage. Fox would never concede this point. Fox then refuted Harwood's various accusations of bad management, and declared that there had been nothing amiss in his relations with Margaret Fell, as many Friends could witness.

On the wearing of hats, Fox was on the defensive. He said that in the pamphlet *The Honour amongst the Jews* he had only referred to the practice of removing one's hat before a magistrate, but it was difficult to argue that, if hats were "earthly" and unimportant in a secular setting, that they mattered so much in Friends' meetings. Fox could only argue from church order, that a spirit-based church, especially in a time of persecution, must have a firm structure or it would collapse, and if this meant observing some practices that some people disliked, then so be it.[23] However, Fox's genius did not lie in conducting a clear argument. His justification for his position is odd:

And so you would bring all men to sit like a company of women, and so you would bring all into a form under the penalty of a curse; for J.P.s law was never called in, which many observes, like a company of women sits covered, of whom thou learned it, of the woman not of the man, and so it is your law and your curse that we oppose, who stands in our liberty in the power of God before hats was . . . and the fellowship which stands in hats, and thy unclean actions and carnal things, and your forms you set up . . . is denied.[24]

Making sense of this is not easy. At the back of Fox's mind was Genesis 3:14–20 and especially verse 16, where God cursed the serpent, Eve and Adam for disobedience, and 1 Corinthians 11:3–16, where Saint Paul discusses the reasons for women keeping their heads covered in church, while men did not. The double meaning of "woman" and "man" is there, where "woman" equals "weak" and "man" equals "strength," but Fox was not necessarily talking about an actual women's meeting. Fox meant that by raising arguments about hats and unimportant matters Perrot was weakening the meeting, causing divisions, and incidentally challenging the leadership, which was the real crime. Fox doubtless approved of Saint Paul's way of dealing with this same issue: "If any man seem to be contentious, we have no such custom, neither the churches of God" (1 Corinthians 3:16).[25]

One of those attracted by Perrot was Isaac Penington. Perrot had stayed at Penington's house after leaving London, and by Perrot's account some unpleasant letters from the Quaker leadership, which Penington may have seen, had followed him there. Penington said nothing at the time, but the matter was upon his mind, and later he published his thoughts for the consideration of Friends, with the title *Many Deep Considerations have been upon my Heart Concerning the State of Israel,* Israel being the true church.

Penington reminded his readers of the high hopes "about the beginning of the late troubles of the nation" that had been disappointed when people became involved in "disputes and contention about forms of worship and church government." Then came "the precious breaking-forth of the Lord (at this dismal time . . .) in some hidden vessels . . . and who can utter what the glory of this light was." These "vessels" had been "for the most part mean, as to the outward, young country lads, of no deep understanding or ready expression." Yet they had prospered, the Lord had "enriched them with gifts and abilities, and in every way fitted them for the service and employment he had had for them." But now they were in danger, more danger than when they had been poor and weak. The enemy was subtle, and some who were good and great in Israel might fall. "If any man, in that day, shall take to himself what belongs to the Lord, or any other shall give it to him, the Lord . . . will find out a way to recover his own." If this were to happen, it would cause "a great shaking and shattering," so Friends must be careful. Then came three queries, the first, how a man, whom the Lord had exalted, could be prevented from falling, the second, if such a thing happened, how could the little ones (i.e., the ordinary Friends) be preserved, and the third, how could such a fallen leader be recovered. It would be difficult, thought Penington, but not impossible, given humility. He ended with an appeal to Friends to abide in the Life, and keep to the Power and the Principle.[26]

The Quaker leaders were appalled at this breach of unity, but Penington had to be handled with care. Among the correspondence in the Penington papers on the Perrot affair are two very cautious letters, one from William Smith and one from Howgill, which put the Quaker establishment position much better than anything that Fox ever wrote. William Smith was another who, like Penington himself, had joined Friends in 1658, after the first rush of enthusiasm was over, and he was a thoughtful and tactful person. After a long preliminary discussion of principles, he came to the nub of his letter, the matter of the hat:

> Though I know, in the true liberty of life, the hat is nothing, yet I also know, that as the keeping of it on is introduced in opposition to the putting of it off, it does not proceed from the healing point of life, but from the point which rather seeks the praises of man. For I had some openings concerning the hat long before I received the truth, and could not at that time put it off to answer the bare formality that was therein observed, but when I came to the true teaching of God's spirit. . . . I was thereby taught to put it off when by the spirit I was moved to pray unto God, or to join in prayer with those who by the same spirit was moved thereunto. Howbeit I do not say that God's spirit is tied or limited to the observation, but may otherwise dispose and order in its own pleasure, yet this practice being brought into the church, by the spirit of God in these latter days, and nothing aimed at thereby but the glory of God alone, I am very careful to close with another thing, until I find by the spirit of God in me, that the propagation of it be from the spirit. . . . The same spirit that did first teach me not to put it off, does rather draw me still to observe the same, knowing that here is yet many weak babes, who are not come to discern from what principle every practice is made manifest. . . . The body is to be considered, and nothing is to be done but in the tender love, by which the body may be edified and comforted.[27]

Hats in themselves did not matter, but the effect on "weak babes" must be carefully considered. Saint Paul had come to much the same conclusion in advising the church of Corinth about the observance of Jewish dietary laws.[28]

Howgill, like Smith, was slow to come to the point, clearly finding it difficult to handle Penington on a matter of discipline. He explained at some length that it was not Friends' practice to dispute publicly with one another, and that Penington's writings were liable to "beget doubts and fears . . . howbeit thou may intend them as for good." It was not helpful for Penington to discuss the possibility that the Lord

> should suffer one or more, who have been eminent in his service, to decline and fall . . . such things . . . weakens us in the sight of our adversaries. . . . Dear Isaac, I do not deal with thee as an enemy . . . as I hope thou wilt not look upon me for speaking plainly unto thee. I would have thee stop writings and papers of this nature, and send them not abroad . . . and banish evil thoughts and surmises, and let them have no place in thy heart, against any whom God hath made serviceable in this work. . . . Divers things more I could say about that business of the hat, but I desire it may die with the people that brought it forth.[29]

Richard Farnworth also took up the question, writing a paper probably intended for limited circulation among Friends, and sending a copy to Penington. He argued that men Friends had always been accustomed to remove their hats "in humility of soul before the Lord," and that the Lord had never shown any disapproval of the practice. Perrot had brought in an "innovation or new doctrine," with the result of "setting many Friends at a distance in spirit one from another." And if anyone should "object and say, that bodily exercise profits little, and so conclude that praying with the hat off is but a bodily exercise and therefore useless and unprofitable," then, Farnworth said, people should understand that the inward and outward are "joined in action," so that "as the inward man is directed and disposed by the eternal power and Godhead, and so directs and disposes of the outward man, as to put off the hat in prayer, [this] is not only a bodily exercise . . . but of some use and service."[30] Farnworth was coming to the conclusion that outward observances did indeed have a place in worship, and that the Quaker emphasis on the spiritual could not and should not exclude all forms. This is a considerable development on primitive Quaker ideas on true worship as being only "in spirit and in truth."

Penington, in the end, accepted the advice given to him, and in spite of misgivings stayed with mainstream Quakerism. In 1666, when he was in prison in Aylesbury, he wrote a general epistle to Friends with his considered thoughts. The Enemy had used three methods to "entangle the minds of the redeemed," first by arousing prejudice against "those whom the Lord has chosen, and pleases to make use of in ministry to his people," second, "To draw men from . . . subjecting to the present dispensation, by an earnest looking after and waiting for another," and third, "under a pretence of sticking to the enlightening and guidance of ones own measure, to set up a sense and judgement in the mind . . . which is not truly of the measure." He ended, "The seed is meek, humble, tender, lowly, sensible of its own state and weakness, and subject to the exaltation, domination and pure authority of life in others where the Lord hath so exalted it."[31] Orthodox Quakerism had little respect for individual judgment, even when the individual was Isaac Penington.

The dispute rumbled on. Epistles from ministers to their flocks contain references to the need to beware of division among Friends. Many leading Friends spoke out on behalf of the stand taken by Fox.[32] Rebecca Travers, a London Friend who had been a close friend of Nayler but was not one of those attracted to Perrot, can be taken as an example:

> Our greatest enemies are those amongst us, who though gathered in the same profession and appearing with us, yet are not of us, for our unity is in the faith, not in any form whatsoever . . . now if one comes who sees you in difficulties and confusion, will he not be hardened? whereas if he see a good order in oneness and stability, not changeable, but firm, may he not then say of a truth God is with them?[33]

The affair dragged on because the fire was continually fed, for Perrot did not accept his dismissal, and indeed, according to his lights, he had done nothing amiss. A letter attempting to clear Perrot circulated in England during 1665, at a time when Fox was held incommunicado in Scarborough Castle, and the response of a group of leading Friends, headed by Richard Farnworth, showed a complete loss of patience, being written in formal quasi-legal language to the effect that Perrot had not repented, and that therefore the fact that he had once been a minister was entirely irrelevant.[34]

The Quaker leaders were reaching the limits of their tolerance. The action that they took is described in the final chapter of this book.

16

POETRY, TESTIMONIES, AND PASTORAL EPISTLES

One result of the political upheavals of the early 1660s was a change in the tone and content of much of the Quaker pamphlet literature. The flood of Quaker political pamphlets dwindled in 1661 and 1662, as hopes waned of influencing the government. Controversial writings, for reasons already explained, decreased to perhaps half a dozen a year. Apocalyptic warnings and pamphlets on sufferings were still produced in quantity, but overall the balance of Quaker writing was changed. The energies of Friends that might have been employed in political pamphleteering, or in disputes with members of other churches, were turned to internal arguments, and also to new forms of expression, descriptions of the Christian life with a

Quaker bias, testimonies to their dead, epistles from ministers to their flocks, and verse.

The quantity of verse is something of a surprise, given the Quaker suspicion of the arts and of any form of writing that needed planning or revision. Quaker poetry of this time has no particular artistic merit, and belongs to the popular ballad tradition.[1] Much of it seems singable, but there is no record of any of the authors singing their verses "in the Spirit" in meetings. The roughness of much of the poetry may be due to the reluctance of Friends to revise what had been given them by the Lord. Humphrey Smith, who had been very sad to give up music on becoming a Quaker, told how he was led to write a song of praise to God.

> As I was walking alone in my prison at Winchester upon the 24th day of the 5th month 1662, in much quietness and inward refreshing by the rising virtue of God's refreshing love; these lines began to run gently through me, with melody in my heart to the Lord, and when I was free in myself to write, it departed not from me, but came so easy and so fast as I could well write, whereby in a very little part of the aforesaid day this was begun and finished with my own hand; yet would I not have it looked upon to be a great thing, nor a pattern nor example for others to run into the like, for since I came into the life and obedience of truth, I durst not write anything in verse until this time.[2]

Between the years 1661 and 1665 over twenty Friends published their verses.[3] Quaker poetry often expressed the same kind of apocalyptic warning, or encouragement to bear suffering, that was also given in prose. One of the more capable of these Quaker versifiers was John Raunce, a doctor from Buckinghamshire, and his broadside ballad in four columns, *A Few Words to all People concerning the Present and Succeeding Times,* is an account of the suffering of the righteous and God's ultimate vindication.

> Who is oppressed save righteous men
> who in vile prisons lie?
> Arise, O God, for these things then,
> yea loud now is the cry
> Of thine elect in every place
> How long Lord, holy, true;

Wilt thou not hasten on thy pace
against this wicked crew?
. . . .
Oh now dear suffering Friends rejoice!
Redemption will not stay
From us who have made Christ our choice
before the evil day.
when prisons, sword, gallows and fire
shall compass us about,
He will help us when in the mire
and guide us when we doubt
. . . .
Yea, in that Love which suffereth long
for ever let us dwell;
And in God's truth let us be strong,
in this I say farewell.[4]

The most prolific writer of verse was Dorothy White. She published
most of her verses in collections of short pieces, often apocalyptic warnings.
This is a specimen of her work, the beginning of a long poem about the
seed arising, ending with the general resurrection of all humankind, "For
the life is come, that reigneth over death":

Who leadeth in the narrow way,
Who bringeth out o' the darkness, unto the perfect day;
Where the light in fulness springeth up,
Where salvation also fills the cup
Of all the faithful, who upon the Lord do wait;
Their consolation always doth abound,
and praises with rejoicing unto God they sound:
With praises sweet they sing to God on high,
Who fills the earth with 's glorious majesty.[5]

Another new literary form was the testimony, an account of the life and
work of a dead Friend. Where appropriate, a testimony would be used to
head a set of collected works; issuing collected editions of works was another new departure. The testimony to Richard Hubberthorne was the
first, published with his works at the beginning of 1663.[6] The "Epistle to
the Reader" is by George Whitehead, and Burrough wrote a contribution

before his own death. The testimony to Burrough, *A Testimony concerning the Life, Death, Trials, Travels and Labour of Edward Burroughs*, by Francis Howgill, George Whitehead, Josiah Coale, and George Fox, was published within a few weeks of his death. Howgill's contribution was a lament in the style of David's lament for Jonathan.

> Oh Edward Burrough, I cannot but mourn for thee . . . thy absence is great, and years to come shall know the want of thee. Shall days or months or years wear out thy name, as though thou hadst had no being? Oh nay! shall not thy noble and valiant acts, and mighty works which thou hast wrought through the power of him that separated thee from the womb, live in generations to come? . . . When I think upon thee, I am melted into tears of true sorrow . . . shall I not say as David said of Saul and Jonathan. . . . *The beauty of Israel is slain upon the high places:* Even so wast thou stifled in nasty holes and prisons, and many more, who were precious in the eyes of the Lord: And surely precious wast thou to me, oh dear Edward. I am distressed for thee my brother, very pleasant has thou been unto me, thy love to me was wonderful, passing the love of women.[7]

This book is also an important document for the history of Quaker beginnings, written from the perspective of ten years afterward. Note the importance given to the message of George Fox, which resulted, according to Howgill's experience, in the coming of the Kingdom of God.

> [The Lord] sent . . . unto us a man of God, one of ten thousand, to instruct us in the ways of God more perfectly, who laid down the sure foundation and declared the acceptable year of the Lord . . . whose testimony reached unto all our consciences, and entered into the innermost part of our hearts, which drove us . . . to a diligent inquisition concerning our state, which we did come to see through the Light of Christ Jesus which was testified of . . . and the Lord of heaven and earth we found to be near at hand, and as we waited upon him in pure silence, our minds out of all things, his dreadful power and glorious Majesty appeared in our assemblies, when there was no language, tongue, nor speech from any creature, and the Kingdom of heaven did gather and catch us all as in a net, and his heavenly power did draw many hundreds to land, that we did come to know a place to stand in, and what to wait in, and the Lord did appear daily to us,

to our astonishment, amazement, and great admiration [wonder] in so much that we often said to one another with great joy of heart, What, is the Kingdom of God come to be with men?[8]

Humphrey Smith died in prison on the May 4, 1663, and the testimony to him was called *The Faithfulness of the Upright made Manifest.*[9] John Crook and Thomas Green wrote the testimony for a fellow minister, John Samm, the following year.[10] Testimonies were not only written for well-known ministers. Mary Page was a Wellingborough Friend who died in Warwick Castle after nearly two years imprisonment, and testimonies concerning her were written by local Friends, several of them women.[11] Testimony writing developed into a standard practice among British Friends, and nowadays, at every Yearly Meeting, testimonies are read "to the grace of God as shown in the lives of deceased Friends."

Pastoral letters giving advice and encouragement to meetings, many written in prison, were regularly printed during the post-Restoration period, no doubt because of the industry of Ellis Hookes. If ministers were prevented from addressing meetings directly, epistles must suffice. These epistles were usually sent out with a note such as "This is only to go among Friends," or "To be read in the assemblies of Friends," or to "the assemblies of the Church of the First-born."[12] Letters of this kind related to the Perrot affair were noted in the last chapter, but Friends wrote on many other subjects.

George Fox the Younger gave advice from prison to others in prison:

> There is a temptation that may be presented to some in bonds (mark) to think highly of themselves, because they are put in prison for the truth. . . . Now where this temptation is joined to, it puffs such up in the fleshly false joy, and leads out of the fear above the cross, so becoming very dangerous to them. . . . Many whose hearts are open, not knowing what you (who are in bonds) may want, may bring or offer you much . . . therefore you need to stand in the pure fear, wisdom and authority of God, . . . or else these things may soon become a snare to you, and so fleshly liberty and ease may be run into. . . . And you who have but little of this world's goods, and do rather want than abound, O Friends, commit your cause to God. . . . Oh do not in any wise do evil, that good may come thereof, the woe will be upon them that keep you from providing for your families.[13]

William Bayly, in prison in Hertford, sent advice on managing Quaker families, which should be ruled, "not with rigour, for that savours of a kind of darkness: nor in a wrong dominion, in conceitedness, self-willedness, or in an impatient brittle spirit, but in the wisdom of God. . . . And when you exhort, admonish or correct them . . . then wait you upon God, to feel his presence and seed to lead, govern and go before you."[14]

William Dewsbury, in Warwick gaol, began a letter, "Dear Children and chosen vessels of the eternal ever-living God, whom he has plucked as brands out of the fire, and has manifested his powerful operating Spirit, to lead you in his holy fear." He warned Friends to take care, that "the enemy never get entrance, to stain your pure garments," and told them, "though the cup look bitter, which many has to drink in this trying day, fear not, you beloved people, but stand approved in the light of Jesus."[15]

William Gibson wrote several short letters from Shrewsbury gaol, including advice to those led to minister.

> Sink down low, to feel his pure powerful presence to arise in you, and to come up and stand over all that is contrary to it in you, and then . . . when you feel the true power rising in you, and words come in, look not out into the words, but keep to the power, and wait, still and low, and let the power work through and over the contrary, forward and subtle will . . . take heed that your souls be not over much lifted up in joy and zeal, for that is very dangerous to lead you out of your measure.[16]

The two early Quaker writers whose works are best known in the present day are George Fox and Isaac Penington. George Fox was the most prolific writer overall during the period 1660–66, with fifty-six titles, but half his output was published during 1660, and most of the remainder in 1661. Much of it was related to the politics of the time, either direct applications to the government or expositions of Quakerism intended for public consumption. His input to other writing that is characteristic of the early 1660s was small.

The writings of Isaac Penington followed a similar pattern, with the bulk in 1660–61, while much of the rest was connected with the Perrot controversy. Penington stood somewhat apart from the main body of Quakers, and was not closely involved with the men's meetings or other organization. He was by far the most polished Quaker writer of the time, and his works read better today than much seventeenth-century Quaker writing, but he may not have been as influential among his Quaker contemporaries as some other writers. He was not a trained theologian, but he could express Quaker beliefs in a distinctive fashion from his personal mystical viewpoint, and it is his mysticism that endeared him to later generations of Friends:

> When God begets life in the heart, there is the savour of it in the vessel, and a secret living warmth and virtue, which the heart in some measure feels, whereby it is known. Lie low in the fear of the most high, that this leaven may grow and increase in thee. This is the leaven of the Kingdom, this is it which must change the heart and nature, and make thy vessel . . . fit to receive the treasure of the Kingdom.[17]

In 1663, when the coming of the Kingdom of God on earth was still delayed, though yet a living hope, he wrote,

> The birth that is now raised is very inward and spiritual, even the seed itself; and its food is the life itself, even that which the earthly birth cannot feed on or digest; and the way and knowledge of life is very inward and spiritual, to cut off the earthly nature and spirit in its closest insinuations and transformings. The Lamb in his appearances this day is very hidden and retired, and none can see his paths and follow him, but such as receive of his present ointment, and feel the guidance of the opening of his eye in them. The Lord is bringing about great things, both inwardly and outwardly, happy are those whose hearts are prepared for them: for great misery, death and destruction is coming upon the earth.[18]

The most prolific Quaker writer of the years 1662–66 was William Smith, who spoke directly to the needs of the time, and, perhaps for that reason, is now forgotten. He was an Independent pastor from Besthorpe, a village between Lincoln and Newark, who came to Friends in 1658, and having transferred his allegiance he wrote from a Quaker point of view while retaining much of the outlook of a professional minister. He understood his work as to bring outsiders to the true faith and to nurture his own flock, and he was a gentle shepherd. His first pamphlet as a Quaker was published in 1658 as a reply to Henoch Howet's last book, *The Doctrine of the Light Within*. Despite the title of his pamphlet, *The Lying Spirit in the Mouth of the False Prophet made Manifest,* Smith answered Howet without misrepresenting his opponent's position or "railing," rare qualities in the Quaker controversial writings, and his final exhortation to Friends is

a good early example of the reflective mood that was coming over Quakerism as its first impetus died down.

> Love one another . . . watch over one another in the meek spirit, and
> be not rash to judge, but ready to admonish, that in love and unity all
> may grow in the measure of God and feel his increase. So all feed
> upon the bread which comes down from heaven, and drink of the
> water which is the living fountain, that you may feed upon that which
> is eternal, while the serpent feeds upon the dust. So in the light
> all dwell, that your hearts and minds may be kept clean and pure to
> the living God, that he may delight to dwell among you, and walk in
> you and have dominion, and reign, whose right it is, and no weapon
> formed against you shall prosper.[19]

William Smith went on to produce a continuous stream of writings until
his death in 1672, the majority of them in the early 1660s. He contributed
to most kinds of Quaker literature, addresses to the government, apocalyptic warnings, descriptions of sufferings, and controversy, but his best writings were epistles to his own meeting and expositions of the Quaker faith
for interested and sympathetic outsiders. Like most Quaker ministers, he
spent some time in prison during the 1660s, but in prison or at liberty, he
continued to write. He did not concern himself with the theological details
of precise relationship between Christ, the Light and the conscience, but
rather with pastoral care.

He wrote many epistles. One came from Nottingham gaol, "to be read
amongst Friends, when in the fear of the Lord they are met together in the
same Spirit." He dealt first with religious experience, which, he said, was
not in itself important. What mattered was the Spirit: "Though many experiences may be declared, which in themselves may be really true, yet at
the highest they are but effects wrought by the Spirit, they are to inform
the minds of all unto the Spirit." Quakers, he continued, were truly experiencing the Day of the Lord. Like Penington, and other Quaker writers, he
tried to show that despite the persecution Quakers really did know the
fullness of the Kingdom of the Lord in the here-and-now.

> And now the day is come that puts a difference between the precious
> and the vile; I do not say it is to come, and is not, but that it is come,
> and also coming . . . and therefore let all upright Israelites walk in the
> day that is come, for it is the day of the Lord, the day wherein the

Son's glory is revealed, whose coming hath caused the night to pass away, and many can say the night is over and gone, and the perfect day is come.[20]

On another occasion, he advised Friends considering marriage:

Run not forth in a hasty eager mind among yourselves, but wait that you may have clearance in the counsel of the Lord. . . . Look not at the sons or daughters of strangers, lest you become one with them, neither look at the world's riches among yourselves, but wait low in God's fear to receive his counsel in every such motion. . . . Let all Friends be exceeding careful in this weighty matter.[21]

Like many other ministers, he gave advice to Friends who might feel called to a similar service.

All you first-born of God, who are risen from the dead, and have received the love and grace of the Father . . . abide in the covenant . . . proclaim his message, keep in heavenly authority, then you will understand when the word of the Lord comes upon you, and when the message of life rises in you. . . . Let all who have received a gift to minister, and are but young in the exercise of it, be watchful in their calling.[22]

Some of his best writings were addressed to people who were not Quakers, whom he tried to lead to the light of Christ in their own consciences. The next quotation comes from a pamphlet written in the early Restoration days, to explain Quaker teaching. Several Quaker authors wrote on this theme, but Smith's pamphlet had his own distinctive flavor.

Whilst the Lord is visiting thee in tender mercy, harden not thy heart gainst him, nor reject his counsel, but be diligent, and ready to receive, and in the quietness of thy mind attend to the word near thee, which is in thy heart, and in thy mouth, that thou mayst obey it, and do it; for it is God's gift unto thee, and stands a witness for God in thy conscience; it is the life, and the life is the light, and the light breaking forth in thee, and making manifest the secrets of thy own heart.[23]

His major work in this genre is *Universal Love*, "An epistle dedicated to the measure of light and life in all people," in which Smith described the various duties of Christians, as parents, masters and dames of families, servants, aged people, people in government, ministers of the church, and people in all kinds of trade and profession, all the time gently directing the reader toward the Quaker understanding of these matters. It is a fine work of pastoral theology, calm and confident to a remarkable degree for a book written in a time of serious persecution.

As so often in publications of this time, he ended with a poem.

> Thou pure life, what is like unto thee?
> Thy path is peace, thy love is full and free:
> Thou art the chiefest good, thy beauty doth excel:
> Blessed are those that in thy bosom dwell.
>
> The fulness of thy springs doth satisfy the poor.
> The freshness of thy streams is always rich in store:
> The plant of thy own hand doth take deep root in thee;
> And thou supplies its tenderness, and sets it wholly free.
>
> Thou art both first and last, and there is not another.
> Who have true liberty in thee, they do not thy life smother;
> But in thy love they spring, and in thy power stand;
> And they rejoice in life and peace, and rest safe in thy hand.[24]

Researching the Quaker pamphlet literature is sometimes a tedious occupation, but discovering William Smith's writings was a delight.

17

METAMORPHOSIS

In the course of a few years, the Quaker movement changed from being one of the most radical of the sects that were looking for the coming of the Kingdom of God on earth, and became an introverted body, primarily concerned with its own internal life, while Quaker theological statements increasingly used the language of traditional Christianity. Several influences led to these developments, some being operative well before the Restoration. Quaker anticlericalism, combined with strict ethical standards, had soon attracted people of the type of Thomas Symonds (see Chapter 9), and many of the men who became leaders of the London meeting were well-to-do businessmen. Members of the gentry class, Margaret Fell, Gervase Benson, and Anthony Pearson, had been adherents from the early days. As a result, the damping-down of Quaker enthusiasm is noticeable from the middle 1650s, as quaking and other extravagant actions practically disappeared, and it was not long before the weight of Quaker opinion came down on the side of solid respectability. Later adherents such as John Crook, Isaac Penington, William Smith, and Thomas Ellwood powerfully reinforced this element.

The changes were accelerated after the Restoration. Quakers had shown during the middle 1650s, when their hope of the Kingdom of God on earth receded, that they could adapt to the current political situation. In the 1660s this capacity became necessary for mere survival. All the nonconforming religious groups that had existed during the Civil War period and that survived the next few years had to make an adaptation, and all were pushed away from the mainstream of British life, and onto their own resources. In one respect this was easier for Quakers, for they had always been looked on by the majority of their countrymen as pariahs, while Presbyterians, Independents, and Baptists had enjoyed respect and had taken part in local and national life. Quakers knew how to cope with persecution and intolerance, but the severity of the persecution in some places, the doubt of any favorable outcome, and the problems of maintaining a national organization, drove the meetings back on themselves, and their vision of the Kingdom of God on earth was reduced to something small, compact and local.

A main concern of Quaker authors was the preservation of their community, and this is evident in many of their writings. An epistle from John Whitehead written in August 1662, "to be read in their meetings," called for Quakers to separate themselves from the world: "And if contention, strife, warring or commotion do arise in the earth . . . dwell you in that power which has redeemed you out of the earth from amongst men . . . *that you may be unto God a peculiar people*. And therefore you shall not defile yourselves with this contention . . . let us sit down in that which keeps us holy and harmless, and separate from sinners."[1] Often, they now spoke of themselves as a faithful remnant, a term deriving from several Old Testament texts, especially such as Isaiah 11:11, and Micah 2:12. The first use of the term "remnant" for the Quaker flock seems to have come from Perrot in 1658, but it is common from 1660 onward.[2] Dorothy White saw the Day of the Lord as a time for rescuing the Remnant, "This is the acceptable day of the Lord God, wherein he is come to gather together his

Fig. 13 "The Quaker Meeting," mezzotint from a painting by Egbert van Heemskeerk, late seventeenth century. Although attempts have been made to identify the individuals in the painting, the figures are most probably caricatures, as was usual in van Heemskeerk's paintings of common life. His Quaker pictures usually include, as here, a gesticulating woman mounted on a tub or box. (Courtesy, Library Committee of the Religious Society of Friends, Britain Yearly Meeting)

Remnant, and to seek the lost sheep of the House of Israel." Thomas Taylor, in a similar apocalyptic work, saw Quakers as "a little Remnant of wheat among such a heap of chaff."[3]

Another example comes from 1665: "Though I say and do still believe that God has a remnant that he will preserve through it [the persecution] to bear witness to his name in a greater trial if it come; And doubtless there is yet a remnant that God will gather to himself, out of all the false ways of the world, and sandy foundations into the true way of God."[4] Later in 1665, in London during the Plague, the word "remnant" acquired a grimmer meaning, in George Whitehead's, *This is an Epistle for the Remnant of Friends and Chosen of God whom he hath yet preserved to bear their Testimony in and about the City of London.*

At the same time as the idea of the faithful remnant was developing, Quaker ideas of their relationship to other Christian bodies were changing, forced on them by the political situation. Toleration for all had not been a major concern of Quakers during the 1650s. Baptists and Levellers had called for universal toleration in the 1640s, but this had been gained, more or less, under the Protectorate. Respectable religious groups had toleration, and Quakers did not care to class themselves with fringe bodies such as Ranters and Fifth Monarchists. In the 1650s the Quakers understood themselves as the one true church, and they believed that ultimately, everyone would come to share their views. Their occasional calls for general toleration related mainly to themselves and to their hope for the triumph of Quakerism through the transformation of society according to their model.[5]

In Chapter 10, signs were noted that, around 1658, Quakers were beginning to recognize the rights of other Christian groups to exist, as churches. In 1659, *The Declaration of the People of God in scorn called Quakers to all Magistrates and People,* signed by John Crook and fourteen others "on behalf of ourselves and the rest of our friends who are of one heart and mind with us," harked back to the stance of those early revolutionaries who had called for liberty of conscience for all.[6] The changed political situation after the Restoration brought this to the forefront of Quaker thinking, for religious toleration was now the chief concern of all nonconforming bodies, especially after Venner's revolt.

Penington had written on this theme before the Restoration, in protest at the persecutions in New England, and went further than any other seventeenth-century mainstream Quaker, in his appreciation of the possibility of the spirit of God appearing in churches other than Quakers:

> It is not the different practice from one another, that breaks the peace and the unity, but the judging one another because of different practices. He that keeps not a day, may unite in the same spirit, in the same life, with him that keeps a day. . . .
>
> And O how sweet and pleasant it is to the truly spiritual eye, to see several sorts of believers, several forms of Christians in the school of Christ . . . performing their own peculiar service . . . and not to quarrel with one another about their different practices. . . . When I walked in the way of Independancy . . . I had more unity with . . . such as were single-hearted in other ways and practices of worship . . . than with divers of such, who were very knowing and zealous in that way of Independancy.[7]

A few months later, as a contribution to discussions about the Prayer Book, he wrote,

> Even in these our days, there was . . . an honest zeal and true sim-
> plicity stirring among the Puritans . . . which was of the Lord and
> very dear to him. . . . But departing from that into some form or
> other, the true simplicity withered. . . . Yet if there be any persons left,
> among any of the forms that have appeared . . . that have not lost
> their sincerity and true zeal towards God, them we own, and have
> unity with, so far as they . . . are kept thereto. If there be any among
> the Episcopal sort, that in truth of heart desire to fear the Lord, and
> look upon the Book of Common Prayer as an acceptable way of wor-
> shipping him, we pity their blindness, yet are tender towards
> them. . . . If there be any among the Presbyterians, Independants,
> Anabaptists, Seekers, or any other sort, that in truth of heart wait
> upon the Lord in those ways, and do not find a deadness overgrown
> there, but a pure, fresh, lively zeal towards God . . . our hearts are one
> with this . . . though in love to them we testify, that their former way
> of worship is their present loss and hindrance.[8]

These passages are given at length because, although often quoted by modern ecumenical Friends, they are not typical of the time. There is not a
great deal of difference between what Penington wrote in 1660 and the
sentiments that caused much trouble for John Perrot in 1662 when he
published *An Epistle for the most pure Unity and Amity in the Spirit and Life
of God: To all sincere hearted soules; whether called Presbyterians, Indepen-
dants, Baptists, Quakers, or Others, Under any other Denomination whatsoever, that desire that God's Truth and Righteousness and Power, may be exalted over all.*[9] Friends were coming to the idea that they were not
necessarily the sole representatives of the true church, but from Perrot this
was too much, and even Penington was not so outspoken again.

Nevertheless, other Quakers also published calls for freedom of worship,
and, even if grudgingly, admitted the right of others to their own views and
practices. This is one example:

> If it be a matter of conscience to one sort of people in this nation, or
> if it be supposed by them that the Book of Common Prayer or divine
> service so called, is the best way of worship, and that they suppose it
> well pleasing and acceptable to the Lord, and from such a persuasion

they do determine to practice it in their families, and in places of public worship, then let them that are so persuaded give liberty to others that are of another persuasion.[10]

Fox's view of the church remained as it always had been: "The Grace of God that brings salvation hath appeared to all men, which if all men minded it . . . would teach them to live righteously, soberly, and godly."[11] Nevertheless, he favored general religious toleration. One of several statements signed by Fox and others and entitled, *For the King and both Houses of Parliament*, includes the request "And let there be no persecution nor imprisonment of them that be in differences in their opinions in religions, which all profess the name of Christ, whose command is . . . that they should love their enemies." Stage-players had liberty to gather together, wrote Fox, so Quakers should have the same freedom. In another pamphlet Fox wrote that it was a sin against Christ to compel anyone against their conscience, "And let him be Jew, or Papist, or Turk, or Heathen, or Protestant, or what sort soever . . . let there be places set up where every one may bring forth his strength, and have free liberty to speak forth his mind and judgement." He went on: "If people be forced and driven contrary to their own consciences, gift and proportion of faith, to make ship-wreck of both, they go . . . into unreasonableness." But Fox always expressed such views in the context of expositions of the truth of the Quaker faith, rather than giving purely pragmatic reasons for toleration.[12]

Whatever their opinions of other churches, from 1660 Quakers frequently published declarations in favor of liberty of conscience, declaring that conscience should not, indeed cannot, be compelled in matters of religion. Edward Burrough called such an attempt "antichrist." Heretics should be admonished, and if necessary cast out of the flock, but he pointed out that there is nothing in the Bible about secular punishments for them. An official Quaker statement, *The Case of Free Liberty of Conscience*, was presented to the King and both houses of Parliament, and was a pragmatic call for freedom of conscience on practical grounds. Crook, Fisher, Hubberthorne, and Howgill, in *Liberty of Conscience Asserted*, found thirty reasons for liberty of conscience, notably that obedience obtained by force would not last, for it creates hypocrites, hardens people against what is imposed, is a matter of the wrath of men, not righteousness of God.[13] There is a shift here in the Quaker understanding of "conscience." In the 1650s it had been the seat of religious illumination, which could not err if properly attended to and would inevitably lead people to a Quaker point of view, but now they were prepared to allow rights of conscience to all kinds of unilluminated people, to accept the existence of a form of "invincible ignorance" that must be respected.

Calls for freedom of conscience continued throughout the period covered by this book and beyond. Richard Farnworth made this point in 1664: "To deny liberty of conscience in point of religion and worship of God to any persons or people, is to deny that right which is given and granted unto them by the Lord . . . it belongs to the Lord to . . . make known his worship both in matter and manner." Quaker practice, of course, was best, and he went on to show how it could be derived from the Bible.[14] A paper of 1665 even included the persecutors under the title "Christian." *For the King and both Houses of Parliament Why should Christians ruinate one another?* is a mildly worded paper asking the government to reconsider the case of those sentenced to banishment.[15]

Quakers and other dissenters now began to develop a certain fellow-feeling in distress, although there is more than a hint of *schadenfreude* in the following verse:

> Priest, thy fiery zeal has made a fool
> Of thee, that thou hast need to go to school
> To learn to plead with conscience 'gainst thy sin,
> Which thou so proudly long hast lived in;
> But now the time is come, when thou and I,
> May both in prison for our conscience lie
> And there may reason what the matter was,
> And how these things so strangely came to pass,
> That we together should so near be brought,
> That were so far asunder as we thought.[16]

Baptists and Quakers, in particular, became aware of common cause and were more reluctant to confront one another publicly. John Wigan, in 1665, expressed such thoughts from the Baptist point of view. After his controversy with Fox (see Chapter 7), and not trusting the Quakers to give a fair description of it, Wigan decided to publish his own account and set out his arguments properly, yet he doubted whether it was right to do so, for, he said, "it was suggested by some, that it was not a season to print against this people, being great sufferers, lest it should add affliction to their bonds."

George Whitehead had similar opinions, and in a doctrinal debate with

a Baptist, wrote that a Baptist teacher should not have started this controversy "at this day, when both he and we are in a suffering state and condition from our adversaries wherein we might rather have comforted one
another in our suffering, than added to one anothers grief and affliction by
fighting with one another before our adversaries, that would rejoice to see
us both destroyed that they might glory over us."[17]

This particular controversy was important for another reason. It was
noted at the end of Chapter 8 that some Quakers were beginning to recognize the need to express their faith in conventional Christian Protestant
terms, and that a pamphlet of George Fox the Younger, dated 1659, showed
the beginning of this tendency. George Fox the Younger died in 1661, but it
may be no coincidence that his close colleague, George Whitehead, was the
first person to write a Quaker statement covering Christian doctrine as a whole,
in a way that made a serious attempt to accommodate criticisms from
outsiders, and to show that Quakerism was compatible with mainstream
Christianity as it was understood in the seventeenth century.[18] Persecution and
the need to mend relations with other dissenting groups no doubt hastened the
trend. Whitehead, answering his Baptist adversary, had to reply to the accusation that Quaker belief in the Light led to denial of a real human Christ. This
was an old charge, and Whitehead picked his words with care, making a
separation between "the light within" and "Christ," while maintaining Arminian doctrine:

> We do not deny either the coming of Christ, or his suffering in the flesh
> . . . [reference to Romans 5:10 and 2 Corinthians 5:19]. We know and
> preach reconciliation through Christ's death, and salvation through his
> life, whose life is the light of men, and this is not any establishing of our
> own righteousness, as falsely we are accused; neither are we strangers unto
> the doctrine of justification by the grace of God through the redemption
> that is in Christ, whom God hath set forth as a propitiation through faith
> in his blood. But how are any justified by the grace of God whilst they
> deny the light within? For is not the light within the free gift of his grace,
> which hath appeared to all men and which by his righteousness hath
> come upon all men [reference to Romans 5:18 and Titus 2:11], which
> righteousness is received where the light of Christ within is obeyed, and
> be thereby made known to be a propitiation through faith in his blood.

Whitehead was clear on his understanding of the two natures of Christ:

> We own the true Christ according to the Scriptures, who according to the flesh was of the seed of Abraham and David, and according to the Spirit is declared to be the Son of God by the resurrection, and that he was the Word which was made flesh and dwelt in the disciples, and his death according to the flesh and his resurrection and ascension according to the Spirit of Truth we own.

This still leaves open the possibility of a spiritual resurrection and ascension rather than a physical one. Also, Whitehead did at one point employ the useful quotation from 1 Timothy 3:16 that Christ was "manifest in the flesh," leaving a possible doubt about Christ's humanity, but he came much closer to standard seventeenth-century theology than most Quaker writers. He continued, emphasizing that the light on its own did not give salvation: "The following of the light within thereby to attain unto righteousness, does not at all render the death of Christ vain, . . . for the saints walking in the light know the blood of Christ to cleanse them from all sin, and purified their souls in obeying the truth through the Spirit (1 Peter 1:22, 1 John 1:7)."[19] This is just a short selection from a solid and well-argued pamphlet. It is the first of a number of doctrinal statements, many part-authored by Whitehead, that followed in succeeding years and show a shift away from the emphasis on "the light within," and an attenuation of the meaning of "the light," together with a move toward finding an accommodation in points of conflict with other Christians.

The political circumstances of the 1660s, therefore, account for the withdrawal of Quakers into their own meetings, for the development of their recognition of other church bodies, and for the rethinking of their theology. Quaker preoccupation with their own church discipline, which can be traced back to very early days, also derived in part from political pressures, since they needed to show a united front to a hostile world and to create a strong structure that would withstand attacks from outside. It also arose from the nature of Quakerism itself. From very early days there was a conflict between the ideas of some free spirits and what the leaders thought acceptable. Limits had to be agreed on, and the case of Christopher Atkinson shows how little these limits were understood even by some trusted ministers. The disciplinary cases of the early years show the limits of Quakerism being defined, and the shock of the Nayler affair tipped the balance right over toward the construction of a strong corporate discipline, underpinned by a strong organization, a process that might well have been completed some years earlier if it had not been for the political upheavals and persecution of the Restoration period. The Quaker disciplinary system was not, in the event, to be completed without a struggle, for although Nayler, after 1656, gave no encouragement to his supporters, many of them were still present in the Quaker movement, blaming Fox for what had happened, and ready to take any suitable opportunity to cause trouble. Fox's abrasiveness made the conflict over John Perrot more acrimonious than it might have been, and was no doubt one cause of the prolongation of these particular arguments for so many years, but if Perrot had not existed, then, almost certainly, some other focus for dissatisfaction would have arisen. The battle between the centrifugal and centripetal forces within Quakerism was still to be resolved.

Dissatisfaction with the Quaker leadership was present in the London meetings at least from 1660. It was focused on Fox, as the most visible and the strongest personality, but Fox would have had little power if he had not been supported by leading London Friends, who included Gerrard Roberts, a goldsmith called John Boulton, and Gilbert Latey, a tailor who was one of the mainstays of the Quaker organization for much of the rest of the century. One of the leaders of the opposition was John Pennyman, a well-to-do self-made draper, who joined with Friends about 1658 and had a love-hate relationship with them for the rest of his long life. He wrote that "a great part of the Quakers had degenerated into mere form, and setting up G. Fox instead of the Spirit of Christ, to be their Lord and lawgiver." As a result, he and some other "sincere men" had diverged from the Quakers "about the year 1660," meeting together in the fields but still frequenting the "civil meetings," as he termed the men's business meetings, in order to help with works of charity, and to stand by Quakers in their sufferings.[20] Burrough, before his death, had noted the presence of dissidents at the men's meeting, and had warned that, "If any person out of the truth and of another spirit . . . come to the meeting, such are not members thereof."[21] There were probably a number of people connected with Quakers who would have preferred a looser organization and more tolerance of other points of view, including keeping on one's hat during prayer, but most of them are not known by name.[22]

Disaffection within the London men's meeting came to a head concerning a perceived conflict of interest between Ellis Hookes's duty to London Friends who paid his salary, and his duty to Friends in the country as a whole, a dispute that may have exacerbated the Perrot affair and vice versa. Some of the London Friends wanted to see all the accounts of sufferings that he had collected, and decide what to do with them, while Hookes took the view that the use made of these records was a matter for the Friends who had sent them in. Hookes was given notice to leave, but George Fox's authority, together with that of the leaders of the London meeting, was sufficient to overcome the rest of the

London men Quakers on that occasion, and no more was heard of Hookes's dismissal.[23] Two years later there was a similar incident.[24]

At the end of Chapter 15, it was shown that, by 1665, Quaker leaders were becoming seriously exasperated by the followers of Perrot, and in addition to the persistence of Perrot's ideas, the indiscipline within the London meetings was a further irritant. Fox was at this time imprisoned in Scarborough Castle and allowed no contact with Friends. No one knew when, or indeed if ever, he would be released, and the Quaker movement had to be managed without his advice. It fell to the Quaker leaders at liberty and within reach of London to take action.

In May 1666, a meeting was held in London, leading to the issue of a lengthy document that was signed by Farnworth, Parker, George Whitehead, and eight others. It is usually called, in short, "The Testimony of the Brethren," and its full title was "A testimony from the Brethren, who were met together at London in the Third Month [May], 1666, to be communicated to faithful Friends and Elders in their counties, by them to be read in their several meetings, and kept as a testimony amongst them." Having referred to "covert enemies . . . who are not afraid to speak evil of dignities, and despise government; without which our society and fellowship cannot be kept holy and inviolable," the Brethren made six points, summarized below.

First, they declared that they had "a true discerning of the working of that spirit, which under a profession of truth, leads into a division from, or exaltation over, the body of Friends, who never revolted nor degenerated from . . . the constant practice of good ancient Friends, who are sound in the faith which was once delivered unto us." Therefore, they declared, "neither that spirit, nor such as are joined to it, ought to have any dominion, office or rule in the church of Christ Jesus . . . but are rather to be kept under by the power of God." This was aimed at the Perrot faction and any other dissidents.

Second, these dissentients "have not any true spiritual, nor gospel authority to be judges in the Church . . . for of right the elders and members of the church, which keep their habitation in the truth, ought to judge matters and things which differ."

Third, giving final authority to the church business meeting, "if any difference arise in the church . . . we declare and testify, that the church, with the Spirit of the Lord Jesus Christ, have power (without the assent of such as dissent from their doctrines and practices) to hear and determine the same. And if any pretend to be of us, and in case of controversy, will not admit to be tried by the church of Christ Jesus, nor submit to the judgement given by the spirit of truth in the elders and members of the same; but kick against their judgement as only the judgement of man . . . then he or she . . . ought to be rejected, having erred from the truth."

Fourth, on the authentication of ministry, "If any go abroad hereafter, pretending to that weighty work and service, which either in life and doctrine grieves good Friends . . . then ought they . . . forbear going abroad and ministering till they are reconciled to the Church, and have approbation of the elders and members of the same."

Fifth, "And if any man or woman that are out of unity with the body of Friends, print . . . anything which is not of service for the truth . . . then we do warn and charge all Friends that love the truth . . . to beware . . . of having any hand in . . . spreading such books or writings."

Sixth, "We do advise . . . that such as are made overseers of the flock of God by the Holy Spirit . . . beware of admitting . . . such as are weak and of little faith, to take such trust upon them; for by hearing things disputed that are doubtful, such may be hurt themselves and hurt the truth. . . . We also advise that not any be admitted to order public business in the church, but such as are felt in a measure of the universal Spirit of Truth." This was important, controlling the appointment of overseers and giving the business meeting power to decide who should or should not be admitted.

The Brethren ended by hoping that their readers would be "one with us in your testimony on behalf of the Lord and his precious truth, against those . . . that reject the counsel of the wise men, and testimony of the prophets, whom God sanctified and sent among you . . . when you were gathered, and would not allow him liberty . . . to appoint a place wherein to meet together . . . but calls this formal, and the meetings of man."[25] This refers to the practice of some of Perrot's followers to insist that Friends should meet only when immediately inspired to do so.

This document marks the end of the early Quaker movement, and it epitomizes the nature of Quakerism for the next two hundred years. The grip of the leaders of the meeting on expressions of the Spirit, which had been implicit in every paper ever written by Quaker leaders on questions of discipline and organization, was formalized as never before. Given the need for discipline perceived and wanted by many Quakers, as a necessary outward expression of the corporate spiritual unity in which they believed, some such development was probably inevitable. The political situation, with the necessity of maintaining unity in the face of persecution, made the imposition of discipline more urgent.

Probably Farnworth was the author of the "Testimony of the Brethren."[26] The change in Quakerism between 1652 and 1666 cannot be better illustrated than by comparing Farnworth's youthfully enthusiastic tracts of 1653 with this cautious, legalistic document. It was Farnworth's last work for Friends; a month later he was dead of a summer fever. Friends published a testimony to his life, but his works were never collected. Perhaps the contrast between his early and late writings was too stark, or perhaps he was never quite forgiven for disappearing to the North for so many years after the Nayler affair.[27]

It is an understatement to say that the "Testimony of the Brethren" was not universally welcomed by Friends. It was regularly quoted by dissidents during internal disputes in later years, as a dreadful example of the lengths to which the Quaker establishment would go to maintain its authority. George Bishop, who had already protested about the tendency of London Friends to make arrangements without consulting the rest of the country (see Chapter 13, page 179) was particularly aggrieved. Whether he was merely piqued, or whether he seriously objected to the contents of the "Testimony," is not certain, but his response was "that it is much that they, so young, so very little in comparison of the body, or those whom they count elder, should take upon them to determine in things of so high a nature, etc., which if they are to be done, ought to be done by the full consent of those who are in authority in the church."[28] This use of the word "young" bears examination. Farnworth and Whitehead were considerably younger than Bishop in years, but Friends usually used terms such as "young" or "ancient" with reference to the length of time that somebody had been a solid and respected Quaker, as in the soubriquet "George Fox the Younger." Farnworth, Parker and Whitehead were not "younger" than Bishop in that sense, so possibly Bishop was ignoring them and concentrating on the supporting signatories.

It cannot be known whether the authors of the "Testimony," unsupported, would have had sufficient authority to enforce their proposals, and given the powerful opposition of George Bishop it is quite possible that their efforts would have led to the disintegration of the Quaker movement. In the event, they were not put to this test, for George Fox was released from Scarborough Castle in September 1666, on the first day of the Great Fire of London, and put his weight behind the new disciplinary measures, while Bishop died a year later and so was not a participant in the next round of internal disputes in the 1670s.[29]

Fox described his imprisonment in a letter to American Friends, "I have been incapable to write or receive writing a long time, or to speak or be spoken to, but have been a man buried alive, and the sepulcher watched with a sword and a gun, for else I should have written to you before now."[30] He traveled to London by gentle stages, and then set about putting heart into London

Friends, who had lost the Bull and Mouth meeting house and their offices with many documents, and probably their stock of books, in the fire, while many Friends had lost their homes. Shortly afterward, he arranged a meeting for Perrot's followers, many of whom returned to the main body of Friends. He then began to reorganize the British Quaker movement in such a way as to make possible the implementation of the "Testimony of the Brethren," providing a strong interlocking structure that would make it very difficult for internal dissent to take root, and that also would stand up to the persecution that continued sporadically into the next century.[31]

During the following years the Quaker movement was completely transformed. Fox overhauled the existing monthly and county meetings, founding new ones where necessary, and renaming the county meetings as Quarterly Meetings, a term already in use in some areas. He coined the phrase "Gospel Order" for the new arrangements. He persuaded Friends to set up women's business meetings alongside the men's, a cause of major controversy for many years. He ordered that careful records should be kept, and in many cases the minutes have been meticulously kept ever since. Many minute books start with a note that Fox was present at the first recorded meeting.

After the Great Fire and the loss of the Bull and Mouth, Friends needed new headquarters. They took rooms in a mansion called Devonshire House, in a part of the city that had escaped the fire, and it suited Friends so well that when the freehold came up for sale they bought it, and built premises that served as Quaker headquarters for 250 years. The London men's business meeting was reorganized, and the powerful Second Day Morning Meeting was set up in 1672. Consisting of leading London men Friends and visiting ministers, and having responsibility for publications, it acquired something of the function of a national executive. Meeting for Sufferings, so called because its original duty was to find legal means of mitigating Quaker suffering, followed in 1676. It survives, in an altered form, as the governing body of British Quakers between sessions of Yearly Meeting. A national meeting, the first since the Restoration, was held in 1668, repeated in most of the ten years following, and has been held annually since 1678.

It was not only the organization that changed. There were new Quakers and books of a new quality, including two major Quaker classics, William Penn's *No Cross no Crown* (1672) and Robert Barclay's *Apology for the True Christian Divinity* (1676). George Fox the Younger, Hubberthorne, Burrough, Fisher, and Farnworth were dead, Francis Howgill died in prison in 1669, and Dewsbury spent much of the rest of his life in prison. George Fox and Margaret Fell were still recognized as pre-eminent, but George Whitehead became increasingly influential, his cautious, careful, conservative nature being well suited to the new age, a leading figure in the shift toward theological orthodoxy and political respectability, that ultimately permitted the Quakers' inclusion in the Toleration Act of 1689.

The charismatic Quaker movement had gone, and was being replaced by the Religious Society of Friends.

APPENDIXES

I. Sources of Information for Early Quakerism

The *Journal* of George Fox

The first published edition was Thomas Ellwood's of 1694, which is reproduced in Fox's collected *Works*.[1] The so-called "Cambridge Journal," edited by Norman Penney, is an exact transcript with copious notes of the Spence manuscripts, volumes 1 and 2, thought to have been dictated by Fox to his son-in-law Thomas Lower in or about 1676. The pages dealing with the years before 1650 are missing. The standard edition has for long been that of John L. Nickalls (1952), but there is now a new transcript of the narrative portions of the Spence manuscript, edited by Nigel Smith and published by Penguin (1998).

When the *Journal* can be checked against other sources it is generally accurate on matters of fact, but there are caveats.[2] If one compares it with the *Short Journal*, which was written about 1664, there is a softening of passages likely to offend. In the *Short Journal* Fox wrote, "I was moved to tell ye man of ye house yt I was ye sonne of God," but in the corresponding passage in the *Cambridge Journal*, "ye" is replaced by "a" before "sonne of God".[3] Fox avoided mention of incidents that discredited Friends, practically eliminating James Nayler from Quaker history and omitting details of the scandal concerning Christopher Atkinson. He said little of the part played by Elizabeth Hooton in the foundation of Quakerism, while his accounts of the convincements of Richard Farnworth, James Nayler, and William Dewsbury are at variance with their own. He played down, probably because of the political situation in the 1670s, the active involvement of Friends in pre-Restoration politics. He described a number of healings that he performed, and quoted early instances of persecutors of Quakers coming to a bad end, but there is little contemporary evidence for these events.

For these reasons, the *Journals* need to be used with care as evidence for the 1650s, although they are essential for the early years of Quakerism, before mid-1652, for which contemporary evidence is rare or non-existent.

George Fox's *Epistles*

Most of the *Epistles* are only known from the edition of 1698, which has been reprinted in Fox's collected *Works*. There is no critical edition. The *Epistles* as published are probably a selection from a larger total, and it is not known how much the texts were edited prior to printing. Epistle 131 is one of a few that also exist in manuscript (Swarthmore MSS 2.95), and by comparing the two versions it can be seen that the epistle was drastically edited before publication. One epistle at least, number 47, has been wrongly attributed to Fox.[4] Some epistles known only in manuscript may have been omitted as not acceptable at the end of the seventeenth century. The collected edition of Fox's *Epistles* is therefore not reliable evidence for the full range of early Quaker belief, though their huge number is evidence for Fox's productivity.

Works of George Fox Partially Recovered by Henry J. Cadbury

The best known of these is George Fox's "Book of Miracles," which was reconstructed by Cadbury from a list of headings. This has been used by some writers as if it were good evidence for the performance of miracles by George Fox, but the "Book of Miracles" only provides evidence for belief, at a later date, that George Fox had performed miracles, and not of the actual performance of miracles.[5]

Cadbury also edited the "Annual Catalogue of George Fox Papers," a chronological listing of Fox's works dating from the later years of the seventeenth century. Many are now lost. As with the *Epistles*, this list provides evidence for the great literary productivity of George Fox, and for the respect his followers gave to his writings.[6]

Sewel's *History of the Quakers*, the Various "Testimonies for Friends," Memoirs, *First Publishers of Truth*, Besse's *Sufferings*, Etc.[7]

These originate from the later seventeenth or early eighteenth century, and were early attempts of Quakers to write their own history. Some, particularly the earlier memoirs and testimonies, have considerable historical value and some incorporate early material. However, since they were written from a later perspective, they can rarely be safely used to establish matters of Quaker faith and opinion before 1660.

Quaker Publications

Some thirteen hundred of these were printed in the period covered by this book, varying from single-page leaflets to substantial books. They provide contemporary evidence for the standard Quaker message, for the treatment meted out to Quaker preachers, and for the names of the leading apologists of the movement. Minority Quaker views are poorly represented.[8] Friends carefully preserved their books, and the collection in Friends House Library, London, is virtually complete.

Collected editions of the works of early Quaker writers that were compiled in the later seventeenth or early eighteenth centuries cannot safely be relied on. They are not necessarily complete and, without careful checking, one cannot be sure that passages unacceptable to the editor have not been amended. Many commentators have noted this fact, most recently Leo

Damrosch, who, in *The Sorrows of the Quakers' Jesus*, found extensive differences between the first and the collected editions of Nayler's writings. The
approach of early editors can be seen in Tract Volume 268 in Friends
House Library, which is a working copy of George Whitehead's works, with
marginal references made when a collected edition was being prepared.
Considerable alterations were planned.

Quaker books were first catalogued by John Whiting early in the eighteenth century, and a more extensive catalogue was produced in 1867 by
Joseph Smith. Some books listed, especially in Smith's catalogue, cannot be
found, and of these some may have been lost and some are probably double
entries or entered on the basis of unchecked reports.[9] The completeness of
Smith's and Whiting's catalogues can be checked to an extent by comparison with the *Catalogue of the Thomason Collection* and Wing's *Short-Title
Catalogue*, and a few books not listed by Smith have been found in this
way.[10]

Whiting did not list books by George Emmott, John Gilpin, John
Toldervy, or Anna Trapnell, but Smith did. This raises the question as to
whether Whiting, and before his time those earlier Friends who started the
Friends House collection, excluded works of doubtful orthodoxy by little-
known writers, who may have joined with the Quakers for a time and then
left or been disowned. However, of these four, only Toldervy was a Quaker
for long enough to write a Quaker book, and it is doubtful if Anna Trapnell should be counted a Quaker at all, so Whiting's judgment was probably correct. Whiting included Christopher Atkinson, George Keith, and
Anthony Pearson, who all left the Quaker movement, the first two doing a
good deal of damage. He omitted some lesser-known writers on the fringe
of Quakerism, authors of one or two obscure pamphlets that they had
printed themselves, and Smith found a few of these, but none is of great
importance.

The filtering would have been done at an earlier stage, when the decisions were made as to what should be printed at Friends' expense. There
are a few Quaker works published "for the Author," which may indicate
that they went beyond the limits of what Friends would officially acknowledge, although ultimately they were included in the list of Friends' books.
One example is Isaac Grayes's *One Outcry More against Tythes,* mentioned
in Chapter 5, which is listed by Whiting as a Quaker book.

It seems highly probable, therefore, that the list of Quaker publications,
as it is known at present, comprises an almost complete corpus of material,
which as a whole gives a good picture of the public face of Quakerism,
although undercurrents and minority views are under-represented.

Anti-Quaker or "Adverse" Publications

A catalogue of the anti-Quaker books, *Bibliotheca Anti-Quakeriana,* was compiled by Joseph Smith.[11] Some of these works exaggerate Quaker peculiarities and caricature their views, but others are valuable in providing a contemporary critique, and may indicate the existence of a more radical "fringe" Quakerism that was denied by the Quaker leaders. Many of these books give information as to those Quakers whose names and reputations were known to the general public. It is not possible to be certain of having a complete list of anti-Quaker works. A few that are not in *Bibliotheca Anti-Quakeriana* have been found, mostly by following references to "Quaker" in Thomason and Wing. A number of the books listed by Smith cannot be found in Wing, and are presumably lost.

Official and Other Non-Quaker Sources

These are official documents and news sheets that mention Quakers. They are an indication of public and official attitudes to Quakers and, like the anti-Quaker books, of names known to the public. A selection of State papers relating to Quakers has been collected and published, but may not be complete.[12]

Manuscripts[13]

There are thousands of relevant manuscripts, most of them in the possession of Friends House Library in London. The following descriptions cover those used in the preparation of this book.

The Swarthmore manuscripts are eight volumes containing some 1,400 letters, papers, and accounts. They were probably sorted by Fox when he was at Swarthmoor Hall (see Chapter 1, note 42 for the two spellings) in 1675–77, for a number of them bear his endorsements. They remained at the Hall with other manuscripts until the Swarthmoor estate was sold in 1759, since when most of them have come into the ownership of Britain Yearly Meeting. The "Letters of John Audland" have been referred to as Swarthmore manuscripts; they are copies made about 1680 of letters, mostly written by John Audland from 1653 to 1656, and include a copy of his travel journal of June–September 1654.

The A. R. Barclay manuscripts are a two-volume collection of 255 letters and other writings dating from 1651 to 1691, previously belonging to Abram Rawlinson Barclay, and used in the preparation of his *Letters of Early Friends*. The first 157 items were printed, imperfectly, in the *Journal of the Friends Historical Society* between 1930 and 1963.

The Caton manuscripts are three volumes of copies of early letters said to have been made by William Caton. Some of them are copies of letters also known from the Swarthmore collection, and Caton has in some cases smoothed the language of the original. Volume 2, once in the possession of Boswell Middleton (c 1668–1763) is sometimes known as the Middleton MSS.

The Spence manuscripts volumes 1 and 2 comprise the original manuscript of Fox's Journal, and volume 3 consists of 162 letters and papers, mainly relating to Margaret Fell. They were also originally at Swarthmoor Hall, passing successively to the Abraham and Dodgson descendants of Margaret Fell, and in 1861 to the Spence branch.

The Thirnbeck (sometimes known as Grace) manuscripts consist of thirty items, 1654–1720, being letters to or by members of the Fell family. Two are important for the early period: (1) Margaret Fell's epistle setting up the Kendal Fund; and (2) from John Lilburne to Margaret Fell.

The John Penington manuscripts are four volumes of copies of Isaac Penington's papers, made by his son John.

The Crosse manuscripts are a volume of copies of some eighty letters and papers, 1661–71, mostly relating to the Perrot controversy, and apparently put together by Edmond Crosse, a supporter of Perrot.

Other Named Collections

There are some other less important collections relating to the early period. I have followed up some references but not systematically searched them. One interesting volume, the Samuel Watson MSS, consists of copies of Friends' papers said to have been made by a Yorkshire Friend, Samuel Watson, and started in 1654 during his imprisonment in York Castle.

Portfolios 1–42. These are miscellaneous papers dating from the seventeenth to the twentieth century. They were bound in their present form during the first thirty years of the twentieth century, but the arrangement into groups is in some cases considerably earlier. I have some references to portfolio MSS, but have not investigated further.

The main collections have been calendared and microfilmed and in part transcribed, but no doubt new discoveries could still be made in the small collections and portfolios that are rarely searched.[14] As regards the reliability of the manuscripts, it is necessary to allow for bias in letters connected with Swarthmoor, certainly a bias toward George Fox and Margaret Fell, and probably a bias against Nayler. Most of the correspondence that was carried on directly between Friends in other parts of the country, bypassing Swarthmoor, has not survived. Some London records were lost in the Great Fire, and for this and, maybe, other reasons, the annual numbers of surviving letters diminish after 1657. Therefore, in using the Quaker manuscript collections, as when using Fox's collected *Works*, one should be aware of what may be missing.

II. Research Methods

This book developed from a Ph.D. dissertation that was an attempt to bridge the divergence between the theological and historical approaches to the study of early Quakerism, which at that time had reached a situation described by one commentator as "historiographical schizophrenia."[1] It seemed possible that the varied ideas about the nature of early Quakerism that had been put forward, at different times and by different scholars, were in part the result of biased selection of source material. I therefore attempted to design a survey that would not impose any preconceived notions on the material. I hoped in this way to throw light on some of those aspects of early Quakerism that were especially in dispute, notably the importance of the political element in early Quakerism that had been identified by Christopher Hill and others, and the related question of George Fox's position within the Quaker leadership before 1660.

What was required was something of the nature of a public opinion poll, to find out how early Quakers came to decisions and whose advice they most respected, to gather their opinions on a wide range of subjects, and to estimate how widely and how strongly the different views were held. These questions are of the kind "How much?," "To what extent?," and "What is the relationship?" In dealing with such questions, which are at least partly quantitative, the information-handling power of a computer database is particularly useful.

Since the questions at issue included the position of George Fox, and differences between the Quakerism of the 1650s and its later forms, Fox's *Journal,* his printed *Epistles,* and all other sources of information that did not belong to the 1650s would have to be treated as suspect.[2] The most complete body of material relating to early Quakerism, as described in Appendix I, is the pamphlet literature. It is an advantage to deal with a complete, or nearly complete, corpus when attempting research with a quantitative element, for missing material may lead to results being skewed in ways difficult to evaluate. The pamphlets provide contemporary evidence for the Quaker message as it was officially proclaimed, for the treatment meted out to Quaker preachers, and for the names of the leading apologists of the movement. The inbuilt bias, that the publications reflect the views of the Quaker establishment and of the more articulate Quakers, mostly men, is not a critical defect provided one is aware of it, and to some extent it can be counteracted by the use of evidence from other sources.[3]

I compiled a list of Quaker books of the 1650s, a year at a time, with author and most probable date.[4] Since I finished my dissertation, a list of Quaker women authors, by Rosemary Foxton, has been published, and when I checked my list against Foxton's, I found that she listed five books by women authors that I had missed.[5] This suggests that the number of books by male authors that I did not find is probably in double figures, but with such small numbers one cannot make a reliable estimate. It is unlikely that they include anything of great importance. Even if these possible unknown books are by fringe authors with a different outlook from mainstream Quakerism, it is quite certain that they made no stir when written. Mainstream Quakers were very quick to answer what they regarded as heresy.

I decided that my unit for counting would be the tract as published, irrespective of length or number of contributing authors. This is what interested members of the public would pick up from the bookstall, or have put into their hands. In cases of multiple authorship, clear differences of opinion or approach by different authors, if any, could be noted, while a short succinct pamphlet may be more influential than a long and tedious book. Some prolific authors would be heavily represented, but this would approximate to their importance in the public eye, and their position within the Quaker movement could be counterchecked from other sources.

If a tract was reprinted it was obviously influential and important, but not necessarily twice as important as another. In the end, I made the rather arbitrary decision that reprints in the year of original publication would not be counted, and that reprints in subsequent years would be listed, but tagged so that they could be identified and used as seemed appropriate. A preliminary study was made of ten early pamphlets, eight by Quakers and two by opponents, and a list made of all themes mentioned, a total of forty-one. These were combined according to type until they were reduced to seven general ideas. Ideally, this work should have been repeated by another person to reduce the risk of observer bias, that is, my personal interests and preconceptions, creeping in and affecting results. It was not possible to guard against this entirely.

A questionnaire was then constructed. The normal questionnaire of a modern pollster, with cross-checks to determine the truth of responses, was of course out of the question; the pollster, that is, myself, not only had to put the questions but also to find the answers. The questions were put to the publications, as if they were being put to the authors, and answers extracted as far as possible from their own words. Most of the pamphlets are short, so it was not difficult to find representative quotations. Longer pamphlets posed more of a problem, but, fortunately, most of them are extremely repetitive. Again, it would be excellent if somebody, sometime, repeated this exercise.

These are the seven thematic questions, in no special order, with cross-references to the chapters in this book where the answers now appear.

1. *How is salvation effected for the individual?* (Chapters 6 and 8). This was mainly concerned with the Quaker experience and its consequences for belief, including their conception of God and the work of Christ.

2. *What is the eschatological standpoint?* (Chapters 5 and 13). This question looked for evidence as to whether the "end-times" were thought to be present or beginning, or to be wholly in the future, or to be both present and future, and for evidence as to the nature of the "end-times" as conceived by Quakers.

3. *How does the publication regard the Church, the saved community?* (Chapters 1, 10, and 11). This was concerned both with positive views, the nature of the Quaker community, and with negative views, what was considered to be wrong with the established church and other religious groups.

4. *What does it say about the conduct of worship?* (Chapter 11). As with question 3, this included both positive and negative aspects, the Quakers' reasons for disagreeing with conventional forms of worship, and any information about the conduct of their own meetings, including business meetings.

5. *What use is made of the Bible, and what view is taken of the Bible?* (Chapter 4).

6. *What does it say about the way of life of believers?* (Chapters 9 and 12). This included all personal consequences of becoming a Quaker, that is, rules of conduct and their likely consequences, and, for some individuals, the call to public witness.

7. *Does it have anything to say about government and civil law?* (Chapters 5 and 13). This covered appeals to the government and army authorities on behalf of Quakers, and anything relating to political issues. In the course of the study it became clear that the Quakers' eschatology varied according to their current relations with the government, so that in the book as finally written most of the material relating to questions 2 and 7 was combined in the same chapters.

There were three further questions. The first asked the purpose of the publication, and was answered from the title-page, the "Epistle to the Reader" (if any) and from a general overview. The most numerous group consisted of tracts proclaiming the Quaker faith. In the earlier years most of these were attacks on the established church, combined with an apocalyptic proclamation of the Quaker faith, but presently they began to modulate to more measured descriptions of Quakerism. There were also numbers of accounts of disputes with opponents, descriptions of Quaker sufferings, and addresses to the government.

A further question inquired about particular key words, if any, and was used to estimate the importance of words such as light, conscience, covenant, and truth. The final question asked if there was anything special to be noted, not covered by the other questions, about this particular tract.

Thus there were ten general information categories in the eventual computer data files, seven concerning themes and three concerning purpose and style. In addition to bibliographic data, this was as much as could be conveniently handled. The questionnaire was tried out, using the tracts of 1652–54 for a pilot study. If necessary, the questionnaire could then have been refined before proceeding further, but no problems arose. Many tracts provided little useful information, and with experience I learnt what to look for. Therefore, when I came to extend the study to 1666, I did not complete questionnaires for every tract, but simply listed and classified them, noting points of importance. This may have resulted in some loss of detail, but probably not to a serious degree.

The Quaker manuscripts could not be treated in the same way because they do not form a complete, discrete body. The risk of built-in bias in the manuscript collections, resulting from the interests and opportunities of the various collectors, was noted in Appendix I. I used the manuscripts for background information, particularly on personal relationships and discipline, but was cautious in drawing general conclusions from them. I made full use of calendars and transcriptions where available, as width of coverage was important, and this may have led to some minor errors and loss of detail. I noted the main purpose of each relevant document, and also made notes on a further nine possible categories, leadership, church organization and mission, disputes, publications, political and social attitudes, personal conduct, and finally theology. When I came to work on the 1660s I found less relevant manuscript material.

When I started this work I had not realized the value of the anti-Quaker books as a source of information, particularly by providing information as to the Quakers whose names and reputations were best known to the general public, and highlighting the objections to Quakerism that pressurized Quakers into refining and developing their ideas. I checked as many as possible of the adverse books, but they were not numerous enough to require full computer database treatment. This source of material practically disappears after 1660.

Since the object of the study was to throw light on Quaker thought rather than on historical detail, I did not attempt fresh work on other possible sources of information.

My study involved counting occurrences of ideas, and working out the relations between them, and there was little information available about the use of computers for this purpose. A contributor to the Proceedings of the Association for History and Computing wrote of his "creation of a number of small specialized databases each fulfilling limited objectives. These files are simply computerized cardboxes, with the advantages of rapid sorting and record linkage which a computer gives."[6] I decided to limit myself to "computerized cardboxes." To avoid loss of information, complete words and phrases were entered into the database rather than symbols, and in consequence the statistical conclusions that could be drawn were limited. By keeping each individual data file small it was possible to inspect it by eye, so that information as to the importance or otherwise of a particular theme, and of the people associated with it, could easily be extracted.

The leading Quakers, their varying ideas, and their interrelationships could be discerned in the Quaker correspondence, and by references in publications, both Quaker and anti-Quaker. The subjects that most concerned Quakers could be discovered mainly from their publications, but also from letters and anti-Quaker works. The possible existence of a "fringe" Quakerism could be estimated from correspondence and from anti-Quaker books. The development of Quaker organization could be followed in correspondence and to some extent in Quaker publications and in references in State papers. As these topics were considered year by year, a three-dimensional model of early Quakerism was built up, showing variations in Quaker ideas with respect to particular people and to time, and a picture of changing Quaker faith and practice was gradually developed.

III. Table of Publications

Year	Quaker Books		Classification					Authors			Anti-Quaker Works	
	Total Books	Women[a]	Q	D	G	S	E	Men	Women	3 Main Authors[b]	Known	Extant
1652/3	36	1	23	6	7	11	1	19	3	Farnworth 13 / Fox 11 / Nayler 9	14	10
1654	61	0	29	18	13	6	1	18	0	Fox 15 / Nayler 14 / Farnworth 8	16	13
1655	91	7	51	38	10	13	3	38	7	Nayler 15 / Farnworth 9 / Parnell 6	34	28
1656	85	7	47	23	7	11	0	39	7	Fox 18 / Nayler 12 / Burrough 8	41	38
1657	81	5	43	17	11	11	3	35	4	Fox 22 / Burrough 14 / Hubberthorne 4	23	20
1658	88	3	41	25	7	8	5	45	3	H. Smith 12 / Fox 11 / Burrough 10	18	11
1659	194	20	59	32	59	23	3	54	14	Burrough 21 / Fox 15 / Nayler 10	35	27
1660	191	16	79	25	49	17	18	57	8	Fox 28 / Penington 13 / Burrough 10	39	33
1661	118	6	62	6	33	10	11	44	5	Fox 14 / Perrot 11 / Burrough 9	7	6
1662	90	12	38	10	16	16	17	39	9	D. White 7 / H. Smith 6 / W. Bayly 5 / Perrot 5	6	4

III. Table of Publications (continued)

Year	Quaker Books		Classification					Authors			Anti-Quaker Works	
	Total Books	Women[a]	Q	D	G	S	E	Men	Women	3 Main Authors[b]	Known	Extant
1663	102	8	49	3	16	5	28	46	8	W. Smith 10 W. Bayly 7 Fox 7	5	4
1664	85	5	14	7	28	16	21	43	2	W. Smith 12 Farnworth 7 4 with 4 each	6	4
1665	65	7	17	5	11	7	19	31	6	T. Green 4 Howgill 4 Several With 2 each	4	4
1666	30	3	13	1	3	2	7	16	1	Fox 4 Margaret Fell 3 Several with 2 each	0	0

NOTES: Reprints are not included. These figures should be understood as best approximations. Apart from the possibility of error, no two people would agree on all the doubtful cases. Especially in the case of lost adverse books, whose existence is deduced from Quaker replies, it is impossible to make more than a guess at dating them. Some of the works answered by Fox in *The Great Mistery* cannot be even tentatively identified, and are not counted here. A few undated works to which not even a probable date can be assigned are omitted.

The Classification is derived from that in the statistical appendix to *Early Quaker Writings*, but it is simpler, and the pamphlets have been re-checked and re-counted. Abbreviations:

Q = Expositions of the Quaker faith for the general public. These changed considerably in content during the period covered.
D = Doctrinal disputes.
G = Addressed to the Government or other authority.
S = Descriptions of Quaker Sufferings.
E = Epistles to the Quaker faithful.
Some publications have more than one author, and some are classified under more than one heading.

[a]Number of books with a woman as author or joint author
[b]The three leading authors of the year, according to the number of books of which they were sole or joint author, with the number of books involved.

NOTES

List of Abbreviations

ARB   A. R. Barclay MSS, Friends House, London.

BA-Q   Joseph Smith, *Bibiotheca Anti-Quakeriana* (London: Smith, 1873).

BDER   Richard L. Greaves and Robert Zaller, eds., *Biographical Dictionary of English Radicals*, 3 vols. (Brighton: Harvester, 1982–84).

BQ   William C. Braithwaite, *The Beginnings of Quakerism* (1st ed., London: Macmillan 1912; 2d ed., revised by Henry J. Cadbury, Cambridge: University Press, 1955).

Cal.   M. A. Green, ed., *Calendar of State Papers*, Domestic Series, 1650–1665, 13 vols. (London: Longman, 1857–1972).

Caton   Caton MSS, Friends House, London

CJ   George Fox, *The Journal of George Fox*, 2 vols., ed. Norman Penney (Cambridge: Cambridge University Press, 1911).

CR   A. G. Matthews, *Calamy Revised* (Oxford: Clarendon Press, 1934; reissued 1988).

DQB   "Dictionary of Quaker Biography," Friends House, London; Haverford College, Pennsylvania.

EQL   Geoffrey F. Nuttall, "Early Quaker Letters," typescript 1952, in Quaker and other major libraries.

EQW   Hugh Barbour and Arthur Roberts, eds., *Early Quaker Writings* (Grand Rapids, Mich.: William B. Eerdmans, 1973).

ESP   Norman Penney, ed., *Extracts from State Papers Relating to Friends, 1652–1672* (London: Headley, 1913).

FF   H. Larry Ingle, *First among Friends: George Fox and the Creation of Quakerism* (New York and Oxford: Oxford University Press, 1994).

FPT   Norman Penney, ed., *First Publishers of Truth* (London: Headley, 1907).

JFHS   Journal of the Friends Historical Society
LEF   A. R. Barclay, ed., *Letters of Early Friends* (London: Harvey and Darton, 1841).
NJ   George Fox, *The Journal of George Fox,* ed. John L. Nickalls (Cambridge:
            Cambridge University Press, 1952).
QFP   Quaker Faith and Practice: The Book of Christian Discipline of the Yearly
            Meeting of the Religious Society of Friends (Quakers) in Britain (London: The
            Yearly Meeting, 1994).
QPE   Hugh Barbour, *The Quakers in Puritan England* (New Haven: Yale University
            Press, 1964; reprinted Friends United Press, 1985).
SJ   George Fox, *Short Journal and Itinerary Journals of George Fox,* ed. Norman Penney
            (Cambridge: Cambridge University Press, 1925).
SPQ   William C. Braithwaite, *The Second Period of Quakerism* (1st ed., London:
            Macmillan, 1919; 2d ed., revised by Henry J. Cadbury, Cambridge University
            Press, 1961).
Smith   Joseph Smith, *Catalogue of Friends Books,* 2 vols. (London: Smith, 1867).
Spence   Spence MSS, Friends House, London.
Sw.   Swarthmore MSS, Friends House, London.
Thomason   *Catalogue of the Thomason Collection* (London: British Museum, 1908).
Wing*   Donald Wing, *Short-Title Catalogue of Books . . . , 1641–1700,* 2d ed., 3 vols.
            (New York: Modern Languages Association, 1978–88).
Works   George Fox, *The Works of George Fox,* 8 vols. (Philadelphia: Gould, and New York:
            Hopper, 1831). Reprinted with new introductions and edited by T. H. S. Wallace
            (State College, Pa: New Foundation Publications, George Fox Fund, 1990).
WTUD   Christopher Hill, *The World Turned Upside Down* (London: Temple Smith, 1972;
            Penguin, 1991).

Unless otherwise stated, early books were printed in London, and manuscripts are kept in
the library of Friends House, London.

*The letter and number in the citation of each early book is the Wing reference number.

Chapter 1

1. Thomas Edwards, *Gangraena or a Catalogue . . . of the Errors, Heresies of the . . .
Sectaries of this Time,* 3 parts (London: Smith, 1646), E228, part 1, 34. See also Ephraim
Pagitt, *Heresiography* (London: Lee, 1645), P174. The 5th edition of 1654, P180, mentions
Quakers.

2. For accounts of this movement, see Alistair Hamilton, *The Family of Love* (London:
James Clarke, 1981), and Christopher W. Marsh, *The Family of Love in English Society,
1530–1630* (Cambridge: Cambridge University Press, 1994).

3. Notably the anonymous *Theologica Germanica,* and the works of Jacob Boehme,
Nicholas of Cusa, Sebastian Franck, and Hans Denck. The translator was John Everard,
preacher and teacher. See Theodor Sippell, *Werdendes Quäkertum* (Stuttgart: Kohlhammer,
1937), 1–34.

4. The standard work on the position of Quakers in the spectrum of seventeenth-
century religion is Geoffrey F. Nuttall, *The Holy Spirit in Puritan Faith and Experience*
(Oxford: Basil Blackwell, 1946; reprinted with new introduction by Peter Lake, Chicago
University Press, 1992). Also see Melvin B. Endy Jr., "Puritans, Spiritualists and Quakerism:

An Historiographical Essay," in Richard S. Dunn and Mary Maples Dunn, *The World of William Penn* (Philadelphia: University of Pennsylvania Press, 1986) 281–301.

5. For the continued use of the English Prayer Book, see John Morrill, "The Church in England 1642–1649," in Morrill, ed., *Reactions to the English Civil War* (London: Macmillan, 1982).

6. For Baptist and Quaker relations, see Ted Leroy Underwood, *Primitivism, Radicalism, and the Lamb's War: The Baptist-Quaker Conflict in Seventeenth-Century England* (New York and Oxford: Oxford University Press, 1997). For possible early contacts between Fox and Baptists, see H. Larry Ingle, *First Among Friends* (hereafter cited as *FF*), 31.

7. Christopher Hill, *The World Turned Upside Down* (hereafter cited as *WTUD*), 184–96; J. F. McGregor, "Seekers and Ranters," in J. F. McGregor and B. Reay, *Radical Religion in the English Revolution* (Oxford: Oxford University Press, 1984), 121–29; Douglas Gwyn. "Joseph Salmon, from Seeker to Ranter and Almost to Quaker," *Journal of the Friends Historical Society* (hereafter cited as *JFHS*) 58, no. 2 (autumn 1998): 114–16.

8. George Fox, *Journal*, 1st ed., ed. Thomas Ellwood (London: Sowle, 1694); also vols. 1 and 2 of *The Works of George Fox*, 8 vols. (hereafter cited as *Works*). *The Journal of George Fox*, 2 vols., ed. Norman Penney (hereafter cited as *CJ*), is a transcription of the original manuscript. *CJ* 1:xxxiv–xxv, gives the probable date of compilation of the *Journal* as 1675–77, and Joseph Pickvance, *A Reader's Companion to George Fox's Journal* (London: Quaker Home Service, 1989), 147, suggests 1674–76.

For the making of Ellwood's edition, see Henry J. Cadbury, "The *Editio Princeps* of Fox's Journal," *JFHS* 53 (1972–75): 199–218. *The Journal of George Fox*, ed. John L. Nickalls and with introduction by Geoffrey Nuttall (hereafter cited as *NJ*), is the edition most generally used. The new edition, *George Fox: The Journal* (London: Penguin, 1998), ed. Nigel Smith, is a transcript of the narrative parts of Spence MS vols. 1 and 2. The *Short Journal* (hereafter cited as *SJ*) was written while Fox was imprisoned in Lancaster Castle in 1663–64.

9. *NJ* 27.

10. First printed in Fox's *Epistles*, no. 10, part in *CJ* 2:338, *NJ* 709. William C. Braithwaite, *The Beginnings of Quakerism* (London: Macmillan, 1912; rev. ed. Cambridge: Cambridge University Press, 1955), 42. This book, hereafter cited as *BQ*, is still essential for detailed facts, and never likely to be superseded. See also Henry J. Cadbury, *Narrative Papers of George Fox* (Richmond, Ind.: Friends United Press, 1972), 1, for a similar note from about 1690.

11. Material for Fox's early life derives from *NJ* 1–9 (where the meeting with Hooton is dated early 1647). See also the "Testimony of George Fox concerning Elizabeth Hooton," 1690, Portfolio 16.74, extracted in *Quaker Faith and Practice: The Book of Christian Discipline of the Yearly Meeting of the Religious Society of Friends (Quakers) in Britain*, hereafter cited as *QFP*, 18.02. See also *NJ* 43, for another mention of Elizabeth Hooton, 1600–72. Emily Manners, *Elizabeth Hooton* (London: Headley, 1914) is informative, but underrates Hooton's early importance.

12. *FF* 27–28; for Fox avoiding the army draft, 35; for a probable identification of this Pickering, who was one of those Baptists who objected to oaths, 297.

13. From *Oxford English Dictionary*.

14. The fragment of Oliver Hooton's lost "History" was copied onto a scrap of paper, probably in 1686–87; MS Portfolio 10.42. Transcribed Manners, *Elizabeth* Hooton, 4. All manuscripts referred to in this book are held at Friends House Library, London, unless otherwise stated.

15. *NJ* 11.

16. *CJ* 1:10. Quakers were uncertain about the status of these people. Early records include a note that the Rhys Jones group had once been enlightened but had turned from the light

(Samuel Watson MS 81), and a note in Fox's handwriting on Portfolio 10.42 that Rice Jones was one of the chiefs of the Baptists and that his followers were never called Quakers or Children of Light. The final reference to the group appears to be William Smith's account of dealings with them in 1669, *A Few Words unto a Peculiar People*. See *CJ* 1:396.

17. The term "Rump" was actually coined in 1659. See Ronald Hutton, *The Restoration: A Political and Religious History of England and Wales, 1658–1667* (Oxford: Oxford University Press, 1986), 88.

18. A contemporary guide to the subject of tithe is William Sheppard, *The Parson's Guide: or the Law of Tithes* (Lee, Pakeman and Bedell, 1654), S3204. See *FF* 47, for tithe agitation.

19. See George H. Sabine, ed., *The Works of Gerrard Winstanley* (New York: Cornell, 1941), introduction, esp. 74; Christopher Hill, *The Religion of Gerrard Winstanley* (Oxford: Past and Present Society, 1978), 57; W. S. Hudson, "Gerrard Winstanley and the Early Quakers," *Church History* 12/13 (September 1943): 177–94, is an early approach to the subject. Richard T. Vann, "From Radicalism to Quakerism: Gerrard Winstanley and Friends," *JFHS* 49 (1959–61): 41–46.

20. There is an extensive literature on mid–seventeenth-century sects. Among the more important works are *WTUD*, and other books by Christopher Hill; McGregor and Reay, *Radical Religion in the English Revolution*; A. L. Morton, *The World of the Ranters* (London: Lawrence and Wishart, 1970); Nigel Smith, *Perfection Proclaimed: Language and Literature in English Radical Religion 1640–1660* (Oxford: Clarendon Press, 1989); Christopher Hill, Barry Reay, and William Lamont, *The World of the Muggletonians* (London: Temple Smith, 1983); J. C. Davis, *Fear, Myth and History: The Ranters and the Historians* (Cambridge: Cambridge University Press, 1986), and the debate that followed, Davis, "Fear, Myth and Furore," *Past and Present*, no. 129 (1990): 79–103.

21. For these and others, who flourished from 1649, see Richard L. Greaves and Robert Zaller, *Biographical Dictionary of English Radicals*, 3 vols., hereafter cited as *BDER*.

22. Abiezer Coppe, *Selected Writings* (London: Aporia, 1987); Roger Crab, *Dagons Downfall* (originally printed 1657; reprinted, Aporia Press, 1990, ed. Andrew Hopton), 42.

23. *NJ* 39–40. Nickalls has conflated the Ellwood *Journal* version with an extract from manuscript Portfolio 36.172.

24. The Blasphemy Act of 1650 required magistrates to proceed against any who maintained "him or her self . . . to be very God, or to be Infinite or Almighty, or in Honor, Excellency, Majesty and Power to be equal, and the same with the true God, or that the true God, or the Eternal Majesty dwells in the Creature and nowhere else." See C. H. Firth and R. S. Rait, *Acts and Ordinances of the Interregnum*, 3 vols. (London, 1911). An account of the trial was published in 1654 in the anonymous *Answer to a Book which Samuel Eaton put up to the Parliament*, together with a copy of the mittimus, or charge-sheet, and is the only contemporary record of Friends' message as it was in 1650. The mittimus was included in Fox's *Journal*; see *NJ* 52. Eaton was a well-known Separatist minister; see *BDER*, and A. G. Matthews, *Calamy Revised* (Oxford: Clarendon Press, 1934; reprinted, 1988), hereafter cited as *CR*.

25. Hooton's imprisonment is mentioned in Joseph Besse, *Collection of the Sufferings of the Quakers*, 2 vols. (London, 1753), i.137. Her letter to the mayor of Derby is Swarthmore MSS (hereafter cited as Sw.), 2.43.

26. Fox, *The Great Mistery of the Great Whore* (Simmons, 1659), F1832, 109, in *Works*, 3:196: "And the first nicknamer of the Quakers that ever I heard, was a corrupt justice in the year 1650, whose name was Gervase Bennet, in Derby. He was the first that ever named the people of God Quakers, though the mighty power of the Lord had been known years before." See also *CJ* 1:4; *NJ* 58; *SJ* 5. Martha Kate Peters, "Quaker Pamphleteers and the

Development of the Quaker Movement, 1652–1656 (Ph.D. diss., University of Cambridge, 1996), 132–40, discusses the spread of the term. I would agree that it was the usual word at the time to apply to such charismatics, but I do not think the Quakers welcomed it. *BQ* 58 n. 1 for earliest known use of the term in print.

27. For Rhys Jones' visit, see *CJ* 1:10 and *NJ* 63. *CJ* 1:16–17 and *NJ* 73 record the visit of a man from Selby in Yorkshire while Fox was in prison in Derby.

28. Sw. 1.373, Thomas Aldam to George Fox, July 1652; Geoffrey F. Nuttall, "Early Quaker Letters," hereafter cited as EQL.

29. For Thomas Aldam, 1616–60, see memoir by his son, Thomas Aldam Jr., *A Short Testimony concerning that faithful Servant of the Lord Thomas Aldam* (London: Northcott, 1690), and Geoffrey F. Nuttall, *Studies in Christian Enthusiasm* (Lebanon, Pa.: Pendle Hill, 1948), "Moral Enthusiasm: Thomas Aldam"; also "Dictionary of Quaker Biography" (hereafter cited as DQB), and *BDER*.

30. Richard Farnworth, c. 1630–66, see Geoffrey Nuttall, "Notes on Richard Farnworth," *JFHS* 48 (1956): 80, and "Didactic Enthusiasm: Richard Farnworth," in Nuttall's *Studies in Christian Enthusiasm, BDER*. A letter from Fox of 1652 (Sw. 2.55) asked Farnworth to return letters that Fox had written to him during his Derby imprisonment, and is evidence for their early acquaintance.

31. Richard Farnworth, *The Heart Opened by Christ* (1654), F485, 3, 8. For seventeenth-century spiritual autobiography, see Owen C. Watkins, *The Puritan Experience* (London: Routledge and Kegan Paul, 1972), 160–79, for Quakers.

32. William Dewsbury, *The Discovery of the Great Enmity of the Serpent against the Seed of the Woman* (Calvert, 1655), D1264, from his personal story, 16–17. See also *BQ* 59–61; *QFP* 19.05, 19.45.

33. James Nayler, 1618?–60. The most recent study and the best on Nayler's thought is Leo Damrosch, *The Sorrows of the Quaker Jesus: James Nayler and the Puritan Crackdown on the Free Spirit* (Cambridge, Mass.: Harvard University Press, 1996). William Bittle, *James Nayler, the Quaker Indicted by Parliament* (York: Sessions; and Richmond, Ind.: Friends United Press, 1986) is good for the constitutional aspect of Nayler's trial, less satisfactory otherwise. See also Geoffrey Nuttall, *James Nayler, a Fresh Approach* (London: Friends Historical Society, 1954), and the chapter on Nayler in Nuttall's *Studies in Christian Enthusiasm*; James Mason, *James Nayler and the Protectorate* (York: Longman, 1980), in the Longman Case Studies in History series, though intended for children, is an excellent introduction. A new popular biography by Vera Massey, *The Clouded Quaker Star: James Nayler, 1616–1660* (York: Sessions, 1999), is based on secondary and incomplete sources, but is useful in that the two older biographies of Nayler are long out of print. These are Mabel Richmond Brailsford, *A Quaker from Cromwell's Army: James Nayler* (New York: Macmillan, 1927) and Emilia Fogelklou, *James Nayler: The Rebel Saint*, translated from the Swedish by Lajla Yapp (London: Benn, 1931). The transcript of Nayler's examination at Appleby, from *Saul's Errand to Damascus*, is reproduced in Hugh Barbour and Arthur Roberts, *Early Quaker Writings* (Grand Rapids, Mich.: William B. Eerdmans, 1973), hereafter cited as *EQW*, 260–61. For Nayler's letters, see Geoffrey F. Nuttall, "The Letters of James Nayler," in Michael L. Birkel and John W. Newman, eds., *The Lamb's War, Quaker Essays to honour Hugh Barbour* (Richmond, Ind.: Earlham College Press, 1992), 38–75.

34. Hill, Lamont, and Reay, *The World of the Muggletonians*, esp. 23–42, 111–53, for the character and personality of Lodovick Muggleton.

35. Quaking is frequently mentioned in the early Quaker correspondence that was preserved from the late summer of 1652.

36. Hooton's imprisonment is known from references in letters, one from Aldam, A. R. Barclay MSS (hereafter cited as ARB) 16.

37. David Boulton, *Early Friends in Dent* (Sedburgh: Dales Historical Monographs, 1986), 24, and *FF* 81–83.

38. DQB, *BQ* 91–92 *FF* 82, 99.

39. *CJ* 1:40–44; *NJ* 104–10. For John Audland, 1630–64, and Francis Howgill, 1618–69, see DQB, *BDER*.

40. Hugh Barbour, *The Quakers in Puritan England* (New Haven and London: Yale University Press, 1964; reprinted with a new preface by the author, Friends United Press, 1985), 72–84. Hereafter cited as *QPE*.

41. Norman Penney, ed., *First Publishers of the Truth* (hereafter cited as *FPT*) (London: Headley, 1907), 242, 244, referring to Sedbergh and Preston Patrick meetings. These congregations are often called "Seekers," a term that derives mainly from William Penn's preface to Fox's *Journal*. Fox himself called them "Separated." Boulton, *Early Friends in Dent*, 21, considers that these small congregations may have been survivors of Laud's purge in the 1630s, who then had to flee from Royalists in the 1640s, but says that more work needs to be done on their origins. Christopher Hill, *The Experience of Defeat* (London: Faber and Faber, 1984), 130, suggests that these groups probably retained some of their original traditions after being swept up by the Quakers, thereby adding to the diversity of early Quakerism.

42. Roger Brerely, Brierley, or Brearley, 1586–1637, Antinomian, emphasized the Holy Spirit. See *BDER* and Nuttall, *Holy Spirit*, 178–80. For John Camm, 1605–58, partner of John Audland in the Quaker ministry, see Craig W. Horle, "John Camm, Portrait of a Quaker Minister," *Quaker History* 51, no. 2 (1970): 69–80, and vol. 52, no. 1 (1971): 3–15.

43. For Margaret Fell, 1614–1702, see Bonnelyn Kunze, *Margaret Fell and the Rise of Quakerism* (Stanford: Stanford University Press; and London: Macmillan, 1993), and Isabel Ross, *Margaret Fell, Mother of Quakerism* (London: Longmans, 1949). Note the spelling "Swarthmoor." It is "Swarthmore" for the College, the manuscript collections, and the Monthly Meeting, but nowadays "Swarthmoor" for the Hall, and also for the local Quaker Recognised Meeting.

44. *BQ* 36–37, Spence MSS (hereafter cited as Spence), 3.24.

45. An adequate study of Margaret Fell's religious position awaits a full examination of her letters in the Spence vol. 3. Elsa Glines, who is working on an edition of Fell's letters, kindly sent me transcripts of several important letters on which I have based my estimate of Fell's religion. For a suggestion that Margaret Fell was known in radical religious circles before the summer of 1652, see H. Larry Ingle, "A Letter from Richard Farnworth," *Quaker History* 79, no. 1 (spring 1990): 35–38.

46. See, e.g., *WTUD* 234–35.

47. ARB 70.

48. Sw. 1.372 (EQL 3); see also Sw. 3.45 (EQL 13), for another letter of general advice from Farnworth. This is Barclay's *Letters of Early Friends* (hereafter cited as *LEF*) 121; *LEF* 122 and 123 are similar, originals for these not found by me.

49. Sw. 3.58 (EQL 12, which does not mention this passage), November 1652.

50. Samuel Watson MSS, postscript on p. 129 to a document that begins on p. 126.

51. Sw. 3.3 and 3.67 (EQL 8), November 1652, note use of both "thou" and "you." See Nuttall, "The Letters of James Nayler." There were several early Quakers called Myers; see DQB.

52. Sw. 3.65 (EQL 11), November 1652. See also Chapter 3, note 28, p. 255.

53. Fox, Epistle 14; see *BQ* 133n. For Fox's *Epistles* as evidence for early Quaker thinking, see Appendix 1.

54. *CJ* 1:187; *NJ* 215. The bound collection of pamphlets is described in John Stalham *Contradictions of the Quakers* (Edinburgh, 1655), S5184.

55. For Burrough, see E. Brockbank, *Edward Burrough* (London: Bannisdale, 1949), and DQB, *BDER*.

56. For Hubberthorne, see E. Brockbank, *Richard Hubberthorne* (London: Friends Book Centre, 1929), and DQB, *BDER*. See also Chapter 14, note 8, p. 284.

57. Richard Hubberthorne, *A True Testimony of Obedience to the Heavenly Call* (1654), H3239, 2; *EQW* 155–60. See also Sw. 4.4, 3.1 (EQL 1, 2), June 1652, Hubberthorne to Fox and Fell.

58. ARB 71, Aldam to Fox, after May 1652, concerning printing arrangements of four books that Farnworth had sent to him, and Farnworth to Fell, Sw. 3.45 (EQL 13), December 1652.

59. Fox and Nayler, *Saul's Errand to Damascus* (Calvert, 1653), F1894; *The Querers and Quakers Cause at the Second Hearing* (Nathaniel Brooke, 1653), Q163, and Francis Higginson, *A Brief Relation of the Irreligion of the Northern Quakers* (1653), H1953, which was an answer to *Saul's Errand*. Higginson (d. 1673) was the vicar of Kirkby Stephen.

60. *Querers and Quakers*, 39, 44. The Malton incident is described in Sw. 1.373 (EQL 4), a letter from Aldam to Fox in July 1652.

61. Higginson, *Irreligion*, 2, 3, 6, 18; *Querers and Quakers*, 12–49.

62. Pagitt, *Heresiography*, 5th ed. (1654), 143.

63. For examples of unpopular persons or groups being accused of popery, see Robin Clifton, "The Popular Fear of Catholics during the English Revolution," *Past and Present*, no. 52 (August 1971): 23–55; and Ian Y. Thackray, "Zion Undermined: The Protestant Belief in a Popish Plot during the English Interregnum," History Workshop no. 18 (autumn 1984): 28–52.

Chapter 2

1. The nature of the relationships between the various leaders of the primitive Quaker movement is a subject of debate. W. C. Braithwaite, writing in 1911 on the situation at the end of 1654, wrote, "Fox, Farnsworth and Dewsbury exercised real leadership" (*BQ* 137). His omission of both Nayler and Fell is typical of the older understanding of Quaker history. Christopher Hill (*WTUD* 231) thought that it was not clear whether Fox was the Quaker leader in the 1650s. Melvin B. Endy (*William Penn and Early Quakerism* [Princeton: Princeton University Press, 1973], 54ff.) thought that Fox was just one among several other leaders, most of whom had arrived at a Quaker position before meeting Fox. Barry Reay, in *The Quakers in the English Revolution* (London: Temple Smith, 1985), 8, considered that in the 1650s Nayler, Farnworth, Dewsbury, Hubberthorne, and Burrough were all as influential as Fox. Certainly, they were all at least as well known as Fox to the general public, but all of them, with the possible or probable exception of Nayler, were under Fox's general direction. More recently, the pendulum has swung back toward Fox with the publication of Richard Bailey's *New Light on George Fox and Early Quakerism: The Making and Unmaking of a God* (San Francisco: Mellen, 1992), which looked at the evidence that Fox was treated by his followers as divine, and with H. Larry Ingle's *First Among Friends* (*FF*), which shows Fox as consistently the leader and planner. Both Bailey and Ingle acknowledge the importance of Nayler, but only Ingle, of all these authors, gives sufficient weight to Margaret Fell. I query Ingle's suggestion (*FF* 85–89) that Nayler and Fell were effectively Fox's appointees, as it is not certain that long-term plans for the Quaker movement were so far advanced in mid-1652. There may rather have been a process of ad hoc development, as the talents of individual Quakers became clear. It is clear, however, that the joining together of a number

of small northern churches in 1651–52, thereby providing the critical mass that permitted the later Quaker expansion, was largely due to the influence of Fox.

2. Sw. 3.75 (EQL 93). For Rhys Jones, see Chapter 1, page 7.

3. See especially the series of letters that Nayler wrote to Fox in the summer of 1653, Sw. 3.64, 3.2, 3.62, 3.60, 3.61, 3.59 (EQL 26–31).

4. Sw. 4.130 (EQL 33), September 1653, where Nayler is twice mentioned before Fox.

5. Included in Nayler, *A Discovery of Faith* (Calvert, 1653), N270, 14.

6. ARB 159, probably 1654.

7. Spence 3.125. See other good examples of Margaret Fell's style in Spence 3:144–46, 138–39, and 155.

8. Thirnbeck Mss. 1, Margaret Fell: "To all my dear brothers and sisters."

9. Caton MSS (hereafter cited as Caton) 3.160, probably early 1654; Spence 3.7, November 1654.

10. In the first instance by Bonnelyn Kunze, "The Family, Social and Religious Life of Margaret Fell" (Ph.D. diss., University of Rochester, New York, 1986). In the abstract Kunze wrote, "Fell's work in early Quakerism has been fettered by a hagiographic approach that fails to define her roles and influence precisely."

11. Farnworth to Fell, Sw. 4.83 (EQL 20), January 1653; Sw. 4.46 and 47 (EQL 25), June 1653; and Farnworth to Fox, Sw. 3.53 (EQL 34), October 1653.

12. ARB 15, quoted *EQW,* 473.

13. *CJ* 141; *NJ* 174. *CJ* gives the number as "seventy," referring to Luke 10:1 and 17. Editor Ellwood changed this to the less contentious "sixty."

14. Information scattered in many letters, and in *FPT.* See *FPT* 208, for a Seekers' group as the origin of a Quaker meeting in Sussex.

15. Phyllis Mack, *Visionary Women: Ecstatic Prophecy in Seventeenth-Century England* (Berkeley and Los Angeles: University of California Press 1992) is a wide-ranging study of women, Quakers and others, in the Civil War sects and in the Restoration period. Christine Trevett, *Women and Quakerism in the Seventeenth Century* (York: Sessions, 1991), covers the same period from a more explicitly Quaker angle.

16. Ralph Farmer, *The Great Mysterie of Godlinesse and Ungodlinesse* (S.G. for Ballard, 1655), F441, introductory epistle to Thurloe, Cromwell's Secretary of State. See John Audland, *The Innocent delivered out of the Snare* (Calvert, 1655), A4196, for reply to Farmer.

17. Endpiece by Fox to Farnworth's *Message from the Lord to all who despise the Ordinances of Christ* (1653), F491A. For the importance of the printed pamphlets in the early Quaker movement, see Peters, "Quaker Pamphleteering."

18. Sw. 3.39; *BQ* index, "Quaker Literature, Censorship," also Thomas O'Malley, "Press and Quakerism, 1653–1659," *JFHS* 54 (1976–81): 169–84, in which several examples are given of Fox being asked to check books.

19. See Kate Peters, "Patterns of Quaker Authorship, 1652–1656," in Thomas N. Corns and David Loewenstein, *The Emergence of Quaker Writing: Dissenting Literature in Seventeenth-Century England* (London: Frank Cass, 1995), 1–24, and esp. 14–16. See Appendix 1 for occasional exceptions to the rule.

20. Caton 3.62, 66, ARB 21.

21. John Audland's Journal in "Letters of John Audland" MS.

22. Caton 3.62 and *LEF* 5, p. 18, Howgill to Robert Widders. Original not found.

23. Caton 3.160; "Letters of John Audland," 10. Anne Audland was one of the most forceful ministers. See Anne Audland, *The True Declaration of the Suffering Innocent* (London: Calvert, 1655), A4195; *BQ* 199; Trevett, *Women and Quakerism,* 71, 98, 117, 150. See also Sw. 3.93, Sw. 3.192, and ARB 161.

24. Sw. 3.82 (EQL 274); ARB 38.

25. Epistle 116, 1656; Sw. 4.1 (EQL 65), May 1654.

26. ARB 161. The two Quakers concerned were Thomas Castle and Elizabeth Williams, in gaol at Stafford. See *BQ* 159 and note.

27. Giles Calvert (d. 1663), printer, bookseller, and leading publisher of spiritual and radical writers, including Collier, Saltmarsh, Dell, Erbury, Coppe, Hugh Peters, Winstanley, and many counted as Ranters. See *BDER* and Altha E. Terry, "Giles Calvert: Mid–Seventeenth-Century Bookseller and Publisher" (M.A. thesis, University of Columbia, 1937, summarized in "Giles Calvert's Publishing Career," *JFHS* 35 (1938): 45–49; entry on Calvert in Henry R. Plomer *Dictionary of Booksellers and Printers, 1641–1667* (London: Bibliographical Society, 1907). See Spence 3.7, Willan to Fell, November 1654, for his financing of Quaker ministers.

28. Sw. 1.162, Parker to Fell, July 1655.

29. Sw. 1.3 (EQL 98), Thomas Killam to Margaret Fell. Swannington is in Leicestershire between Coalville and Ashby-de-la-Zouche. See *FF* 47, 300 n. 22, for the probable identification of the host as Edward Muggleston, a well-to-do farmer and noted tithe rebel.

30. *BQ* 177–78, refers to *CJ* 1:151 and 424 n. 2; Thurloe, *A Collection of State Papers of John Thurloe*, 7 vols. (London: 1742) iii.94, 116, reprinted *JFHS* 8 (1911): 148–50, records the presence of the printer Giles Calvert. See also Sw. 1.7 (EQL 114), Audland to Fell, on the presence of Ranters. Bauthumley, counted as a Ranter, was a pantheist, author of *The Light and Dark Sides of God* (1650), condemned for blasphemy (*BDER*).

31. *QPE* 58 and 58 n. 55. The discussion would have concerned the development of the existing system rather than, as Barbour suggests, its inauguration.

32. For instance, John Jackson, *Strength in Weakness* (London: Maycock, 1655), J78B, 34, asked that the private letters between him and Nayler might be "publickly manifested before . . . any or all the children of the light, that they might impartially give evidence to the plainess, or obscurity, which will appear to be in the same." By "children of light" Jackson meant persons considered to be faithful Christians. Ingle in *First among Friends* (*FF*) overuses the term, which he always writes as "Children," or "Children of the Light." Quakers did not often refer to themselves as "Children," and overall, "Children of Light" is probably commoner than "Children of the Light."

33. *BQ* 179–81, referring to *CJ* 1:161–62.

34. For more detail on this period, see *BQ* 180–240, *FF* 134–41.

35. See William Beck and T. Frederick Ball, *The London Friends Meetings* (London: Bowyer Kitto, 1869). A later hotel of the same name on this site is marked by a plaque on the wall in St Martin-le-Grand.

36. Sw. 3.22 (EQL 106); "Letters of John Audland," John Audland's Journal.

37. Fox and Nayler, *Several Papers* [1653] F1903, "Epistle to the Reader" by A. P., presumed Parker.

38. See, for example, Pagitt, *Heresiography,* 136. Nayler and Fox called "the chief Quakers"; Fox, Hubberthorne, and Thomas Atkinson, *Truths Defence against the Refined Subtilty of the Serpent* (York: Thomas Wayte, 1653), 56, referred to an opponent who knew Fox; Thomas Weld, *The Perfect Pharisee* (London: Tomlins, 1654), 27, described Fox as "their grand master," and in *A Further Discovery of that Generation of Men called Quakers* (Gateshead: S. B., 1654), showed knowledge of both Fox and Nayler.

39. *BQ* 560, citing British Museum Pamphlets no. 636.

40. Note especially such letters as Sw. 4.234 (EQL 124), February 1655, Caton and Parker to Fell, where it is unclear whether Fox or the Lord is meant; and Caton 3.91, May 1655, Parker to Fell concerning Fox's visit to London, when he was doing his best to gloss over problems regarding Fox's reception by London Friends.

41. Caton 3.149, June 1656, Audland to Fell; Sw. 1.81 (EQL 300), August 1656, Henry Fell to Margaret Fell.

42. James Parnell, 1636–56, considered by Quakers to be their first martyr; *BQ* 189–93.

43. ARB 120 and 123, February 1655, printed in *JFHS* 48 (1957): 126–30.

44. John Wilkinson and John Story gave their names to a major revolt against George Fox later in the century, the so-called Wilkinson-Story Separation. See W. C. Braithwaite, *The Second Period of Quakerism* (hereafter cited as *SPQ*), 290–323; and *FF* 252, 261–64.

45. ARB 28, April 1655, printed in *JFHS* 31 (1934): 55.

46. Henry Fell (no relation to Margaret as far as is known, but from the Swarthmoor household) to Thomas Rawlinson, before taking ship for Barbados in August 1656, Sw. 1.42 (EQL 305).

47. Caton 3.110, from Hubberthorne; Sw. 1.310 (EQL 186), Anne Cleaton to Fell, October, probably 1655; Spence 3.8, presumed from Fell, to Friends, probably 1655.

48. For Taylor on Lancelot Wardell, Sw. 1.278, 282 (EQL 290, 298), July and August 1656; Wardell's defense, Sw. 1.284 (EQL 318); Holme to Fell in May and June 1656, Sw. 1.203 (EQL 262), Sw. 3.32 (EQL 263), Sw. 1.205 (EQL 276), and Sw. 1.204 (EQL 281). Thomas Holmes, c. 1627–66, married Elizabeth Leavens, who had been attacked by students and then whipped at Oxford in 1654 (*BQ* 158 and Hubberthorne *A True Testimony of the Zeal of Oxford Professors* [1654], H3240). For Thomas Holme, see Nuttall, *Studies in Christian Enthusiasm*, part 4, "Emotional Enthusiasm."

49. Spence 3.41, undated. See *CJ* 1:245–46, 1656, giving Humphrey Norton's letter of complaint.

50. Barry Reay, *Quakers in the English Revolution,* 8, considered Hubberthorne a leader of similar status as Fox, but this ignores Hubberthorne's emotional dependence on Fox.

51. Salthouse, 1630–91, had been a member of the Swarthmoor household (DQB). Judge Fell still looked after his interests when he was imprisoned in Exeter; see Sw. 1.112 (EQL 236), February 1656, Salthouse to Fell, telling Margaret that Judge Fell had asked if they needed anything, but they did not.

52. For Bishop, see Maryann Feola, *George Bishop: A Seventeenth-Century Soldier turned Quaker* (York: Ebor Press, 1996).

53. Caton 3.92, Parker to Fell, May 1655; Sw. 1.255 (EQL 181), Willan to Fell, September 1655.

54. Samuel Fisher, *Rusticus ad Academicos* (Wilson, 1660), F1056.

55. Thomas Curtis 1630?–1712, and Ann, 1631?–1703, cared for Fox during his illness in 1659, see Chapter 13, page 170. They were involved in the Wilkinson-Story Separation of the 1670s, and therefore did not receive their due in Fox's *Journal* (DQB).

56. John Crook, J.P., 1617–99, was a wealthy gentleman and a leading Friend over a long period (DQB). For early meetings at Crook's house, see Sw. i:161 (EQL 140), Parker and Howgill to Fell, April 1655; Henry J. Cadbury, ed., *Letters to William Dewsbury* (London: Bannisdale, 1948), 43, no. 19, John Whitehead to Dewsbury, November 1655, and several references in *BQ*.

57. George Bishop and others, *The Cry of Blood* (Calvert, 1656), B2990.

58. For effectiveness of Quaker censorship in the middle of the decade, see Thomas O'Malley, "The Press and Quakerism," *JFHS* 54, no. 4 (1979): 169–84, esp. 172, where he refers to this letter, Sw. 1.277 (EQL 288), July 18, 1656, Lancelot Wardle to Fell.

59. Further details *FF* 126 and 126 n. 45.

60. Discussed in works of Christopher Hill, Barry Reay, and others, esp. Reay, *The Quakers and the English Revolution,* 20–26. Richard Vann, *Social Development of Early Quakerism 1655–1755* (Cambridge, Mass.: Harvard University Press, 1969), 50–57, deals with the social background of the earliest Quakers, but is otherwise less applicable to the very early period.

61. Dewsbury, *The Mighty Day of the Lord is Coming* (Calvert 1656), D1271, was written for colonists, and printed on light-weight paper. Burrough, *A Description of the State and*

Condition of All Mankinde (1657), B5998, was intended for "the dark parts of the world, among those called heathens."

62. Sw. 4.77 (EQL 282), Edmondson to Fell, June 1656. See Kenneth Carroll, "Quakerism and the Cromwellian Army in Ireland," *JFHS* 54, no. 3 (1978): 135–54. William Edmondson, 1617–1712, was the founder of Irish Quakerism, a soldier who settled in Ireland in 1652, and heard Nayler speak when on a visit to England the following year (DQB, *BQ* 210–11).

63. William T. Hull, *The Rise of Quakerism in Amsterdam*, Swarthmore College Monographs no. 4, 1938, and *Benjamin Furly and Quakerism in Rotterdam*, ditto no. 5, 1941, are solid comprehensive studies, but more material may now be available. A fresh study is needed by someone able to access both Dutch and German sources. For Italy, see Stefano Villani, *Tremolanti e Papisti: Missioni Quacchero nell'Italia del Seicento* (Rome: Edizione di Storia e Letteratura, Uomini e Dottrine 3).

Chapter 3

1. An example of a letter praising Nayler's ministry is Sw. 4.88 (EQL 157), John Killam to Margaret Fell. See Chapter 1, page 20, for Higginson.

2. Caton 3.64, about July 1655, Burrough and Howgill to Fell.

3. Sw. 3.80 (EQL 195), November 1655.

4. Caton 2.4, May 1655, Richard Nelson to Nayler, quoted *BQ* 243.

5. Jeremiah Ives, *Quakers Quaking* (Cottrell, 1656), I1103, 9–10, and *Innocency above Impudency* (Cottrell, 1656), I1028–29. Ives, fl. 1646–74, was a General Baptist Preacher and former Leveller, a London box-maker and cheesemonger (*BDER*). Bailey, *New Light*, 144, and Bittle, *James Nayler*, 102, think that Nayler needed a sign to prove himself equal to Fox, that and his failure with Ives may have precipitated the events that followed. However, there are several other records of Quakers being challenged to perform miracles and no drastic consequences followed. See Chapter 10, pages 131–32, for miracles as a sign of the true church.

6. Sw. 3.82 (EQL 274), and also Sw. 4.137 (EQL 280), from Dewsbury to Fell

7. See Chapter 1, note 32, for literature on Nayler. Trevett, *Women and Quakerism*, 29–41, and Phyllis Mack, *Visionary Women* (Berkeley and Los Angeles: University of California Press, 1992), 197–206, look at the parts played by Martha Simmons and others. Bailey, *New Light*, esp. 137–78, considers the influence of the affair on Quaker development. *FF* 140–49 relates the story to the life of Fox. Authorities do not always agree with each other.

8. There is an informative article by Kenneth L. Carroll, "Martha Simmons, A Quaker Enigma," *JFHS* 53 (1972): 31–52.

9. Martha Simmons, *A Lamentation for the Lost Sheep of the House of Israel* (Calvert, 1655), S3791, 5, 6. She wrote three tracts during 1655 and 1656.

10. Cadbury, ed., *Letters to William Dewsbury*, 40, no. 18.

11. Donald Lupton, *The Quacking Mountebank or the Jesuit turned Quaker* (E.B., 1655), L3493, 19. Other tracts that mention her are Matthew Caffyn, *The Deceived and Deceiving Quakers Discovered* (Smith, 1656), C206, 19; and Christopher Wade, *Quakery Slain Irrecoverably* (1657), W159, 12.

12. *BQ* 144–245, and likewise *QPE* 63, and John Punshon, *Portrait in Grey* (London: Quaker Home Service, 1984), 75. There are other examples in Trevett, *Women and Quakerism*, 29–30.

13. Caton 3.116, Hubberthorne to Fell, August 26, referring to an earlier letter from Howgill on the same subject.

14. William Markey coll. MSS, Friends House, 120. The Bible reference is to Matthew 25:32–33.

15. Burrough, *Trumpet of the Lord Sounded out of Sion* (Calvert, 1656), B6048, 25: "To all you who say you want, or believe for the Coming of Christ to Reigne in Person upon Earth."

16. Caton 3.118, Caton to Fell, January 1657.

17. Martha Simmons, Hannah Stranger, Nayler, "WT," *O England thy time is come,* S3793, 5, 7. Presumably written late 1656, as it refers to Nayler's imprisonment at Westminster.

18. See, for instance, George Bishop and others, *The Cry of Blood*, esp. 49, 98, 116.

19. Burrough and Howgill to Fell, Caton 3.73, probably early 1655, with reference to London, "many precious women which every week are stirring abroad and getting meetinges," and, with reference to Ireland, ARB 176, March 1656, where Elizabeth Fletcher and Elizabeth Smith are described as "noble and serviceable."

20. For example, Sw. 4.163 (EQL 334), November 1656, Arthur Cotton to George Fox, rather apologetic about Cornish Friends preference for men. In this instance it may have been his own wife rather than Martha Simmons who occasioned this prejudice (see Chapter 4, page 57, for Priscilla Cotton).

21. Mack, *Visionary Women*, 197, considers that Simmons was disciplined for attempting to dispute with male ministers, conduct not permissible in a woman. There is no real evidence for this. "Speaking in her will" would be ministry considered out of order. Quakers were not expected to argue with leading ministers or elders on any matter of substance; note the fate of Collinson (Chapter 10, pages 133–34, and note 24, p. 275) and the furor caused by Isaac Penington (Chapter 15, pages 200–203). Quakers differed in this respect from other separated churches, where public dispute with ministers was a normal practice.

22. Fogelklou, *James Nayler*, 149, thinks that Nayler went through a period of vacillation rather than breakdown. Bailey, *New Light*, 143, thinks that he was in a trance preparing for what lay ahead. Damrosch, *Sorrows of the Quaker Jesus*, 131–32, notes that Nayler had some kind of collapse and that, as always in this story, it is difficult to find out exactly what happened. Contemporary descriptions in Bishop, *The Throne of Truth Exalted over the Powers of Darkness* (Calvert, 1657), B3008; Ralph Farmer, *Sathan Inthron'd in his Chair* (Thomas, 1657), F444; Nayler's own description of his "hour of darkness and temptation," in *To all the people of God* (written 1658), N320, 2; and the concerned correspondence of various Friends in the summer of 1656 are all compatible with mental disturbance. See, e.g., the following letters to Margaret Fell, all written during August 1656: Sw. 3.86 (EQL 306), August, from John Braithwaite; Sw. 3.12 (EQL 307), William Rawlinson; Caton 3.61, Howgill and Burrough; Caton 3.116, Hubberthorne.

23. Ingle considers that Fox deliberately delayed the meeting, perhaps because he was unsure how to handle the situation. *FF* 143–46.

24. Sw. 3.195 and 193 (EQL 317 and 322), Fox to Nayler, September and October. The second of these was found on Nayler when he was arrested, and probably saved Fox from legal proceedings.

25. For the most sensitive insight into Naylers actions, the best interpretations are probably Damrosch, *Sorrows of the Quaker Jesus*, 115–76, and Douglas Gwyn, *The Covenant Crucified: Quakers and the Rise of Capitalism* (Wallingford, Pa.: Pendle Hill Publications, 1995), 161–88. Damrosch thinks that the apparent folly of Nayler's actions was part of a deliberately planned prophetic sign, for as Christ had been weak, so must Nayler be in his re-enactment of Christ's sufferings.

26. See Bittle, *James Nayler*, for the constitutional implications of Parliament's actions.

27. Mason, *James Nayler*, 17–20, from the diary of a Member of Parliament, Thomas Burton.

28. See *FF* 140–41, on the early relations between Fox and Nayler. An old error has unfortunately resurfaced in Damrosch, *Sorrows of the Quaker Jesus*, 139, and again in Massey, *The Clouded Quaker Star*, 23, expressing the view that Nayler treated Fox as Messiah. This rests solely on an anonymous scrap of manuscript beginning: "My Father my Father" (Sw. 3.63), endorsed JN but not in the usual hand of Nayler's letters, and not included in Nuttall, "The Letters of James Nayler."

29. Caton 3.91, Parker to Fell, May 1655, that Friends in London "begin to know George, though at first, he was strange to them . . . at the first, they would rather have heard any of us than him."

30. Farmer, *Sathan Inthron'd*, 39.

31. Spence 3.38. This letter was sent via Bristol, where George Bishop intercepted it. Sw. 1.188 (EQL 326), October, Bishop to Fell, explained that Bishop had withheld Fell's letter because he considered that the messianic references to Fox that it contained were liable to cause trouble if it fell into government hands. This letter is the nearest contemporary account of the happenings in Bristol, and is reproduced in full in *EQW* 481–85.

32. Etting MSS 30, in *The Swarthmore Documents in America*, ed. H. J. Cadbury, *JFHS* Supplement 20 (1940).

33. Note in this connection William Haller, *The Rise of Puritanism* (Philadelphia: University of Pennsylvania Press, 1938), 179: "Whenever in any given sect or congregation, two leaders of something like equal force arose, there would generally occur sooner or later a serious clash of opinion and then a split."

34. *Copies of Some Few of the Papers Given into the House of Parliament at the Time of James Nayler's Trial There* (1657), N268. Robert Rich, in *Hidden Things brought to Light* (Francis Smith, 1678), R1356, said that he prepared the collection at Fox's request. Rich (d. 1679) was a wealthy London merchant and shipowner. He went to live on his property in Barbados in 1659, but kept in touch with Quakers and supported John Perrot in his dispute with Fox in the 1660s. For a study of Rich, see Nigel Smith, "Hidden Things Brought to Light: Enthusiasm and Quaker Discourse," in Corns and Loewenstein, *Emergence of Quaker Writing*, 57–69.

35. Bishop, *The Throne of Truth Exalted*, 16.

36. Caton 3.103, June 1658.

37. As so often, the details are obscure. Robert Rich in *Hidden Things*, 37, says that Fox required Nayler to kneel before him. Dewsbury's letter to Margaret Fell, describing the occasion, Sw. 4.134, does not say so explicitly. See FF 182 and 331 n. 69. Ingle considers that such behavior would not have been out of character in Fox, though Fox later denied that he made such a requirement.

38. *History of the Life of Thomas Ellwood* (1st ed., Sowle, 1714; modern edition, ed. Graveson, Headley, 1906).

39. Nayler, *What the Possession of the Living Faith is* (Simmons, 1659), N328, 11–13, 24.

40. Collier, *A Looking-Glasse for the Quakers* (Brewster, 1657), C5290, 17; Edward Dodd, *Innocents No Saints* (Tyton, 1658), D1790, 3.

41. Farmer, *Sathan Inthron'd*, 29, 39, 40.

42. Bishop, *The Throne of Truth Exalted*, 13. Farmer wrote a reply to this in 1658, *The Imposter Dethron'd* (Thomas, 1658), F441A, and Bishop replied again with *A Rejoinder Consisting of Two Parts* (Simmons, 1658), B3004A. These books did not add much to the argument, but served to keep the controversy alive.

43. ARB 38. This was a letter about the arrangements for the meeting that produced the "Epistle from the Elders of Balby"; see Chapter 10, page 137.

44. For example, Sw. 3.185 (EQL 357), Salthouse to Fell; Sw.1.316 (EQL 372), Caton to Fell; Sw. 1.69 (EQL 381), Henry Fell to Margaret Fell; Caton 3.15, Caton to Fell (all January–May 1657). There are many other references to repercussions of the Nayler affair throughout the spring and summer of 1657.

45. See *FF* 150–52.

46. Epistle 131. The MS version is Sw. 2.95, and it was heavily edited before printing. A letter from Thomas Turner to Margaret Fell concerns the release of the Launceston prisoners and the holding of a general meeting in Cornwall, Sw. 4 123 (EQL 323), and *CJ* 1:326.

47. Caton 3.118. Parker also wrote about the same occurrence, Caton 3.100.

48. Caton 3.119.

49. Caton 3.172 and Sw. 4.12.

50. These pamphlets included, in 1657, *A Catechism for Children* F1756, *Concerning Good Morrow and Good Even* F1766, *An Instruction to Judges and Lawyers* F1848, *Of Bowings* F1869, *The Priests Fruits Manifest* F1883, *This to all Officers and Souldiers* F1935, and *A Warning to all Teachers of Children* F1983, and, in 1658, *Here is Declared the Manner of the Naming of Children* F1840, *The Law of God the Rule of Lawmakers* F1856, *To the Protector and Parliament of England* F1961, and *A Warning to all the Merchants in London* F1985.

51. George Fox, *The Great Mistery of the Great Whore* (*Works* 3). For the date of compilation, see *CJ* 2:338, quoted in *BQ* 301, stating that "this year [1657] G. F. drew up the mad priests principles, being collected out of their own mad books," which appears to be a reference to *The Great Mistery*. The book was not completed in 1657, as it dealt with ten books published in 1658. Burrough's "Epistle to the Reader" is dated the ninth month (November), so the book probably went to the press during the winter of 1658–59. For a fuller discussion of *The Great Mistery*, see my Ph.D. dissertation, "The Faith of the First Quakers" (University of Birmingham, 1993), 195–202, and tables 1 and 2.

52. There is little on *The Great Mistery* in *BQ, QPE,* Douglas Gwyn, *Apocalypse of the Word: The Life and Message of George Fox* (Richmond, Ind.: Friends United Press, 1986), or Punshon, *Portrait in Grey.* Bailey, *New Light,* 179, has a useful short summary within the context of his own point of view. I can find no reference to *The Great Mistery* in *FF*.

53. I am grateful to Dr. Geoffrey F. Nuttall for a copy of his own unpublished notes on the books answered by Fox in *The Great Mistery.*

54. W. C. (presumed Caton), *The Moderate Enquirer Resolved* (1658), C1515, title-page. Quoted in Chapter 8, page 110.

55. Penington, *Many Deep Considerations have been upon my Heart* [1664], 3; see also Ellwood's "Testimony" prefacing the first, 1681 edition of Penington's *Works; EQW* 230–34, and other accounts in Penington's writings. Penington was a prolific writer, and extracts are often reprinted in modern Quaker books and pamphlets; Isaac Penington, *Works,* 4 vols., new ed. (Glenside, Pa.: Quaker Heritage Press, 1995).

Chapter 4

1. For the political use of the Geneva Bible, see Christopher Hill, *The English Bible and the Seventeenth-Century Revolution* (London: Allen Lane, Penguin, 1993), 58–62.

2. The area of disagreement among commentators regarding the Quaker attitude to the Bible is not large, though some, such as Nuttall and Barbour, stress the continuity between Quakerism and the radical end of Puritanism, while others, such as Hill and Reay, stress the similarity between Quakerism and more radical sects. Comments on Quakerism and the Bible include Nuttall, *Holy Spirit,* 20–33; *QPE* 157–59; *WTUD* 261–68; Gwyn, *Apocalypse*

of the Word, 118–25. See also James L. Ash, "Oh No, It is not the Scriptures!: The Bible and the Spirit in George Fox," *Quaker History* 63, no. 2 (1974): 97–107; Henry J. Cadbury, *A Quaker Approach to the Bible* (Guilford College, N.C.: Ward Lecture, 1953); T. Canby Jones, "The Bible, Its Authority and Dynamics in George Fox and Contemporary Quaker-ism," *Quaker Religious Thought* no. 4 (1962): 18–36; Dean Freiday, "Early Quakers and the Doctrine of Authority," *Quaker Religious Thought* no. 15 (1973): 4–38, and *The Bible: Its Critics, Interpretation and Use in Sixteenth- and Seventeenth-Century England* (Pittsburgh: Catholic and Quaker Studies no. 4, 1979); Hill, *The English Bible.* T. L. Underwood, *Primitivism, Radicalism, and the Lamb's War: The Baptist Quaker Conflict in Seventeenth-Century England* (New York and Oxford: Oxford University Press, 1997), 20–33, for a comparison between Quaker and Baptist views of Scripture.

3. Thomas Rosewell, *An Answer to Thirty Quaeries* (1656), R 1941, 5.

4. Pagitt, *Heresiography,* 5th ed., 142.

5. Nuttall, *Holy Spirit,* 27, makes the same point. See Hill, *The English Bible,* 231–36, for radicals other than Quakers who did not accept the Bible.

6. Bunyan, *A Vindication of a Book called Some Gospel Truths Opened* (Newport: Cowley, 1657), 23. Ann Blackley is Ann Blaykling, a leading traveling minister in Cambridge and East Anglia, who "ran out" for a time but later returned to the Quaker fold (DQB). There are similar accusations in Ellis Bradshawe, *The Quakers Quaking Principles* (Lloyd, 1656), B4148, 3–4, and Jeremiah Ives, *Innocency above Impudency* (Cottrell, 1656), I1102, 29.

7. Sw. 4.52, Edward Bourne to Fox. It would be interesting to know Fox's reaction.

8. *QPE* 157: "In many Quaker tracts, letters and even Journals, 70 per cent of the phrases are biblical quotations and paraphrases." Making an accurate estimate is extremely difficult.

9. This exercise has been done for Nayler's letters; see Nuttall, "The Letters of James Nayler."

10. Catherine M. Wilcox, *Theology and Women's Ministry in Seventeenth-Century English Quakerism,* Studies in Women and Religion Vol. 35 (Lewiston/Queenstown/Lampeter: Mellen, 1995), includes a valuable account of Quaker use of biblical texts. An earlier study based on a large number of early texts is Pamela M. C. Oliver, "Quaker Testimony and the Lamb's War" (Ph.D. diss., University of Melbourne, 1977), esp. chapter 2 on Quaker use of the Bible, and appendix C, "A Select Glossary of Scriptural Images most used by Early Friends," 271–71.

11. Hebrews 5:5–10, 6:20–7:10. The writer of Hebrews was using Genesis 14:18–20, the story of the priest-king Melchizedek.

12. Farnworth, *A Discovery of Truth and Falsehood* (Calvert, 1653), F479A.

13. Farnworth, *Truth Cleared of Scandals* (1654), F512, 8.

14. Burrough and Howgill, *Fiery Darts of the Divil Quenched* (1654), H3159, Howgill's introduction.

15. See, for instance, Romans 1:16, 1 Cor. 4:15, 2 Cor. 4:4, and many others.

16. Fox, *Paper sent forth into the World* (Simmonds, 1653), F1872, 2; Fox and Nayler, *Saul's Errand to Damascus,* 7.

17. *NJ* 34.

18. Thomas Atkinson, Fox and Hubberthorne, *Truth's Defence against the Refined Subtilty of the Serpent* (York: Thomas Wayt, 1653), F1970, 6; Fox, *Warning to all in this proud city called London* (about 1654), F1892, broadside.

19. William Tomlinson, *Word of Reproof to Priests or Ministers* (York: Wayte, 1653), T1855, 23.

20. John Stalham, fl. 1617–77, an Independent minister from Essex who often preached in Edinburgh (*BDER, CR*), a very careful commentator, thought that Nayler's attitude to the

Bible was less extreme than Fox's. Stalham, *Contradictions of the Quakers* (Edinburgh, 1655), S5184, 23.

21. Nayler, *Discovery of the Man of Sin* (Calvert, 1654), N274, 32, 34. See Chapter 8, page 101, for the controversy.

22. Burrough, *Truth Defended* (Simmons, 1654), B6049, 11, 17; and Burrough and Howgill, *Fiery Darts of the Divil Quenched*, 27.

23. Hubberthorne, *Reply to a Book set forth by one of the Blind Guides* (Calvert, 1654), H3231, 2.

24. Sw. 2.74, "To Friends in the Truth," 1653.

25. Pagitt, *Heresiography*, 5th ed., 136.

26. Fox and others, *Declaration against all Popery* (1654 from context), F1783, esp. 14f.; Fox, *Here is declared the manner of the naming of Children* (Simmons, 1658), F1840.

27. See Miriam Slater, *Family Life in the Seventeenth Century: The Vernons of Claydon House* (London: Routledge and Kegan Paul, 1984), 82, an occasion when a business deal was not concluded, "the other parties being women," or in other words, unbusinesslike.

28. Priscilla Cotton and Mary Cole, *To the Priests and People of England* (Calvert, 1655), C6474, 6–8. See also Fox, *The Woman Learning in Silence* (Simmons 1656), F1991, 2; Mack, *Visionary Women*, 175–76 for similar examples.

29. Margaret Fell, *Womens Speaking Justified, Proved and Allowed by the Scriptures* (1666), F642.

30. This example was used on several occasions by Fox, the earliest I have found being his trial at Launceston in 1656, but the text was used in this sense in 1655 by Humphrey Smith, when he was prosecuted at Evesham. *CJ* 1:212; *NJ* 243–44; and Humphrey Smith, *The Cruelty of the Magistrates of Evesham* (Calvert, 1655), 5.

31. William Haller, *Liberty and Reformation in the Puritan Revolution* (New York: Columbia, 1955), 27, 61, gives examples from the early Civil War period.

32. This particular translation "defiled" is not in either the Authorised nor the Geneva Bible. Norwich Friends must have been using one of the other versions circulating at that time. See Henry J. Cadbury, "George Fox and Seventeenth-Century Bibles," *JFHS* 21 (1924): 1–8.

33. Keith Thomas, *Religion and the Decline of Magic* (London: Weidenfeld and Nicholson, 1971), 82–92, on the seventeenth-century understanding of ill-fortune.

34. William Prynne, *The Quakers Unmasked* (Thomas, 1655), P4045, 1.

35. Audland, *The Innocent Delivered out of the Snare* (Calvert, 1655), A4196, 22.

36. Samuel Fisher, *The Scorned Quakers True and Honest Account* (1656), F1057, 21, and *Rusticus ad Academicos* (Wilson, 1660), F1056. Christopher Hill thinks that Fisher was the first thorough-going advocate of this view, though it was touched on by other seventeenth-century writers, *WTUD* 214–15. See *BQ* 288–94, for Fisher's theology.

37. Whitehead and Burrough, *The Son of Perdition Revealed* (Simmons, 1661), 58. See Chapter 17, note 18, for discussion of authorship.

Chapter 5

1. Alexander Ross, ΠΑΝΣΕΒΕΙΑ *or, a View of all Religions in the World* (Saywell, 1653), 413. This includes a useful survey of sects and opinions, less prejudiced than *Gangraena* or *Heresiography*.

2. William Erbery, *The Lord of Hosts* (Calvert, 1648), title page.

3. B. S. Capp, *The Fifth Monarchy Men* (London: Faber and Faber, 1972), 76, 224, and 137–56, for the political program.

4. Bryan W. Ball, *A Great Expectation: Eschatological Thought in English Protestantism to 1660* (Leiden: Brill, 1975), 160, 196–200, points out that millenarians were not necessarily radicals, but they were always theologians, and Quakers were not theologians in this sense. Among works dealing with mid–seventeenth-century eschatology are Christopher Hill, *Antichrist in Seventeenth-Century England* (Oxford: University Press, 1971); P. Toon, ed., *Puritans, the Millennium, and the Future of Israel* (Cambridge and London: Cambridge University Press, 1970), esp. T. L. Underwood, "Early Quaker Eschatology"; the debate between Capp and Lamont regarding the nature and extent of millenarianism in *Past and Present*, no 52 (August 1971): 106–17; no. 55 (May 1972): 68–90; and no. 57 (November 1972): 156–62; H. Larry, Ingle, "George Fox, Millenarian," *Albion* 24, no. 2 (1992): 261–78.

5. ARB 15, 125.

6. Fox, *Newes Coming up out of the North sounding towards the South* (Calvert, 1653), F1867, 4, 5, 19, 21.

7. David Underdown, *Fire from Heaven* (London: Harper Collins, 1992), describes the attempt to put a similar programme into practice in Dorchester.

8. Benjamin Nicholson, *Blast from the Lord* (Calvert, 1653), N1104, 9–10.

9. Farnworth, *Voice of the First Trumpet* (1653), F512B, 1–2; *The General Good and Gods Covenant* (Calvert, 1653), F483, 27; idem, *Brief Discovery of the Kingdom of Antichrist*, [1659], F472A, 1, 2. See Revelation 12:7–12 and 20:7–10; for Gog and Magog, Ezekiel 38, 39.

10. Farnworth, *Brief Discovery of the Kingdome of Antichrist*, 15–16.

11. Parnell, *The Trumpet of the Lord Blowne* (Calvert, 1655), P539, 1. The first six pages are all in this vein.

12. Higginson, *Brief Relation*, 10.

13. Nayler, *A True Discoverie of Faith* (Calvert, 1655), N322, 13–14.

14. Gerrard Winstanley, *The True Levellers Standard Advanced* (1649), T2716, available in Andrew Hopton, ed., *Selected Writings* (London: Aporia, 1989), 10–11.

15. Hubberthorne, *The Mittimus Answered, by which Richard Hubberthorne was sent prisoner to Norwich Castle* (broadside, 1654), not found in Wing.

16. Historians such as Alan Cole, Christopher Hill, and Barry Reay found many examples from the Quaker pamphlet literature relating to social justice and political concern. This was an important new emphasis, in that this aspect of early Quakerism had been almost entirely missed by earlier commentators, but the new approach was also misleading in a different way, in that the historians did not indicate that such passages make only a small proportion of the total Quaker pamphlet literature.

17. *FF* 21 and 393 nn. 37 and 38, for Fox's finances. Tomlinson's *Seven Particulars: The Word of the Lord against Oppressors* (Calvert, 1657), T1851, is worth noting as a later statement of the Quaker view of wealth. Very fierce against "the oppressors of the earth, who grind the faces of the poor, who rack and stretch out their rents till the poor . . . can scarce get bread to eat," Tomlinson said that the duty of the rich was "to support the distressed; to ease the heavy burdens . . . and so to succour by your riches such as are oppressed . . . this is the improvement of your estates" (1, 4).

18. Isaac Grayes, *One More Outcry Against Tythes* (for the author, 1657), G1626, 4. Isaac Grayes, c. 1614–75, convinced in Cumberland 1654, wrote an earlier pamphlet against tithes in his pre-Quaker days, *Tithes—A Curse* (for the author, 1654), G2167.

19. Nayler, *Lamentacion over the Ruines of this Oppressed Nation* (York, 1653), N292, 3, 9. See also Christopher Hill, *The Experience of Defeat* (London: Faber and Faber, 1984), 139–40.

20. Nayler, *The Power and Glory of the Lord* (1653), 1, which is dated August 13 in the Thomason catalogue (hereafter cited as Thomason). See also an earlier reference in the letter of advice Sw. 3.3 and 3.67, November 1652, telling Friends that they should be "waiting for the kingdom of God in you."

21. For the Kingdom of God in the gathered churches, see Geoffrey F. Nuttall, *Visible Saints: The Congregational Way 1640–1660* (Oxford: Blackwell, 1957), 157–59.

22. The theological term for this kind of belief is "realised eschatology," which derives from New Testament studies and refers to the strand of New Testament teaching that shows the Kingdom of God as already present, in a sense, in Jesus and his followers.

23. Fox, *Vials of Wrath Poured Forth* (Calvert, 1654), F1975, 4; *Warning from the Lord to such as hang down their head for a day* (1654), F1980, 8.

24. Nayler, *Few Words Occasioned by a Paper lately Printed* (1654), N279, 10.

25. Burrough, *For the Souldiers and Officers* (1654), B6003, broadside. Howgill's writing was similar, e.g., *An Answer to . . . Ellyson* (1654), H3154, 7: "Christ is come and made manifest . . . he shall confound the mighty and the lofty . . . now is war proclaimed betwixt Michael our Prince and all inhabitants of the earth." Commentators often call the cosmic battle "The Lambs War," a phrase deriving from the title of a pamphlet by Nayler and used also by Fox. It is not, however, common in the Quaker pamphlet literature of the time.

26. Dewsbury, *A True Prophecy of the Mighty Day of the Lord* (Calvert, 1654), D1279, 1; *The Discovery of Mans Return to his First Estate* (Calvert, 1654), D1259, 20. See Hill, *Antichrist in Seventeenth-Century England*, 142–43, for internalization of the concept of Antichrist by Erbury, Salmon, Coppin, Winstanley, and others.

27. All these views can be found in Fox's writings. The variation of the understanding of the Kingdom of God among Quakers as a whole can be judged from 1655 onward from the many authors now writing a few tracts apiece. In 1655 and 1656, authors strongly inclining to a future kingdom were Thomas Aldam, John Harwood, who was in York Castle with Aldam, Christopher Taylor, a former Independent preacher, Samuel Fisher, an ex-vicar and ex-Baptist minister, George Fox the Younger, who was an ex-soldier and colleague of George Whitehead, and John Rous, son of a Barbados merchant who married a Fell daughter. Those strongly inclining to a present Kingdom were Christopher Atkinson, of near Ranter views, John Audland, Francis Ellington, who was a well-to-do cloth merchant, Thomas Lawson, who was a parish minister turned Quaker after hearing Fox in 1652 and noted for his learning, Martin Mason, one of the most learned of early Friends, "RW," presumed Robert West, who appears to have been well-educated, and lastly John Whitehead, a soldier convinced in 1652. See DQB for all of these.

28. Melvin B. Endy Jr., *William Penn and Early Quakerism* (Princeton: Princeton University Press, 1973), esp. 53, 61–62.

29. Farmer, *The Great Mysterie of Godlinesse and Ungodlinesse*, 28.

30. B. S. Capp, *The Fifth Monarchy Men*, 192, has an account of John Tillinghast's *Knowledge of the Times* (Chapman, 1654), T1179, calculating that the world would end in 1656; Collier, *A Word in Season* (1655), C5302, for concern about civil war breaking out among the Saints in an attempt to force the coming of the Kingdom of God.

31. Nayler, *Love to the Lost* (Calvert, 1656), N294, 20. See also Nayler's other 1655 tracts, including: *The Boaster Bared* (Calvert, 1655), N266, 2; *The Royal Law and Covenant of God* (Calvert, 1655), N308, 4; *The Secret Shooting of the Wicked* (1655), N315, broadside; *A Salutation to the Seed of God* (Calvert, 1655), N309, 2. The first edition of *Love to the Lost* omitted to consider the Last Judgment. Because Quakers said that the Kingdom of God was actually present or arriving, they were often accused of disbelieving in the final resurrection of all dead people, which was part of the standard Christian faith of the time and derives

mainly from 1 Corinthians 15. A second edition, with a chapter on the final resurrection, was brought out almost immediately.

32. Burrough, *Trumpet of the Lord*, 25–26. Calvert, the printer, was questioned by the Council of State about this book, and George Taylor wrote to Margaret Fell in May that there was "much rage" about it; however, Nayler was able to write to her the month following that "the affair of E.B.'s book is over." George Taylor to Fell, May 1656, Sw. 1.272 (EQL 262); and Nayler to Fell, June 1656, Sw. 3.81 (EQL 273).

33. *Querers and Quakers* 11.

34. Quoted in Dewsbury, *Discoverie of the Ground from which Persecution did arise . . . in Northamptonshire* (1655), D1266, 13. See also Capp, *The Fifth Monarchy Men*, 143–44, for similar behavior by Fifth Monarchists.

35. For example, Howgill, *Particulars Concerning the Law sent to Oliver Cromwell* (1654), C391; Howgill, *A Short Answer to be set forth to Seven Priests* (Calvert, 1654), P36; Howgill, *Answer to a Paper of . . . Thomas Ellyson* (1654), H3154, 2, 3, 9; Hubberthorne, *The Antipathy betwixt Flesh and Spirit* (Calvert, 1654), H3220, 4.

36. Burrough, *Truth Defended*, 14. See also Burrough and Howgill, *Fiery Darts of the Divil Quenched*.

37. Hubberthorne, *The Mittimus answered*.

38. *A Declaration against all Popery*. Catalogued under Fox and probably written by him, but signed by a number of London Friends.

39. Burrough, *For the Souldiers, and all the Officers* [1654]. See Capp, *Fifth Monarchy Men*, 113–14, for other attempts to subvert the army in 1655–56

40. Caton 3.63, August 1654.

41. Fox and Nayler, *A Word from the Lord to all the Faithless Generation of the World* (1654), Part 4, by Fox (not found in Wing). The burial of a Gerrard Winstanley, a corn chandler, is listed in the records of Westminster Meeting. However, if Winstanley died a Quaker, he never took any known part in Quaker activities.

42. See in *FPT*, Braithwaite's note on "Penal Laws Affecting Friends," 347–49. Note also a reference in Norman Penney, ed., *Extracts from State Papers Relating to Friends, 1652–1672* (London: Headley, 1913) (hereafter cited as *ESP*), 6–10, which suggests that relations between Quakers and the State were not uniformly poor, as the Council of State in 1655–56 was holding lists of Quakers to serve as magistrates. Braithwaite in *BQ* 460 n. 2, also as a note in *ESP*, considers this is an error, and that these lists belong with others from 1659. Braithwaite's view may be justified, in that Cromwell is hardly likely to have favoured new Quaker magistrates during 1655–56, especially as Fox says that it was about this time that some Friends were expelled from the office of justice (*CJ* 1:263; *NJ* 280).

43. For example, in Caton 3.72, Howgill to Fell, March–April 1655, he had delivered her two letters to Cromwell but did not expect much benefit from them; see also Caton 3.69, 72, 2, for other contacts with Cromwell, and a number of letters throughout 1656, many concerned with Fox's imprisonment at Launceston. *CJ* 1:259–60 (*NJ* 274) describes Fox's meetings with Cromwell in October 1656.

44. *CJ* 1:161, and in Chapter 2, pages 28–29.

45. Fox and Nayler, *To Thee, Oliver Cromwell* (Calvert, 1655), F1962, 1. This consists of three short pieces concerning freedom of conscience. The quotation is from a section by Fox.

46. See, for instance, J. Harwood, R. Clayton, and G. Whitehead, *The Path of the Just Cleared* (London: Calvert, 1655), W1944, 10, for a clear declaration of principle on the lines of Romans 13:1–7.

47. Francis Ellington, *True Discoverie of the Grounds of Imprisonment* (Calvert, 1655), T2683, 6.

48. Burrough and Howgill, *To the Camp of the Lord in England* (Simmons, 1655), H3182, 8. This is a collection of several short pieces, republished 1656 in a different order under the title *This is Onley to Goe Amongst Friends*.

49. Halhead and Salthouse, *The Wounds of an Enemy in the House of a Friend* (Calvert, 1656), S476, 1. See *BQ* 171 for the Bristol riots.

50. George Rofe, *The Righteousness of God to Fallen Man* (Calvert, 1656), R1788, 11.

51. Thomas Higgenson *A Testimony to the True Jesus* (Brewster, 1656), 28. This was actually an attack on Quakers, whom Higgenson thought had caused much of the trouble.

52. Fox, *To the Protector and Parliament of England* (Calvert, 1658), F1961, 62, 63.

53. Capp, *Fifth Monarchy Men,* 116–17. See Ball, *A Great Expectation,* 196–201, for the divergence in attitude between Fifth Monarchists and Quakers regarding violence: "One cannot imagine John Rogers being in 'ye love of God' to a mob who had just beaten him unconscious [*CJ* 1:58] or Thomas Venner advising an armed soldier to 'putt uppe his sword' [*CJ* 1:59]."

54. *ESP* 29.

55. Burrough, *A Measure of the Times* (Simmons, 1657), B6012, 34–35 (written in July).

56. Daniel Baker, *A Thundering Voice out of Sion* (Simmons, 1658), B488, 43, 45.

57. Thomas Zachary, *A Word to the Officers of the Army* (Calvert, 1657), Z4, 1, 2.

58. Fell, *For Manasseh ben Israel* (Calvert, 1656), F632, and *A Loving Salutation to the Seed of Abraham* (Simmons, 1656), F634; and Fox, *A Visitation to the Jews* (Calvert, 1656), F1978. For background, see Peter Toon, "The Question of Jewish Immigration" in Toon, ed., *Puritans, the Millenium and the Future of Israel* (Cambridge: Cambridge University Press, 1970) 115–25, and Christopher Hill, "Till the Conversion of the Jews," in Christohper Hill, ed., *Religion and Politics in Seventeenth-Century England: Collected Essays,* 2 vols. (Brighton: Harvester, 1986), 2:269–300.

Chapter 6

1. *CJ* 1:161 and 381, not in *NJ. SJ* 17, not in corresponding passages *CJ* 1:41, *NJ* 105.

2. See Chapter 1, note 21.

3. Sw. 2.55, and Caton 2.48–9, ed. H. Larry Ingle and pub. in *JFHS* 55, no. 8 (1989, issue 2). See also Henry J. Cadbury, *The Annual Catalogue of George Fox Papers, compiled in 1694–1697* (Philadelphia: Friends Book Store, and London: Friends Book Centre, 1939), 23, 13A, a letter from Fox, probably from around the same date, beginning "I am the light of the world and do enlighten every man that cometh." This is cited by Geoffrey F. Nuttall in "A New Letter of George Fox," *JFHS* vol. 57, no. 3 (autumn 1996): 223–24.

4. Sw. 2.48; undated, but placed with 1652 writings. For 2 Peter 1:4, see Chapter 4, page 54. Friends did not invent this kind of theology, see, e.g., Erbery, *Lord of Hosts,* 3–4: "What is the house of God, but God dwelling in the flesh of his saints, or the saints filled with all the fulness of God?" Erbury, however, thought that this state had not yet come to pass.

5. Sw. 3.58, 1652.

6. "Letters of John Audland," 10.

7. Caton 3.431.

8. ARB 138, September 9, 1654, and ARB 157, September 13, 1654.

9. Richard Bailey in *New Light on George Fox and Early Quakerism* (San Francisco: Mellen 1992), which is the only major study of this topic, puts forward the view that Friends' attitude to Fox amounted to treating him as divine, in a different sense from the

way they were all divine by virtue of their incorporation into Christ. This is probably taking things too far. Moreover, Bailey makes much use of late and uncertain sources, and does not, in my opinion, give enough weight to the very strong messianic language used to Margaret Fell. Also there is no need, as Bailey does, to use the terminology of Eastern religion in describing the Quaker phenomenon. Nevertheless, Bailey's analysis of the Quakers' under-standing of their relationship to Christ (esp. 92–99) is probably as nearly accurate as it is possible to come. For a similar conclusion, see Nigel Smith, "Hidden Things Brought to Light: Enthusiasm and Quaker Discourse," in Corns and Loewenstein, *The Emergence of Quaker Writing*, 63–66.

10. Christopher Atkinson, *The Sword of the Lord Drawn* (Calvert, 1654), A4129, 4–5.

11. Fox, *This for each Parliament Man* (Simmons, 1656), F1933, 1. The Bible reference is to John 1:12. See also Underwood, *Primitivism* 38–40, for the Baptist tendency to separate the Spirit from the individual.

12. Fox, *To all that make mention of the Name of the Lord* [1655] 6, also in *The Great Mistery of the Great Whore* (Simmons, 1659), F1832, 1831 ed., 396. The reference to "flesh and bones" in Eph. 5:30 has been deleted as spurious in modern translations. It referred back to Genesis 29:14.

13. For example, Gwyn, *Apocalypse of the Word*, 103–9, 120.

14. Nayler, *Discovery of the First Wisdom from Beneath and the Second Wisdom from Above* (Calvert, 1653), N272, 2, 10.

15. Burrough and Howgill, *Answers to Several Queries* (Calvert, 1654), B5984, 12, from the answers to John Reeve.

16. E. Reyner, *Precepts for Christian Practice* (Newberry, 1655, 8th ed.), R1224, 64, 69. This is a 600-page treatise on Christian faith and life, with preface by Edmund Calamy, addressed to the mayor and aldermen of Lincoln. "Godded" and "Christed" is Familist language.

17. Most of these were collected in the second volume of the Swarthmore manuscripts.

18. Note the chapter heading in *QPE*, "The Terror and Power of the Light," 94.

19. Fox did not make regular use of the phrase "the light within" until 1657, when, quite suddenly, it begins to appear frequently in his pamphlets.

20. See Jackson I. Cope, "Seventeenth-Century Quaker Style," in Stanley E. Fish, ed., *Seventeenth-Century Prose: Modern Essays in Criticism* (New York: Oxford University Press, 1971), 200–235. Cope described Quaker style as "the epistemology of verbal incantation" (211).

21. Farnworth, *The Generall-Good to People / Gods Covenant* (Calvert, 1653), F483, tail-piece, "An Exhortation to all that desire to know the Truth, to mind the Light of God within." The "day of small things" is a reference to Zechariah 4:10, a favorite Quaker text.

22. Key texts include John 1:14, 17, 14:6, 16:13, 17:17–19, 18:37; Romans 2:8; 1 Corinthians 5:8; 2 Corinthians 4:2, 11:10, 13:8; Galatians 2:5, 14, 5:7; Ephesians 4:15, 21, 5:9, 6:14; Hebrews 10:26; James 5:19; 1 Peter 1:22.

23. For example, Fox, Epistles 24 and 25, 1653; ARB 161; Samuel Watson Collection 42 and others.

24. Early references are in epistles such as Sw. 2.8, 2.64 and 2.72. Fox made more use of "seed," to mean the people of God and Christ within them, from the 1660s onwards. It would be worth investigating possible cross-fertilisation with Penington's use of "seed."

25. Sw. 3.14 (EQL 49), 1654, Burrough and Christopher Atkinson to Fox.

26. Parnell, *The Watcher* (Calvert, 1655), P541, 51. This imagery was especially favoured by Fox.

27. Smith, *Perfection Proclaimed*, 107–225.

28. Dewsbury, *Discoverie of the Great Enmitie of the Serpent against the Seed of the Woman*

(Calvert, 1655), D1264, 13–14, 16, 19. Compare John Whitehead, *A Reproof from the Lord* (Simmons, 1656), W1980, 4, and Nayler, *An Answer to a Book called the Quakers Catechism* (1655), N258, query to Baxter; *NJ* 27.

29. Farnworth, *Moses Message to Pharaoh* (1653), F491B, 19.

30. A. J. Beachy, *The Concept of Grace in the Radical Reformation* (Nieuwkoop: B.de Graaf, 1977), 4–5, "Grace is for the radical reformers not so much a forensic change in status before God as an ontological change in the individual believer."

31. Fox, *Newes coming up out of the North*, 15–17, 25, 29, 40.

32. Farnworth, *Message from the Lord to those who despise the Ordinances of Christ*, 10–11.

33. The earliest instance I found is in Nayler's set of queries in Fox and Nayler's *Several Papers* (1653), F1903, 30. Instances of "Covenant of Light" in Fox's writings include: *Declaration of the Difference of the Ministry of the Word* (Calvert, 1656), F1790, 4, "The Ministry of the Word held forth a Covenant of Light to the Gentiles"; *A Discovery of some Fruits of the Profession of this Nation* (Simmons, 1656), F1795A, 8, "Christ . . . who is the Covenant of light, of peace, and of life"; other Quaker writers also used the phrase.

34. London Particular Baptist Confession, 1646, quoted in B. R. White, *The English Baptists of the Seventeenth Century* (London: Baptist Historical Society, 1983), 12. For early Baptist confessions of faith, see E. B. Underhill, *Confessions of Faith and other Public Documents illustrative of the History of the Baptist Churches in England* (London: Hanserd Knollys Society, 1854).

35. *NJ* 2–3, *FF* 24–25, for Fox's drinking episode with his cousin, a formative experience.

36. Farnworth, *Message from the Lord to all who despise the Ordinances of Christ*, 20–21.

37. Nayler, *Love to the Lost*, 22.

38. Nayler, *The Railer Rebuked* (1655), N306, 5, answering Ellis Bradshawe's, *The Quakers Whitest Divil Unveiled* (1654), B4148.

39. Martin Mason, *The Proud Pharisee Reproved* (1655), M933. Mason was the author of several pamphlets, and was evidently educated as he could discuss the Greek text, but little is known of him. The phrase in 1 John 3:9 is ποιειν 'αμαρτιαν, "to do sin," and biblical scholars have spilt much ink over its interpretation.

Chapter 7

1. As in Joseph Smith, ed., *Bibliotheca Anti-Quakeriana* (London: Smith, 1873), hereafter cited as *BA-Q*. See Underwood, *Primitivism*, 17–18, for the high proportion of Baptist works.

2. Thomas Underhill, *Hell Broke Loose—An History of the Quakers* (Simon Miller, 1660), U43, which George Thomason had on November 13, 1659, answered by Howgill with *The Mouth of the Pit Stopped* (Simmons, 1659), H3172.

3. Fox and Nayler, *Saul's Errand to Damascus*. There is an introduction to *Saul's Errand* and a lengthy extract in *EQW* 251–61.

4. *Humble Petition of many Thousands of the County of Worcestershire* (Tyton and Underhill, 1652), B1285, included with Richard Baxter's works.

5. The Quaker attack is a set of queries by Ben Nicholson in Thomas Aldam and others, *A Brief Discovery of the Threefold Estate of Antichrist* (Calvert, 1653), A894B. Baxter's reply is *The Worcestershire Petition . . . Defended* (Underhill 1653), B1455, answered by Nicholson, *Truths Defence against Lies* (1654), N1107.

6. Thomas Collier, *To all the Churches of Jesus Christ* [1658], C5300A, 19.

7. Salthouse, *An Epistle to the Church of the Anabaptists (so-called)* [1658], S472, 1; Collier, *To all the Churches of Jesus Christ*, 20; Salthouse, *The Line of True Judgement* [1658], S474, 15.

8. E. B. Underhill, ed., *The Records of a Church of Christ meeting in Broadmead, Bristol* (London: Hanserd Knollys Society, 1847), 42–57. See also *BQ* 170.

9. Denis Hollister, *The Skirts of the Whore Discovered* (Calvert, 1656), H2508; Thomas Ewens and others, *The Church of Christ in Bristol* (Brewster, 1657), E3556, 20; Hollister, *The Harlots Vail Removed* (1658), H2507.

10. John Gilpin, *The Quakers Shaken* (1653), G769.

11. The 1655 edition of Gilpin's *The Quakers Shaken* has this story. See also *Strange and Terrible Newes from Cambridge* (London: Brooks, 1659), S5827; and *A Relation of a Quaker that attempted to Bugger a Mare near Colchester* (1659), R794.

12. *The Quakers Dream, or, the Devil's Pilgrimage* (Horton, 1655), Q22. Other titles were William Prynne, *The Quaker Unmasked* (Thomas, 1655), P4045; Donald Lupton, *The Quacking Mountebank or the Jesuite turned Quaker* (E.B., 1655), L3493; *Quakers are Inchanters and Dangerous Seducers* (Dodd, 1655), Q13.

13. Lupton, *The Quacking Mountebank*, 4, 17.

14. O'Malley, "The Press and Quakerism," 181, states that between January and October 1655 there was hardly a fortnight without one reference in the periodical press, usually concerning interruptions to church services, supposed witchcraft, or breach of the peace. The individual Quaker most often mentioned by name was James Nayler. Replies to these accusations were *Declaration from the Children of Light* (1655), D588, and *Slanders and Lies cast upon the Children of Light* (1655), S3956.

15. Thomas Weld, *A Further Discovery of . . . Quakers* (Gateshead: S.B., 1654). The similarities found were the denial of the imputed righteousness of Christ, assertion of justification by inherent righteousness, the possibility of perfection, or of keeping the whole law, Scripture not the supreme judge of spirits, Scripture a dead letter, truth established by revelation and miracles, and the practice of fasting and wearing "beggarly apparel."

16. Prynne, *The Quakers Unmasked*. Prynne had been branded and had his ears cropped during the reign of Charles I for writing pamphlets against the English church. The Quaker answer is in *Slanders and Lies cast upon the Children of Light*. See *BQ* 172–73, for further material of this kind.

17. Samuel Watson Coll. MSS 159, dated February 1655.

18. Sw. 4.216 (EQL 471), January 1659, Thomas Patching to "George Fox the older and younger, Edward Burrough and Francis Howgill." Matthew Caffyn was a leading General Baptist minister and Messenger with area responsibilities (*BDER* and Michael R. Watts, *The Dissenters from the Reformation to the French Revolution* [Oxford: Clarendon Press, 1978], 298–300).

19. Description of Taverner from note on Taverner's book in *BA-Q*, quoting Palmer, in E. Calamy, *Nonconformist Memorial*, abridged and corrected by Samuel Palmer, 3 vols. (London: Button, 1802), 2:183. Taverner, *The Quakers Rounds* (Lodowick Lloyd, 1658), T248, "Epistle to the Reader," and 14, 25, 29, 34, answered by Burrough, *Something of Truth made Manifest* (Simmons), B6026, and *Some of the Principles of Quakers Vindicated* B6024 (both 1658). Taverner gives Burrough's companion as William Fisher, but this is presumably an error for Samuel Fisher. For Goodenough see *BDER*.

20. EQL 293–97 has a useful note on the Manifestarians. Their leaders were Thomas Moore senior and Thomas Moore junior, and John Horne, and their beliefs were Arminian and Antinomian.

21. Nayler, *A Second Answer to Thomas Moore* (Calvert, 1655), N314, 29, replying to Moore's *Antidote against the Spreading Infection of Antichrist* (Chapman, 1655), M2599, and

A Defence against the Poyson of Satan's Design (Chapman, 1656), M2600. Nayler's reply has an earlier printer's date than the book it answered, probably a year-end anomaly.

22. Richard Hickocke, *The Saints Justified and their Accuser found out* (Simmons, 1660), H1917A, "Epistle to the Reader."

23. The county of Shropshire and its county town Shrewsbury are in the remote rural West Midlands, near the Welsh border.

24. Thomas Smith, *A Gagg for the Quakers,* S4231bA, and *The Quaker disarm'd,* S4231B (both 1659); Richard Blome, *The Fanatick History, or, an Exact Relation of the Old Anabaptist and New Quaker* (Simms, 1660), B3212, 149–50; George Whitehead, *The Key of Knowledge not found in the University Library of Cambridge* (Wilson, 1660), W1939, 1. Audience "laughter" is mentioned several times in the anti-Quaker books. The meeting house where this debate took place was on or near to the site of the present Friends Meeting House in Jesus Lane, Cambridge.

25. John Wigan, *Antichrist's Strongest Hold Overturned* (Printed for the author, 1665), W2096, answered by Thomas Curwen and others in *This is an Answer to John Wigans Book* (1664), C7703; see *CJ* 2:63–64, *NJ* 471–72. For Wigan (d. 1665, in the plague), *CR* 529; W. T. Whitley, *A Baptist Bibliography,* 2 vols. (London: Kingsgate, 1916), 1:90–91, and *BDER. NJ* 351–52 (not in *CJ*), for an earlier dispute between Wigan and Fox in 1658.

Chapter 8

1. Serious criticisms of Quakerism included John Stalham, *Contradictions of the Quakers to the Scriptures of God* (Edinburgh, 1655), S5184, which shows knowledge of a great range of Quaker writing and also of the oral message; Magnus Byne, *The Scornfull Quakers Answered* (Crook, 1656), B6402; and Thomas Higgenson, *A Testimony to the True Jesus* (Brewster, 1656), H1950.

2. Key texts of uncertain interpretation included Romans 6:1–11 and 7:21–8:4, and 1 John 3:4–10 and 5:18.

3. Nuttall, *Holy Spirit,* 134–49, and Endy, *William Penn and Early Quakerism,* 29–30, 35–46, for the life of the Spirit as understood by spiritual Puritans.

4. For Clarkson, who later turned Muggletonian, see A. L. Morton, *The World of the Ranters* (London: Lawrence and Wishart, 1970), 115–42. There is an excellent account of Arminianism and Antinomianism in Dewey D. Wallace Jr., *Puritans and Predestination: Grace in English Protestant Theology 1525–1695* (Chapel Hill: University of North Carolina Press, 1982), chap. 3, "Arminian Controversies," 79–111, and chap. 4, "The Antinomian Catalyst and the Further Formation of Theological Parties, 1640–1660," 112–50. Gertrude Huehns, *Antinomianism in English History with special reference to the period 1640–1660* (London: Cresset, 1951), is still valuable, especially with regard to political issues. See Underwood, *Primitivism,* 65–66, for theological similarities beween Quakers, Seekers, and Ranters.

5. The four books were: (1) Thomas Weld, *The Perfect Pharisee* (Gateshead: Tomlins, 1653), W1268A; (2) Nayler, *An Answer to the Booke . . . called the Perfect Pharisee* [1654], N261; (3) Weld, *A Further Discovery of that Generation of Men called Quakers* (Gateshead: S.B., 1654), W1268; and (4) Nayler, *The Discovery of the Man of Sin* (Calvert, 1654), N274.

6. Nayler, *Discovery of the Man of Sin,* 21–22.

7. Nayler, *Discovery of the Man of Sin,* 18, 21.

8. Weld, *The Perfect Pharisee,* 13, 14.

9. Weld, *Further Discovery of . . . Quakers,* 51.

10. Nayler, *Discovery of the Man of Sin,* 6, 28.

11. See Underwood, *Primitivism,* 101–14, for a full discussion of Quaker and Baptist concepts of "light."

12. John Stalham, *Contradictions of the Quakers,* "Epistle to the Reader."

13. Farnworth, *Scriptures Vindication against Scotish Contradictors* (Calvert, 1655), F503, 27, in reply to Stalham, *Contradictions of the Quakers,* 23.

14. Farnworth, *AntiChrists Man of War* (Calvert, 1655), F470, 36. This answered Edward Skipp, *The Worlds Wonder, or, the Quakers Blazing Star* (1655), S3949.

15. This phrase and others like it are very common in Quaker writings. Here it is from Burrough and Howgill, *Answers to Several Queries . . . of Philip Bennett* (Calvert, 1654), B5984, 3.

16. Joseph Kellet, Christopher Feake et al., *A Faithful Discovery of a Treacherous Design* (London: Brewster, 1654), F568, 30.

17. Farmer, *The Great Mysteries of Godlinesse and Ungodlinesse,* 63.

18. Underwood, *Primitivism,* 52–57, for Quaker and other seventeenth-century ideas of atonement. Wilcox, *Theology and Women's Ministry,* chap. 1, found various accounts of the work of Christ in the Quaker literature, but these were not points of issue at the time.

19. The pamphlets are Baxter, *The Quakers Catechism* (Underhill, 1655), B7362, and Nayler, *An Answer to the Book called the Quakers Catechism* (1655), N258. For extracts from the Nayler/Baxter pamphlets see *EQW* 262–89, and further extracts from Baxters' disputes with Quakers *EQW* 294–98.

20. Nayler, *Love to the Lost,* 2, 35, 54.

21. (1) John Bunyan, *Some Gospel Truths Opened* (Wright, 1656), B5598, with introductory epistle by John Burton, minister at Bedford. (2) Edward Burrough, *True Faith of the Gospel of Peace Contended for* (Calvert, 1656), B6046, 17. (3) Bunyan, *A Vindication of a Book called Some Gospel Truths Opened* (Newport: Cowley, 1657), B5605, 4. Introductory epistles by several others. (4) Burrough, *Truth (The Strongest of All) Witnessed Forth in the Spirit* (Calvert, 1657), B6051.

22. Burrough, *A Declaration to All the World* (Simmons, 1657), B5995, 2–5.

23. Burrough, *A Generall Epistle and Greeting* (Simmons, 1657), B6004, 3.

24. Fox, *An Epistle to All the People on the Earth* (Calvert 1657), F1805, 7, 5.

25. Fox, *The Pearle found in England* (Simmons, 1658), F1878, 4.

26. *Great Mistery,* 297, *Works* 3:469 (refs. to 1st ed. and collected ed.).

27. John Gilpin, *The Quakers Shaker* (S. B., 1653), G769; Atkinson, *The Standard of the Lord Lifted Up* (Calvert, 1653), A4128; Benson, *An Answer to John Gilpins Book* (Calvert, 1655), B1899.

28. Richard Baxter, *The Quakers Catechism* (Underhill, 1655), B7362, answered by Nayler, *Answer to a Book called the Quakers Catechism* (1655), N258; Thomas Collier, *A Looking Glass for the Quakers* (Brewster, 1656), C5290, answered by John Pitman and Jasper Batt, *Truth Vindicated* (Simmons, 1658), P2299.

29. Examples are Baxter, *Quakers Catechism,* referred to in *Great Mistery* 27, *Works* 3:74; and Higginson, *Irreligion,* referred to in *Great Mistery* 66, *Works* 3.132.

30. Books attacking quaking that were answered in the *Great Mistery* include Samuel Eaton, *The Quakers Confuted* (White, 1654), E125; George Willington, *The Gadding Tribe Reproved* (for the author, 1655), W2802; Joshua Miller, *AntiChrist in Man* (Lodovick Lloyd, 1655), M2061; Francis Harris, *Some Queries proposed to the Quakers* (Fletcher, 1655), H844; Higginson, *Brief Relation*; Weld, *Perfect Pharisee*; Giles Firmin, *Stablishing against Shaking* (Webb and Grantham, 1656), S967.

31. *The Great Mistery* 48, *Works* 3:104.

32. *The Great Mistery* 9, 11, *Works* 3:46, 51, and elsewhere. See Chapter 6, page 79, and

note 12, page 263, where the reference to Ephesians 5:30 (older versions) and to Genesis 29:14, meaning close kinship, was noted. A stronger phrase than "spiritual unity" may be needed for the relationship; Bailey, *New Light,* coined the phrase "celestial inhabitation."

33. *The Great Mistery* 131, *Works* 3:227.

34. Fox, *The Priests and Professors Catechisme* (Calvert 1657), F1882, 3.

35. Fox, *To all People that meet in Steeplehouses* (London: Simmons, 1657), F1951, 5, and many other such examples.

36. Examples in Hubberthorne, *The Cause of Stumbling Removed* (London, Simmons, 1657), H3222, *The Rebukes of a Reviler* (Calvert, 1657), H3229, and *Truth and Innocence Clearing Itself* (Calvert, 1657) (not found in Wing); and George Weare, *The Doctrines and Principles of Priests of Scotland* (Calvert, 1657), W1190.

37. Most commentators who approach from a Quaker position, or from one sympathetic to Quakerism, make such assertions, including Barbour, *QPE,* Gwyn, *Apocalypse of the Word,* and Nuttall, *Holy Spirit.* Maurice Creasey, "Early Quaker Christology with special reference to the thought of Isaac Penington" (Ph.D. diss., University of Leeds, 1956), saw the weakness in Quaker Christology but insisted that Quakers really accepted the importance of the human life and death of Christ. It is my opinion that confessional considerations were at work. T. L. Underwood, in his Ph.D. dissertation, "The Controversy between the Baptists and the Quakers" (University of London, 1965), made similar points to mine, but his conclusions remained unpublished and little known until *Primitivism* appeared in 1997. See *Primitivism,* 34–50, for a detailed discussion of early Quaker Christology.

38. This was a form of Wisdom Christology, based on texts such as John 1:1–14, Philippians 2:5:11, and passages from the first three chapters of Hebrews. The figures come from data collected for my Ph.D. dissertation, "The Faith of the First Quakers." It is not possible to be certain of exact numbers, but there is no doubt as to the general trend.

39. Fox, *A Catechism for Children* (Calvert, 1657), F1756.

40. The young George Whitehead was a possible exception to this tendency. See Chapter 17, note 18.

41. Robert Barclay, *An Apology for the True Christian Divinity* (Sowle, 1676), Proposition 7.

42. *The Great Mistery* 13, *Works* 3:52.

43. Burrough, *A Declaration to all the World of our Faith* (Simmons, 1657), B5995, 4.

44. Caton, *The Moderate Enquirer Resolved,* 25.

45. Fox the Younger, *The Words of the Everlasting and True Light* (Simmons, 1659), F2021, 8.

Chapter 9

1. Some early examples were Farnworth in 1654, Dewsbury, Parnel, Martha Simmons, and John Whitehead in 1655, and William Ames, Francis Howgill, John Lilburne, George Rofe, Thomas Symonds, "RW," who may be Robert West, and George Whitehead in 1656. See Watkins, *The Puritan Experience,* for the habit of keeping spiritual journals.

2. Francis Harris, *Some Queries Proposed to the Quakers* (Fletcher, 1655), H844, 22. Harris, fl. 1652–72, a Gloucestershire curate who contended with Quakers, was one of those who signed a petition to Cromwell in 1656 not to accept the crown (*BDER, CR*).

3. It is worth noting that in Baptist circles "disorderly walking" usually meant a sin against church order, not against morality, see B. R. White, ed., *Association Records of the Particular Baptists of England, Wales and Ireland to 1660* (London: Baptist Historical Society,

1971–74), 26, 61, 68, 126. The Baptist antonym was to "walk orderly," whereas, for Quakers, the antonym was to "walk in the light."

4. Sw. 2.79, 1654.

5. These sins were also particular targets of many contemporaries of Quakers. See Underdown, *Fire from Heaven*, 72–78, 104, for the efforts of Dorchester authorities to deal with such practices.

6. Fox and Nayler, *A Word from the Lord, unto all the Faithless Generations of the World* (1654), 13. See also Farnworth, *Light Risen out of Darkness* (Calvert, 1653), 57, F490: "All Ranters and Libertines, who are without order and spiritual government . . . we disown."

7. "Letters of John Audland," 3; cf. *CJ* 1:416.

8. Thomas Symonds or Simonds, *The Voyce of the Just Uttered* (1656), S3804, 3. He was a master weaver (d. 1665).

9. Such phrases were frequently used, especially in the second half of the 1650s. See Parker, *To all ye who be called Baptists* [1657], P387; Batt and Pitman, *Truth Vindicated* (Simmons, 1658), P2299, 6; Penington, *The Way of Life and Death* (Lloyd, 1658), P1219, 69. See also Mary Penington, *Experiences in the Life of Mary Penington*, ed. Norman Penney (Philadelphia: Biddel, and London, 1911, reprinted, London: Friends Historical Society, 1992), 44–45, also in *QFP* 19.13.

10. For example, Thomas Ollive, in difficulty at home, to Fox, Sw. 4.166, 1658; Thomas Ellwood, *The History of the Life of Thomas Ellwood* (Sowle, 1714), for many problems with his father; also *BQ* 488–93.

11. Some Baptists also witnessed against tithes. White, *Association Records of the Particular Baptists of England, Wales, and Ireland to 1660* (London: Baptist Historical Society, 1971–74), 69, 151, 157, 158, shows that Baptist churches left it to the individual to pay tithes or not, but those who refused should "be passive under it, taking joyfully the distraining of their goods."

12. Fox, *A Paper sent forth into the World, why we deny teachers* (London: Calvert 1653), F1872, 8.

13. Camm, *Some Particulars concerning the Law sent to Oliver Cromwell* (1654), C391, and Howgill, *Answer to . . . Ellyson* (1654), H3154, 5, 9. Mary Forster, *These Several Papers was sent to the Parliament* (1659), F1605, is a huge petition on tithes from Quaker women.

14. In East Anglia in 1658 Ann Blaykling was found to be teaching that impropriated tithes should be paid, and that civil taxes should not be paid, so Hubberthorne and George Whitehead went to the area, and explained that she had Quaker teaching back to front; see Sw. 4.91 (EQL 367), February 1657, George Whitehead to Fox; Sw. 4.10 (EQL 440), April 1658, Hubberthorne to Fox. See also Billing, *Word of Reproof and Advice to my late Fellow-Soldiers* (Simmons, 1659), B2903, 18; Crook, *Tythes no Property nor Lawful Maintenance* (Simmons, 1659), C7225, 1; and Hubberthorne, *The Real Cause of the Nations Bondage* (Simmons, 1659), H3228. The lack of clarity regarding impropriated tithes is such that Braithwaite (*BQ* 346) thought that Quakers objected to paying impropriated tithes, while Barbour (*QPE* 156) suggested that Quakers had no such objection.

15. Pearson, *To the Parliament of the Commonwealth of England* (1653), P992, 31, 34.

16. Byne, *The Scornfull Quakers Answered*, 62. Sheppard, *Parson's Guide*, "Epistle to the Reader," notes that proposals to abolish tithe concerned "only the Tithes in the hands of Ministers, and in relation to their Maintenance, and not the tythes in the hands of other men."

17. Fox, *An Answer to Dr. Burgess His Book* (Simmons, 1659), F1743, 20, answering Cornelius Burgess, *A Case Concerning the Buying of Bishops' Lands* (1659), B5670. Burgess's book described a long-running dispute concerning the disposal of church lands. Fox may have chosen it as a convenient peg on which to hang a discussion of tithe.

18. John Pearson, *Antichristian Treachery* (c. 1678, Wing reference erroneous), 138–39, claimed that about 1657 Fox had advised someone to buy out an impropriator. In view of the strong evidence for this attitude among Friends of the 1650s, and also Fox's pragmatic attitude to anything that he did not consider a matter of principle, he may well have done so.

19. For possible origins of the testimony on oaths, see Christopher Hill, *Society and Puritanism* (London: Secker and Warburg, 1964), 382–419, where it is related to social protest, in that oaths were usually only required of the poorer section of the community.

20. See William Tallack, *George Fox, Friends and the Early Quakers* (London: Partridge, 1868), 70–74, for similar Baptist testimonies. White, *Association Records*, 126, gives a date as "8th day, 8th month (vulgarly, October), 1652."

21. Henry Clarke, *Englands Lessons Set to be Learned by her Rulers* (Calvert, 1656), C4454, is an early pamphlet on this subject. See especially Fox's *Battledore*, mentioned in Chapter 13, page 177.

22. For Fox's views on setting one fair price, see *A Warning to all the Merchants in London* (Simmons, 1658), F1985.

23. Fox, *Concerning Good Morrow and Good Even* (Simmons, 1657), F1766, 1, 2. See also Fox, *Of Bowings* (Simmons, 1657), F1869.

24. Ellis Bradshaw, *The Quakers Whitest Divell Unvailed* (1654), B4148, 6; Byne, *The Scornfull Quakers Answered*, 1; Richard Baxter, *One Sheet against the Quakers* (1657), 4.

25. Billingsgate reference from Thomas Collier, *A Looking Glass for the Quakers* (Brewster, 1656), C5290, 1. See Jeremiah Ives, *Innocency above Impudency* (Moon, 1656), I1102, 9, for a similar comment.

26. *QPE* 162–66 discusses possible regional differences.

27. *BQ* 162. Capp, *The Fifth Monarchy Men*, 143, mentions a hat testimony and use of "thou" among Fifth Monarchists.

28. Fox, *An Instruction to Judges and Lawyers* (Simmons, [1657]), F1848, 25, 27.

29. Farnworth, *An Easter Reckoning* (1653), F480, 25.

30. Burrough, *A Declaration to all the World of our Faith* (Simmons, 1657), B5995, 5.

31. George Fox the Younger, *Exhortation to Families* [1659], F2001; cf. Hubberthorne, *Rebukes of a Reviler*. For social relations in the seventeenth century, see, for example, A. Fletcher and J. Stevenson, eds., *Order and Disorder in Early Modern England* (Cambridge: Cambridge University Press, 1985), and P. Griffiths, A. Fox, and S. Hindle, eds., *The Experience of Authority in Early Modern England* (Basingstoke: Macmillans, and New York: St Martins, 1996).

32. Mack, *Visionary Women*, 225–32; Trevett, *Women and Quakerism*, 43–74.

33. Caton 3.95, July 1655. Fox wrote a diatribe against fashionable dress, published twice under different titles, *The Priests Fruits made manifest and the Fashions of the World*, F1883, and *The Priests Fruits made manifest and the Vanity of the World*, F1833A (both Simmons 1657)

34. Thomas Ellwood, *History of the Life of Thomas Ellwood* (London: Sowle, 1714), 15.

35. Humphrey Smith, *To the Musicians, the Harpists . . .* (1659), S4082.

36. Solomon Eccles, *A Musick-Lector* (1667), E129.

37. Sw. 2.1, cf. *NJ* 1–2, for Fox's youthful practice; Thomas Howsegoe, *A Word from the North sounded to the South* (London: Calvert, 1657), H3197, 2; Ellwood, *History of the Life*, 14. Cf. Richard Bauman, *Let Your Words Be Few: Symbolism of Speaking and Silence Among Seventeenth-Century Quakers* (Cambridge: Cambridge University Press, 1983, new ed. London: Quaker Home Service, 1998), 20–31, on the control of speech as a Quaker testimony.

38. Mad Tom, *Twenty Quaking Queries* (1659), T3416, 7.

39. Hubberthorne, *The Antipathy betwixt Flesh and Spirit* (Calvert, 1654), H3220, 4.

40. Thomas Symonds, *The Voyce of the Just Uttered*, 6. Such views were present in the Quaker movement from the beginning, see Sw. 3.3 and 3.67 (EQL 8), November 1652, when Nayler advised a rather disorganised meeting, "abide every one in your calling, be not slothful in business."

41. Sw. 2.95; Fox, *Epistles,* 131.

42. Possibly Dewsbury, see Chapter 1, page 11. The earliest clearly pacifist statement is probably Sw. 4.228, Agnes Wilkinson to Friends in 1653: "Strip yourself naked of all your carnal weapons . . . for the Lord is coming to judge men . . . and carnal weapons shall be broken."

43. Howgill and Burrough, *A Visitation of the Rebellious Nation of Ireland* (Calvert, 1656), H3188, 12–13.

44. Note Camm's letter about the great meeting at the Bristol Fort in 1654 (Caton 3.79), Chapter 11, page 148, and Miles Halhead and Thomas Salthouse *The Wounds of an Enemy in the House of a Friend* (Calvert, 1656), S476, 1, regarding the Captain of the Fort at Bristol who provided them with a certificate, "concerning them and their good affections to the Commonwealth."

45. Fox and Nayler, *To thee, Oliver Cromwell* (Calvert, 1655), F1962, 7.

46. Fox, *To the Council of Officers of the Armie, and the Heads of the Nation* [1659], F1955, title, 2, 5; cf. Fox's earlier paper Sw. 2.66, to soldiers, governors and officers, where soldiers were advised that their swords should "be laid upon all that do violence." See also Fox and Burrough, *Good Counsel and Advice Rejected* (Simmons, 1659), B6006, esp. 27, 35.

47. "Letters of John Audland," 11; *To the Generals, and Captains, Officers and Souldiers of the present Army* [1658], T1396, 6: "We do now declare, that not for any offence, or breach of the law, martial or civil, were we cast out from among you, but only by the injustice of men for the exercise of our consciences towards God . . . and could not respect persons, nor flatter men, nor let them have lordship over our conscience . . . for we were never otherwise minded, than to have stood in defence for the nations against their enemies." Cf. Christopher Hill and Edmund Dell, eds., *The Good Old Cause* (London: Lawrence and Wishart, 1949), 406–7, quoting a letter from Colonel Daniel to General Monck, July 16, 1657: "My Captain-Lieutenant . . . is much confirmed in his principle of quaking, making all soldiers his equals (according to the levelling strain) that I dare say in a short time his principles in the army shall be the root of disobedience." See also *WTUD* 241–42, and *BQ* 218–19, for Quaker soldiers.

48. Thomas Lurting, *A Fighting Sailor Turned Peacable Christian* (Sowle, 1710), 18–21. See also *ESP* 14; *Cal.* (1656–57), 441, October 1656, possibly referring to Lurting, and Kenneth Carroll, "Quakerism and the Cromwellian Army in Ireland," CJFHS 54/3 (1978), 135–54, for a record of one soldier in Henry Cromwell's force who objected to fighting.

49. Sw. 2.2, also *CJ* 1:161.

50. John Lilburne, *The Resurrection of John Lilburne* (Calvert, 1656), L2175, 14. See the discussion of Lilburne's conversion in Nuttall, "Overcoming the World," in Baker, *Sanctity and Secularity: The Church and the World,* Studies in Church History 10 (Oxford: Oxford University Press, 1973), 156–59. It was not Lilburne's ends but his methods of gaining them that changed

51. Note Fox's avoidance of the army draft, Chapter 1, page 6, and Bryan Ball's comparison between Fox and the Fifth Monarchists, Chapter 5, note 53.

52. Vann, *Social Development of Early Quakerism,* 10–12, refers to Baptist and army contacts, and to Ann Blaykling, who was carrying "divers papers . . . containing directions for travels into several counties and places in this commonwealth" when she was arrested in Cambridge. See also Luke Howard, *Love and Truth in Plainness Manifested* (London: Sowle,

1704), 19, for the list of names and addresses, including Samuel Fisher's, which he gave to Caton and George Whitehead.

53. "Letters of John Audland," 18, the Journal of John Audland. Thomas Ayrey (fl. 1654–79) was later disciplined for taking an oath. (DQB).

54. Sw. 3.53 (EQL 34), October 1653. Cf. Sw. 4.1 (EQL 65), Hubberthorne to Fox, May 1654; Caton 3.66, Howgill to Fell, July 1654.

55. Robert Turner, *Truths Defence* (1658), T3333, 1. This happened at Bandon Bridge in Ireland. Turner became a friend of Penn and went to America, where he was disowned in 1692 for his association with George Keith.

56. See Mack, *Visionary Women*, 106–7, for women ministers in other churches, and 165–90, for differences between the men's and the women's calls to ministry. In my opinion, Mack tends to exaggerate this. Wilcox, *Theology and Women's Ministry*, preface, thinks that the explanation for the Quakers' attitude to women lay in their theology, but it is more probable, given the development of Quaker theology as described in Chapters 6, 7, and 8, that the attitude to women came first, possibly deriving from Fox's encounters with Elizabeth Hooton and Margaret Fell, and, maybe his relationship with his mother, and that the theological justification was thought out afterward.

57. Mary Garman, Judith Applegate, Margaret Benefiel, and Dorth Meredith, eds., *Hidden in Plain Sight: Quaker Women's Writings 1650–1700* (Wallingford, Pa.: Pendle Hill Press, 1996) is an annotated anthology of these publications. The first, dated 1650, is Seeker rather than Quaker. The importance of Quaker writings in the women's literature of the seventeenth century is well documented, but it should be remembered that this is but one aspect of Quaker pamphlet productivity. In 1655 and 1656, over 14 percent of the pamphlets collected by George Thomason were written by Quakers, most of them men.

58. Hubberthorne, *A True Testimony of the Zeal of the Oxford Professors* (1654), H3240.

59. Sw. 3.16. This was attended to; a later letter, ARB 176, mentions another woman with Elizabeth Fletcher.

60. Sw. 4.163 (EQL 334), November 1656; cf. Priscilla Cotton on women's ministry, Chapter 4, page 57.

61. Caton 3.29, Caton to Fell, probably early October 1658.

62. Fox, *A Reply to the Pretended Vindication of the Quakers Twenty-three Queries* (Simmons, 1658), F1890, 12.

63. *Quakers are Inchanters and Dangerous Seducers* (Dodd, 1655), Q13, 7; Giles Firmin, *Stablishing against Shaking* (Webb and Grantham, 1655), S967

64. Sw. 1.383, about 1656. "Country" could mean another part of Britain, rather than a foreign land.

65. Sw. 2.95, original version of Epistle 131, 1656.

66. See David Underdown, *Revel, Riot and Rebellion: Popular Politics and Culture in England 1603–1660* (Oxford: Clarendon Press, 1987), 252. Underdown considers that there is no need to look beyond normal human reactions for hostility to Quakers.

67. ARB 129.

68. See Jeremiah 27 and 28, for the working of prophetic signs, when two prophets disagreed about God's message. For Quaker signs, Kenneth L. Carroll, "Early Quakers and 'Going Naked as a Sign,'" *Quaker History* 67, no. 2 (autumn 1978): 69–87, and also "Sackcloth and Ashes and Other Signs and Wonders," *JFHS* 54 (1957): 314–25. Bauman, *Let Your Words Be Few*, 84–94, underestimates the importance of the Old Testament influence.

69. William Simpson, *Going Naked, a Signe* (Wilson, 1660), S3844, broadside.

70. The Holmes incident caused considerable scandal and is mentioned in Higginson and other anti-Quaker books. For Elizabeth Fletcher, *FPT* 259. See also the case of Ann Nicholson, recorded by Agnes Wilkinson in the "Letters of John Audland," 1; *BQ* 126, 135.

71. Examples are *The Quacking Mountebank*, 16, and Francis Fullwood, *A True Relation of a Dispute* (Roper, 1656), F2520, 75.

72. Bishop, *The Cry of Blood*, 98, 116; Cadbury, ed., *Letters to William Dewsbury*, 18, for Parnell's letter.

73. Nayler mentioned Howgill's fast in a letter to Fell, Sw. 3.66. For Parnell, see Henry Glisson, *The True and Lamentable Relation of the Desperate Death of James Parnell, Quaker* (1656), T2510, answered by *The Lambs Defence against Lyes* (Calvert, 1656), L249. There are also a number of references in Fox's *Journal* to Quakers fasting.

74. Fox, *An Answer to a Paper which came from the Papists* (Simmons, 1658), F1742, 3. Internal evidence shows this anti-Catholic pamphlet to have been partly written by a woman, who may have been Margaret Fell, for the style is similar to her letters, and the content agrees with the description of fasting at Swarthmoor in the letter Sw. 4.267 (EQL 493), October 1659, Caton to Fox. Also, Thomas Fell at least on one occasion objected to his wife publishing a book, which might have led her to publish anonymously (Spence 3.49, October 1657, Fell to Gerrard Roberts).

75. *BQ* 147, referred to in *The Quakers Shaken* and in *Saul's Errand*.

76. σαρξ and πνευμα, contrasted in many Pauline epistles, see, for instance, Romans 8:1–17, Galatians 5:13–24. σαρξ is a difficult word to translate into modern English; the *New International* and *Good News* Bibles have "sinful nature." Quaker usage needs more attention from Quaker theologians than it has yet had. Douglas Gwyn, *Apocalypse of the Word*, 98–99, touches on it, saying that Quakers were not matter/spirit dualists.

77. Farnworth, *A Discovery of Truth and Falsehood* (Calvert, 1653), F479A, 51.

78. Nayler, *Two Epistles* (1654), N325, 5, cited by Nuttall, "The Letters of James Nayer," in Birkel *The Lamb's War*, 49. Cf. *How Sin is Strengthened* (London: Simmons, 1657), N285, and *Message from the Spirit of Truth* (London: Simmons, 1658), N298. Penington had similar views, see, for example, *The Way of Life and Death made Manifest* (London: Lodowick Lloyd, 1658), P1219, 70–71.

79. Fox, *Concerning Good Morrow and Good Even* (Simmons, 1657), 12.

80. Fox on "unity with creation," see *CJ* 1:44, *NJ* 110.

Chapter 10

1. For example, Hubberthorne, *A True Testimony to the Zeal of the Oxford Professors* (1654), H3240, 13–14. Note the incomplete explanation in Mack, *Visionary Women*, 177.

2. For example, Nayler, *The Discovery of the Man of Sin* (Calvert, 1654), N274, 12. Hubberthorne, *Immediate Call to the Ministry of the Gospel* (1654), H3225, tells of his own call to the ministry.

3. Such phrases were used in many pamphlets. See, for example, Fox, *A Paper sent forth into the World* [1653], F1872; *A Short Answer to a Book by Seven Priests* (Calvert, 1654), P36; Dewsbury, *True Prophecy*; Farnworth, *Character Whereby the False Christs . . . may be known* (Calvert, 1654), F475.

4. Paid ministry, especially if funded by by tithes, was an issue for many radicals. See, for example, William Haller, *The Rise of Puritanism* (New York, 1938), 350–51, for Milton's opinions. Nicholas Morgan, *Lancashire Quakers and the Establishment 1660–1730* (Halifax: Ryburn Academic Publishing, 1993), for post-Restoration period Quaker objection to tithe, on religious rather than social grounds.

5. Thomas Aldam, Elizabeth Hooton, William Pears, Benjamin Nicholson, Jane Holmes, and Mary Fisher, *False Prophets and False Teachers Described*, internal date 1652,

which could mean early 1653 new style, A894B, 1, 2, 3, 4, 8; see *EQW*, 359–62. Many Quaker pamphlets of 1653 and 1654 make similar complaints, see especially Fox, *A Paper sent forth why we deny the Teachers of this World* (Calvert, 1653), F1872, and many reprints.

6. Hubberthorne, *The Rebukes of a Reviler Fallen on his Own Head* (Calvert, 1657), H3229, 52–56, answering Stalham, *The Reviler Rebuked* (Hills, 1657), S5186.

7. Nayler, *A Few Words Occasioned by a Paper lately printed* [1654], 18; see Watts, *The Dissenters*, 185.

8. Baxter, *Quakers Catechism*, 31; Nayler, *Answer to a Book called the Quakers Catechism*, 44. See Chapter 14, pages 191–92, for the Quakers' changing attitude to earlier martyrs during the 1660s.

9. Henry Clarke, *Description of the Prophets, Apostles, and Ministers of Christ* (Calvert, 1655), C4453, 1. Henry Clarke (fl. 1655–61) was from Southwark (DQB).

10. Henry J. Cadbury, *George Fox's "Book of Miracles"* (Cambridge: University Press, 1948), a reconstruction of a lost book by Fox. Cadbury's introduction covers most of the evidence for early Quaker miracles, and of miracle-working by other religious leaders, and he notes that on several occasions Quaker ministers were challenged to perform miracles. See Reay, *Quakers and the English Revolution*, 36–37; Bailey, *New Light*, 48–58; *FF* 103, all of which accept the evidence for Quaker miracles rather uncritically. It is quite possible that some of the stories of healings were introduced into the Quaker kerygma some years after they were alleged to have happened. Bailey notes the existence of a rearguard pro-Fox movement, in retreat before the rationalising processes of the later seventeenth century, and Ingle in *FF* makes much of Fox's problems in maintaining his position in later years. It would be worth investigating whether the Quaker miracle stories were developed and recorded in connection with such problems, rather than as strictly contemporary records.

11. Sw. 1.372, July 1652. Nayler's healing of Dorcas Erbury is another possible instance (see any book on Nayler for the story), but this was outside the Quaker mainstream, and the circumstances are most doubtful.

12. See Bailey, *New Light*, 54. Hubberthorne's, *A True Separation between the Power of the Spirit and the Imitation of Antichrist* (Calvert, 1654), H3238, 7, has a definite reference to Matthew 11:5, and one cannot be sure how literally Hubberthorne expected to be understood. Fox, *A Reply to the Vindication of the Answer to the Quakers Twenty-three Queries* (Simmons, 1658), 14, claims "visible miracles," but nothing specific.

13. The painless childbirth is quoted by Reay in *Quakers and the English Revolution*, 37 n. 39, with reference to Sw. 3.158. The fasting challenge came up in his dispute with Thomas Moore and John Horne; see Chapter 7, page 95, and *BQ* 108.

14. *Great Mistery* 3, *Works* 3:37, cited by Cadbury, "Fox's '*Book of Miracles*,'" which has a full discussion of such Quaker "miracles," 19–27.

15. See Chapter 16, note 12, for "church of the first born."

16. Higginson, *Irreligion of the Northern Quakers*, Introductory Epistle, "To the Seduced Followers of George Fox, James Nayler, etc., living in Westmorland and some adjacent parts."

17. Caton 3.106, summer 1654. Note references to 1 Corinthians.

18. *The Great Mistery*, 31; *Works* 3:80.

19. Bishop, *A Rejoinder Consisting of Two Parts*, 102. See also Hubberthorne, *The Cause of Stumbling Removed* (Simmons, 1657), H3222, 26.

20. Salthouse, *The Line of True Judgement* (Simmons, 1658), S474, 15, quoted in Chapter 7, page 90.

21. Fox, *An Instruction to Judges and Lawyers* (Simmons, 1657), F1848, 21.

22. *FF* 104 notes several early epistles of Fox calling for unity, and for the first time using the word "minister" for Quaker leaders.

23. Sw. 3.40 (EQL 7), Aldam to the Brethren and Sisters.

24. Sw. 1.341 (EQL 32), September 1653. Robert Collinson (fl. 1653–56) caused trouble again in 1656, making a similar charge against Howgill and Burrough, and was formally disowned by them. See also Sw. 1.88, *BQ* 345, and DQB.

25. Sw. 1.245 (EQL 44) (1653), Lawson to Fell; Sw. 3.2 (EQL 27) July (1653), Nayler to Fell, not to Fox as in EQL. Thomas Lawson (1630–1691) was a parish minister who resigned his living on becoming a Quaker, later becoming a schoolmaster and a noted botanist (DQB). Nothing is known of Ellen Parr.

26. Sw. 4.232 (EQL 111), John Grave to Margaret Fell [1654]. See Chapter 11, pages 152–53, for singing in meetings.

27. Sw. 4.202 (EQL 99), Thomas Robertson to Fox, December 1654, and ARB 58, from Bristol, July 1655, which also mentions Anne Wilson.

28. Examples include Sw. 4.149 (EQL 156), June 1655, Camm to Fell, trouble in the North and with Thomas Ayrey; Sw. 4.35 (EQL 197), November 1655, John Wilkinson to Fell, arguments in Somerset; Sw. 4.103 (EQL 269), May 1656, Caton to Wardle, trouble over a meeting house in Scotland; Sw. 4.137 (EQL 280), June 1656, Dewsbury to Fell, Farnworth bringing back Friends who had "run out."

29. Burrough and Howgill, *To the Camp of the Lord in England* (1655), H3184, 16.

30. *BQ* 64–65. Braithwaite only touched lightly on this unsavoury story. It would not have been appreciated in 1911, and, like Fox, he preferred not to dwell on Quakers' faults. Arthur Eddington, "The First Fifty Years of Quakers in Norwich" (typescript 1932, in Quaker libraries), gives a full account. See especially the letter from Richard Clayton to Margaret Fell, Sw. 1.30 (EQL 164), in Appendix 7 to "Quakers in Norwich." Vann, *Social Development,* 18, found a reference in Norwich Quarter Sessions records, that Atkinson disowned Quakerism in open court on August 1, 1955.

31. Sw. 1.347(EQL 133), expressing repentance, is Atkinson's reply to what had evidently been a sharp letter from Fell.

32. ARB 36, Burrough to Fox, 1657, for the "little short maid." Mack, *Visionary Women,* 205–7 and n. 120 for other examples of women under discipline. See Chapter 3, pages 36–37, for Martha Simmons. Two letters to Fox in the summer of 1664, Sw. 4.52 from Edward Bourne, and Sw. 4.201 from Thomas Robertson, concern a Katherine Crooke in Hereford whom they could not handle (see Chapter 4, pages 52–53).

33. Sw 4.206, Robertson to Fox, 1658; Sw 4.177, Hall to Fox the Younger, June 1660.

34. Sw. 2.17, Dewsbury, *Works,* 1–4, Sw. 3.19. See *BQ* 140–43, *FPT* 244. *FF* 103 gives a 1653 date for these developments in Durham, but 1654 is a possibility, allowing more time after the convincement of Anthony Pearson. The 1653 references may refer to Yorkshire, where Dewsbury was definitely active.

35. Quakers were like General Baptists in that they were organised in areas rather than as congregations. General Baptists appointed persons whom they called "Messengers" to care for several local churches, similar to Quaker "overseers" (page 136), but having less authority. See Tallack, *George Fox,* 70–76, and Watts, *The Dissenters,* 298.

36. Caton 3.156, Camm to Fell, August 1655.

37. Sw. 2.28, May 1655. *CJ* 2:118 refers to an earlier paper of Fox, from 1653. See *BQ* 144–46, for fuller details of arrangements, and *FF* 105–6, for the political background.

38. Sw. 1.195 (EQL 89), Holmes to Fell, October 1654; and Willan and Taylor to Fell, Sw 1.214, February 1655, expressing their doubts.

39. *BQ* 175 n. 7 has a reference for the word "elder" for January 1655.

40. There is evidence for such arrangements in a number of letters, including Caton 3.91, 156, 157. Quakers with knowledge of Greek would have known that "overseer" is *episkopos,* a bishop. John Pendarves, *Arrowes against Babylon* (Chapman, 1656), P1136, 44, remarked that Quakers did have Masters or Masterly Teachers.

41. Sw. 2.18, 1656, for suggestions for extending general meetings to the whole country.

42. Katherine Crook had the right to "appoint meetings." Sw. 4.52, Edward Bourne to Fox; and Chapter 4, pages 52–53, for Crook. The main exceptions to the rule that women did not sign official statements are the women's tithe petition of 1659, introduced by Mary Forster, *These several papers was sent to Parliament* (1659), F1605, and Margaret Fell's letter to Charles II in 1660, in *A Declaration and Information from the People called Quakers* (Simmons and Wilson, 1660), F628.

43. The Bristol minute book refers to the women's meeting as if it was already established when records begin in 1667.

44. ARB 38, October 1656, to Burrough and Howgill, published in *JFHS* 32 (1935): 62.

45. The best copy is considered to be the one from the Marsden Monthly Meeting record book, now in the Lancashire Records Office in Preston. There is another copy in Caton 1.90, and it is also reproduced in *LEF*. Other similar disciplinary documents in *LEF*; see also *BQ* 310–39.

46. *QFP*, at the end of section 1.01.

47. For example, Pendarves, *Arrowes against Babylon,* 44. Note also comments made by opponents after the Nayler affair, Chapter 3, page 43.

48. *BQ* 314–39 has a detailed discussion of these developments. Dates and details not always clear. Caton 3.104, Parker to Fell, July 1658, described the setting up of county and regional meetings and the new financial arrangements.

49. Sw. 2.95, Fox at a general meeting in the autumn of 1656.

50. Sw. 2.97.

51. Burrough, *Message Proclaimed by Divine Authority* (Simmons, writer's date 24th of 8th month [October] 1658), B6013A, 3. This date does not coincide with any of the meetings identified by Braithwaite (*BQ* 325–35), and needs further investigation.

52. Examples of letters to Fox asking for help or advice include ARB 36, January 1657, from Burrough, a problem about ministry; Sw. 4.91 (EQL 367), February 1657, from George Whitehead, payment of impropriated tithes; Sw. 4.146 (EQL 457), September 1658, from Henry Fell, difficulties in Barbados; Sw. 4.166 (EQL 459), October 1658, from Thomas Ollive about the difficulties faced by young people whose families disapproved of their becoming Quakers.

53. Humphrey Wollrich, *The Unlimited God* (about 1659), W3303; Sw. 1.4 (EQL 504), December 1659, Wollrich to Fox; also see *BQ* 393.

54. Sw. 3.112 (EQL 473), February 1659, John Sands to Fox.

55. Sw. 4.103 (EQL 215), 1655.

56. Sw. 1.241 (EQL 214), 1655. See note at EQL 214 for the link between the letter and the accounts, which are reproduced in *JFHS* 6 (1909): 49–52 and 82–85 (85 for payment to Lawson). Thomas Lawson (1630–91) had been vicar of Rampside, near Sedbergh, and became a noted schoolmaster and botanist.

57. Halhead and Salthouse, *The Wounds of an Enemy in the House of a Friend* (Calvert, 1656), S476, 56.

58. This persecution caused angry reactions from European Protestant governments, and Cromwell called for a national fast day in support of the Waldensians.

59. Sw. 1.237, 239, 263 (EQL 159, 165, 212), June–December 1655, Taylor to Fell. See Fox's epistle, Sw. 2.93.

60. For the setting-up of the men's meetings, see John Penington MSS 4.29–34, Friends House Library, a letter written by Burrough shortly before his death. Full text, *LEF* 287–310; William Crouch, *Postuma Christiana, or, a Collection of some Papers of William Crouch* (Sowle, 1712), 22, describes the beginnings of both men's and women's meetings, reproduced in *LEF* 285–86; see also *BQ* 340–42. See Watts, *Dissenters,* 319–20, for women in gathered churches.

61. Mentioned in John Harwood, *To All People that Profess the Eternal Truth,* 7; and Fox,

The Spirit of Envy Lying and Persecution, 10 (both 1663). See Chapter 15, pages 198–99, for the dispute between Fox and Harwood.

62. *BQ* 306–42 gives an account of what was happening. The main manuscript references are ARB 160, Howgill to Burrough, 1657; Sw. 1.297 (EQL 385), May 1657, and Sw. 1.302 (EQL 411), September 1657, both Taylor & Willan to Fell; Sw. 1.317 (EQL 448), June 30, 1658, Caton to Fell; Sw. 1.303 (EQL 455), September 1658, Taylor to Fell.

63. Sw. 2.97 and 99. The title "Quarterly Meeting" was in use in Yorkshire by 1666 (Yorkshire Quarterly Meeting minute book).

64. See *ESP* 31, 39, and *Cal* 1658–59, 147, 148, for references to Roberts.

65. Little St. Thomas Apostle is not to be found in the modern London street map, for it lies under the western part of Cannon Street. Gerrard Roberts moved to another part of the city after the Great Fire, so it is possible that his property was affected by the construction at that time of a new road, Queen Street. If so, the house at the sign of the Fleur-de-Lys probably stood close to the Cannon Street/Queen Street intersection.

66. *LEF* 248, cited *SPQ* 672, mentions the destruction of documents. A count of letters recorded in EQL, made in connection with my Ph.D. dissertation, "The Faith of the First Quakers," showed some 120 Swarthmore letters for 1656, 80 for 1657, around 40 for 1658, and the same in 1659. The ARB collection showed a similar effect, although total numbers are much smaller.

67. There are many examples of reports on the ministry.

68. *BQ* 317 and n. 1.

69. Sw. 1.176 (EQL 402), Thomas Barcroft, and Caton 3.103, Parker, both to Margaret Fell.

Chapter 11

1. See especially Farnworth, *The Heart opened by Christ* (1654), F485, 8, which is referred to in Chapter 1, page 11, and note 31, page 247.

2. Tallack, *George Fox*, 66–67, for Baptist opinions; Nuttall, *Holy Spirit*, 66–74, 82–85, 96–100.

3. Hubberthorne, *The Antipathy betwixt Flesh and Spirit* (Calvert, 1654), H3220, 3. See also Fox, *Declaration against all Popery* [1654], F1783, 2; and Nayler, *The Discovery of the Man of Sin* (Calvert, 1654), N274, 11–12. See Underwood, *Primitivism*, 77–81.

4. Farnworth, *Easter Reckoning* (Calvert 1653), F480, 9; Camm and Howgill, *This was the Word of the Lord . . . to Oliver Cromwell* (1654), C392, 2. See John 4:24, I Corinthians 12:13 and 10:17, and other such texts.

5. Watts, *The Dissenters*, 306.

6. Nuttall, *Holy Spirit*, 75–89. Watts, *The Dissenters*, 34, 205.

7. Ross, ΠΑΝΣΕΒΕΙΑ, 413.

8. Charles Marshall, *Sions Travellers Comforted and the Disobedient Warned* (London: Sowle, 1704), unpaginated introduction, "A Short and Brief Narration of my Pilgrimage in this World."

9. *FPT* 52 and 124, for similar precursors of Quaker worship. Higginson, *Irreligion of the Northern Quakers*, 11.

10. Long silences in Quaker meetings, according to Higginson, appeared to be a well-established form. Bauman, *Let Your Words be Few*, analyses the Quaker attitude to silence and speech, but does not deal with the historical roots. Charismatic groups, from Saint Paul's church at Corinth up to the present day, are not usually noted for silence. More research is needed.

11. Sw. 1.189 (EQL 55), Holmes to Fell, March 1654; Sw. 4.83 (EQL 20), Farnworth to Fell, January 1653; Margaret Fell, "Testimony . . . concerning her late husband," published as preface to Fox's *Journal*; Sw. 1.373 (EQL 4), Aldam to Fox and others, July 1652; Sw. 1.43 (EQL 16), Widder to Fell, about 1652.

12. Watkins, *The Puritan Experience*, 145, refers to some individuals who shook, especially George Foster. See *BQ* 57–58 and notes, for early use of the term.

13. Until recently the importance of these charismatic phenomena was underestimated by most writers on early Quakerism. Barbour, for instance, devoted two pages to "quaking," but this was in connection with a general discussion of the process of convincement, *QPE* 99–102. See Reay, *The Quakers and the English Revolution*, 35: "People are not always aware that the early Quakers were essentially an ecstatic movement." Ingle in *FF* gives quaking its rightful importance.

14. Hubberthorne and Lawson, *Truth Cleared and Deceit made Manifest* (1654), H3241, 8, answering Vavasour Powell.

15. Nayler, *Discovery of the Man of Sin*, 44.

16. Higginson, *Irreligion of the Northern Quakers*, 12.

17. Sw. 3.50, 51 (EQL 35), November 1653, see *BQ* 198; Sw. 4.25 (EQL 272), May 1656. Bauman, *Let Your Words be Few*, 120, considers that the meeting for worship in early days was secondary to the ministry out in the world "as a directed focus of Quaker energy and initiative." This is to put the cart before the horse. Public ministry, Fox's included, grew out of the meetings for worship and the aim of public meetings was to bring people, ultimately, to the silent meetings; see, for instance, the very early instructions of Fox and Farnworth quoted in Chapter 1, page 18.

18. Higginson had made the same observation in *Irreligion of the Northern Quakers*, 12. See Bauman, *Let Your Words Be Few*, 24–25, for the significance of the word "speak."

19. John Gilpin, *The Quakers Shaken* (Gateshead, 1653), G769.

20. Sw. 3.192 (EQL 61). This may have been John Toldervy, who told much the same story of himself, with other details of his Quaker experience, in *The Foot out of the Snare* (1656), T1767.

21. Dewsbury et al., *Several Letters to Saints* (1654), D1272, Fox's letter, 13–14.

22. ARB 157.

23. Farnworth, *A Woman Forbidden to speak in the Church* (Calvert, 1654), F514, 4; Priscilla Cotton and Mary Cole, *To the Priests and People of England* (Calvert 1655), C6474, 6; and Fox, *The Woman Learning in Silence* (Simmonds, 1656), F1991, 2.

24. Examples include Francis Harris, *Some Queries proposed . . . to the Quakers* (Fletcher, 1655), H844, 18, 26; Drayton and Parker, *An Answer According to Truth* (1655), D2147, 23; George Willington, *The Gadding Tribe Reproved* (Hunt, 1655), W2802, 8; Byne, *The Scornfull Quakers Answered*, 67; Giles Firmin, *Stablishing against Shaking* (Webb and Granham, 1656), S967, 28.

25. Fisher, *The Scorned Quakers True and Honest Account*, 25; Halhead and Salthouse, *The Wounds of an Enemy in the House of a Friend* (1656), S476, 2.

26. Fox, Sw. 2.95

27. Harris, *Some Queries proposed . . . to the Quakers*, 18.

28. Farnworth, *Antichrists Man of War* (Calvert, 1655), F470, 28.

29. Bishop, *The Cry of Blood*, 27 (describing events of 1654); *Jesus Christ, the Same Today as Yesterday* (Calvert, 1655), B2995, 4.

30. Caton 3.69, Burrough and Howgill to Fell, March 1655.

31. Caton 156, 157, Camm and Audland to Fell, August 1655; John Timson, *The Quakers Apostacie from the Perfect Rule of Scripture Discovered* (Williams, 1656), T1295,

"Epistle to the Reader." There is also a mention of divided meetings in Sw. 2.95, but the text is unclear, and the printed version, in Epistle 131, appears to be a gloss.

32. Fox, "Epistle to Friends about Christ having the best room," Sw. 2.94 (1656).

33. *CJ* 1:223, quoted at greater length in *BQ* 310.

34. Thomas Underhill, *Hell Broke Loose*, 3.

35. Crouch, *Postuma Christiana*, 17, purchase of land for a meeting house in Horsley-down, Southwark; *FPT* 208, referring to the first Banbury meeting house.

36. Fox, *An Epistle to All the People upon the Earth* (Calvert, 1657), F1805, 2–3.

37. Henry Lavor, *Replies to the Antiquaeries of Thomas Lye* (Daniel White, 1657), L628, 42.

38. Burrough, *The True Christian Religion Again Discovered* (Simmons, 1658), B6043, 9. See also Anthony Mellidge, *True Relation of the former Faithfull and Long Service* (1657), M1648, 4.

39. Caton, *The Moderate Enquirer Resolved*, 14, 15. See also Fox, *Something Concerning Silent Meetings* [1657], F1909A, broadside. Fox explains them much less clearly than Caton.

40. ARB 57, Richard Waller to Fell, August 6, 1657.

41. Hubberthorne, *Rebukes of a Reviler,* 52; John Whitehead, *The Enmitie Between the Two Seeds* (1655), W1975, 20; Farnworth, *Truth Exalted and Deceit Abased* (Calvert, 1658), F512A, 18,19. See also Portfolio 36.138, quoted by Kenneth L. Carroll, "Singing in the Spirit" (*Quaker History* 73, no. 1 [spring 1984]: 1–13, which lists many other references to the practice of singing in meeting. See also Nuttall, *Holy Spirit,* 66–67, for attacks on pre-arranged singing by members of other religious groupings.

42. George Whitehead and Edward Burrough, *Son of Perdition*, 39; John Whitehead *A Small Treatise* (Wilson, 1661), 20; Leek MSS 66–76, a disciplinary document of 1675. The Yearly Meeting statement of 1675, the time of the Wilkinson-Storey dispute, says that Fox supported "singing, sighing and serious groaning."

43. Thomas Salthouse and Alexander Parker, *A Manifestation of Divine Love* (Simmons, 1660), S475, 15–19, this section by Parker. This pamphlet was published early in 1661 according to our calendar; the printer's date is old style. *QFP* 2.41.

44. It was thought that voting would not necessarily produce the will of God; this was why the Nominated Parliament was not elected. For a Quaker view on voting, see George Fox the Younger, *A Few Plain Words to be considered by those . . . who would have a Parliament* (Simmons, 1659), F2002, 1–3.

45. Russell Mortimer, ed., *Minute Book of the Men's Meeting of the Society of Friends in Bristol,* 2 vols. (Bristol, Bristol Record Society, 1971), introduction, xi, notes that many Friends of this meeting came from the Broadmead church, which kept records, and also that the new Quaker minute book, starting 1667, appears to begin in the middle of business. Other early minute books have been transcribed and are available in Friends House Library. For Baptists, see E. B. Underhill, ed., *The Records of the Churches of Christ gathered at Fenstanton, Warboys and Hexham, 1644–1720* (London: Hanserd Knollys Society, 1854), and B. R. White *Association Records of the Particular Baptists.*

46. See Chapter 10, page 140. John Penington's coll. MSS 4.29–34, *LEF* 287–310, extract in *QFP* 2.87.

47. Harold Fassnidge, *The Quakers of Melksham* (Bradford on Avon Friends, 1992), 55, quoting Thomas Beaven.

48. Michael J. Sheeran, *Beyond Majority Rule: Voteless Decisions in the Society of Friends* (Philadelphia: Philadelphia Yearly Meeting, 1983) has a useful first chapter on the early period, but beware error page 20 n. 4 regarding Perrot's supporters. See also Chapter 15, page 198.

Chapter 12

1. Francis Howgill and James Nayler, *A Woe against the Magistrates, Priests and People of Kendal* (1654), H3189, 1.

2. For Quaker attacks on particular places, see Burrough, *A Warning from the Lord to the Inhabitants of Underbarrow* (London, Calvert, 1654), B6057; Henry Gill, *A Warning and Visitation to Godalming* (1658), G742A; Fox, *To the People of Uxbridge* (London: Simmons, 1659), F1959; and many others.

3. Pearson, *To the Parliament of the Commonwealth* [1653], P992, 2.

4. Humphrey Smith and others, *A Representation of the Government of the Borough of Evesham* (1655), R1104, broadside.

5. Humphrey Smith, *Something Further of the Cruel Persecution at Evesham* (1656), S4072, 2.

6. This aspect of the Quaker attitude to suffering was similar to that of continental Anabaptists. See Harold S. Bender, "The Anabaptist Vision," in *The Recovery of the Anabaptist Vision*, ed. Guy F. Hershberger (Scottdale, Pa.: Herald Press, 1957), esp. 33, 45, 49; and Geoffrey F. Nuttall, "The Church's Ministry of Suffering," in *The Puritan Spirit* (London: Epworth, 1967), 288–303.

7. For example, Thomas Salthouse and Robert Wastfield, *A True Testimony of Faithfull Witnesses Recorded* (1657), W1036, 40: "Most of us . . . are men that have . . . conscientiously engaged for the Commonwealth interest . . . some of us in places of Trust and Concernment."

8. Sufferings pamphlets form a separate section in Joseph Smith's *Catalogue of Friends Books* (hereafter cited as Smith), 2:644–86, entitled "Sufferings of Friends for the Testimony of the Truth." The first true example of this genre is probably Hubberthorne, *A True Testimony of the Zeal of the Oxford Professors* (1654), H3240, an account of the beating-up and whipping of two women preachers at Oxford. I am grateful to Dr. Geoffrey F. Nuttall for permission to consult his unpublished survey of this literature, "Record and Testimony: Quaker Persecution Literature, 1650–1700" (1982).

9. Anne Audland and others, *The Saints Testimony Finishing through Sufferings* (Calvert, 1655), S365.

10. William Caton and John Stubbs, *A True Declaration of the Bloody Proceedings of the Men in Maidstone* (Calvert, 1655), S6072, 3. Caton (1636–65) was a former inmate of the Swarthmoor household and close to both Fell and Fox (DQB). Stubbs (b. about 1618) was a soldier and Baptist preacher convinced by Fox during his Carlisle imprisonment (*BQ* 186).

11. Sw. 4.162 (EQL 169), Gervase Benson and Anthony Pearson to Margaret Fell, August 1, 1655. Followed by the published book of Gervase Benson, Fox, and others, *The Cry of the Oppressed from under their Oppressions* (Calvert, 1656), B1900.

12. Sw. 2.97 and 2.99, Fox to Friends, 1657. A document issued in Hampshire in 1659 is in *LEF* 283. Two other 1657 epistles of Fox, Sw. 2.88 and 89, refer to the collection of sufferings records, and this was followed by the publication, with an introduction by Richard Hubberthorne, of *The Record of Suffering for Tithe in England* (1658), H3230. *BQ* 311–15 includes summaries of early documents describing these arrangements

13. Anonymous, *To the Parliament of England now sitting at Westminster* (Calvert, 1659), T1579A.

14. The reasons for the use of this process, and its working in practice, are explained by Alfred W. Braithwaite, "Early Tithe Prosecutions—Friends as Outlaws," *JFHS* 49 (1959–60): 148–56. The letters concerning this case, which date from 1655 and 1656, are, in chronological order: Sw. 4.41, 29, 30, 102, Sw. 1.63, Sw. 4.101, and Sw. 1.380 (EQL 221–25, 240, 246). See also Benson et al., *Cry of the Oppressed*, 23f.

15. For Quaker dealings with the law during the Restoration period, see Craig W. Horle, *Quakers and the English Legal System* (Philadelphia: University of Pennsylvania Press, 1988).

16. *SPQ*, 282–85.

17. Isaac Penington and William Dewsbury both took this view, according to *SPQ* 284.

18. Keith Thomas, *Religion and the Decline of Magic*, chap. 4 ("Providence," 78–112), discusses the belief in God's punishment of evildoers.

19. Pamphlets expressing this viewpoint include *Copie of a Paper presented to Parliament* (Calvert, 1659), C6185; *To the Parliament of England who are in Place to do Justice* (Simmons, 1659), T1581; and William Morris, *To the Supreme Authority of the Commonwealth* (Simmons, 1659), M2813.

20. Edward Billing, *A Word of Reproof and Advice to my late Fellow-Soldiers* (Simmons, 1659), B2903. The Examples are appended to the main pamphlet, 79–84. A reconstruction of a collection of Examples attributed to George Fox has been attempted by Henry J. Cadbury in his *Narrative Papers of George Fox* (Richmond, Ind.: Friends United Press, 1972), 209–31, but this should not be used as firm evidence for happenings in the 1650s.

21. Sw. 1.168 (EQL 496), November 1659.

22. The "Little Apocalypse" of Mark 13, many similar texts in the Synoptic Gospels, and much of Revelation.

23. Sw. 3.18 (EQL 406), August 25, 1657.

24. John Higgins, *To All Inhabitants of the Earth* (1658), H1 2. Higgins (1632/3–67) traveled in Germany with William Ames, published pamphlets in Dutch as well as English.

25. George Whitehead, John Whitehead, and George Fox the Younger, *A Brief Discovery of the Dangerous Principles of John Horne and Thomas Moore jnr* (1659), W1896, 30, answering Horne and Moore, *A Brief Discovery of the People called Quakers* (1659), H2795.

26. See, for instance, Nicholas Morgan, "The Social and Political Relations of the Lancaster Quaker Community, 1688–1740," in Michael Mullett, ed., *Early Lancaster Friends* (University of Lancaster, 1978), 27–31.

27. For the influence of John Foxe, see William Haller, *Foxe's Book of Martyrs and the Elect Nation* (London: Cape, 1963).

28. Pearson, *The Great Case of Tithes Truly Stated* (Calvert, 1657), P989, 24. See also Crook, *Tithes no Property nor Lawful Maintenance* (Simmons, 1659), C7225.

29. Edward Burrough, *A Declaration of the Sad and Great Persecution and Martyrdom of the People of God* (Wilson, 1660), B5994, 29. The better-known version of Mary Dyer's last words, in *QFP* 19.18, comes from Besse's *Collection of Sufferings*, 2:201–2. See also Francis Howgill, *The Heart of New England Hardened* (1659), H3166; George Bishop, *New England Judged* (Wilson, 1661), B3003.

30. Humphrey Smith, *Man driven out of Earth and Darkness* (1658), S4068, 38.

31. Humphrey Smith, *The True and Everlasting Rule of God Discovered* (London: Simmons, 1658), S4083, 27.

32. Humphrey Smith, *The Sounding Voyce of the Dread of Gods Mighty Power* (London, 1658), S4075, 7–8. Also in *The Fruits of Unrighteousness and Injustice* (London, 1658), S4061, 53.

Chapter 13

1. The best account of the events of 1659 as they affected Quakers is given by Barry Reay, *The Quakers and the English Revolution*. For the general history of the Restoration

period, see Ronald Hutton, *The Restoration: A Political and Religious History of England and Wales, 1658–1667* (Oxford: Oxford University Press, 1986).

2. There are further details of the 1659 pamphlets in my Ph.D. dissertation, "The Faith of the First Quakers" (Birmingham University, 1993), 242–53. Not only Quakers were bursting into print; Thomason had 652 titles in 1659 and 976 in 1660, against 282 in 1658 (Thomason xxi). Very few of these were Quaker pamphlets, as by this time Thomason had wearied of Quakers.

3. These included Hubberthorne, *The Good Old Cause briefly demonstrated* (Simmons, 1659), H3223A, dated "3rd month"; Penington, *To the Parliament, the Army and all Welaffected* (Calvert, 1659), P1215, dated "3rd month"; and George Fox the Younger, *Honest Upright Faithful Plaindealing* (Simmons, 1659), F2005A, dated "former part of 3rd month." The "third month" was May.

4. These included John Crook and others, *The Declaration of the People of God in scorn called Quakers to all Magistrates and People* (Simmons 1659), C720; *To the Parliament of England now sitting at Westminster* (Calvert, 1659), T1759A; and *To the Parliament of England who are in place to do Justice* (Simmons 1659), T1581.

5. Fox, *To the Parliament of the Commonwealth of England—Fifty-nine Particulars laid down for Regulating Things* (Simmons, 1659), F1958. Often known as the *Fifty-nine Particulars*.

6. Dorothy White, *Friends, you that are of the Parliament, hear the Word of the Lord* (1659), W1749. From the tone it probably dates from the autumn of 1659, shortly before Lambert's army expelled the Rump Parliament.

7. *ESP* 105–15; *Cal.* 1658–59, 351.364.

8. Sw. 1.84 (EQL 485), Parker to Margaret Fell, June 22, and ARB 60, Howgill to Burrough, August 8. See *BQ* 580–81; and Cole, "The Quakers and the English Revolution," *Past and Present,* no. 10 (November 1956): 39–54, esp. 43, for Fox's reaction to these suggestions, and for his letters Sw. 7.157 and 165.

9. For Quaker involvement in the militia, see *BQ* 461–63; Reay, *The Quakers and the English Revolution,* 87–91.

10. Sw. 2.103.

11. See Burrough and Fox, *Good Council and Advice Rejected* (Simmons, 1659), B6006, 27; Fox, *To the Council of Officers of the Army* (1659), F1955.

12. Spence 3.61, 59, 63, 65, Margaret Fell junior to Margaret Fell senior, August–December 1659. See also Sw. 4.185 (EQL 490), Loveday Hambly to Fox, regarding his illness.

13. See H. Larry Ingle, "Richard Hubberthorne and History: The Crisis of 1659," *JFHS* 56, no. 3 (1992): 189–200, for an account of all Hubberthorne's writings in 1659. Hubberthorne was, in fact, less exceptional in his attitude to the political situation than Ingle implies.

14. Crouch, *Postuma Christiana,* 26.

15. *Cain's Offspring Demonstrated* (London: Simmons, 1659), C269, 1.

16. Barry Reay, "The Quakers and 1659, two newly discovered broadsides by Edward Burrough," *JFHS* 54 (1976–82): 101–11. (Rawlinson collection, Bodleian Library, D 397, folios 13 and 17). Reay thought that they were written during the first period of the Rump, that is, between May 7 and October 13, and not printed either because they were to be delivered by hand, or else because they were out of date before they could be printed. It is the second that is quoted here.

17. Burrough, *To the Parliament of the Commonwealth of England who are in place of Authority to do Justice* (1659), B6039, 1–3. Reay, *The Quakers and the English Revolution,* 82 nn. 6 and 9, does not clearly distinguish between this and B6038.

18. Hutton, *The Restoration*, 62, for soldiers attending Quaker meetings, 67–71, for Monck's motives.

19. Burrough, *A Message to the Present Ruler of England* (Calvert, 1659), B6015, 14.

20. See Hill, *The Experience of Defeat*, 143–53, on Burrough's politics and faith in the army.

21. *A Declaration from the People called Quakers to the Present Distracted Nation of England* (London: Simmons, 1659), B5989, 8–9. There were fifteen signatures.

22. Many Friends were in doubt. For instance, Sw. 3.259 (EQL 511), January 1660, is a letter to Fox from Francis Gawler, a Welsh Friend, asking if Friends were free to serve in the army.

23. Hutton, *The Restoration*, 76, 83.

24. Penington, *Some Considerations proposed to the Distracted Nation of England* (1659/1660), P1191, author's date, January 19.

25. Sw. 3.145 (EQL 542), August 1660.

26. Penington, *A Question propounded to the Rulers, Teachers and People of England* (Lodovick Lloyd, 1659/1660), P1183. Hutton, *The Restoration*, 93 and 96–122 for the highly complex events of the following months.

27. Penington, *Some Queries concerning the Work of God in the World* (Wilson, 1660), P1200, 2.

28. Sw 5.93, *LEF 75*, addressed to "W.M.," attributed to Edward Billing.

29. A copy of Monck's order is in Sw. 4.265.

30. *The Fanatick History*, B3212.

31. About 194 new pamphlets in 1659, and about 190 in 1660.

32. Fox, Stubbs, and Furly, *A Battledore for Teachers and Professors* (Wilson, 1660), F1751.

33. Burrough, *A Visitation and Presentation of Love unto the King* (Wilson, 1660), B6056, dated third week of May. Spence 3.3 is a copy of a letter "To the King and Council," presumably from mid-1660, signed by Ames, Nayler, Fisher, George Whitehead, John Copestand, Henry Fell, Caton, Gilbert Latey, and Hookes, to the effect that Quakers are peaceable people who pay their taxes, but there is no indication whether or not it was delivered. It is an odd collection of signatories.

34. George Fox the Younger, *The Dread of God's Power* (Wilson, 1660), F1999, 5, 8, 9, 17. Nearly in full in *EQW* 388–404. For a milder approach, see Bishop, *To Thee, Charles Stuart, King of England* [1660], B3010, 2–3. Other Quaker messages to the King included John Collens (J.C.), *A Word in Season to all in Authority* (Wilson, 1660), C5235; Penington, *Three Queries to the King and Parliament* [1660]; William Smith, *To the present Authority, or Heads of Nations in England* (Wilson, 1660), S4538; Martin Mason, *Charles King of England*, M925, and *To Both Houses of Parliament* (Wilson, 1660), M934; *The Copies of Several Letters that were delivered unto the King* (Simmons, 1660), F1778, by Fox, Nayler, Parker, Henry Fell, John Sowter, William Smith and William Caton.

35. Thomas Goodaire, *A Cry of the Just against Oppression* (1660), G1087, 2. For testimonies on oaths, etc., see, for example, Penington, *A Brief Account of some Reasons why Quakers cannot do things* [1660], P1154. Hubberthorne and Nayler, *An Account of the Children of Light in Several Particulars* (Simmons, 1660), H3216A, is a careful, moderate account of Quakerism, probably belonging to the autumn discussions on public worship.

36. Burrough, *A General Epistle to all the Saints* (1660), B6005, 15.

37. Margaret Fell and others, *A Declaration and Information from us the People of God called Quakers, to the present Governors, the King and both Houses of Parliament, and all whom it my concern* (Simmons and Wilson, dated June 5, "delivered into the King's hand 22 4th month"), F628. Presumably, Fox had agreed in advance that his name should be attached.

38. Bishop, *A Few Words in Season, or, a Warning from the Lord to Friends of Truth* (Wilson, 1660), B2993, 2.

39. The pamphlet *For the King and both Houses of Parliament. for you (who have known Sufferings) now (in the day of your prosperity)* (Simmons, 1660), F1436, gives a full list of current sufferings updated to December.

40. For the radical underground during the period of this book, see Richard L. Greaves, *Deliver us from Evil: The Radical Underground in Britain, 1660–1663* (Oxford: University Press, 1986), and *Enemies under his Feet: Radicals and Nonconformists in Britain, 1664–1677* (Stanford: Stanford University Press, 1990).

Chapter 14

1. *ESP* 130, *Cal.* (1660–61), 569. For relations between Quakers and the general underground movement, and the authorities' reactions, see Greaves, *Deliver us from Evil*, 54–55, 68.

2. Fox and others, *A Declaration from the Harmless and Innocent People of God* [1661], F1786.

3. Penington, *Somewhat Spoken to a Weighty Question* (Simmons, 1661), P1206, 1–3, 8. Larry Ingle (*FF* 195–96) thinks that Penington was opposing Fox, but in my opinion he was clarifying, and pointing out the difficulties, rather than contradicting. Compare William Smith, *A Right Dividing* (Simmons, 1659), S4325, which approached very close to Penington's position, and Fox's Epistle 177, also of 1659, which proposes a similar arrangement.

4. Quaker Act Ann. 13 Caroli II cap. 1. *LEF* 95–114 has several letters from this period.

5. *ESP* 156, from a memorandum on plans to seize the Tower and kill the King. *Cal.* (1661–62), 464.

6. This letter, dated November 25, was intercepted; *ESP* 153, *Cal.* (1661–62), 568.

7. *Briefe Declaration of the People of God called Quakers,* January 1663, B1520. Signed by a number of Friends and included in William Bayly's works.

8. Since Hubberthorne is one of those mentioned by Reay (*Quakers in the English Revolution,* 9) as equal to Fox, his subordinate position should be established. See Chapter 1, page 20, and note 57, page 249, for his emotional dependence on Fox and Fell. See also letters at the time of his imprisonment in Norwich for the persistence of this relationship to 1655, esp. Sw. 1.344. I agree with Ingle (*FF* 193) that he probably wrote much of Fox's peace declaration of 1661, and may have performed the same service for Fell the previous summer, see Hooke's comment, quoted on page 183, which puts Hubberthorne before Fell as author. He was at Fox's side throughout the confrontation with Perrot (see Chapter 15, page 196). He was a valuable lieutenant, but not an independent thinker. For Hubberthorne as controversialist, there are two opposed assessments, Adam Martindale's, cited in *BQ* 303, that Hubberthorne was "the most rational calm-spirited man of his judgement [i.e., among the Quakers] that I was ever publicaly engaged against," and Thomas Danson's *The Quakers Folly made manifest to all Men* (John Allen, 1659), D217, 53, in that he was "a right Quaker, whose discourse wanted all the ingredients that should have made it savoury, viz. truth, sense, and pertinence," and who thought that George Whitehead had more "mother-wit."

9. *NJ* 437, not in *CJ*. See Chapter 16, page 207, for Howgill's "Testimony" for Burrough.

10. Greaves, *Deliver us from Evil*, 173, 177, 181–82, 190, and esp. 200–201, for Quaker involvement in the Northern plot.

11. *ESP* 171, July 23, 1663, *Cal.* (1663–64), 216.

12. ARB 93, September 3, 1664, reproduced in *JFHS* 46/2, Autumn 1954, 78, also *SPQ* 31.

13. Hutton, *The Restoration.* 208, 264–65, thinks that Charles II withdrew his protection from Quakers after the Northern plot, because they had not justified his faith in their pacifist intentions. By 1666, he was prepared to favor them again.

14. *SPQ* 50 and notes.

15. The Quakers' account of the transportation that failed was given by Nicholas Lucas and others, *A True and Impartial Relation of the Remarkable Providences of the Living God* (1664), T2496, and the opposition's account by Edward Manning, *The Masked Devil, or Quaker* (1664), M484.

16. William Bayly, *An Epistle General containing Wholesome Exhortations* (1664), B1524, 3, 9, 12.

17. Fox and Fell, *The Examination and Trial of Margaret Fell and George Fox* (1664), E3710; *For the King and both Houses of Parliament a Declaration of the present Suffering and Imprisonment of above 600 of the People of God called Quakers* (1664), F1432; see also Josiah Coale, *A True and Faithful Relation from the People of God called Quakers in Colchester* (1664), T2475; William Smith, *The Innocency and Conscientiousness of Quakers asserted and cleared* (1664), S4308; Billing, *A Faithful Testimony for God and my Country* (1664), B2900, and others.

18. *For the King and Both Houses of Parliament the True State and Condition of the People of God called Quakers,* two versions one with Wilson's imprint, neither found in Wing; *For the King and his Council at Whitehall* (Wilson), F1436A.

19. *The Cry of the Innocent and Oppressed for Justice* (1664), C7450, *Another Cry of the Innocent and Oppressed for Justice, or a second relation* . . . (1664), A3255, and *Another Cry of the Innocent and Oppressed for Justice, or a third relation* . . . (1664), A3256.

20. Chapter 1 of Greaves, *Enemies under his Feet,* describes connections between English radical plotters and the Dutch.

21. William Smith, *Some Clear Truths particularly demonstrated unto the King and Council* (1664), S4329; *A Testimony from us the People of God whom the World calls Quakers* (1664), signed by Fox and other leaders, not found Wing; *A Remonstrance of the Suffering-People of God called Quakers* (1665), R1016.

22. Ellis Hookes postscript to Fox's pamphlet, *Friends the matter concerning not putting off the Hat at Prayer* (1663).

23. Dewsbury, *The Word of the Lord to his Church and Holy Assembly* (1666), D1284.

24. Greaves, *Deliver us from Evil,* 216–25, for the government's attack on the radical press, which led to the imprisonment of several printers and the execution of one for treason; 212, for the raid on Wilson.

25. Greaves, *Enemies under his Feet,* 169.

26. Hookes to Fell, Sw. 1.48, September 1664; Sw. 1.45, April 1665.

27. For the rest of the century, the annual output of pamphlets rarely exceeded fifty, and the reasons for this need investigation.

28. Mostly in connection with the Perrot dispute, see Chapter 15, and pages 140, 154.

29. *CJ* 2:111.

30. *SPQ* 41–42, 223–28; Hutton, *The Restoration,* 211–12.

31. Richard Crane, *The Cry of Newgate* (1662), C6809, 3. See also Burrough and others, *To all dear Friends and Brethren* [1662], T1320; Salthouse and Baker, *To all the Christian Congregations* [1662], T1332; Crook, *Glad-tydings Proclaimed* (1662), C7211; Ambrose Rigge, *To All who Imprison and Persecute the Saints* (Mary Westwood [1662]), R1495; Humphrey Smith, *Sound Things Asserted* (Mary Westwood, 1662), S4074; Anne Gilman

"An Epistle to King Charles II," in *An Epistle to Friends* (1662), G768; Christopher Bacon, *A Trumpet Sounding an Alarm* (1662), B266A; William Brend, *A Short Declaration of the Everlasting Counsel of God's Heavenly Host* (printer's date 1662, author's date "8th month" 1663), B4360, and others.

32. Robert Wastfield, *The Great Objection concerning the Quakers Meetings* (1662), W1034.

33. Albertus Otto Faber, *A Remonstrance in Reference to the Act* F69; William Smith, *A Few plain Words concerning Conformity,* S4301, and *Some Clear Truths particularly demonstrated unto the King and Council,* S4329; Crook, *A True Information for the Nation,* C7216 (all 1664).

34. Farnworth, *Christian Religious Meetings allowed by the Liturgy are no Seditious Conventicles* (1664), F476. Sw. 4.148, Dewsbury to Fell, October 1661, for Farnworth's return to activity: "Richard Farnworth is raised up in great power, and has been abroad among Friends, the sweet presence of the Lord has gone with him."

35. A few examples are William Bayly, *A General Epistle to all Friends* (W.M., author's date: November 1662), B1527; Ambrose Rigge, *To all who Imprison and Persecute the Saints and Servants of God* (Wilson, [1662]), R1495; Christopher Bacon, *A Trumpet sounding an Alarm* (1662), B266A; Dorothy White, *An Alarum sounded forth from the God of Vengeance unto Englands Rulers* (1662), W1744. Michael A. Mullett, *John Bunyan in Context,* Keele: Keele University Press, 1996), 91–92, notes in John Bunyan's writings of this time a similar combination of assurances that his church presents no danger to the State together with fierce apocalyptic attacks.

36. Margaret Fell, *A Call to the Universal Seed of God,* November 1664, F625A16.

37. William Bayly, *The Great and Dreadful Day of the Lord God Almighty (which is hastening like a flood . . .)* (1664), B1528; George Whitehead, *The Conscientious Cause of the Sufferers, called Quakers, pleaded and expostulated with their Oppressors* (September 1664), W1916, 15; Bishop, *to the King and both Houses of Parliament* (November 1664), B3009.

38. Some of the Quaker pamphlets ascribing the Great Plague to the Lord's vengeance, all 1665: Josiah Coale, *England's Sad Estate Lamented and her Abominations Discovered which are the Cause of the Present Visitation of God's Judgements upon her Inhabitants,* C4752; Richard Crane, *A lamentation over Thee, O London* and *God's Holy Name Magnified,* C6814; Alexander Parker, *To the Mayor and Aldermen, with all others in Authority . . . in . . . London,* P388; Salthouse, *A Brief Discovery of the Cause for which this Land Mourns,* S470; Ambrose Rigge, *A Lamentation over England,* R1485; George Whitehead, *No Remission without Repentance,* W1943.

39. Sw. 4.121.

40. George Whitehead, *This is an Epistle for the Remnant of Friends* (1665), W1963; cf. Whitehead, *A Few Seasonable Words to all the Tenderhearted* (August 1665), not found Wing; Howgill, *A General Epistle to the Dispersed and Persecuted Flock,* October 1665, H3161; Thomas Green, *A Voice of Comfort Sounded Forth,* G1846.

41. Sw. 3.159.

42. Rebecca Travers, *This is for any of those that resist the Spirit* (1664), T2063, 7; cf. Morgan Watkins, *A Lamentation over England* (1664), W1066, another of the same type.

43. Ellis Hookes, *The Spirit of the Martyrs Revived,* H2663A, and *The Spirit of the Martyrs is Risen,* H2663. Both undated, but probably written around 1664–65. Burrough also wrote approvingly of the Marian martyrs in *Persecution Impeached* (1661), B6019, but this was an answer to an anonymous Catholic propaganda pamphlet, *Semper Iidem.* John R. Knott, *Discourses of Martyrdom in English Literature, 1563–1694* (Cambridge: Cambridge University Press, 1993) has a chapter on "George Fox and the Quaker Sufferings," but this is largely derived from Besse, *Collection of Sufferings.*

44. William Bennitt, *Some Prison Meditations of an Humble Heart* (1666), B1893, 6, 24.

Chapter 15

1. The standard account is Kenneth L. Carroll, *John Perrot, Early Quaker Schismatic* (London: Friends Historical Society, 1970). See *SPQ* 228–44, 247–50; *FF* 197–206; Nigel Smith, "Exporting Enthusiasm: John Perrot and the Quaker Epic," in Thomas Healy and Jonathan Sawday, eds., *Literature and the English Civil War* (Cambridge: Cambridge University Press, 1990). For Vatican records, see Villani, *Tremolanti e Papisti.*

2. Ellwood, *History,* Graveson ed. 207, says that Luffe died. Villani, *Tremolanti e Papisti,* 61–62 n. 31, found no record of Luffe's being condemned to death, either in the list of condemned prisoners in the Roman State Archive or elsewhere. Stefano Villani thinks that Luffe died from excessive fasting, and I am grateful to him for sending me a note about this in English.

3. *SPQ* 229–31 has examples of Perrot's style, including his poetry.

4. Perrot, *Glorious Glimmerings of the Life* (Wilson, 1663), P1612, 5. This, said Perrot, was written in prison in Rome, but not published until after his arrival in Barbados, "from whence it is sent a second time to the Lord's lambs." Robert Wilson the printer was a Quaker, and the regular printer of Quaker books at this time. Was he one of Perrot's supporters? Did establishment Quakers fall out with Wilson? Crosse MSS 28 is a pro-Perrot letter signed by one R.W. and dated from Jamaica. There are no Quaker books with Wilson's imprint after 1663, and nothing more is heard of him.

5. Crosse MSS 12, cited by Carroll, *John Perrot,* 45.

6. *CJ* 1:244, *NJ* 268; cf. references in Gangraena part i, 65 and part iii, 96, to soldiers keeping their hats on during church prayers that they disapproved of. Mucklow *Tyranny and Hypocrisy Detected* (Smith, 1673), M3036, 10, for variations in practice; apparently, in East Anglia it was usual in all churches to keep one's hat on during prayer. Burrough, *Trumpet of the Lord,* 29, said of Seekers that, "Your form is inward, and your chiefest idol is in your hats," but does not make it clear whether they kept hats on or off.

7. Carroll, 51 nn. 1 and 2, identifies this reply with Cadbury, *Annual Catalogue* 74, item and as probably the same as the letter in *CJ* 2:5, and mentions a second letter from Fox in Rich, *Hidden Things,* 3.

8. Sw. 2.95.

9. Fox's Epistle 214 mentions Nayler at one time keeping his hat in for prayer, but says that he quickly "judged" it, and Mucklow, *Tyranny,* 70, alleges Fox at one time did the same. Carroll, 58–59, and *FF* place Epistle 214 in 1662, contemporary with events and possibly one of the papers that Fox sent to Bristol after Perrot's departure from London. However, the reference to "Jo Perrot, whose end was according to his work" suggests that it was written after Perrot's death in 1665. It was first published with John Bolton, *Testimony in that which separated between the pretious and the Vile* [1673], B3510, and may well date from that year, when "hats" again became a live issue. About the same time there is evidence for "the hat party" rejecting the Bible (Carroll, 85).

10. Replied to by Fisher, αποκρυπτα αποκαλυπτα, *velata quaedam revelata* (Wilson, 1661), F1047. The original queries, by pseudonymous authors, do not survive and may not have been printed.

11. Sw. 5.17

12. Perrot's account of what happened is in Rich, *Hidden Things,* which has circumstan-

tial detail and is probably reliable as regards the order of events, but may exaggerate Fox's unpleasantness to Perrot.

13. Burrough's reconsideration is in his *Two General Epistles*, B6052, published post-humously in 1663. Poor John Crook was still explaining himself in 1673, in William Penn, *Judas and the Jews* (1673), P1307, 71.

14. Cited by Carroll, *John Perrot*, 63, from William Penn, *Judas and the Jews*; Burrough, Howgill, Crook, and Perrot, *To all dear Friends and Brethren* (writers' date June 1662), T1320.

15. Fox, *Friends, the Matter concerning not putting off the Hat at Prayer*, 3, 4, and post-script 3. This is Epistle 199.

16. Sw. 4.95.

17. Crosse MSS 22, Furly to Friends, undated.

18. William Salt, John Perrot, and George Fox the Younger, *Some Breathings of Life from a Naked Heart* ("may be enquired for of Thomas Simmons," 1663), S460.

19. Fox, Epistle 214.

20. John Harwood, *To all People that profess the Eternal Truth of the Living God* (1663), H1102A. Only one copy of this pamphlet is known, in the British Library. There is an erroneous reference in Wing to another copy in Friends House under the title *The Cause why I deny the Authority of George Fox*. The pamphlet is followed in the British Library volume by a manuscript copy of an unpublished paper by Harwood, dated March 1667: "The Life of Innocency vindicated that was manifested in two former ministers in these days, viz, JN and JP, who are both deceased." I am grateful to Kenneth Carroll for drawing my attention to this manuscript.

21. Marmaduke Storr, *To Friends of Truth in London* (1663), T1340A.

22. Harwood, *To all People*, 6.

23. Contrast John Bunyan, who a few years later was arguing against a rigid requirement for believers' baptism (Michael A. Mullett, *John Bunyan in Context*, 177–81). But Bunyan had only to deal with one church with a congregational constitution. Fox was dealing with a national church.

24. Fox, *The Spirit of Envy Lying and Persecution* (1663), F1916A, quotation from p. 7.

25. See *FF* 199, where Ingle gives his opinion that this passage displays Fox's "deepest assumptions about women and their nature." Yes and no. Fox was a man of his time in that he accepted the woman/weak, man/strong dichotomy, but this one passage must be set against the many instances of Fox's support for the position of women in the church. See his argument with Harwood on this very point, Fox, *Spirit of Envy*, 10.

26. Penington, *Many Deep Considerations have been upon my heart concerning the State of Israel* (Wing [1664], should be 1663, as it is mentioned in Howgill's letter of June 20, 1663), P1178.

27. John Penington MSS 4.7, June 11, 1663.

28. 1 Corinthians 8:1–13.

29. John Penington MSS 4.3, also Portfolio 3.83, June 20, 1663. *SPQ* 263.

30. John Penington MSS 4.40, August 1663, "Concerning putting off the hat in prayer."

31. Penington, *To Friends in England* (1666), P1211, 3, 4, 9. He gave a second explana-tion in Penn, *Judas and the Jews*, 68–70, which concerned a later episode in the Hat saga.

32. Carroll, *John Perrot*, 87, "A listing of those who took Fox's side . . . reads like a Quaker *Who's Who*." The reverse explanation is that someone like Benjamin Furly, a very able man, never gained the influence among English Friends that might have been his due. Note Sheeran's misreading of Carroll in his *Beyond Majority Rule*, 20 n. 4.

33. Rebekah Travers, *A Testimony to the Light and Life of Jesus* (1663 T2061), 3, 4.

34. Farnworth and others, *Truth Vindicated, or, an Answer to a Letter* (1665) (Wing T3165, but often catalogued under Farnworth).

Chapter 16

1. For the contemporary ballad literature, see Peter Burke, "Popular Culture in Seventeenth-Century London," and Bernard Capp, "Popular Literature," in Barry Reay, ed., *Popular Culture in Seventeenth-Century England* (London: Croom Helm, 1985, reprinted, Routledge, 1988).

2. Humphrey Smith, *A Paper showing who are the True Spouse of Christ, and who are not* (M.W.), S4070, 4.

3. Writers of published verse include Dorothea Gotherson, William Smith, Dorothy White, William Bayly, Francis Ellington, Richard Greenway, Josiah Coale, John Raunce, Andrew Robeson, Daniel Baker, John Collens, John Grave, Humphrey Smith, William Brend, John Gibson, Ambrose Rigge, John Whitehouse, John Crook, John Ives, Rebekah Travers, and John Swinton.

4. John Raunce, *A Few words to all People concerning the Present and Succeeding Times* (1662), R320.

5. Dorothy White, from *A Trumpet sounded out of the Holy City* (1662), W1755.

6. Hubberthorne, *A Collection of the Several Books and Writings of Richard Hubberthorne* (Warwick, 1663), H3216.

7. Howgill and others, *A Testimony concerning the Life, Death, Trials, Travels and Labour of Edward Burroughs* (Warwick, 1662, old-style date), T809; cf. David's lament for Jonathan, 2 Samuel 17–27, esp.19, 26.

8. *Testimony concerning the Life . . . of Edward Burroughs*, 5. See QFP 19.08.

9. Nicholas Complin, *The Faithfulness of the Upright made Manifest* (M.W., 1663), C5561.

10. John Crook and Thomas Green, *A True and Faithful Testimony concerning John Samm* (1664), C7215.

11. Daniel Wills and others, *A Relation in part of what passed through Mary Page* (1666), R782.

12. The phrase "Assembly of the Church of the First Born" derives from Hebrews 12:23 (note the apocalyptic context). For this or similar usage in Quaker epistles, see, for example, Ambrose Rigge, *To the Whole Flock of God Everywhere* (Simmons 1660), R1497; Dorothy White, *An Epistle of Love and Consolation unto Israel* (Wilson, 1661), W1748; Dewsbury, *To All the Faithfull in Christ* (1663), D1277; Crook, *An Epistle of Peace and Goodwill* (1664), C7205. The earliest reference found, Caton 3.80, Howgill to Fell, 1654, sends love to "the whole church of the firstborn with thee." The reason this term did not persist as a title for Friends is, probably, that it became associated with Quaker dissidents. After the Great Fire of London, Robert Rich, a wealthy Barbados merchant who had been a friend and supporter of both Nayler and Perrot, sent a gift of £210 to be divided between seven London churches, one being Quakers, and one being the "Church of the First Born," which consisted of fringe Quakers of like mind to himself. They were probably not an organised group, and most likely, Rich merely used the term as suitable for a group of his friends "whose names are written in Heaven," contrasting them with orthodox Quakers, whom he considered to have lapsed. The Quakers were much annoyed, and turned the gift down. Several pamphlets refer to this episode, and the story is summarized by Geoffrey Nuttall, "The Last

of James Nayler, Robert Rich, and the Church of the First Born," *Friends Quarterly* 60 (1985): 527–34.

13. George Fox the Younger, *Two General Epistles* (Warwick, 1663, both written from prison in January 1661), F2016, 7, 8.

14. William Bayly, *The Lambs Government to be Exalted* (1663), B1531, 11–12.

15. William Dewsbury, *The Breathings of Life to God's Spiritual Israel* (printers date 1663, written January 1664), D1257, 3, 5.

16. William Gibson, *A Salutation of the Fathers Love unto all Young Men and Virgins* (1663), G687, 6–7.

17. Penington, *Some Directions to the Panting-Soul* (Wilson, 1661), P1193, 7.

18. Penington, *Some of the Mysteries of God's Kingdom* (1663), P1197, preface.

19. William Smith, *The Lying Spirit in the Mouth of the False Prophet made Manifest* (Simmons, 1658), S4313, 16. Howet's book is lost, and a reference in the first edition of Wing was deleted in the second edition.

20. William Smith, *An Epistle from the Spirit of Love and Peace* (1663), S4296, 5, 7.

21. William Smith, *Joyful Tidings to the Begotten of God in All, with a Few Words of Counsel to Friends concerning Marriage* (1664), S4309, 6, 7, 8.

22. William Smith, *The Glory of the New Covenant* (1664), S4305, 6.

23. William Smith, *The Morning Watch* (Wilson, 1660), S4317, "Epistle to the Reader."

24. William Smith, *Universal Love* (1664), S4343. "Streams" in verse 2 is taken from Smith's collected works, as there is an impenetrable misprint in the first edition.

Chapter 17

1. John Whitehead, *For the Vineyard of the Lord of Hosts* (1662), W1977, 9, 8. The Bible reference is not an exact quotation but refers to Deuturonomy 14:2, Psalms 135:4, and Titus 2:14.

2. Perrot, *Immanuel the Salvation of Israel* (Simmons, 1658), P1619, 10: "And as for us, the Remnant of God, and his seed."

3. White, *A Visitation of Heavenly Love unto the Seed of Jacob* (Wilson, 1660), W1759, 8; Thomas Taylor, *a Faithfull Warning to Outside Professors* [1661], T572, 1.

4. S.H. (Hubbersty), *England's Lamentation, or her Sad Estate Lamented* (1665), H3213, 6.

5. For example, Fox and Nayler, *To Thee, Oliver Cromwell* (Calvert, 1655), F1962, esp. 2, 6–7. John Coffey, "Puritanism and Liberty Revisited: the Case for Toleration in the English Revolution" (*The Historical Journal* 41, no. 4 [December 1998], 961–85), gives an account of the calls for general toleration, as distinct from toleration only of the godly, during the 1640s and 1650s, and quotes in this connection Samuel Fisher's *Christianismus Redivivus*, written in his Baptist days.

6. Crook and others, *The Declaration of the People of God* (Simmons, 1659), C7201, 6.

7. Penington, *An Examination of the Grounds and Causes, which are said to induce the Court of Boston in New England, to make that Order or Law of Banishment upon Pain of Death against the Quakers* (1660), P1166, 82, 84. See *QFP* 27.13.

8. Penington, *An Answer to that Common Objection against Quakers* (Wilson, 1660), P1151, 3.

9. Perrot, *An Epistle for the most pure Unity and Amity in the Spirit and Life of God* (1662), P16.

10. Thomas Salthouse, *A Candle Lighted with a Coal from the Altar* (dated October 14, 1660), S471, 13.

11. Fox, *A General Epistle to be read to all the Christian Meetings in the World* (1663), F1825.

12. Fox and others, *For the King and both Houses of Parliament* (1661), F1821; Fox, *Truths Triumph in the Eternal Power* (Simmons, 1661), F1971, 14, 18.

13. Burrough, *Antichrists Government Justly Detected* (Wilson), B5985; Burrough, *The Case of Free Liberty of Conscience* (Simmons), B5986; Crook, Fisher, Hubberthorne, and Howgill, *Liberty of Conscience Asserted* (Wilson), L1960, all 1661. See also Crook, *An Apology for the Quakers* (1662), C7196; Richard Crane, *The Cry of Newgate*, C6809, and *A Hue and Cry after Bloodshed*, C6813 (both 1662), and others. Burrough, *A Discovery of Divine Mysteries*, B5999, is a collection of short pieces, and though issued in 1661 some were written earlier. Here liberty of conscience is described as being freedom from sin, an idea of conscience as the seat of religious illumination typical of the 1650s rather than the 1660s.

14. Farnworth, *Gospel Liberty sent down from Heaven in a Suffering Time* (1664), F484. See Gwyn, *The Covenant Crucified*, 258–63, for an account of Farnworth on toleration.

15. *For the King and Both Houses of Parliament—Why should Christians ruinate one another?* [1665] (not in Wing), "From us called Quakers."

16. John Collens, *Something written after the Manner of a Discourse or Dialogue betwixt a Rigid Presbyterian and Good Conscience, which begins to be roused up and awakened these TRYING TIMES* (For I.C., 1662), C5233A, 21. See also George Whitehead, *The Pernicious Way of the Rigid Presbyter and Antichrists Minister detected* (Wilson, 1662), W1945.

17. George Whitehead and Edward Burrough, *The Son of Perdition Revealed* (Simmons, 1661), W1962, introduction. Answer to Joseph Wright, *A Testimony for the Son of Man* (Dover, 1660), W3704.

18. Burrough wrote the "Epistle to the Reader" for *The Son of Perdition*, where he states that Whitehead had begun the book but that he himself had finished it. The cross-reference to Burrough has been deleted in the third edition of Wing. Overall, the flavor of the book has more of Whitehead than Burrough, especially the emphasis on the human Christ, rare in early Quaker writings but present in Whitehead's earlier works: *Path of the Just Cleared* (1655), W1944, 4, "Christ come in the flesh we own and witness"; *Jacob found in a Desert Land* (1656), W1936, 14, "his death and suffering witness against you: and whose sins Christ has nailed to the Cross, they are crucified and blotted out"; *Seed of Israel's Redemption* (1659), W1955, 33–34, account of human Jesus and relation between divinity and humanity of Christ. Hugh Barbour, "The Young Controversialist," in Dunn and Dunn, *The World of William Penn*, 19–20, also notes this tendency of Whitehead. However, Underwood, *Primitivism*, ascribes *Son of Perdition* to Burrough.

19. *The Son of Perdition Revealed*, 1, 9, 10. See also John Whitehead, *A Small Treatise* (Wilson, 1661), W1981, for a similar theological approach and striking evangelical theology. Fox's use in several epistles of the advice that Friends should "meet in the name of Jesus" dates from the same period, and would be part of the same tendency. I am grateful to Ursula Windsor for drawing my attention to this phrase.

20. John Pennyman, *A Short Account of the Life of Mr. John Pennyman* (1696), 10. See L. H. Higgins, "John Pennyman" *Quaker History* 69 (1980): 102–18.

21. *LEF* 304, from John Penington MSS 4.29–34, 1662.

22. Robert Rich was in touch with some of them, see Chapter 16, note 12, and Nigel Smith "Enthusiam and Quaker Discourse," esp. 64.

23. Ellis Hookes letter to Fell describing these events was intercepted, see *ESP* 153–55, *Cal.* (1661–62), 569. See Pennyman, *Short Account*, 10–11, for his version of what happened. See also *FF* 199–200.

24. Sw. 4.96, George Whitehead to Fox, May 1664.

25. There are several known ms. copies; I used Portfolio MS 41.94 and John Penington MSS 4.43–45, in Friends House Library. The document is printed in *LEF* 318–24, with a few differences from the manuscript, of which the only one of importance is the phrase "society and fellowship" in the preamble, where Barclay has "safety." If "society" is original, this would be an early use of the term for the whole body of Friends.

26. His name stands first among the signatories, and the style is similar to his late pamphlets, especially the anti-Perrot tract, *Truth Vindicated*.

27. Farnworth's "Testimony" was written by Josiah Coale, *The Last Testimony of that Faithful Servant of the Lord, Richard Farnworth* (1667), F488, also in Coale's collected works, *The Books and Divers Epistles of the Faithful Servant of the Lord Josiah Coale* (1671), C4751. Coale states that Farnworth was thought by some to be "under a cloud." The meaning of this is uncertain, but may refer to reservations that Fox probably entertained about Farnworth's reliability. See *SPQ* 247.

28. Bishop, January 3, 1667. Known from the quotation, possibly not word for word, in William Mucklow, *Tyranny and Hypocrisy Detected*, 34. The source is suspect, but the authenticity of the letter was not denied by Friends.

29. Since it has been suggested that one reason for the change in the nature of Quakerism after the Restoration, is that Fox survived most of the other early Quaker leaders and so was unchallenged, it is worth emphasizing that the "Testimony of the Brethren" was conceived and issued without any input from Fox. However, the death of Bishop may well have affected subsequent events. If he had lived a few years longer, and had decided to challenge Fox on the centralizing and unifying tendencies of the reforms of those years, then the schism of the 1670s might well have ended differently.

30. Fox, *To Friends in Barbados, Virginia, Maryland, New England and Elsewhere* (dated November 29, 1666), F1953.

31. The first major test of this system, the Wilkinson-Story Separation of the mid-1670s, needs a thorough study. Overall, the structure held, though for some years there were two Monthly Meetings in Reading, and Bristol was in revolt.

Appendix I

1. See Chapter 1, note 8, for the history and various editions of the *Journal*.

2. See Larry Ingle, "George Fox: Historian," *Quaker History* 82, no. 1 (spring 1993): 261–78.

3. *SJ* 17; *CJ* 1:41

4. Geoffrey F. Nuttall, "A Letter by James Nayler appropriated to George Fox," *JFHS* 55 (1983–89): 178–79.

5. Henry J. Cadbury, *George Fox's "Book of Miracles"* (Cambridge: Cambridge University Press, 1948).

6. Henry J. Cadbury, *The Annual Catalogue of George Fox Papers, compiled in 1694–1697* (Philadelphia: Friends Book Store; and London: Friends Book Centre, 1939). See also Cadbury, *The Narrative Papers of George Fox* (Richmond, Ind.: Friends United Press, 1972), for a collection of unpublished Fox papers.

7. Willem Sewel, *The History of the Quakers* (London: Sowle, 1696); FPT; and Besse, *Collection of the Sufferings*.

8. See the account of early censoring of books in Chapter 2, page 26.

9. An example is Richard Abell, *Deceit made Manifest* (1659).

10. Thomason, Preface, xxiv. This collection of nearly fifteen thousand books and pamphlets was made between 1640 and 1661 by the London bookseller George Thomason.

11. Cited as *BA-Q.* See also Moore, "Quaker and Anti-Quaker Publications."

12. *ESP.*

13. I am grateful to Malcolm Thomas, the Librarian of Britain Yearly Meeting, Friends House, London, for assistance with these notes.

14. Even in one of the better researched collections, I came across one important document whose existence was not generally known—a copy of the "Epistle to the Elders of Balby" in Caton 1.90.

Appendix II

1. Larry Ingle, "George Fox, Millenarian," in *Albion* 24, no. 2 (1992): 261–78. This controversy should now be buried. Quaker theologians have accepted that there was a strong political element in early Quakerism (see, for instance, Douglas Gwyn, *The Covenant Crucified*), while the "Marxist" school of history, which produced so much excellent work on the mid–seventeenth-century sects but emphasized the political element in Quakerism to the near exclusion of anything else, now has to compete with other interpretations of the period suggesting that the "English Revolution" was less revolutionary than supposed. See David Underdown, *A Freeborn People* (Oxford: Clarendon Press, 1996), 68–69, for a summary of views.

2. The question of whether Quakers rewrote their own history later in the seventeenth century was first raised by W. S. Hudson in "A Suppressed Chapter of Quaker History." He was answered by Henry J. Cadbury, "An Obscure Chapter of Quaker History," and made a further reply with a "Reply to Henry J. Cadbury." The three articles are in *Journal of Religion* (April 1944, 24/2, 108–18; July 1944, 24/3, 201–13; and October 1944, 24/4, 279–81). Cadbury was dismissive of Hudson, and the weight of Cadbury's reputation was such that the question was not looked at again for a number of years. See Larry Ingle, "George Fox, Historian."

3. See Kate Peters, "Patterns of Quaker Authorship."

4. At this time, the first month of the year was March, but printers frequently began their year in January. Where it was possible to check the date of a winter publication more exactly, by reference to internal dates or to the date in the Thomason collection, year-end dates were found between the middle of November and the middle of February. A considerable number of pamphlets had to be dated from internal evidence. Compilation of this list was greatly helped by Hugh Barbour, who made available the raw data gathered by his pupil David Runyon for the appendix, "Types of Quaker Writing," in *EQW*. This listed the numbers and literary types of publications for each author in chronological order, but not titles. Considerable adaptations were made when using this data for the present purpose, and the original compiler is not responsible for any errors that may have crept in.

5. Rosemary Foxton, *Hear the Word of the Lord: A Critical and Biographical Study of Quaker Women's Writing, 1650–1700* (Melbourne: Bibliographical Society of Australia and New Zealand, 1994).

6. Donald A. Spaeth, "Computerising the Godly: The Application of Small Databases to Anecdotal History," in Evan Mawdesley, ed., *History and Computing III: Historians, Computing and Data* (Manchester: University of Manchester Press, 1990), 156.

BIBLIOGRAPHY

For reasons of space, most books on related subjects, including all standard histories and most primary sources, are not included here. Lists of the Quaker and anti-Quaker publications from the years 1653–66 are available on the Internet: www.wood-brooke.org.uk/resources/rmoorebiblio/html.

Manuscript sources are described in Appendix I, pages 233–55.

Works of Reference and Listings of the Main Printed Primary Sources

Barbour, Hugh, and Arthur Roberts, eds. *Early Quaker Writings*. Grand Rapids, Mich.: William B. Eerdmans, 1973.
Barclay, A. R., ed. *Letters of Early Friends*. London: Harvey and Darton, 1841.
Benson, Lewis, and Arthur Windsor. "Notes on the Works of George Fox." Typescript in Quaker libraries, 1981.
Cadbury, Henry J. *The Annual Catalogue of George Fox Papers, compiled in 1694–1697*. Philadelphia: Friends Book Store,; and London: Friends Book Centre, 1939.
———. *George Fox's "Book of Miracles."* Cambridge: Cambridge University Press, 1948.
———. *The Narrative Papers of George Fox*. Richmond, Ind.: Friends United Press, 1972.
"Dictionary of Quaker Biography." Many loose-leaf typescript volumes regularly up-

dated. Duplicate copies in Friends House, London, and in Haverford College, Pennsylvania.

Fox, George. *The Works of George Fox.* 8 vols. Philadelphia: Gould; and New York: Hopper, 1831. Reprinted with new introductions. Edited by T. H. S. Wallace. Pennsylvania: New Foundation Publications, George Fox Fund, 1990.

———. *The Journal of George Fox.* 2 vols. Edited by Norman Penney. Cambridge: Cambridge University Press, 1911.

———. *Short Journal and Itinerary Journals of George Fox.* Edited by Norman Penney. Cambridge: Cambridge University Press, 1925.

———. *The Journal of George Fox.* Edited by John L. Nickall. Introduction by Geoffrey F. Nuttall. Cambridge: Cambridge University Press, 1952.

———. *George Fox: The Journal.* Edited by Nigel Smith. London: Penguin, 1998.

Garman, Mary, Judith Applegate, Margaret Benefiel, and Dorth Meredith, eds. *Hidden in Plain Sight: Quaker Women's Writings 1650–1700.* Wallingford, Pa.: Pendle Hill Press, 1996.

Greaves, Richard L., and Robert Zaller, eds. *Biographical Dictionary of English Radicals.* 3 vols. Brighton: Harvester, 1982–84.

Green, M. A., ed. *Calendar of State Papers.* Domestic Series, 1650–1665. 13 vols. London: Longman, 1857–1972.

Matthews, A. G. *Calamy Revised.* Oxford: Clarendon Press, 1934. Reissued, 1998.

Milligan, Edward H. "Appendix: Quaker and Anti-Quaker Writers, 1660–1665." In Geoffrey F. Nuttall, "The Beginnings of Nonconformity 1660–1665, a Checklist." Typescript, 1960. Then obtainable from Dr. Williams Library.

Moore, Rosemary. "An Annotated Listing of Quaker and Anti-Quaker Publications 1652–1659." Computer printout, Quaker libraries at Friends House, London, and Woodbrooke, Birmingham, 1994. Available from the author as hard or soft copy.

Nuttall, Geoffrey F. "Early Quaker Letters." Typescript, 1952. Available in Quaker libraries in the United Kingdom and the United States, and main national libraries in the United Kingdom, United States, and several continental countries. There are nineteen in all.

———. "The Letters of James Nayler." In Michael L. Birkel and John W. Newman, eds., *The Lamb's War: Quaker Essays to Honour Hugh Barbour.* Richmond, Ind.: Earlham College Press, 1992.

Penney, Norman, ed. *The First Publishers of Truth.* London: Headley, 1907.

———, , ed. *Extracts from State Papers Relating to Friends, 1652–1672.* London: Headley, 1913.

Smith, Joseph. *Catalogue of Friends' Books.* 2 vols. London: Smith, 1867.

———. *Bibliotheca Anti-Quakeriana.* London: Smith, 1873.

Wing, Donald. *Short Title Catalogue of Books printed in England, Ireland, Wales and British America . . . 1641–1700.* 3 vols. New York: Modern Languages Association, 2d ed., 1978–88.

Whiting, John. *Catalogue of Friends Books.* London: Sowle, 1708.

Some Primary Printed Sources Not Listed Elsewhere, and Selected Secondary Sources

Bailey, Richard. *New Light on George Fox and Early Quakerism: The Making and Unmaking of a God.* San Francisco: Mellen, 1992.

Barbour, Hugh. *The Quakers in Puritan England.* New Haven and London: Yale University Press, 1964. Reprinted with a new preface by Barbour. Richmond, Ind.: Friends United Press, 1985.

Bauman, Richard. *Let Your Words Be Few—Symbolism of Speaking and Silence among Seventeenth Century Quakers.* Cambridge Studies in Oral and Literate Culture No. 6. Cambridge: Cambridge University Press, 1983.

Birkel, Michael L., and John W. Newman, eds. *The Lambs War: Quaker Essays to Honour Hugh Barbour.* Richmond, Ind.: Earlham College Press, 1992.

Bittle, William. *James Nayler, 1618–1660: The Quaker Indicted by Parliament.* York: Sessions, and Richmond, Ind.: Friends United Press, 1986.

Braithwaite, William C. *The Beginnings of Quakerism.* 1st ed., London: Macmillan 1912; 2d ed., revised by Henry J. Cadbury, Cambridge: University Press, 1955.

———. *The Second Period of Quakerism.* 1st ed., London: Macmillan, 1919; 2d ed., revised by Henry J. Cadbury. Cambridge: Cambridge University Press, 1961.

Carroll, Kenneth. "Sackcloth and Ashes and other Signs and Wonders." *Journal of the Friends Historical Society* 53/4 (1975): 314–25.

———. "Martha Simmons: A Quaker Enigma." *Journal of the Friends Historical Society* 53, no. 1 (1972): 31–52.

———. "Singing in the Spirit." *Quaker History* 62, no. 1 (1973): 1–12.

———. "Early Quakers and 'Going Naked as a Sign.'" *Quaker History* 67, no. 2 (autumn 1978): 69–87.

Corns, Thomas N., and David Loewenstein. *The Emergence of Quaker Writing: Dissenting Literature in Seventeenth Century England.* London: Frank Cass, 1995.

Crouch, William. *Postuma Christiana, or, a Collection of some Papers of William Crouch.* London: Sowle, 1712.

Damrosch, Leo. *The Sorrows of the Quaker Jesus: James Nayler and the Puritan Crackdown on the Free Spirit.* Cambridge, Mass.: Harvard University Press, 1996.

Eccles, Solomon. *A Musick-Lector.* 1667. E129.

Edwards, Thomas. *Gangraena or a Catalogue . . . of the Errors, Heresies of the . . . Sectaries of this Time.* London: Smith, 1646. E228.

Ellwood, Thomas. *History of the Life of Thomas Ellwood.* 1st ed., Sowle, 1714; modern edition edited by S. Graveson, London: Headley, 1906.

Endy, Melvin B., Jr. *William Penn and Early Quakerism.* Princeton: Princeton University Press, 1973.

Gwyn, Douglas. *Apocalypse of the Word: The Life and Message of George Fox.* Richmond, Ind.: Friends United Press, 1986.

Hill, Christopher. *The World Turned Upside Down.* London: Temple Smith, 1972; Penguin, 1991.

———. *The Experience of Defeat.* London: Faber and Faber, 1984.

———. *The English Bible and the Seventeenth-Century Revolution.* London: Allen Lane, Penguin, 1993.

Hill, Christopher, Barry Reay, and William Lamont. *The World of the Muggletonians.* London: Temple Smith, 1983.

Horle, Craig W. *The Quakers and the English Legal System.* Philadelphia: University of Pennsylvania Press, 1988.

Ingle, H. Larry. "From Mysticism to Radicalism: Recent Historiography of Quaker Beginnings." *Quaker History* 76, no. 2 (1987): 79–94.

———. "George Fox, Millenarian." *Albion* 24, no. 2 (1992): 261–78.

———. "George Fox: Historian." *Quaker History* 83, no. 1 (spring 1993): 28–35.

———. *First among Friends: George Fox and the Creation of Quakerism.* New York and Oxford: Oxford University Press, 1994.

Kunze, Bonnelyn. *Margaret Fell and the Rise of Quakerism.* Stanford: Stanford University Press, and London: Macmillan, 1993.

Mack, Phyllis. *Visionary Women: Ecstatic Prophecy in Seventeenth Century England.* Berkeley and Los Angeles: University of California Press, 1992.

Manners, Emily. *Elizabeth Hooton.* London: Headley, 1914.

Massey, Vera. *The Clouded Quaker Star: James Nayler, 1618 to 1660.* York: Sessions, 1999.

McGregor, J. F., and Barry Reay. *Radical Religion in the English Revolution.* Oxford: Oxford University Press, 1984.

Morgan, Nicholas. *Lancashire Quakers and the Establishment, 1660–1730.* Halifax: Ryburn Academic Publishing, 1993.

Morton, A. L. *The World of the Ranters.* London: Lawrence and Wishart, 1970.

Nuttall, Geoffrey F. *The Holy Spirit in Puritan Faith and Experience.* Oxford: Basil Blackwell, 1946, reprinted with new introduction by Peter Lake. Chicago: University Press, 1992.

———. *Studies in Christian Enthusiasm.* Lebanon, Pa.: Pendle Hill, 1948.

———. *James Nayler, a Fresh Approach.* London: Friends Historical Society, 1954.

Peters, Martha Kate. "Quaker Pamphleteers and the Development of the Quaker Movement, 1652–1656." Ph.D. diss., University of Cambridge, 1996.

Punshon, John. *Portrait in Grey.* London: Quaker Home Service, 1984.

Reay, Barry. *The Quakers and the English Revolution.* London: Temple Smith, 1985.

Rich, Robert. *Hidden Things Brought to Light.* London, 1678. R1358.

Ross, Isabel. *Margaret Fell, Mother of Quakerism.* London: Longmans, 1949; reprint York: Sessions, 1986.

Sippell, Theodor. *Werdendes Quäkertum.* Stuttgart: Kohlhammer, 1937.

Tallack, William. *George Fox, the Friends, and the Early Baptists.* London: Partridge, 1868.

Thomas, Keith. *Religion and the Decline of Magic.* London: Weidenfeld and Nicholson, 1971.

Trevett, Christine. *Women and Quakerism in the Seventeenth Century.* York: Sessions, 1991.

Underwood, Ted Leroy. *Primitivism, Radicalism and the Lamb's War: The Baptist-Quaker Conflict in Seventeenth-Century England.* New York: Oxford University Press, 1997.

Vann, Richard T. *The Social Development of English Quakerism, 1655–1755.* Cambridge, Mass.: Harvard University Press, 1969.

Villani, Stefano. *Tremolanti e Papisti: Missioni Quacchero nell'Italia del Seicento.* Rome: Edizione di Storia e Letteratura, Uomini e Dottrine 3.

Watts, Michael. *The Dissenters—From the Reformation to the French Revolution.* Oxford: Clarendon Press, 1978.

Wilcox, Catherine M. *Theology and Women's Ministry in Seventeenth-Century English Quakerism.* Studies in Women and Religion Vol. 35. Lewiston, Queenstown, Lampeter: Mellen, 1995.

INDEX